The Following True story is dedicated to my Brothers in Arms, members of 101st Airborne Division, British Airborne-Special Forces and all the members of the American, British, Canadian, Australian, French and Military Forces who have lost their lives on Operations in the Middle-East, Afghanistan and Africa.

This book is also dedicated to the members of the American CIA and British SAS who gave their lives for Freedom.

Important note to readers: Money raised from the Honour Bound Trilogy of books will go to Military Charities in America, Britain, Canada and Australia. An International legal team is overseeing this task.

Note to readers: As this book is being published, members of the British FCO (Foreign & Commonwealth Office) are using their official positions to try to discredit Anthony Malone by putting pressure on close friends and members of the British Military who are witnesses to this story. Question to the British Home Secretary Theresa May and the British Prime Minister David Cameron; "Why are you still allowing these disgraceful actions?" There should be a public enquiry into key points within my book. Karen Todner the head of Anthony Malone's legal team in 2015 sent an official legal letter to the British Home Secretary Theresa May, this requested guidance on the book manuscript and a request for Anthony Malone and several other former Military NCOs and officers to be officially de-briefed. No official response by the British Government. (Anthony Malone has "never" been officially interviewed by the British police and no Government de-brief has ever taken place?)

Introduction

Chances are, you've never heard of Anthony Malone. Yet the chances are also good that you're a little safer because of him.

Malone, a former British Paratrooper, had set up a private security contracting company that made use of his extensive contacts in the Middle East. In the wake of the US and British invasions of Afghanistan in 2001 and of Iraq in 2003, he found his services much in demand.

He also soon found himself at the heart of a story so incredible that it seems borrowed from the likes of the TV series Homeland or the novels of John Le Carré: incarcerated in Afghanistan's most notorious prison on false charges, Anthony Malone became the only known Western intelligence agent to ever infiltrate the inner circles of a major terrorist network with close links to both al-Qa'ida and the Pakistani Taliban.

Before he was extracted from Afghanistan in 2010, Malone personally intervened – at huge risk to his own life – to prevent a staggering number of terrorist acts in the US and UK. The intelligence he collected from within the fearsome Islamist Haqqani Network was, in fact, a contributing factor to the assassination of Usama bin Laden in 2011.

***

As a security contractor, Malone was often asked to do the jobs that the US and UK militaries couldn't – or wouldn't – handle. He was a fervent believer in the field basics of proper tradecraft, teamwork, planning, organisation and equipment, and especially in the cultivation of local relationships in order to obtain the highest-quality intelligence. This combination brought results, and earned him a reputation as someone who could get the job done.

In 2002, Malone used his Syrian connections to track twenty-eight high-value targets ('HVTs') along the Syria–Iraq border, all tied to al-Qa'ida. In a record-setting operation, Men from the American elite pathfinders from 101st Airborne Division captured all the men on the list in a single night – alive – and discovered critical information in their vehicles. This outstanding success attracted the attention of the United States Central Command (CENTCOM), and Malone was approached with a proposal to begin working with the Americans to convert his private relationships into an active intelligence network.

(Above from Author with American Military) Terrorists captured in an IED factory and Terrorist safe house in Northern Iraq. Evidence found during sensitive site exploration indicated this Terrorist cell was about to attack British and American soldiers.

So began the next phase of Malone's career. Working closely with the US to undermine al-Qa'ida and Taliban operations, he progressed from being an agent under cover as an 'embedded photographer' with the US military to being a 'Grade A Intelligence Source', responsible for handling and training intelligence assets.

Malone did not lack for motivation: 'I lost nearly two dozen close friends to al-Qa'ida,' he would explain years later. 'And I wanted to take their network apart.' Malone had heard the story of how now-General David Petraeus, early in his career, had lost eight men under his command in one night, and how a soldier, recognising how low this incident had brought the General and future CIA director, had galvanised him again by telling him: 'Now you've got eight reasons to get the mission right and get the guys who did this.' Said Malone: 'I had twenty-three reasons.'

(Above Left) Malone with Special Operations Northern Iraq. (Above Right) General David Petraeus (Former Director of the American CIA) with Brigadier General Joe Anderson.

His journey as an intelligence agent would see him collaborate with the cream of US forces in the region associated with rising military leaders such as Petraeus and now-Lieutenant-General Michael Linnington. Malone coordinated activities with the Regional Security Officers stationed at several US embassies in the Middle East, intelligence officers who themselves answered to the director of the CIA. This journey would end with Malone's release from an open sentence in the heart of darkness: Pul-e-Charki, Afghanistan's most notorious prison, near Kabul.

***

In 2006, the governor of Kandahar contacted Malone through a mutual acquaintance, with a request to purchase an armoured vehicle. Malone brokered the deal, but later realised that the vehicle was outfitted with stolen US equipment that he and his team had been tasked with tracking down. Further investigation, later confirmed by a senior SAS officer, revealed that the governor was feeding information on US and British Special Forces positions and safe houses to the Taliban.

Malone confronted the man and filed a report with US and UK authorities. The governor was removed from his post – but, this being Afghanistan, he was soon promoted to an even more powerful one, by dint of being a business associate of President Hamid Karzai's brother. The former governor later accused Malone of having pocketed a $50,000 deposit for the armoured car. (In fact, the deposit was forfeited when the order was cancelled following discovery of the illegal weapons.) In 2007, Malone was kidnaped by Afghan authorities, charged with theft and incarcerated in Pul-e-Charki: a medieval, hellish and extremely precarious place, overrun with drug traffickers and terrorists and prone to riots and killings.

Once there, he was soon informed that the British government would make no special effort to free him: they did not know he was working with US intelligence, and believed him to be a collaborator with elements close to the Pakistan Taliban and Al-Qadea. The US, for its part, denied knowledge of his activities – but such plausible deniability, Malone knew, came with the job, and was expected. Officially forsaken by both governments, it appeared that he was to remain in Pul-e-Charki. Malone endured the torture and desperately poor conditions that were routine in the charnel house of the prison.

Yet here was an opportunity: alone amongst a rogue's gallery of Taliban and al-Qa'ida detainees, Malone spotted several HVTs – dangerous men for whom the Americans and British had long been searching. The prison, he realised, was serving as a base of sorts for a core group of senior figures from the Haqqani Network, one of the most powerful jihadist groups in the world. The Network had begun in the 1970s and was nurtured by the CIA and Pakistan's ISI during the war against the Soviet occupation of Afghanistan in the 1980s. 'Salahuddin', one of the group's most forbidding leaders, was now directing operations from deep within Pul-e-Charki. A British Embassy mentored prison.

When one of Malone's key associates visited him in prison and conveyed a message that his team was organising a raid in conjunction with off duty US and British Special Forces, including British Para's to break him out of the prison, Malone shocked him by refusing the offer. Instead, he said, he would stay a month and gather critical information on the Network for passing on to US military intelligence. This Dangerous Task went on for three years.

Official British antagonism toward Malone had not gone unnoticed within the prison and made him the object of special curiosity. Yet he knew his life was under threat just by virtue of his presence and decided to confront the beast in his own lair. Marching through a gauntlet of intimidating al-Qa'ida enforcers in a narrow corridor of the prison, he went straight to Salahuddin and told the terrorist leader: 'If you're going to kill me, do it now – but I want you personally to do it.'

Instead, Salahuddin offered him tea and a chance to talk. For the next few hours, the terrorist leader interrogated Malone calmly. Had he ever worked for the British military? For the CIA? What was his full name, rank and number? Malone answered each question honestly and truthfully, and when the questioning was over, Salahuddin showed him the dossier he had already compiled on Pul-e-Charki's newest Western inmate. Fortunately, Malone's replies had matched the information; had they not, Salahuddin assured him, he would indeed have killed him.

Malone's Saudi and Hizbullah connections, in addition to the fact that the British Foreign Office believed he had crossed over to the 'other' side, ensured that he had a minimum of respect and credibility. As his relationship with Salahuddin deepened, so did the possibility of penetrating the terrorist network further.

A month passed quickly; Malone realised that in order to do the maximum amount of good, he would have to remain for the long haul – even if it killed him. He converted to Islam and began to pray five times daily, grow out his beard and study the Qur'an, and had daily conversations with Salahuddin and his circle. When US authorities raided Pul-e-Charki, Malone was beaten as badly as his jihadi neighbours – though not without receiving an apology, in private, from one of the soldiers, who let him know his patrons in US intelligence hadn't forsaken him. As Malone's credibility increased, so did his access.

Malone was able to smuggle messages out and to have the equipment he needed smuggled in: mobile phones were as common inside the prison as in the streets of Kabul, only he used the camera on his to take covert images of the lists of phone numbers, names and other data. While others slept, Malone was active, taking extreme risks to amass key details of al-Qa'ida's membership and directives worldwide.

Then came Major Bill Shaw, a British military veteran of nearly three decades' service who had been awarded an MBE. Shaw, working in Afghanistan for a major security firm, had been falsely indicted on charges of bribery in 2009 after trying to ransom vehicles under his command that had been seized arbitrarily at a checkpoint. A major effort was underway back in Britain to get Shaw released and in 2010 he was. Malone had used his status within the prison to protect Shaw, invoking the Pashtun warrior code: Shaw was considered his ward and therefore could suffer no deliberate harm – the bounty on his head that had been placed by hostile Afghans in the prison was thus cancelled. When Shaw was freed, Malone himself could no longer be ignored by his homeland. Within a year, he too was brought back to the UK. Again falsely imprisoned and asked in an official meeting in Stoke Newington police station London 18.00hrs on September 10th 2010, (Witnessed by DCI Benton/Senior Police Officer) with three senior members of British Intelligence for Malone to continue working as an deep undercover operative inside British prisons, only later due to politics for them to go back on their word, due to orders from high up in the British Government. Which was not a good precedent for future undercover operatives or NOC None Official Cover Operatives.

Unbeknownst to his countrymen, Malone had been working behind the scenes for many years, compiling the best picture of a functioning terrorist network that had existed to date and saving countless British and American lives in the process. He did so on his own initiative and at the behest of US military intelligence, capitalising on an opportunity that would be unlikely to occur again. It was extraordinarily dangerous work for scant reward, for which Malone has never been officially recognised.

***

Anthony Malone's deep-cover infiltration of active terrorist networks within Afghanistan between 2007 and 2010 has been estimated to have prevented or disrupted over 100 attacks in the US, Europe and throughout the Arab World, saving hundreds of lives, as well as suicide bombings and IED placements aimed at American, British and Canadian forces in the country.

His intelligence ranged cross the Middle East and Africa, revealing details of weapons and explosives shipments; hostage locations; HVT and safe-house positions; terrorist leaders' travel plans and routes; financing systems, including bank account numbers and the names of front companies used for money laundering; the location of IED factories and training camps; the names of bomb-makers; and much more.

Highlights from the 'Malone dossier' include the painstaking copy of an operational notebook containing hundreds of names and phone numbers used within al-Qa'ida and the Taliban; the 2010 plot to detonate a car bomb in New York's Times Square, which was foiled as a result; plans to attack members of the British Royal Family in Buckingham Palace London – and the identification of a certain villa in Abbottabad, Pakistan, as Usama bin Laden's residence and base of operations, eight months before the al-Qa'ida leader's assassination by Seal Team 6 in 2011.

Malone was able to acquire much of this information directly, having gradually won the trust of the inner circle of the Haqqani Network and of al-Qa'ida in Iraq and the Pakistan Taliban. He gathered a great deal after hours, covertly and at mind-boggling risk. (In one daring act of sabotage, Malone short-circuited the electric mains supply in his prison block as terrorist operatives were charging their mobile phones, satcoms and laptops in preparation for coordinating an attack on Kandahar International Airport. There, fresh from a secret visit to Camp Bastion in Helmand Province, British Prime Minister David Cameron was aboard a C-130 Hercules transport aircraft 400 metres from the intended blast site.)

All told, Malone's record of high-quality, high-risk intelligence operations during his incarceration in Afghanistan's worst prison – lasting three years – is without precedent. It is a story known within the higher echelons of the international intelligence community, but which has not been possible to reveal in detail – until now.

Anthony Malone's story is unique in the annals of intelligence operations. Since his return to the UK, he has been lauded privately by very senior figures in US and British military, law enforcement and political circles, many of whom are prepared to go on record in praise of Malone's outstanding service – it is revelatory, in the tradition of Spycatcher, but substantiated, unlike the majority of such works.

In addition to preparing to write this book, Anthony is also working with award-winning documentary filmmaker Paul Jenkins (whose work for BBC, Channel 4, ARTE and PBS has frequently covered political and military themes) on a film about his experiences, to be aired later next year. Video statements from senior British and American military officers and Special Forces including British SAS/SBS/MI6 have already been recorded for the International documentary and copies have been given to Karen Todner, the head of Anthony Malone's British Legal team. Anthony has also been advising Sky News on an in-depth series of stories/programmes about war and intelligence activities in the Middle East.

****Anthony has a wealth of experience in conflict zones as an intelligence operative and has kept journals and photographs in addition to his excellent powers of recall. Honour Bound will be just the first in a series of books.****

Author Biography: Anthony Stephen Malone

Anthony Stephen Malone is a fifth-generation soldier and was the second-youngest since the Second World War to earn his wings with the British Army's elite Parachute Regiment, at just seventeen years old. A few years later Malone would also be awarded his French Wings.

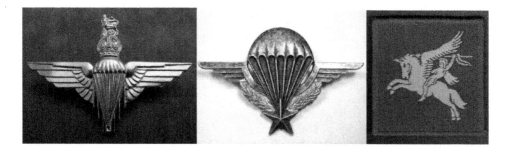

(Above) British Parachute Regiment Cap Badge. French Military Parachute Wings. British Airborne Pegasus Patch.

Since his return from Afghanistan, he has continued to cultivate a lifelong passion for photography, and serves as a special advisor for the United Nations and the United States military, amongst others, consulting on ongoing operations in places such as Syria, Iraq and the territory known as Islamic State.

Anthony Malone's extraordinary record of his infiltration of a major al-Qa'ida cell whilst incarcerated in one of the worst prisons in the Middle East is a story for our time. For nearly all of the twenty-first century, we have been at war. Even as we commemorate the centenary of World War One, and as we continue to set novels and films during World War Two, and as the Cold War – including its Korean and Vietnamese iterations – recedes further into memory, the climate of war has enveloped us completely. From the events in New York of 11 September 2001 to the execution of Charlie Hebdo magazine staffers in Paris barely a week into 2015 and the tragic events across Paris later in the year with over 129 people losing their lives, to barbaric terrorist attacks that rocked the French Capital and in which all Western countries shared the pain and grief of the French people. We are reminded regularly if not daily that our countries are at war, overtly or otherwise.

Anthony Malone has been a soldier in that war, both officially and under deepest cover. Honour Bound will not merely tell of his tense and daring exploits, but will also provide insight into how the secret wars of our era are waged.

(Top) Malone operating Behind Enemy Lines in Western Iraq. (Middle) VIP Close Protection at St James London. (Bottom) SWAT Special Weapons and Tactics instructor in Africa. (Below Left) Operating out of American FOB Western Iraq. (Right) Weapons instruction for VIP on PKM at American Special Forces Base Afghanistan.

This manuscript is based on my recollection of events, which may not be exactly as others recall them. Where conversations cannot be remembered precisely, I have recreated them to the best of my ability. Where people need to be protected or to avoid offence I have altered names. Any mistakes are my own.

Contents

Introduction - Background - International Terrorism

Anth Malone (The Rogue Warrior) Part One

London – England   Page 9

Diplomatic meetings and scheduled trip, Dubai, Tajikistan, Afghanistan   Page 12

Meet and greet with Mujahedeen Commanders   Page 14

Crossing the legendary Oxus River   Page 16

Picked up by the Vice President's motorcade   Page 18

The Salang tunnel of ghosts   Page 18

The Panjshir Valley – Massoud – Ambassador   Page 20

Kabul   Page 23

The Mustafa Hotel - Meetings with CIA - SAS – Chief of Staff – SOCA   Page 23

Trafalgar night celebration at the Gandamack Lodge – Peter Jouvenal   Page 24

Assadullah the Governor of Kandahar   Page 26

Kidnapped   Page 27
Plausible deniability   29

Tawqeef prison – Guantanamo bay detainees – Suicide bomber   Page 29

Pul-i-Charkhi mass graves   Page 30

Anth Malone (The Rogue Warrior) Part Two

Pul-i-Charkhi prison – Hell on earth   Page 31

Russian dungeon – Torture chamber   Page 34

Maximum security – Afghan Guantanamo bay   Page 36

Jack CIA   Page 38

Al-Qaeda – Taliban run the inside of Pul-i-Charkhi   Page 43

Torture and murder   Page 58

Prime Minister David Cameron – Attack on Kandahar airfield   Page 66

Truth Justice Freedom Liberty and the pursuit of all that threaten it   Page 68

My team planned my escape from Pul-i-Charkhi   Page 70

Al-Qaeda – Osama bin Laden villa location – Taliban – Pakistan Taliban - Afghanistan   Page 71

Kabul Bank runs out of money – Corruption   Page 76

The man who never was 1953 – Balls of British Steel   Page 78

Meeting with Al-Qaeda – Saladin – Taliban   Page 79

Taliban collateral damage – Murder   Page 84

Iraqi insurgents – IED - Airstrike   Page 88

Dubai – United Arab Emirates   Page 90

The Airborne Brotherhood needed someone inside the terrorist network   Page 92

Women and children executed in Mosul Iraq by terrorists   Page 97

Interrogation – Water boarding - The moral high ground   Page 98

Abdul Aziz – Al-Qaeda Commander – Afghan Chief Prosecutor changing official
terrorist prison files for money, so they can be released   Page 100

CIA signature drone strikes in Waziristan - CIA revenge strike – Pakistan Taliban
Commander Hakimullah Mehusd (Hakimullah Mehsud) – Times Square New York Car Bomb –
Camp
Chapman   Page 103

Prisoners tortured by Afghan NDS Security Services – Finger nails ripped out   Page 108

For Evil to triumph, all it takes is for good men to do nothing – Standing

up to the Taliban   Page 110

Four British soldiers killed - Once more into the breach dear friend   Page 116

Sin City - 1st June 2010 'top cover' from American Intelligence – Infiltrating

Al-Qaeda, Taliban   Page 119

They will never be forgotten - SOE (Special Operations Executive) and Bletchley

Park   Page 122

The Airborne Brotherhood – Why we do the job we do   Page 124

What Manner of men are these that wear the maroon beret   Page 124

Anth Malone (The Rogue Warrior) Part Three

The Road Not Taken   Page 126

God son of Ayman al Zawaniri (Ayman al-Zawahiri) the leader of Al-Qaeda   Page 128

Allah-Odin "Means 'God' in Arabic and 'Odin' is the 'Greek God of war'"   Page 130

Beatings and torture by Afghan Authorities – Screams and blood on the ceiling   Page 132

British Nationals ill-treated and killed   Page
132

Hunger Strike – Credibility with the terrorist network – Red Cross war hospital   Page 135

The bloodbath of a Taliban suicide attack   Page 143

The Hurt Locker   Page 146

Abandoned and betrayed (Poem by Author)   Page 146

Fear   Page 148

Strictly need to know and the British Embassy did not need to know   Page 149

Dead drops by American intelligence - lost American specialist weapons
Equipment, including; Stinger missiles   Page 152

Every terrorist bomb maker at some point, gets bitten by his own work   Page 154

Bedouin of Arabia desert – Moody camel   Page 155

Air Power; AC130 Combat Talon, Apache helicopter gunships and parachuting   Page 155

American soldier (Bowe Bergdahl), official POW Prisoner Of War   Page 160

Converting to Islam – Cold courage   Page 162

I accused by name members of the 'British Foreign Office, British Embassy
Kabul' of treason   Page 164

The British stiff upper lip, it's important to keep this when faced with adversity   Page 165

Honouring my promise to fallen friends and soldiers who gave their lives protecting
America and Britain from International Terrorism   Page 166

My actions had been responsible for the elimination of over 100 bad guys, terrorists   Page 168

Afghanistan, a text-book example on how to lose a war   Page 163

British PM Margaret Thatcher called the Para's her Dogs of War   Page
170

British Embassy, Consulate and Vice Consulate are removed from their jobs   Page
171

Update meeting with senior American Intelligence   Page 174

Iranian Missiles and IED's (Improvised Explosive Device and) FMSC
(Factory Made Shape Chargers) being used by terrorists to kill American and
British soldiers   Page 176

Al-Qaeda Commander – British and American soldiers killed   Page 177

Al-Qaeda international Terrorist network   Page 177

Hawala money changers   Page 179

The darker side of terrorist networks smuggling routes, human trafficking and

human "children" organ trafficking   Page 181

Dinner with Senior Al-Qaeda Commanders and the Pakistan Taliban   Page 181

Children being groomed to fight in the Jihad   Page 186

Hunting Al-Qaeda international terrorists, the best fun you could have

with your clothes on   Page 189

Taliban and Al-Qaeda narcotics smuggling routes   Page 190

All terrorist foreign fighters, sanitized within the Al-Qaeda, Taliban safe-house

network   Page
191

The Crusades and the age of the Assassins, Saladin and Richard the Lion Heart   Page 191

The Bank of Al-Madina, international scandal   Page 192

Terrorist Afghan narcotics shipments are processed in drug refineries hidden in

the mountains of Lebanon and black market arms deals in Beirut and Damascus   Page
194

Al-Qaeda and Terrorist Funding   Page 195

Emeralds and illegal mining operations   197

Al-Qaeda, CBC (Cross Border Communications) - American military base destroyed
by suicide truck bomb   Page 198

Cold Zero, resulting in a "clean kill"   Page 200

Helmand Provence Southern Afghanistan   Page 201

International Terrorism, Foreign Fighters and the Global Jihad   Page 202

Rudyard Kipling's 'Barrack-room ballads' published in 1892   Page204

The unprecedented British High Court ruling in 2013, 'Every British soldier has a right
to life in a war zone'   Page 205

Shariah (Sharia) law through terrorists eyes   Page 206

Terrorist martyrdom operations   Page 206

Prisoners of War and Shariah law   Page 207

Terrorist Commander Saladin gets captured, betrayed by another Afghan.
"Have faith in Allah but always tie your camel up" (John Noel)   Page 209

Correspondence with HRH Queen Elizabeth and the British Royal family   Page 210

Al-Qaeda death match between the bad arse scorpion and the fierce camel spider   Page 211

My reports were evolving from being just high level intelligence reports from a trusted grade 'A' source, into full on target packages, including my personal opinion on such things as military mission options and recommendations   Page 213

Major Bill Shaw MBE, put into an Afghan prison hell   Page 214

British SAS Hero, Andy McNab would later state; that Bill Shaw was an honourable man treated in the most dishonourable way   Page 216

Terrorists fighting for who controlled the inside of Pul-i-Charkhi Prison   Page 217

Afternoon tea and biscuits with Al-Qaeda and International Terrorists   Page 218

Taliban barber who cuts heads off   Page 219

Disrupting and stopping a terrorist IED attack and ambush on British and American soldiers and saving lives   Page 221

CIA Extreme rendition protocol, 'Bio-metrics', retina scans, digital finger prints, voice analyst   Page 222

Outside terrorist meetings being held in Pul-i-Charkhi Prison   Page 223

British Prime Minister David Cameron, Mission Accomplished?   Page 225

An open invitation to British Muslims to come and join their Jihad and join the brothers of Al-Shabab – Terrorists targeting America, Britain and expanding Al-Qaeda   Page 226

The Escalation in Violence across the Middle-East, Afghanistan, Pakistan and Africa - Where are we? Where are we going?   Page 228

God save us from the short-sighted politicalization of intelligence   Page 230

The British Embassy Kabul was about to blow almost three years of covert intelligence work of a Grade 'A' source inside the international terrorist network   Page 232

An historical first, British National Anthony Malone was the first person in

history to be extradited from Afghanistan to Britain. (Without Habeas Corpus)   Page 232

Sir Peter Gibson OBE, documents indicate that Government or its Agencies

may have been inappropriately involved in some cases of Rendition   Page 233

The murder in Syria of Doctor Abbas Khan, British national   Page 234

Confirmation of my previous report on barbaric torture and Genocide

inside Syria (see Authors introduction, Syrian torture chambers) – Carter

Ruck report on Syria – International war crimes   Page 235

Personal note to the reader   Page 236

Wounded Mind (Poem) From 'Theo Knell SAS' book 'a hell for heroes'   Page 237

Phil Young's official statement about Pul-i-Charkhi prison   Page 243

Main Glossary and navigational aid   Page 246

Terrorist Groups   Page 305

Arabic Glossary   Page 306

Islamic customary prayers and praises   Page307

Acknowledgements   Page 309

Bibliography   Page 311

Exclusive; future publications by Anthony Malone   Page 313

Synopsis of Anthony Malone's deep covert infiltration of the Al-Qaeda and Taliban, Pakistan
Taliban networks from within Afghanistan (Continuation of counter-terrorism and intelligence
work carried out between 2002-2007)

     Page 290

Sergeant Trevor Cooper Statement   Page 296

Major Bill Shaw MBE Statement   Page 298

Major Bevan Campbell Statement   Page 299

Official Letter from Afghanistan Government   Page 304

ISIS Islamic State Terrorist Group Report   Back

Al-Qaeda and other terrorist groups and networks operate across the globe and are involved with numerous personalities, organisations and ethnic groups, crossing all geographical boundaries. The comprehensive navigational aid at the rear of this manuscript is meant to assist the reader of this book-report, in maintaining focus, gain in-depth knowledge and to use for future reference. A report on ISIS is included at the rear of this book.

"London-England"

After living and operating for many years in and across conflict zones and hostile environments worldwide, I had returned to the UK from the Middle-East to conduct refresher courses, including communications, specialist weapons and physical endurance training. I had been contacted and asked by a Captain within the British Special Forces to come and join a specialist recruitment course that was about to start, with '63 SAS' Territorial Signals Regiment, based in the South of England. The timing of this was perfect for me on many levels, I wanted to get my fitness back up to scratch again. This would also give me a respite from the operational high tempo that I had become accustomed to while operating in and across the Middle-East and Africa. My body and mind were fatigued and my time, several years spent on the ground, had taken its toll on me physically. The SAS Captain had also told me that my knowledge and experience would be valuable to new recruits. I spent the next 12 months living in London and training, getting my personal skills and fitness back to their peak. Living in London was convenient, close to 63 SAS training locations and bases. I would like to make it clear that I never officially served in the SAS. I did, however, train with the Regiment and had the honour to work alongside senior SAS members on sensitive tasks and target packages across the Middle-East. I was not allowed to become an official member of the SAS due to sensitive politics, even after I was security cleared. I was living just 5 minutes' walk from the Houses of Parliament and the River Thames. My week day mornings were spent running along the Embankment next to the river and over Chelsea Bridge and taking the footpath past MI6 headquarters at Vauxhall Cross, along and past the corridors of power at Whitehall and the British Ministry of Defence. The London Eye, an oversized fairground wheel is a prominent fixture along the Embankment and modern addition to the London skyline. Running beneath and passing the Eye and on, through historic old London, whose buildings are steeped in history and historic architecture, gave me a sense of being back home in my beloved England. Running through the morning rain, through all the hustle and bustle of the vibrant city was quintessentially English and always a great experience and stark contrast compared to the stifling heat and open vast golden deserts of Arabia and the snow-capped majestic mountains of the old Persia Empire. Other early mornings I would spend silently running around Green Park, passing prominent landmarks, such as St James Park and Buckingham Palace, then though and around the warren of paths and vast green open spaces within

Hyde Park, the bright lights from the luxurious Dorchester Hotel on Park Lane, pointing the way to Speakers Corner in the early morning gloom. Further around Hyde Park, past the lake and Serpentine, the grandeur that is Kensington Palace marked the half-way point of one of my running routes. Many a morning was spent relaxing after training; enjoying the aroma of freshly ground Columbian coffee and fruit smoothies along the cosmopolitan high streets of Chelsea and Kensington. On my cool down and walk back to my accommodation, I would browse through the enchanting bookshops along old Church Street, where very old and fragile early copies of "A Thousand and One Nights" and the classic T.E Lawrence (Lawrence of Arabia) "Seven Pillars of Wisdom", could be found among the dusty shelves where other hidden forgotten literary treasures lay waiting to be re-discovered. Some afternoons in the city I would enjoy catching up over Cuban cigars and a gin-and-tonic with old friends in the many discreet venues, including the Officers Club and other locations along Pall Mall and St James Street. My weekends away training included time down at Thorny Island and the Brecon Beacons Wales and sometime training and exploring the wild Isle of Sky and rugged Outer Hebrides, Scotland. During my extensive time training I managed to develop and cultivate my international contacts with short trips to Singapore, India, UAE Dubai, New York, Venice, Paris and Geneva in Switzerland. I even managed to fit in a few two week trips and bodyguard tasks in Afghanistan were I met Afghan and American military personnel including several Colonels and members of American Special Forces. After a year of gruelling physical and refresher training with some old military, MI6 friends and the British SAS, I was back to being at my peak fitness again. Not bad considering that I was 36 years old and contemplating operational retirement, I had previously operated across five war zones and had been involved and carried out well in excess of 120 successful missions, including; locating terrorist training camps in Syria, Iraq and long range reconnaissance patrols across the Western desert of Iraq with the American military and hunting, helping to locate terrorists and outlaws, including covertly working within the local population acquiring intelligence and working to locate Saddam Hussein and his barbaric and belligerent sons Uday and Qusay. One mission that was actioned using my human intelligence network resulted in 101st Airborne Division, Pathfinder platoon Commanded by my 'blood brother' and fellow paratrooper Colonel Linnington (who would go on to become Brigadier General of West Point military academy). We captured a record 28 HVTs international terrorists alive in one night, as they crossed the border illegally between Syria and Iraq. Another stunning result was when I accompanied an American military fighting patrol; we raided an Iraqi location, a compound in the Northern city of Mosul. The compound and the villa within were tactically assaulted in the dead of night, after the lightning fast raid, items recovered included documents linked to the insurgency and false passports, AK47s and the target of the raid, an illegal printing press and engraving plates, which were a high priority due to them being used to print thousands of American $100 bills, which were in turn being used to finance the insurgency in Iraq. In Basra during meetings with the American J2 intelligence officer, based at the British military intelligence HQ 'The Hotel' located within Basra airport, (See photographs). We had put together, working steadily through the night, compiling and substantial 'target packages' for locations in and across Syria, Iraq and Lebanon, these had been sent to and then authorised by Washington DC within 24hrs. American surveillance aircraft were tasked to photograph locations within Syria that were of great interest to American intelligence (the locations are still classified, but were linked to Saddam's sons Uday and Qusay). My life was never dull. Years of training when I was younger in the Elite British Parachute Regiment had conditioned me and moulded my body so it could endure pain and extreme physical demands. I had always tried to look after my body regardless of where I found myself, this was important because a person is only as strong and durable as your body, your body dies, you die. So it's best to stay as fit as circumstances allow you to. After the 12 month rest gap, it was now time for me to get back to the sharp end of security operations. I had always enjoyed working at the tip of the sword of military, and intelligence, operations. The terrorists and bad guys are still out there and needed stopping and in some far off distant location Osama bin Laden was just waiting to be found and taken out of circulation, it was just a case of when and by whom. My sources were telling me that Osama bin Laden was somewhere in Northern Pakistan, no one could get a fix on his precise location at that time. In the not too distant future I would dramatically change that. My next trip had been planned back to Afghanistan, for some reason I always ended up back in this lawless country. No one knows when the hands of the Gods intervene in the destiny of us mere mortals, but fate was about to intervene in my destiny. My next trip to the Middle-East would include stopovers in the United Arab Emirates (UAE) and Tajikistan, ending in a month in Afghanistan meeting VIPs, Diplomats and other international dignitaries including Mujahidin Commanders. The trip had been formulated by Colonel Muslim Hyatt, the Afghan Defence and Military Attaché based in the Afghanistan Embassy, London. He had coordinated our trip with his good friend Wali Massoud the former Afghan Ambassador to London who had just taken up the post as Afghan Ambassador to America, in Washington DC. Col Hayatt had also contacted the Vice President Massoud of Afghanistan whose official motorcade would meet us at the Afghan border to Tajikistan and then bring both Col Hayatt and I to Kabul. This trip was supposed to be a fact finding exercise with several high level meet and greets. I was also going to meet and re-establish my intelligence connections and HumInt 'Human Intelligence' network across the region. I would meet and end up working closely with the Chief of Staff, a Major in the SAS operating out of the British Embassy. I would also touch base with American intelligence that had a big contingent covertly working across Afghanistan, Pakistan and the Middle-East. The intelligence agencies still had the same old topics of interest and agenda. The 'war on terror' and stopping SAMs (Surface to Air Missiles) and 'dirty bomb' material (see Glossary, Dirty Bomb) from falling into the hands of Al-Qaeda, their franchise and other radical Islamic terrorists groups. With the escalation in violence across the Islamic world, focus was also on stopping and disrupting terrorist attacks including IED and suicide bombings and saving American and British soldiers lives. The blades, the name given to SAS teams, were locating and neutralising terrorist leaders and Commanders. 'Task Force Black' had been closed down in Iraq; emphasis was now back on Afghanistan. All the SOF 'Special Operations Forces' teams and Task Forces from Britain and American wanted to find Osama bin Laden and other terrorist leaders. Everyone wanted payback for the 9/11 and 7/7 terrorist's attacks. The Afghan AO (Area of Operation) was like the 'Wild West' pistols strapped to our thighs and AK47s or M4A1 assault rifles with a M203 under barrel 40mm grenade launchers at hand. It was great to operate during this time, when 4X4s could not be used due to the extreme mountainous terrain, we would use horses. Western political agendas had not yet started to interfere in military operations, this fact would change dramatically in the not too distant future when everything went politically correct. I had been away from operations for over a year and being back in the loop and on the ground felt good, as if I had never left, nothing had changed, Just another mission.

"Scheduled trip and Diplomatic meetings in Dubai, Tajikistan, Afghanistan"

After having Afghan diplomatic multi entry visa's put in my British passport, during meetings at the Afghan Embassy, I flew out of London for an unscheduled meeting with American intelligence in Dubai. One of the HVTs (High Value Targets) terrorists that I had helped track in the past was thought to be travelling through the UAE with a stopover in Dubai. I was helping an old American intelligence friend out with his latest intelligence task. After this had been completed I booked into my suite at the exclusive Jumeirah Beach Resort. I also booked Col Hayatt into an adjoining suite. I picked Col Hayatt up at Dubai international airport 48hrs later. We spent the next couple of days entertaining VIP's and guests within the beach complex's vast array of Arabian tea shops, bars, restaurants and private beach. The exclusive marina was another location for some of our meetings, with the back drop against million dollar penthouses and yachts that were the toys and playground for the elite wealthy Arabs and the young Arab playboys and millionaires. Over the pleasant aroma of Arabian water pipe, chi and strong sweet Arabian coffee, old acquaintances were met and past relationships were re-kindled and re-established. I was back working, developing and cultivating my Arab contacts and intelligence assets. All was squared away and ready to go within a couple of days. My next stop was to be Tajikistan. The low key flight was booked from Sharjah airport located 30 minutes outside Dubai city, to Dushanbe the Capital of Tajikistan. At Sharjah airport, while we were waiting to board a very precarious looking, small and rusty old Russian plane, Col Hayatt had commented that this was the same airport that British MI6 had ferried him to while he was fighting in the old Jihad against the Russians in Afghanistan in the 1980s. Col Hayatt had been flown out of Afghan without a passport and when he landed at Sharjah he was stuck, British intelligence had turned up and got him onto a plane and flight to the United Kingdom where he was to undergo training at the British Military Collage at Sandhurst. Col Hayatt had even been awarded a medal from HRH Queen Elizabeth II of England for his military service during the Soviet Jihad. Col Hayatt would often share little private snap shots into his life. We had become good friends over the previous year, he had trusted me with sensitive intelligence files of Taliban fighters living in Britain, at his request I had passed these highly sensitive files and information on to MI6 and British Intelligence. We also shared many old military friends, some of which were 'old school' Para's and SAS who had taught and worked with Col Hayatt and his men on the ground in Afghanistan in the 80s. Almost all of his life had been spent fighting in one Jihad or another in Afghanistan. He had even once been a POW (Prisoner Of War) the Taliban had captured him, he had been a prisoner in Kandahar before quickly escaping, he had not appreciated Taliban hospitality. Col Hayatt and I landed one late overcast afternoon in the small airport in Dushanbe the capital city of Tajikistan. It was a relief that we made it that far in the old Russian plane, I could have sworn that I saw a piece of metal fall off the plane as we landed. The Col looked as relieved as I was when we walked down the gangway and finally stepped on to the tarmac, it was good to have 'terra ferma' under our feet again. The pilot walked passed us holding a bottle of vodka, I don't know if it was full or empty, but from the standard of the flying during our flight I would have a bet the latter. Not to worry we were alive and in Dushanbe. Col Hayatt had phoned ahead prior to our flight arriving, airport security met us off the plane and ushered us through the small airport building, taking our passports and giving us strong coffee in the little cafe outside the airport terminal. After about 15 minutes a security officer brought our passports out, all stamped and ready to go. A driver was waiting; he drove us to a house that had been put at our disposal for the duration of our visit. Weapons and maps were waiting for us at the safe house.

After unloading our kit from the vehicle, we checked our personal belongings over to make sure nothing had been damaged during the flight. After carrying out the checks ensuring all kit, satellite phones and laptops 'Panasonic tough books' were serviceable and working, weapons were stripped, oiled, reassembled and loaded. All were ready to rock and roll if needed, just in case we had any unexpected hostile guests crashing through our front door. I was very aware that there was an escalating bloody war just across the border in Afghanistan. I was constantly aware of our precarious security situation, the worse normally happens when you least expect it. So being a good boy scout 'I was always prepared'. For stopping bad guys from crashing in to kill you in the dead of night, my weapon of choice has positively got to be an AK47, except no substitute, 30 bullets of red hot lead, will discourage even the most determined extreme bad guys. We chilled out for the rest of the night, hot shower and a good night's sleep. The next 3 days schedule was packed with meetings at different locations across Tajikistan. I woke early the next morning, my Breitling Emergency watch showed the time 05:30am. I always wore my Breitling Emergency when working overseas, yes it looked good and was strong and practical, but more importantly it had a built in emergency transmitter, it was a good piece of kit to have on the end of my wrist in case of emergencies. When activated the transmitter, built into the watch, would send out its first signal to a satellite on a frequency of 406 MHz, after that further signals would be sent out on the international emergency frequency of 121 MHz over land, sea and air. The watch had saved my life in the past so was a priceless addition to my personal kit. I had a spare Breitling Emergency watch so I made sure Col Hayatt wore one. Kidnapping by heavily armed terrorists groups was a real threat and was on the increase in these parts of the world due to the lucrative ransoms being paid by Western Governments and private companies. The powerful aroma of fresh coffee and gun oil drifted into my room, Col Hayatt was also an early riser. I found him in the kitchen, he welcomed me with a big smile, he asked did I want coffee, I answered, 'hell yes, is the Pope Catholic', Col Hayatt laughed at my early morning humour, we sat at the small kitchen table and tucked into traditional bread and Arabian coffee, a freshly oiled AK47 lay on the table between the bread and jam. We went through the schedule for the day, the first meeting was at 08:00am at the house, there was time for a quick shower to freshen up and go over the notes of who we were meeting. I always like to do background on anyone that I am to meet, this is just standard procedure, I don't like surprises during any meetings. My beard was coming on well; I was going 'native' to blend in with the local population. My close friends would always comment that I looked more Arabian than the Arabs. I always say; if you're going to do something, do it properly or don't bother.

"Meet and greet with Afghan Mujahedeen Commanders"

The coming days were spent attending sensitive meetings with dignitaries from several countries and Mujahedeen Commanders. We travelled north through the staggeringly beautiful snow-capped mountains and lush green fertile lands where wild fast flowing rivers ran through the valleys. I was taken aback by how wild and untouched this country was, there are not many places in this world that are untouched by man, this mountain range was one of the last of them. Travelling through villages and small hamlets, along dusty single lane tracks, we came across an isolated village, situated high on a mountain plateau. In the village squire stood an oversized brass statue of Joseph Stalin, this was a stark reminder that I was travelling through a former Soviet bloc country, which had once been ruled with an iron fist from Moscow. The look of suspicion and weariness on the villagers faces as we past slowly through the village was evident. Their life under Soviet rule had been harsh and unforgiving, past dark memories still haunted them, they also feared the unknown. We moved on with our journey, towards our next location and our planned meeting with one of Col Hayatt's old friends and the Japanese Ambassador. The location of this meeting was to be in a mountain retreat, which looked more like a medieval impregnable fortress nestled in the shadow of two snow-capped mountains. As we approached the entrance I noticed an Eagle owl circling above us, we took this as a good omen that the meeting was going to go well. We entered the fortress on foot, after leaving the vehicles outside the vast walls. Seeing such a structure was like stepping back in time, we made our way inside. We were met with warm traditional greetings and shown to a seated area. After 'confidential' meetings and discussions, which included, politics and military matters, we all had lunch, which was more like a medieval banquet that had been prepared on large long wooden tables. The tables were filled with a vast variety of plates and dishes, roast meats and local game, vegetables and fish which had been caught from the local river. Giant bowls of colourful and fragrant fruits filled the far end of the table. The aroma of freshly baked traditional flat bread filled the air. The local hospitality was outstanding, on a par with the warm greetings we received on our arrival. Four hours later we were saying our traditional goodbyes and we started on our long ride back through the mountain passes to Dushanbe. I noted the spectacular sunset during our decent down the mountain. The whole sky was awash with bright golden colours and warm glooms that stretched across the sky. This was truly an ancient and enchanting land.

05.00am the next morning, we were up all bright eyed and bushy tailed. Today we were to meet Col Hayatt's old Mujahedeen Commanders; the day was to combine meetings with a trip to the hot springs at Obi Garm, located in the Karotegin district, east of Dushanbe, the Karotegin or Rasht valley is rarely visited by foreigners. The valley and in particular Gharm, was the scene of intense fighting during the civil war. The land and the valleys are notably scarred by all the past fighting. Derelict factories, resistance hideouts and abandoned personnel carriers are poignant reminders of the violent recent history. In some parts there are many similarities to its neighbour, war torn Afghanistan. After the 150km drive to Obi Garm, we enjoyed the hot baths, springs and pools, taking in all the therapeutic qualities that these natural hot spring waters were supposed to have. Even we old soldiers need a little bit of TLC upon occasion. Because all the Commanders were old friends of Col Hayatt, the atmosphere was relaxed, friendly and jovial. They sat around in the steam room telling old war stories and other long forgotten funny events, like when one of their friends got his foot blown off in a mine field; he still managed to hop over to his weapon and re-joined the fight against the Russians. Laughter filled and echoed around the rooms where we were sat; this was a little surreal and unexpected, given to the seriousness of all the meetings the day before. However this was a welcome break, the former Afghan Northern Alliance, Mujahedeen had a very relaxed attitude towards life in general. The conversation turned to politics; every Afghan and Mujahedeen has his own opinion on politics and is not shy in venting their opinions. Military matters also came up, Col Hayatt wanted to get an update on the real situation of what the state of play was in and across Afghanistan. The truth was that the new Afghan Government was so corrupt that this was strengthening the hand of the Taliban, who were gaining ground right across Afghanistan, politically and militarily. The unstable situation in Afghanistan has a direct effect on many of its surrounding and neighbouring countries, including Tajikistan and Pakistan. Due to the close professional bond and trust I had with Col Hayatt, I was treated as an equal by the other Mujahedeen Commanders, who after finding out from the Col that I was a former paratrooper, talked openly and treated me as one of them. Their updates and insight into the security and political situation across Afghanistan and their personal opinions were more accurate, in-depth and informative than any intelligence report I had read over the past weeks. These people who I was sat with really knew their subject matter. I listened attentively, asking questions when appropriate, they also asked my opinion on several subjects, I always answered honestly and to the point, I was not shy of presenting my personal opinion during the conversation. My 22 years of experience had given me comprehensive knowledge of Unconventional Warfare and their politics. My directness and frankness was met with approval from the Mujahedeen Commanders, who liked straight talking people; obviously they did not like Western politicians much for some reason? From the tone of the conversation I knew that we would all meet again in the future. These like-minded old Mujahedeen fighters also wanted to take the fight to the Taliban. After a pleasant and informative afternoon we set off back, driving through the Surkh mountain range and along the mountain passes and tracks that snaked through the valleys. We passed over bridges where wild rivers stormed through beneath; covering the vehicles we were driving in spray. The staggering raw beauty and power of the mountains was forever enchanting. The wild life across the mountains we were passing through was also staggering. Majestic snow leopards and Marco polo sheep are residents of the high mountains. Grey wolves also roam freely around the mountains, alongside Brown Bears and Wild Boar. Red Deer and the Siberian Ibex also roam through the Tugai forests. Across the sky, the vulnerable Pallass fish eagle and European Eagle-Owl soar to great heights watching over their domain. We arrived back in Dushanbe late into the night. After saying our goodbyes to the Commanders we retired for the night. I typed up all my notes and updated my personal diary of the day's events and points of interest, names, dates, places. I liked to keep an accurate record and log of every small detail. From past experience I have found that little details can become very important in the future. I had also kept a photograph log of all the places and people we had met since our arrival, since the Iraq 2003 conflict I had always kept a camera handy when I was working. I personally favoured the Nikon D2H professional digital camera, with my D100 as my backup camera. I also carried a good selection of lenses; these included the normal standard 35mm lens and the 100 to 300 meters, VR 'Vibration Reduction' zoom lens. This was very good at taking head shots of people, this helped to identify HVT's and people of interest, I had used my camera kit throughout Iraq, Saudi Arabia, Syria, Lebanon, Afghanistan and across Africa. I was proficient with any and all equipment that I carried, like any weapon I used; it was always clean and ready to go at a moment's notice. It can be quite amazing and surprising when terrorists just pop up, they turn up when they're least expected.

"Crossing the legendary Oxus River in the footsteps of Marco Polo and Alexander the Great"

Another early 0500am start the next morning, it's cool at this time of day and is the best time to start a long overland journey; by midday the heat from the sun would be stifling. Today was the day of the epic overland journey from Tajikistan, over the mountains of the Hindu Kush, then on into Northern Afghanistan. After a quick, light breakfast of coffee and bread with yogurt, we loaded our kit into the waiting car that was going to ferry us along the 200km main highway to the South of the country, we travelled through, Obikiik, Kurgan Teppa, Urtabuz, Isoev, Dusti and onward through the Tigrovaya Balka Nature Reserve and down to the river crossing at the Tajikistan border to Afghanistan. The ancient Oxus River runs along the Southern border of Tajikistan, it marks the geographical border to Afghanistan. We de-bussed the vehicle when we reached the border point, I grabbed my personal kit and stepped off the dusty track, finding shade under a solitary tree, I was on the high ground which over looked the green and fertile lands which were the border area. The Oxus River snaked its way across the landscape, far into the distance laid the land that was Northern Afghanistan. Viewing from the Tajikistan side of the border gave me a whole new perspective of how Afghanistan is perceived from this part of the world. From where I was standing, there was no visible sign of war anywhere. No burned out tanks, no IEDs, no sound of gunfire, fighting or explosions. All was quiet, the locals and the traders were going about their daily business, transporting food, animals and fresh fruit, as if there was no war going on in Afghanistan, life had to go on, people had to eat and live. What struck me as surreal was that the locals were just going about their daily business peacefully, completely oblivious to the killing and carnage that was going on only 50km over the border and across Afghanistan. The locals were just crossing the border to trade in the local Souq, Bazaars 'markets'. They and their ancestors had been trading like this for hundreds of years, through many wars and conflicts. We shouldered our rucksacks and made our way down the dusty track to the border crossing office, which was a small grey concrete two story house, built during the Soviet era and had seen better days. The old green paint flaking off the outer walls and the broken windows, the old red window shutters hanging off gave it a derelict look; it would have been at home on the set of some old forgotten cowboy film. After a quick conversation with the border guard, our passports were stamped and handed back to us with a friendly smile. With the appropriate exit stamp in our passports we bordered a small green Soviet era bus that was on its last legs. I could have sworn that I saw bullet holes in one of the doors as we boarded. We were driven down to the border crossing point which was the river bank 600 meters away. After a short drive down yet another dusty track, snaking through the mine fields on both sides, we pulled up on the river bank, next to an old small grey Russian diesel powered boat; this was how people were ferried back and forth across the border. The shadow of the construction of the new bridge, which was going to connect the two countries in the future, could be seen in the distance. It looked completely out of place, people crossing the Oxus River by boat had been a tradition for hundreds of years, once the bridge was completed yet another old tradition would come to an end, this thought saddened me. Change is sometimes good, but a lot can be said about the old ways and traditions. For me personally I prefer many of the old ways across this part of the world. After carefully storing our bags and rucksacks on the boat, I stood on the bow of the boat looking out across the Oxus River, for years I had read about this river and the historic people that had crossed it on their adventures. The sun was high in the sky and the cool breeze blowing in my face as we moved slowly off from the river bank. The fast flowing river ran all around and beneath us. We crossed the historic Oxus River in the footsteps of Marco Polo and Alexander the Great. We landed on the Afghan side of the river 15 minutes later. After disembarking, being careful not to fall into the river, Col Hayatt and I picked up our bags and rucksacks and started to walk along the river bank.

"Picked up by the Vice President of Afghanistan's personal motorcade and security team"

Five bearded Afghan men who were heavily armed and wearing military fatigues approached us brandishing AK47s. Col Hayatt stepped forward and greeted them and introduced me. This group of soldiers were his men, all hardened fighters of the Afghan Mujahedeen, they were also the Vice President of Afghanistan's personal motorcade and security, and this was our ride and security. They had been assigned to meet us and get us safely to Kabul. We mounted the waiting armoured B6 Toyota 4X4, then quickly we sped through the Afghan border post without stopping, leaving a cloud of dust in our rear view mirror, we pushed on into Northern Afghanistan. We made our way driving through the low lying farmer's fields, small villages and hamlets. On up through the valleys and passes, the majestic, dominant and daunting snow-capped mountains lay to our front. After a few hours we ascended into the mountains, there was a sharp change in temperature, the warm temperatures of the low lands were left behind within 25 minutes of our assent, due to the sharp increase in altitude it was now freezing, thick ice covered the roads to our front and 8 feet of snow was at each side of us, the road had been cleared of snow just hours before. This was the main historic route and road through the mountains; it was the life line of supplies coming through from the north. Snow chains were fitted to our vehicles to give them some grip and traction on these perilous roads during our assent. Many people died every week on these icy mountain roads, attempting to cross these mountains. The remains and skeletons of their vehicles littered the sides of the road, others could be seen down at the bottom of 300 feet shear drops at the side of the road, the battered and burned out vehicles at the bottom of these ravines was a testament to many failed journeys. This was a haunting sight, crosses and flowers marked the sight of where people had been killed, so many lives lost and people killed tragically. We slowly and carefully made our way, snaking through the mountain roads and passes. The rugged beauty of the mountains took my breath away; this was a truly wild and untouched mountain range. Our vehicles made their way over and through the mountains until we stopped at the mouth of the Salang tunnel, located in the Salang Pass.

"The Salang Tunnel of Ghosts"

We stopped 50 meters from the mouth of the tunnel to stretch our legs. The entrance to this notorious tunnel was dark and foreboding; it had a medieval look and presence about it. Even the locals did not like to travel through it; some locals felt that strongly about it, they would walk over the mountain on foot, which took a full day, instead of travelling on through the tunnel. The locals said that 'Jin' ghosts lived within the tunnel. A large number of people had died in the tunnel over the years, frozen to death within their broken down vehicles, when an avalanche had sealed of both ends of the tunnel, the bodies of men, women and children were recovered, their bodies were frozen solid, with the look of terror etched onto their faces. The whole tunnel had a dark sinister ghost-like feel to it. As we started back on our journey and entered the mouth of the tunnel, the hairs on the back of my neck stood up as we progressed through the mouth under the vast, old grey weathered concrete structure that marked the entrance. The limited light gave the inside of the tunnel an eerie feel and look, small light bulbs every 100 feet give off a distant yellow glow for a second before the toxic petrol fumes from the vehicles completely smothered the light. This place had the feel of a gas chamber and tomb. If the freezing temperatures did not kill you, the overwhelming petrol and engine fumes would. The air inside the tunnel was extremely toxic. I felt that I was in a graveyard, dark shadows moved up and along the walls, following us as we made our way slowly forward. Visibility was down to 20 feet, I could just make out the red break lights of our escort vehicle to our front. The temperature inside the tunnel was well below freezing, the road beneath us was sheet ice, the repetitive sound of the vehicle's snow chains cutting into the ice echoed through the darkness of the tunnel. All of a sudden there was a blinding ray of light to our front; we had turned through a bend in the tunnel. Then in a flash we were surrounded and flooded by brilliant sunlight, we slowly exited the tunnel, the sunlight reflecting off the surrounding snow was blinding, it took us all a few seconds to re-adjust our eyes after the darkness and gloom of the tunnel. We breathed a silent breath on exiting the tunnel; we all became conscious that we had been holding our breath a little towards the end. It had taken us 15 minutes to drive through the Salang tunnel; it had seemed like a lot longer. We all enjoyed breathing in the cold, clean and crisp mountain air, we continued on our journey south. Col Hayatt received a phone call from his good friend Wali Massoud, brother of Ahmad Shah Massoud, Mujahedeen leader, inviting us to stop at the Panjshir valley, the strong hold of the Mujahedeen, for refreshments during our journey to the capital, Kabul. We accepted - our ETA to the Panjshir valley was three hours. Col Hayatt would point out places of interest as we travelled down through the mountain passes and valleys, including the locations of battles and sights of where he had ambushed Russian tank convoys during the Russian Jihad. He told me that many Russian bodies were buried in and across these mountains. Over the next several hours we made our way through the mountains of Northern Afghanistan and down to the flat open plains and lush green fields of Panjshir Province. We travelled across the fertile farmlands and through the villages located close to the entrance to the Panjshir valley.

The Panjshir valley (also spelled Panjsheer or Panjsher) is a valley in North-Central Afghanistan, 150 km north of the capital Kabul, near the Hindu Kush mountain range. Located in the Panjshir Province, it is divided by the Panjshir River. The valley is the home to more than 140,000 people, including Afghanistan's largest concentration of ethnic Tajiks. As of April 2004, it became the heart of Panjshir Province. The Panjshir was the sight of the Panjshir offensives, fought between the DRA and the Soviets against the Mujahedeen during the Soviet war in Afghanistan from 1980-1985. The valley again witnessed renewed fighting during the civil war in Afghanistan 1996-2001 between Taliban and the Northern Alliance under the Command of Ahmad Shah Massoud. Col Hayatt had been one of the key Northern Alliance Commanders during the fighting against the Russians and then later the Taliban. The name Panjshir, literally meaning "Five Lions", refers to five Wali protectors. The valley is steeped in history, the later part being that the Panjshir was the location of some of the most intense and brutal fighting, during the conflicts of modern times. The Mujahedeen of the Panjshir are famous world-wide for their fighting skills. American CIA and British SAS had trained and equipped them back in the 1980s. The Mujahedeen back then had been a formidable fighting force; they had also fought alongside the British and the Americans in 2001 when the Taliban were overthrown from power. After the fighting, the Mujahedeen drifted away, some had entered politics within the new government in Kabul, some had left the country, and others just went back to farming. Groupings within the tribal system meant that some Mujahedeen leaders and Commanders became war lords, ruling over their own small part of Afghanistan. The Panjshir has always been an important location and highway. Nearly 100km long, it leads to two passes over the Hindu Kush, the Khawak Pass (3848m) leading to the northern plains, and Anjoman Pass (4430m) that crosses into Badakhshan, used by the armies of Alexander the Great and Timur. The Red Army had some of its darkest and horrific days in Afghanistan here.

"The renowned Panjshir valley"

We entered the Panjshir valley at 1500hrs this sunny afternoon; the sky was blue and cloudless. The entrance to the valley is small with a single road, flanked with high mountains to each side. The wild fast flowing river runs next to the road, the force of the water being channelled out and through the small entrance was staggering. The noise was deafening from the volume of water thundering down the valley and into the plains below. This location was a natural bottle neck and excellent defensive position. After seeing and experiencing the entrance to the valley for myself, it was no wonder that the Russians were never able to take the Panjshir valley. The mountains surrounding the Panjshir valley were heavily mined with both anti-personnel and anti-tank mines. The only safe route in for vehicles was through the only entrance at the mouth of the valley, the entrance narrowed to just 10 meters in places. We travelled on through to our meeting with Wali Massoud. We passed through the Mujahedeen checkpoints, with heavy machine gun positions overlooking, carefully monitoring all the people and traffic, going in and out of the valley. The threat from Taliban suicide bombers was all too real. After we stopped at every check point for the Col to say his hello's to all the other Mujahedeen fighters, we made our way up the valley. I noted all the old rusting Russian tanks and armoured vehicles in and around the river and along the road side. Col Hayatt saw me taking note; he leaned over and said in a matter of fact voice, they were the ones who did not make it. He smiled; the whole place looked like a graveyard for Old Russian military vehicles, not forgetting all the Russian bodies that must have been buried all around and through the valley.

(Above) The Panjshir Valley

The Panjshir is a very picturesque place, with its lush green fields and wild Blue River, framed with mountains on each side, however, there is an undercurrent of military and hard mountain life, with violence, just bubbling away under the surface. We pulled up outside Ahmad Shah Massoud's house. It looked a little out of place, it was of French design in nature, the late Massoud had put his architectural and engineering skills to good use by building his own house, nestled between the mountains. Ahmed Shah Massoud had been an ethnic Tajik and the most famous Commander of the Afghan Jihad, Massoud was also a master media manipulator and had kept a number of prominent Western correspondents on his leash for more than twenty years. Massoud consistently misled these journalists and some American and European politicians, to believe that he was a pro-Western Muslim who would install democracy, diversity and feminist policies in Afghanistan. His assassination appears to have been planned and executed by Al-Qaeda, on 9th September 2001 only three days, before the 9/11 terrorist attacks on New York.

Wali Massoud came out to greet us, after warm embraces and traditional greetings, we walked over to an outside seating and meeting area, and chi-tea was brought out and served with nuts and dates. After light conversation about our overland trip down from Tajikistan, Afghanistan politics became the subject of choice. President Karzai was feeling threatened by the Panjshir people who, after the fall of the Taliban in 2001, had positioned themselves in almost all of the main and prominent jobs within the new Afghan Government. The Panjshir tribe had pushed out almost all of the other ethnic groups from the South of the country. This had led to no trust and bad blood and feelings of hatred between the Pashtun's in the south and the Panjshir tribe. There was no love lost between the Panjshir tribe and President Karzai who was Pashtun and who was also backed and supported by the Americans. President Hamid Karzai in the previous weeks recalled all his Panjshir Defence attachés, back from Afghan Embassies around the world. Col Hayatt was one of these attachés. News had just leaked out that all the Panjshir Defence attachés were going to be sacked in one hit, all at the same time by President Karzai, who had plans to replace them with attaches who were Pashtun. This bombshell of news had sent shockwaves through the former Mujahedeen and Northern Alliance. The Panjshiri's ability to control events within the Afghan Government was being taken away, culled as one Commander put it. The Panjshiri's strength within Western Governments and countries was being deliberately weakened by Karzai. The Afghan Vice President (VP), who was Panjshiri, was next on President Karzai's list of people who he wanted to replace. In the future, 2014, President Karzai would go one step further in ostracising the Panjshir tribe, by negotiating a power sharing agreement with the Taliban, who were sworn enemies of the Panjshiri tribe. Karzai would also place known drug dealers and war lords within his Afghan Parliament; these were the people who would do Karzai's bidding. President Karzai had also sacked his Foreign Minister Abdullah-Abdullah in the past during his official visit to Washington DC, America; it would come to no one's surprise that Abdullah-Abdullah was from Karte Parwan and lived in the Panjshir valley. Abdullah-Abdullah is a skilful politician and a doctor in medicine; he was a close friend, adviser and bodyguard to the late Ahmad Shah Massoud. The on-going situation was just another example of Karzai's actions to push members of the Panjshir tribe out of Government; he saw them as a threat to him personally. Pashtuns were now taking over all the key positions within the Afghan Karzai Government. Karzai historically got his way and what he wanted; another example of this was back in 2001, when Karzai called the U.S. Embassy in Rome, and then Islamabad on a borrowed satellite phone, and said, "Look, I need some help. I'm willing to fight the Taliban, but I need equipment and supplies". Two days later Karzai's men lit four fires in four corners of a remote mountain area. U.S. intelligence satellites locked on to the signal. The NRO (National Reconnaissance Office) plotted the grid coordinates and sent the DZ imagery to TFD (Task Force Dagger). The next night Special Operations C-130 started dropping containers of gear and equipment. Karzai was one leader who would do whatever it took to achieve what he wanted. Karzai's attitude would become very problematic in the future for Western Governments, including America and Britain. After what is in excess of 14 years of war, including over

447 British and well in excess of 2000 American soldier's lives lost, while fighting in and across Afghanistan. The Taliban are now operating freely within the Afghan Government's political system and they are coming back into power. So what has been achieved? Why did Western soldiers die in such high numbers? Al-Qaeda is still in Afghanistan, Pakistan, Iraq and Syria. Terrorist attacks are on the increase with every month and year that passes. International terrorism is at an all-time high around the world. Has Western Foreign policy brought terrorism and extremism with all its violence and ideology to the streets of Western cosmopolitan countries, London, Paris and New York, (See Glossary Urban siege)?

After our conversation and updates from Wali Massoud, whose conversation was both comprehensive, informative and intriguing, which was no surprise given that he was the former Afghan Ambassador to Both America and Britain, we thanked him for his hospitality and we promised to return. In the future I would spend a lot of time in the Panjshir Valley with the Mujahedeen and attending meetings with Government officials, including several meetings with Abdullah-Abdullah at his mountain retreat in the Panjshir. We drove at speed out of the valley, with silent nods of acknowledgement from the Mujahedeen fighters who manned the military checkpoints, we drove on. With the new road, it only took 45 minutes to reach the city of Kabul. A big difference from the two hours it used to take back in 2002. Obviously the Panjshiri's made sure a new road was built when the Taliban had been toppled from power back in 2001.

"Kabul"

We entered Kabul as the last light of the day was fading; the heat of the afternoon was being replaced by a cool night. The temperature went down dramatically when the sun went down over the surrounding mountains. The city had not changed since my last visit 6 months before. Many of the old buildings in central Kabul were still in ruin, remnants of the past bloody civil war and bitter fighting that followed. Bullet holes from AK47s and the scars of war, prominently decorated the sides of buildings and scorched ruins, we drove silently past, this was a testament to the cities' violent history of fighting and extreme violence that had plagued the cities' people for over 20 years. In October 2001 the Taliban regime was overthrown by Operation Enduring Freedom including NATO and United Front Forces. If ever there was a city in the world that was war torn, Kabul was it. Western Governments had poured obscene amounts of money into the country; unfortunately most of it had gone straight into the pockets of corrupt Afghan Government officials. The city has got some new additions in the form of a small shopping centre and many new extravagant villas, but the undercurrent of violence and poverty is still very visible. Children and injured Afghan soldiers beg openly in the middle of the streets. The Afghan police try to move them on out of sight in an effort to hide what is really going on. The Afghan Government like to project a new and prosperous country, the reality is very dark and troubling. We made our way through all the military check points. Being in the Vice Presidents cars had its perks, we were never stopped. We made our way to the Intercontinental Hotel, which was located on the hill to which overlooked Kabul city. This was going to be our base for the next couple of days, while we enjoyed a couple of down days, we all had things to do, places to go and friends to meet. I headed down the Mustafa Hotel in the middle of town, to catch up with some old friends.

"Mustafa Hotel"

The notorious Mustafa Hotel's bar had been the known hangout for NGOs, journalists and private military contractors, spooks, spies, mercenaries and off duty SF, (Special Forces). This bohemian hangout I had frequented over the past 10 years during my many trips in the country. The Mustafa had a reputation for being no frills, which was a politically correct term for being rough as old boots. It was renowned for many a night of debauchery and hard drinking, Russian vodka, Russian women and other nocturnal activities; it had all the trademarks of an old American Western saloon, whiskey and weapons always made for an interesting and potent mix for a night out. It was also the 'Go To' place to find out what was really going on around town and across Afghanistan. Give young journalists or NGO's a few beers, flatter their ego and they will give you the information you want. With enough Vodka anything is possible. The manager of the hotel was an old friend of mine, so I just grabbed a bottle of vodka, sat at a quiet table and we caught up on old times. We put our Glock pistols on the table and rested our AK47s next to the seat, then made swift work of the bottle of vodka, some inspiring young journalists came over to join us and within the hour I had all the information and updates that I needed. With the work part of the night completed, another bottle of vodka appeared, complements of the hotel manager, this was going to turn out to be yet another epic night at the Mustafa Hotel.

"Covert meetings with CIA, SAS and SOCA"

After a couple of days, we moved into a villa in Wazir Akbar Khan, the district which most of the Foreign Embassy and Diplomatic missions are located in Kabul, the British Embassy was only 300 meters from the location of our villa. Vehicles, weapons, communications were organised; villa security was provided by the Panjshir Mujahedeen. Col Hayatt lived at the villa and kept an office in the operations and conference building located in a large separate building at the rear of the main villa. Meetings were coming in fast and furious, several a day, the meetings at the villa included covert meetings with British SOCA (Serious Organised Crime Agency) and COS 'Chief of Staff' the MI6 chief of station, British SAS Commanders also attended many meetings at the villa location. The SAS COS (Chief of Station) and Blade team Commander worked closely with me on several sensitive tasks. My old friends from the CIA called in, just to touch base; I always made sure that coffee and cold sodas were at the ready. Former members of the Parachute Regiment would frequently call in for a coffee or a cold soda and intelligence update on terrorist activity in the areas which they were operating within; everyone knew that I had my finger on the pulse of Afghan intelligence; I knew what was going on officially and un-officially. Covert meetings and pickups were also put in place by American intelligence, who would pick me up in the dead of night at pre-arranged RV points, I was then driven to an American safe house where briefs and de-briefs took place, I would receive envelopes of $100 bills to cover operational expenses. The senior SAS officer who was based out of the British Embassy had arranged that some of his local assets were keeping a watch on my villa; this was just a security precaution, given the level and amount of weapons and equipment that were located within. My team operating from the villa, including Trevor, Graham and Mick, were all former NCOs in the British army or Special Forces. We were working in the counter proliferation of weapons such as SAMs (Surface to Air missiles) from falling into the hands of Al-Qaeda and other terrorist groups. Having local SAS assets monitoring my villa was reassuring. It was also nice to know they cared about my personal welfare. Everything was going according to plan. Then Colonel Hayatt invited his friend, the then Governor of Kandahar, Assadullah to the Kabul villa for a meeting.

Assadullah was former Mujahedeen which I had a lot of respect for, but he was also a known drug trafficker, operating out of Kandahar Province, Southern Afghanistan. I ran, and confirmed, this information through both my American intelligence contacts and my contact within the British SAS. Both sources confirmed that Assadullah was being watched because of his illegal activities. Assadullah was also known for selling information to the Taliban on British and American troop movements, and the locations of SF (Special Forces) safe houses in and across Kandahar city. I voiced my concerns about Assadullah, during a meeting with British SOCA, who had turned up at my villa with a large box of maps, tactical pilot charts and a new satellite phone for one of my intelligence sources and contacts who was operating across Afghanistan, Pakistan and India. I was running many such high level sources across the whole Middle-East, Afghanistan and surrounding countries. My HUMINT (Human intelligence) network was comprehensive, prodigious and far reaching; my Saudi Arabian contacts were impeccable, as was the rest of my network. I had already achieved great results within the first couple of months of being back fully operational in Afghanistan, locating several terrorist training camps in Afghan and Pakistan and HVTs (High Value Targets) terrorists. What had started out as a small network had grown exponentially. I was receiving high value intelligence on a daily bases. I would hand over all information gained by my trusted sources to American and British intelligence. I was confirmed by the SAS COS as a Grade 'A' intelligence source, which was a confirmation of the value of the intelligence which I had handed over to the SAS and British SOCA. My standing with American Intelligence was good, I had been Grade 'A' intelligence source for them since the Iraq war in 2003.

"Trafalgar night celebration at the Gandamack"

My social life in Afghanistan orientated around my work and contacts, my good friend Peter Jouvenal, who has probably spent more time in Afghanistan than any other Englishman and any other foreign journalist in the world. He first started filming in the country in 1980 shortly after the Soviet invasion. He's probably the only cameraman to have filmed Mullah Omar and one of the few to film Osama bin Laden, who he described as "rather like a bank manager". He was also the first cameraman to film stinger missiles in Afghanistan. Peter Jouvenal now ran the Gandamack Lodge in Kabul, he had organised a celebration dinner for the historic British battle of Trafalgar. The British Ambassador and Deputy Ambassador would be present, as well as 100 prominent people and other dignitaries and VIPs. The MI6 Chief of (Afghan) Station and the SAS Chief of Staff (Afghan Desk) would be present. There were only 100 tickets available, so spaces were limited and sort after. The British Embassy senior staff took most of the tickets. This would have made for a tempting target for a Taliban suicide bomber. I received tickets for my team. We dusted off our tuxedos and attended, everyone looked the 'Bulldogs Bullocks' very sharp and distinguished in formal dress. Peter Jouvenal had made sure that every detail was impeccably presented which made for a memorable evening. The seating for the night was three long wooden tables almost the full length of the small room, 30 people sat each side. The idea of this was to recreate the officer's dinner on Nelsons flag ship, the night before the battle. The small Captains table was situated at the head of the small room. The British Ambassador and Royal Naval Commodore, Peter and his wife Hassina were all seated facing the rest of the guests. The atmosphere was good and got better when the wine started to flow during the meal, followed by decanters of port and speeches by the Commodore, who was the guest of honour. After which the SAS Major and I retired out on the veranda to enjoy a cigar. The night was an outstanding success on every level. Peter Jouvenal had planned and pulled off yet another outstanding night to remember. It was nice to see everyone enjoying themselves; it also felt a little surreal given that we were in Afghanistan, in the middle of a war zone. This just proved that we Brits can put on a good show anywhere, at any time.

(Above) By Author who was sat with senior members of the British SAS; The British Ambassador about to give his after dinner speech.

"Assadullah the Governor of Kandahar"

The first meeting with Assadullah the next morning was when I knew something was not right. I'm experienced enough to know when a potential intelligence contact is lying to me. I have interviewed, developed, cultivated and handled hundreds of sources during my 12 years operating across the Arab world; Assadullah, I knew he had his own hidden agenda and was trying to play on his friendship with Col Hayatt. Assadullah wanted to use Col Hayatt and my credibility with British SOCA and Americans intelligence. One of Assadullah's thoughts was to feed British and American intelligence agencies false and out of date information; while he was giving the Taliban information and intelligence on British and American troop movements and the locations of SF (Special Forces) safe houses across Kandahar city and Province in Southern Afghanistan. Assadullah was playing both sides of the war on terror, when the Taliban and Al-Qaeda found out in the future what Assadullah was really up to, they would try several times to assassinate him for talking to western intelligence. Assadullah had tried to order a specialised B6 armoured Toyota 4X4 with communications equipment fitted, through some of my European contacts. I quickly put an end to that, when I found out that he had lied to me and Col Hayatt about not being still involved in the illegal drugs business. He was involved right up to his neck. Assadullah had the intention of using the armoured 4X4 in his illegal activities. I had informed British SOCA about Assadullah and they agreed with my actions to cancel his armoured 4X4. He lost his small deposit. I could not be seen being connected to Assadullah in any way; I also made my feelings very clear to Col Hayatt, who was not happy when I called his friend a drug dealer and drug lord. I had made it very clear what I thought of Assadullah, he was furious when he found out that I had cancelled his 4X4 and that I had publicly called him a dirty drug lord, I had dented his ego, sometimes the truth hurts. I had confirmed Assadullah's illegal activities through sources in the British SAS and British SOCA. I quickly broke all contact with Assadullah, unbeknown to me at this time; Assadullah continued his meetings with British SOCA and Col Hayatt at locations around the British Embassy and Kabul. Was it now British SOCA and the British Embassy policy to be dealing with and doing business with Afghan drug lords, who were known to be giving intelligence to the enemy, the Taliban? I was about to find out the full meaning of "Plausible Deniability" and how dirty British Embassy internal politics could be. Also unbeknown to me, senior staff within the British Embassy and FCO, wanted to silence me and my team by any means, due to their embarrassment and hidden agenda, their complete betrayal would surface in time, their actions, treachery and cover-up would have future far reaching and lethal consequences. One example of this was when FCO and MI6 HQ London "turned away" would not talk to, two former British Senior NCOs soldiers who had flown from Afghanistan to Britain on my instructions. They had walked into MI6 HQ to hand over files containing sensitive information on terrorists and suicide bombers coming into Europe and the UK, the file contained photographs, names, phone numbers and other sensitive information including locations of terrorist training camps across the Middle-East. When Colonel Bob Stewart British MP found out about this, within 30 minutes of meeting the soldiers he confirmed the Author of the report was Anthony Malone, he phoned another Colonel in MOD then he personally walked the two former British soldiers and my Next of Kin into the MOD HQ in White Hall London to hand over the report to senior British Military Officers. A debrief followed. All the information was acted upon. (Colonel Stewart confirmed the above facts to Sky News in an interview with Lisa Holland) The FCO and MI6 had blocked my team handing over the report due to their internal politics within the agencys and FCO. So I went straight to my British MOD contacts in London to make sure the information was acted upon. Attacks were stopped and lives were saved, job done. People within the British FCO should hold their heads in shame over this, how many other people have they turned away when trying to help or hand over sensitive information?

"Kidnapped by rogue Afghan police and NDS - 22rd January 2008 at 0500hrs"

That early morning started the same as any other, up bright and early. Ready for the meetings that were planned that day in Jalalabad province, east of the capital Kabul. I had travelled to and across Jalalabad city and province many times over the years, I knew the area well. We set off early morning to miss all the Kabul traffic. On route to the location of the planned meeting at American FOB (Forward Operating Base) located at Toukoum, close to the Afghan, Pakistan border. Travelling in a lone unmarked 4X4, with my two Afghan personnel, we approached a group of civilian cars and 4X4s, situated along the side of the main Jalalabad, Kabul highway. Four men, Afghan nationals in police uniforms stepped out and waved my 4X4 over, the police often had a check point at this location. On slowing down, two 4X4s pulled in front of our vehicle and one pulled to our rear to cut off our escape routes. Within seconds, fifteen men in plain clothes surrounded my 4X4, all carrying AK47s and PKMs, all their weapons pointing at me with their safety catches off, ready to fire. I always like going up against good odds, but this was a little one sided. I showed my hands on the dashboard. Within a split second I was dragged from the 4X4, a black hood was placed over my head; I was handcuffed, then again dragged and thrown into the back floor of another 4X4. During my military training and later when I was teaching security personnel and operators, there are some key things to remember, they are, if you do not have any other way of getting out of a kidnap situation alive, do not resist your enemy when you are in a 100% no win situation. I would have been up for shooting my way out of the road block, it would not have been the first time, but something seemed off, these were not terrorists, I did not want to be responsible for shooting or killing several Afghan policemen. In a kidnap situation it is sometimes best to be passive, even if you want to fight back, don't. It's hard to fight if you're shot and you cannot stay switched on if you're knocked out with the butt of an AK47. When the odds are stacked against you, keep your head, stay alert and notice all your surroundings, number of men, weapons, 4X4, locations, direction of travel and movement, pay attention to every detail. My first instinct, I had been snatched, kidnapped by Taliban, even with this thought; something did not seem to fit. I have spent many years operating against terrorists throughout the Middle-East, and I had been in tight situations in the past, my gut instinct told me that something was out of place. I would later find out that I had been kidnapped by rogue NDS (National Directorate of Security) Afghan security services. I was taken to a location in Jalalabad, a disused farm house, interrogation centre, evident from blood stained chains fixed to the walls and metal cage, built into the farm house courtyard, surrounded by bullet ridden 12 foot high blood stained mud walls, with old razor wire and eight armed guards with AK47s circling. I was stripped searched, beaten and thrown into a cage. The cage smelled of death, corpses of decaying animals lay off to one side, rats scurried past me. There was no sign of my Afghan staff. I would also find out later that both of them were working covertly for a rogue member of NDS. They had been threatened by NDS, to co-operate with them or be killed or sent to prison. This was the normal procedure with NDS, using scare and terror tactics on their own people. What is the difference between them and the Taliban; they both have a complete disregard for human life and human rights. My personal rucksack and equipment was stripped and searched. Nothing untoward was found. Luckily my personal combat equipment and new weapons including M-4A1 with M203 fitted, (See Glossary M-4A1) were waiting for me at the American FOB. I managed to distract the Afghan guards while I was being searched and my second small emergency mobile phone and Sim card were not found, it was well hidden in the map lining of my jacket. After 30 minutes the guards and the other personnel calmed down. I was able to crouch down, out of sight and retrieve my small mobile phone. I sent a message to a contact, a British friend. The Panjshir mafia had planned and tried to plant illegal drugs, narcotics in their bags on route to the airport the weeks before, all this had been reported to the British Embassy Kabul. The Panjshir mafia makes a lot of money doing this; they then charge obscene amounts of money to get people released, 'Legal Kidnap for ransom'. This was made possible due to the non-action by people like the British Embassy when this happens and is reported. The British Embassy and SOCA chose to ignore the rampant corruption in the Afghan Ministry of Justice. I told my contact that I had been snatched outside Jalalabad, I instructed them to go to the British Embassy, find the SF, SAS officer 'V' and put a trace and locate my position, using my phone signal to triangulate. This was carried out within the hour. I had been reported kidnapped and my location confirmed by the British Military. When the British officials had confirmed that I had been kidnapped by a rogue team of Afghan NDS, this had been organised by corrupt Afghan politicians, who were members of terrorist groups and drug lords, I had a feeling Assadullah the corrupt Governor of Kandahar had his hand in my kidnapping, time would tell. Because I was British, the NDS, Taliban beat me, this was expected of these animals ???. They even tried to get me to sign a confession, stating that I was working for the American intelligence services, I politely declined their offer and obviously they were not impressed with my not co-operating. It would take a hell of a lot more than a beating from these savages to break me. I was dragged out of the cage, shackled and driven to a police station in Kabul. Because my British military contacts within the Embassy were aware of my situation, they put pressure on the head of the Afghan NDS to explain what the hell they were doing kidnapping a British national. Too many people knew that rogue NDS had me, so killing me was not an option. Their only option was to hand me over to the Afghan police in Kabul. The rogue NDS who had taken me at this point just wanted rid of me, there was heat and questions coming down on them from all over the place. After being locked in a wet cold cell for several hours, I was frog marched into the chief of police office in Kabul police HQ. I saw the British Embassy armoured 4X4s outside, my spirits lifted, at last the situation would be dealt with in a professional manner and boy did I get that very wrong. High level politics were now at play.

"Plausible Deniability"

What happened next both completely floored and astonished me. No help from the British Embassy to get to the bottom of the false Afghan allegation and case lodged against me by corrupt Afghan officials and drug lords. Quote, from the British Embassy staff, 'they cannot get involved with the Afghan Justice system', I informed them that this was all a setup. They did nothing, what about my safety, is that not a concern to the British Embassy? Their answer was the same, 'we cannot get involved in the workings of the Afghan police'. I asked them who was responsible for kidnapping me, a British national; the Embassy said they would look into it? I never got an answer to the question. I commented that the two British Embassy staff sat in front of me, 'did realise that there was a major war going on and that Afghanistan is a full on conflict zone'. Again I got the same monotone response, 'we cannot interfere'. I asked what happened to me now, given the circumstances I thought that this was a relevant question. I would be kept in police custody and put in an Afghan prison, Tawqeef, until the situation was sorted out. I said 'Fuck me, you're joking right. Tawqeef is full of Taliban and other terrorists'. The look on the Embassy staff's faces was a picture, they said slowly looking at me, 'there are Taliban in Tawqeef?', I shook my head, the Embassy was clueless or playing dumb, I couldn't figure which. Either way I had the sensation that I was being hung out to dry. So this was what Plausible Deniability felt like?

"Tawqeef Prison Kabul"

In brief what happened next; I was dropped like a lamb to the slaughter, in the mix with terrorists, into the nuthouse that was Tawqeef. False charges were lodged against me by drug dealers and corrupt Afghan Government officials, no evidence presented, no Afghan prosecution witness able to appear in an Afghan court. My human rights violated on several occasions, beatings and torture by Afghan authorities, because I was British. Afghan Judges and Prosecutors demanding bribes for my freedom and the political situation manipulated by people to keep me quiet and in prison. I was railroaded into prison with Al-Qaeda and Taliban Commanders. The 'long beards' were the ones I needed to watch. The Panjshir mafia also tried to have me killed several times while I was in Afghan prison; they had told the Taliban who I was. This would be confirmed by Al-Qaeda and Taliban Commander Saladin in the future. Locked up in Tawqeef, I learned to adapt and over-come again. I found ways of managing my disgust at the cockroaches and the mould, the rats and spiders that crawled over you as you slept. The overflowing toilets and their stench was gagging, the lack of proper washing facilities. Having been fastidiously clean and tidy all my adult life, I was permanently unshaven, dirty and smelly. I hated that aspect of my incarceration with every fibre of my being. The one 'good' thing was that I met up with Bevan Campbell, an ex-South African Air Force Intelligence Major, with whom I'd had dealings prior to being locked up. Bevan was working for Louis Berger Group (LBG) when we hooked up again in February 2007. His main area of operations as a Security Manager on LBG's REFS project was the hydro-electric scheme at Kajaki Dam in Helmand Province; the area that the British military were responsible for. We had exchanged information on Taliban movements in the area. Bevan's main objective was to ensure that the turbines, necessary for the completion of the scheme, would be able to pass through the village of Sangin, on the Helmand River, and it was this that had brought us together on many an occasion at The

Gandamak. To say it was a 'relief' to see another 'westerner', and someone I knew is an understatement.

One morning while walking around the prison courtyard, there was a loud explosion, a Taliban suicide bomber had just detonated himself next to the prison wall, targeting a passing army patrol. The following detonation had sent a cloud of thick smoke, dust, rocks and metal, hundreds of feet into the air, debris showered down on the prison, shrapnel and bloody body parts, shredded arms and parts of a human torso, landed with a thump on the ground within the courtyard which I was standing. Other debris landed on the surrounding roof tops. The air was thick with dust and smoke, the distinctive smell of burnt human flesh was evident. Sporadic gunfire could be heard across the city. This was a timely reminder of the war escalating across the country. The prisoners swept up the shrapnel and body parts and just put them in the bin.

(Left) By Tim Brown, the leg of a suicide bomber in Kabul Afghanistan, the rest of him was scattered around the whole area.

30 people died in the Taliban attack, JADA (Just another day in Afghanistan). My situation was precarious and extremely dangerous. Officials and prominent people in Afghanistan and the British Embassy Kabul were embarrassed by how successful I had been at my work and my efforts to save British and American soldier's lives. I had always prided myself at doing the right thing and I had steadfast principles. Even under beatings and torture by Afghan authorities, they did not come close to breaking my resolve or spirit, I was steadfast and absolute. My attitude was 'bring it on'. An old friend in the intelligence agencies had once told me; at some point on Task the Western politicians will make you chose, Do good or Do well. I had always chosen to do good, the same as my old friend. I was to experience, however, the shocking betrayals of people close to me, who had flawed characters and no principles or loyalty, which were only focused on their personal gain and careers, regardless of the consequences. These people showed their true colours. My belief system would be tested to breaking point and beyond. I would question who I was and what I had been taught over the years, the very fabric of my being and soul. Only my training, tradecraft, principles and one close friend, Dil 'Pegasus's support would guide me

through the dark, unprecedented journey that was about to start. After 6 months of being held in Tawqeef, abandoned by the British Embassy, I was looking at my options of getting the hell out of there. The name Pul-i-Charkhi came up during conversations with the other Afghan prisoners, they had joked that I would be sent to Pul-i-Charkhi, one of the most dangerous and notorious prisons in the world, filled with thousands of Taliban and Al-Qaeda prisoners. 125 detainees from Bagram detention facility 'Black Prison' ran by the American military in Afghanistan and 250 former detainees from the American Guantanamo Bay detention camp had just been transferred to Pul-i-Charkhi prison. Mass graves close to the prison had been discovered, over 2000 bodies had been found, investigations were still on going, but it looked like they had all been shot, executed. Other mass graves had also been found around the Pul-i-Charkhi prison area. I laughed at the preposterous idea of being sent to Pul-i-Charkhi prison. There was no way the British Embassy would ever allow a British national and former British Paratrooper to be taken to Pul-i-Charkhi. This would be nothing short of a death sentence if it happened. I still had faith that the British Embassy would work its backdoor channels and get me quietly released once the politics surrounding my situation had calmed down. Boy did I get that wrong! One morning out of the blue, Bevan and I were called into the courtyard in the middle of the prison, then shackled and frog marched out at gun point and put on the old Afghan prison bus which was heading to Pul-i-Charkhi prison. I had a dark sense of foreboding, that I was being driven to my death.

Anth Malone (Rogue Warrior) Part Two

"Pul-i-Charkhi - Ill-treatment, torture & Corruption"

Pul-i-Charkhi prison, hell on earth.

Approaching the notorious prison in an old, beat up, bullet ridden, blue Afghan prison van, full of armed guards carrying AK47's with their safety catches off. Several prisoners painfully shackled and being thrown around with every bump, pot hole and bomb crater in the road. The van crawled and snaked around machine gun nests, firing points and mud walls of bombed out buildings, smouldering where rubbish and blood stained clothes were being burned. The pungent smell of rotten, burning rubbish filled the air. The quiet eerily silence as we drove past skeletons of old Russian military vehicles was deafening, as if we were passing graves, which from the look of it, we were. We turned past a sand bank, the dark grey shadows of the old decaying concrete prison structure and gun-watch towers came into view. It was like a scene from an epic old horror movie. We passed massive amounts of rusty old razor wire scattered across the desert, attached was old, blood stained clothing, blowing in the wind, obviously people trying to escape but did not make it, old broken grave stones protruding through the desert sands and razor wire. This was the prison graveyard; I would find out later that the whole desert around the prison was a mass graveyard.

The sheer size of this barbaric place sent a chill down my spine; the 40 foot outer solid stone walls gave Pul-i-Charkhi the dark appearance of a medieval fortress. It's shadow casting an eerie chill across the surrounding desolate desert landscape. Dark foreboding thoughts filled my mind. Were all the horrific stories I had heard about this place true? I always thought they were just stories, now I was not so sure. My darkest nightmares were about to become a reality.

Pul-i-Charkhi is one of the most dangerous and notorious prisons in the world, its reputation is well deserved, it made Alcatraz look like Disneyland and Saddam Hussein's Iraqi torture chambers were nothing in comparison; I have seen them first-hand, so I know. It is a well-known fact that the prison guards in Pul-i-Charkhi run the outside of the prison, the Taliban and Al-Qaeda run the inside. Swift 'Sharia' Islamic law is implemented throughout the prison. Prisoners are killed or executed weekly. The inside of the prison is run like an Al-Qaeda training school, 'Madrasah', over half of the prison population are recruited and trained in Al-Qaeda ideology. Top Al-Qaeda and Taliban Commanders are located within the prison and other top Al-Qaeda and Taliban Commanders visit weekly on visitor's day for operational meetings and planning attacks. Including IED and suicide bombings on Western, British and American 'ISAF' soldiers across Afghanistan, including Jalalabad and Helmand. British and American soldiers died as a result of what was going on from inside Pul-i-Charkhi prison. Built to house 2,000 prisoners, Pul-i-Charkhi now housed over 5,000 terrorists and Afghan prisoners, who called this overcrowded hell 'home'. The Prison was mentored by the British Embassy Kabul, who for years was in denial of what was really going on. Over 10 years of sustained cover-up of the horrific truth, due to internal British Embassy, FCO politics. As a former British soldier this was unacceptable. The more I spoke out on this point, the less help I received from the British Embassy Kabul, until there was no help at all. I became 'Persona Non Grata'.

Escape is virtually impossible. The last prisoners who tried to escape, right after being marched out to work in the desert, were shot in the back of the head as they tried to flee and escape. Firing squads were also justified by the Afghan authorities to kill prisoners sentenced to death; they later changed this to hanging, which was rarely carried out currently at the time. Prisoners were left hanging by the neck, dying slowly in agony. I spoke to future victims, prisoners on their way to the gallows; the deep dark look in their eyes was that of a caged animal, about to be slaughtered, they were powerless to prevent it. The sounds of emotional pleading, crying and sobbing by some of these prisoners will stay with me for the rest of my life.

To the prison guards, sadistic abuse and torture even murder were a sport for their personal amusement. Being from a military background I noticed that all the heavy machine guns in the guard towers were facing inwards, towards the prison blocks. The guards seemed to be more worried about the Al-Qaeda and Taliban prisoners inside the prison, than the weekly Taliban attacks on the prison. It is difficult to describe what it felt like going through the heavy black foreboding iron gates of the prison entrance, surrounded by armed Afghans with AK47's and tanks. Imagine walking through the fiery gates of hell with tormented screams in the background and knowing that you will never walk out alive, times that by ten and you're on the way to how I felt at that day and moment in time. The sense, sights and smells of sustained human suffering, torment and death, were shockingly evident on every level. In typical British gallows humour, I turned around to Bevan, who I had got to know well, and said 'do you want to put a bet on who gets beheaded first?' It's quite funny now looking back on it, but it was not at the time. The fact was I was the only British national in the whole prison. The American Embassy and Government would never allow one of its nationals to be put or held here, it was deemed far too dangerous, and obviously the British Embassy did not get that memo...! I gave myself a 10% chance of walking out of there alive, not very good odds, but hell, I liked being the underdog, nothing new there really. The thought did occur to me that certain people in the British Embassy and FCO might not want me to survive my situation. I was obviously expendable, 'plausible deniability' came to mind. I had heard this saying many times during my time working in covert operations in Africa and across the Middle-East, only now did I start to understand the true meaning and implications of these words.

On entering the prison, the transport-van pulled over onto some waste land. Off to one side, the area was full of discarded rubbish and human waste. Several Afghan men in mixed dress army-police uniforms and civilian clothing, some wearing the black turban of the Taliban; suddenly stormed the prison van, shouting-screaming and slapping prisoners at random. The prison guards were carrying AK47s which were loaded and had their safety catches off, ready to fire. The guards hit and pushed the barrel of their weapons into prisoner's chests, just looking for any excuse or reason to fire and kill any prisoner who tried to fight back or retaliate. The vehicle was quickly searched. Me being the only British Western prisoner on the bus, the guards launched into a torrent of verbal abuse at me; 'infidel, kufir' and 'British pig' were shouted at me with venom in their voices. One of the guards was Taliban; his brother had been killed in Helmand province the week before by British soldiers, so he was feeling the love for me in a big way. He finished his onslaught of abuse, spat on me and walked off away from the van, a look of utter hatred in his eyes; I remember thinking that the next time we were to meet would be interesting. Christ, if the guards were anti-British Westerner, then the greeting from the Al-QaedaTaliban prisoners was going to be all warm and fuzzy, greeting me with open arms, 'Not'. In short I was totally and completely fucked, you have to look at the funny side of it, what a way to go, odds 5,000 to 1. I had always liked being the underdog. John Hardy, the RSM, Regimental Sergeant Major of 3 Para, had 'once said' in Helmand; "Paratroopers are meant to be surrounded by the enemy". I was good at looking after myself, but this was getting ridiculous. Even by my own crazy standards. Men I had trained during Special Forces training and during the Iraq War had given me the nickname "Rogue Warrior". I was about to live up to that name and then some. Unknown to me, this was going to be my home from home for the next 3 years. I had no idea of what was about to happen or what a rollercoaster ride and journey I had just embarked upon, but one thing was or sure it was going to be "Emotional".

All prisoners were dragged off the prison van and lined up against an old bullet ridden blood stained wall, so this was the execution wall I had heard about. The guards started to smile at me; this unnerved me, I was in deep crap and not wearing Wellington boots, the sky was a clear blue and the sun warmed my face, I hoped this was not going to be my last sight of this world before a bullet through the back of the head. I noticed another prisoner, stripped to the waist and bare foot, chained to another outer prison wall like an animal. Blood covered the wall and floor around him, he tried turning his back on us, the cuts and whip marks right across his back were horrific, and blood was still seeping from his wounds. This poor Afghan man had been brutally tortured for sport by the Afghan prison guards. The guards just laughed and pointed at him making jokes. The tortured man was so malnourished; his rib cage was visible through his skin. Brutal torture was commonplace across the prison; I found out later that this Afghan man's only crime was to ask the guards for some bread. I would witness hundreds of human rights abuses (many documented by the Red-Cross) within British Embassy mentored Pul-i-Charkhi Prison. The smell of rotten rubbish and human waste was overpowering, orders were barked at the guards by an old boy in military style uniform. We were frog-marched into one of the old prison blocks, dark and dingy, no electricity, no windows and rotten rubbish everywhere. Piercing screams and crying/sobbing could be heard through the darkness. I noticed sunlight protruding through the bullet holes in the wall; this gave the whole corridor an eerie feel, dark shadows moved silently across the floor and between the beams of sunlight, this place gave me the creeps. We were lead into a holding area, the Old Russian dungeon, we were quickly broken down into small groups and our personal kit-clothing was ripped apart and searched, the guards helping themselves to whatever they wanted. One prisoner tried to appeal; he was silenced quickly by slaps and a beating from the guards. I stayed quiet just trying to blend in and assess my surroundings. A lone prisoner walked into the dungeon, he was wearing flowing white Arabic robes and he spoke in classic Arabic. He ordered a group of prisoners, who were also in Arab dress, to be taken up-stairs to one of the accommodation blocks. Al-Qaeda was looking after their own fighters and men. The prison guards carried out all orders that the strange Afghan ordered them to do. I would later learn that this Afghan was called Saladin; Commander within the Al-Qaeda, Taliban network. As he left the room, Saladin, without a word being said, gave me a deep look of utter contempt. From my time spent in the Middle-East including Saudi Arabia, I knew that Saladin was a lot more than just one of the Al-Qaeda Commanders; he was Al-Qaeda Taliban senior leadership. The way people acted around him was with utter respect and loyalty. I was interested in meeting this man again; he is just a man at the end of the day. The first rule in warfare, know your enemy as you know yourself. Anyway if I was going to die, I wanted to look the man in the eye before he gave the order for me to be killed (I am kind of old fashioned when it comes to this sort of thing).

I was in a very dangerous and precarious position, no field manuals taught you how to act or deal with a situation like this. So I did what I do best, improvise, adapt, overcome and followed my gut instinct that had saved my life more times than my Colt 45 pistol. I found out much later that the British Embassy was not even aware that I had been moved to Pul-i-Charkhi. The British Embassy only found out several weeks later when they tried to visit me at the old Kabul Prison 'Tawqeef' so much for British Embassy duty of care?

"Old Russian dungeon and torture chamber"

After my kit had been ripped apart and searched, I was personally strip searched, then told to stand in a dark corner. I complied, carefully assessing and weighing up the prison guards around me. They were not very professional, their kit and uniforms were dirty and not in very good serviceable order. These prison guards were just "gophers" to the Taliban, Al-Qaeda prisoners. On closer inspection the corner of the dungeon had crimson blood stained rusting chains hanging from the walls and old meat hooks hanging from the ceiling. This was definitely the Old Russian dungeon and torture chamber. I had heard about this place, but never in my worst nightmares did I ever imagine I would one day be standing in it. Blood stained the walls and floor, blood sprays were across the ceiling, some looked fresh. The only thing that was missing was the mutilated bodies hanging from the ceilings meat hooks. I later found out that the bodies were all buried out the back of the prison (See Phil Young's official British legal statement, prisoners being hanged, murdered by Afghan prison guards). The Taliban and Al-Qaeda were bringing the horrors of the old torture chamber back to life. Hundreds of prisoners had been tortured to death in this dark foreboding place; this was definitely the place of nightmares and horrific human suffering and death. My only aim was to walk out of here in one piece, so even if you're flapping inside, you must never show any emotion on the outside, the order of the day was to stay cool, calm and collected and take everything in, places, locations, personalities, the whole situation as it unfolded around me and the main players. I knew that every little detail could be very important at a later date. My only option was to stay focused and go as unnoticed as possible, luckily I did not look like the normal Westerner stereotype, so that was one plus at this point.

A loud scream, from down in the dark dungeon corridor jolted my mind-set back to my present time and situation. An Afghan Prison officer, with a big belly spilling over his old Russian belt and bad fitting dirty clothes, which stank of sweat and BO, entered the dungeon; his odour and bad cigarette breath polluted the whole room as he entered, this guy was a sure winner of the prison 'Mr Ugly' contest. He was not just grotesque and ugly, he had an evil demeanour. His entire persona was that of an old, dirty over weight animal. I would later find out the other prisoners nicknamed this guy the 'pig'. My first impressions had been bang on; this prison officer took pleasure in torturing anyone. The word sadist springs to mind, all that was missing from this sadist was the black leather underwear with the studs on the inside. He held a radio in one hand and a cigarette in the other. Another cell phone rang out in the dungeon; a young prison guard pulled out the phone from his top left shirt pocket and moved over to a hole in the outer wall to get a better reception. The guard was silhouetted against the bright sunlight coming into the dungeon from outside. A few words were spoken and exchanged in Pashtun, this drew my attention, Pashtun is the language from Southern Afghanistan and Western Pakistan, all Taliban and some of Al-Qaeda, also speak this language, as well as Arabic. The guard walked over and looked myself and Bevan over. He shouted some orders and me and Bevan where lead outside with our personal kit and quickly put back on the prison van. Col Najib had both Bevan's and my files in his hands and took them to the driver of the prison van where he somewhat ceremoniously handed them over, turned around and gave us a look of total disdain and walked off. We were surrounded by prison guards at this point and I remember thinking 'Now we do have a problem...!' The heat of the midday sun was stifling and you could taste the dust in the air. Several Taliban were walking, swaggering arrogantly past the prison van looking in, aggressively banging on the windows of the prison van and whispering amongst themselves. They wore the standard black head dress, turban of the Taliban and Al-Qaeda. The terrorists were very open about whom they were and it was very apparent that the guards and other prisoners feared them. The Taliban exchanged words in Pashtun with the guards, voices were raised and insults were aimed at us. The normal 'British pig infidel'. It's nice to feel loved at such times. The Taliban spat on the van and then walked away. After 20 minutes of us just sitting there in limbo, several guards entered the van, sat and the van moved off slowly, I don't know who was more relieved, me or the guards.

The van drove around to the back area of the prison, where the American CIA "GIT-MO" is located in Afghanistan. This was the Max-Security facility where the American CIA interrogated terrorists; it had all the hallmarks and characteristics of the original "GIT-MO" Guantanamo Bay, Camp X-ray and Delta located in Cuba. Massive amounts of razor-wire, CCTV cameras and orange boiler suits and black blind folds. I could see the prisoners being walked up the metal stairs twisting up the outside of the tall building. We were ordered off the van and taken into a small court-yard; this was the entrance to another small max-security compound, block 10 next to "GIT-MO". I looked up in the shadow of the foreboding, big blue metal gate towering 30 feet high above me. Topped with razor wire, guard towers and search lights. Through a small gap in the wall I could just make out metal cages 'chicken runs' used for prisoner exercise inside. OMG; this was going to be like the bloody war movie "The great escape", the only difference was, being surrounded by terrorists and terrorists were also the guards? In the true time served words of a combat veteran and paratrooper, this was a 'dear diary' moment. I was totally 'fucked'. This was turning into one hell of a day. Due to the tight shackles around my ankles, I shuffled through the large metal gates, guarding the entrance to the inner compound, towards the prison accommodation block. I shuffled past the metal cages on the left. I noticed a lone Afghan prisoner handcuffed to the cage in a painful stress position, his hands cuffed high behind his back so high that the prisoner was standing on his tip-toes trying to relieve the forced pressure and pain on his arms and shoulders. Blood trickled down the prisoners face, from his nose, mouth and alarmingly from his eyes. He had been severely and brutally beaten and tortured by the guards and left in the scorching Afghan midday sun. The prisoner's demeanour was that of someone who had resigned himself to his fate, urine ran down his legs and pooled with blood around his bare feet. The smell was over powering, he was begging and whimpering for help and water, the guards ignored him. Treating him with complete contempt and indifference?

"Maximum Security, Afghan Guantanamo Bay"

(Above) Exclusive Photographs of inside Afghanistan's Guantanamo Bay.

The guards manhandled me into the prison block and removed the metal shackles, blood flowed painfully back into my hands and feet, we were roughly given a standard rub down search. The guards spread our personal kit and clothing across an old table and started to search our kit again. One of the guards did not know what shaving gel in a can looked like, so he ended up spraying it all over our kit and himself, the other guards laughed and called him a donkey. From first impressions, the guards at this location were not too bright on any level. As the British Defence Minister 'Fox' once said "Afghanistan is a 13th Century broken country" never have truer words ever been spoken. I would later find out that the guard 'donkey' as the other guards call him, was in fact the guard Commander, Abdul Khan 'Taliban'. The name given to him by the other prisoners was 'Candy Man', he would and could get hold of anything you wanted for a price, phones-food-medical supplies, if he could make money he would sell it to you.

Prison rules were more like guide lines than rules; this was what the guards told me as they laughed. These were the same prison guards, trained and mentored by the British Embassy Kabul. It wasn't until much later (3 years) that proper vetting and security checks were carried out and implemented on Afghan prison guards. The fact was that most of the guards were

Taliban. A little golden nugget of information that the incompetent British prison mentors, conveniently kept on overlooking? (My highlighting this small, but I felt significant point made me very popular with the British Embassy prison mentors over the coming years) which would end up with an official petition on the British Government '10 Downing Street' website. Officially authorised by the British Government; The Prime Minister's office, calling for an independent investigation into FCO/BEK. Obviously the FCO/BEK was all warm and fuzzy towards me?

The prison guards searched through all our kit and taxing us 50% of the food and drinking water we had. It's common practice that guards always take half of any food that prisoners have, they called it free tax? The only people who did not ever get taxed on anything were the Al-Qaeda and Taliban prisoners. One guard made the mistake of trying; he was never heard of or seen again. Most, if not all of the prison guards, are on the Al-Qaeda-Taliban payroll; depending on their rank depended on how much the Al-Qaeda, Taliban prisoners would pay them. Payments were given monthly always at the start of the month. The corrupt Afghan Government often did not pay their prison guards for 3 to 4 months. The corrupt Afghan Government officials would just keep the money given to them by the Americans and British Governments. The guards had to live and feed their families, for several months without any pay, Al-Qaeda exploited this fact to the full. The British Embassy was fully aware of all this but did not follow information up or complain, because the British Embassy/FCO 'did not want to upset the politics within the corrupt Afghan Government'; this was just how things worked in Afghanistan.

For years the British Embassy Kabul would try to cover-up and even deny that the Afghan Government and Ministry of Justice was corrupt. Gross incompetence and neglect of duty, are just two ways people used to describe the actions of the BEK/FCO, their 'duty of care' was non-existent. The corruption was epidemic throughout the prison, guards sold anything and everything to prisoners including; mobile and satellite phones at a premium, $150 up to $1,000, a laptop would set you back $2,000, even copies of prison keys for cells and gates could be bought for the right price; an example of this was the $10,000 paid by the Taliban, when several Taliban, Al-Qaeda terrorists escaped from Max-security block 10. 20 Afghan prison guards and Commanders were later put into prison in Pul-i-Charkhi Block 10, due to the terrorist escapes. This serves as an example of how 'disconnected from reality' the British Embassy prison mentors were. All they seemed to care about was turning up at the prison to hand out expensive prison clothing, jackets, boots, belts, and riot equipment (all supplied by Britain). The Afghan prison guards had not been paid for over three months at this point, by the end of the day; most if not all of the expensive prison equipment had been sold by the Afghan guards down the local market (bazaar). The small amount of money received by the Afghan prison guards was just 5% of the value of the equipment bought by the British Embassy, British tax payers. The guards used the money from the sale of their British equipment to buy food for them and their families. The prison guards commented to me, why the British prison mentors don't just pay them their wages for the past three months, instead of giving them expensive equipment that they did not want or need? This was not an isolated incident, it happened several times, even after I brought the subject up with the British Embassy during one of their rare prison visits.

"Jack CIA..."

The name 'Jack-CIA' was spoken several times by the prison guards. As they pointed at me, one of the guards from Kandahar City, Southern Afghanistan, the spiritual home of the Taliban, stroked his long black beard and asked in his broken English, if we knew or were friends of 'Jack'. Obviously playing completely dumb, there was only one answer for me 'absolutely not'. Who was he, this Jack person; Bevan did not know Jack, but was aware of who he was and what he'd been imprisoned for. I did know Jack, and I also knew his real name. I had met Jack years earlier at the 'Mustaffa Hotel' in Kabul, a place that was a hangout for press-private security personnel and Special Forces types looking for a good time, good whiskey, hot women and reliable firearms. Jack and I had a lot in common. Jack was a Captain in the American Special Forces and had been part of 'Task Force Dagger' hunting UBL (UBL is the standard abbreviation used by the CIA for Osama bin Laden). Jack had returned to Afghan when he 'left' the American Military. Unofficially he was still working for the American Government, CIA and Military Intelligence hunting Al-Qaeda and Taliban terrorists across Afghanistan. Jack and I shared many friends and contacts, also a love of firearms and hunting Al-Qaeda. Jack had been caught running his own private prison-interrogation centre in the Panjshir valley in the North East of the country, about one hour North of Kabul. Jack had been betrayed by some of the Afghan's working for him, nothing new there, you could not trust an Afghan as far as you could throw one. Jack had been yet another victim of what is known as an 'Afghan truth' betrayed by Afghans for money. The Americans and Western Intelligence denied all knowledge of what Jack had been up to, even the American Military ran for cover when he was arrested. All the support and help Jack had received just melted away. No one asked questions of Jack, or how he got his results, just as long as he got them - hunting down the terrorists by any means at his disposal and bringing them to justice. At first the Americans denied all knowledge of Jack and his operations and activities, "Plausible deniability", in other words the Americans politically could not be seen supporting torture, officially in Afghanistan. The number of Afghans and terrorists that were found in Jack's private prison was a little on the high side, even 'water boarding' was a fair sport, slightly controversial but pretty fair, given that these terrorists show no human rights to those killed in the 9/11 attacks on the twin towers, New York. Jack was temporarily cut loose and abandoned by the American Embassy, "Plausible Deniability, Denied Operations" until the politics were sorted out. American Embassy Security Staff were drinking lots of Afghan chi-tea with the Afghan Government trying to smooth things over. Jack had been kept in the same block as I was now standing in. It was also common knowledge throughout the prison that Jack had been American Special Forces-CIA. Which made him 'very popular' with the Taliban and AlQaeda prisoners? The American's had given Jack two large dogs for his own protection (Afghans are scared of dogs) they lived with him in his prison cell, the other little perks Jack had, included; food, whisky and a 'Play Station'. Unlike the British, the Americans looked after their own people. The American's soon retrieved Jack and before long he was back 'hunting crocodiles' (a euphemism for 'bad-guys') Al-Qaeda again. The fact that the prison guards were comparing me to Jack was a little disconcerting, given Jack's history, so I thought it best that I played dumb about the name Jack.

Just when I thought it could not get any worse, we were led up to the first floor and put into a cell, not being split up was a bonus at this point, at least we could watch each other's backs. The other prisoners Taliban and Al-Qaeda were just walking around freely, using mobile phones. This struck me as odd, so much for British Embassy mentored Max-Security? (See statement from Major Bill Shaw MBE). As I walk through the cell door behind Bevan, the guards closed and locked the door behind us. The sound of the locks being slammed shut echoed down the corridor. The bars of the door allowed the other prisoners to walk up and look in, I felt like an animal at the zoo. Lots of curious people looking in; they had never seen a British man before. The cold concrete cell I found myself in was 4m x 3m, a small old rusty metal bunk bed off to one side, with no mattress just metal slates and a small opening with bars high-up the back wall. A mass of green mould was growing down one of the corners from the ceiling, Jihadi graffiti and drawings of Islamists obliterating the Coalition Forces adorned the walls, last messages and names of dead prisoners, some written in their own blood hours before their horrific executions, and cockroaches on steroids ran across the floor to greet us. Welcome to Pul-i-Charkhi.

The whole place was dirty and looked, and smelled, like animals had been living in there. It turned out four Afghan's had lived there, but had just been moved into the cell next door. All the cells were supposed to be one or two man cells. The reality was 4 to 6+ people lived in each cell. The toilet was a hole in the floor in the corner. The smell from the hole was putrid, due to the heat. This was where the big spiders lived and when I say big, I mean big. These hairy fuckers wore trainers and shades, spiders with major attitude. Even the hardened Taliban would run out their cells when these spiders decided to make an appearance and stretch their legs. Bevan and I 'settled' into our new home from home, we cleaned the cell as best we could. Sitting on the top bunk looking out the small barred opening I could just make out Kabul on the horizon, raising from the surrounding desert. It was a clear blue sky, the heat from the sun was stifling outside, but inside the temperature was cool, borderline cold. It was a beautiful afternoon, and typical of Afghanistan always 'the beauty and the beast' wherever you looked. In and across Afghanistan, you found beauty in nature, followed by the beast and bloody carnage of war and killing.

Max-Security Block 10 was right in the heart of the prison. We were surrounded by 5,000+ Taliban and Al-Qaeda prisoners, terrorists; the very same terrorists, who I had hunted down outside. I was well aware that terrorists had and still were ordering terrorist attacks from inside this prison. During my work outside the name Pul-i-Charkhi had come up a few times, from both my Afghan contacts and my HUMINT contacts across the Middle-East and Africa. I had taken it as a given that British Intelligence were not just aware of this but that they were on top of this subject and situation; boy did I get that wrong, they were completely clueless and the British Embassy was in denial. Even when the evidence was put in front of them, they tried to cover it up, something which lead to the deaths of civilians and British soldiers. This was one of the subjects that I would re-visit in the near future, being a former British soldier-paratrooper; I was not going to let this go. The British Embassy had to be held accountable. Britain and America had kicked over a hornet's nest of terrorists in Iraq, Afghanistan, Syria, and across Africa; they were buzzing into every souk and mosque in the Arab world. Western Intelligence analysts, called this proliferation of Iraq and Afghanistan terrorism "bleed out"; this was very apparent and highlighted in the groups of AlQaeda and Taliban, Pakistan Taliban and Haqqani network within Pul-i-Charkhi prison. I witnessed new groupings forming from my first day there, new groupings within existing groups; Pakistan Taliban and Kandahar Al-Qaeda. The Somalian group Al-Shabab were also becoming more involved with Al-Qaeda, AQAP and Hezbollah. This would become clear and a real game changer in future attacks by Al-Shabab; including; Kenya, Westgate shopping Mall, killing 70+ and injuring 300+. Never in my wildest nightmares could I ever have imagined that I would be right in the middle of active Al-Qaeda, Taliban operational cells, networks and International terrorist operations.

My only thought was what the hell I was going to do now. What the hell was the British Embassy doing allowing a British national and former British soldier in a place as dangerous as Pul-i-Charkhi. The thought did cross my mind that maybe; someone within the British Embassy wanted me dead. Whatever possible reason would they have or gain from allowing me to be put in this precarious situation? Did they really want me dead, it would have silenced me and stopped the truth from coming out.

What should I do next? What was my next move? I made the conscious decision to observe and absorb all my surroundings and everything that I was exposed to. To make the most out of being in here; I would normally call this sort of situation character building. My major problem was that I was in here alone with no backup or support, other than Bevan, if things went wrong; and from what I had already seen, things could go wrong very quickly in here. My being surrounded by 5,000 terrorist's left a lot of scope for things to go 'Pete Tong' in a heartbeat. So my first mission was to stay alive, otherwise it was game over. Losing one's head by decapitation was a real risk and game changer, so keeping it was a priority. As it stood, on my first day at Pul-i-Charkhi, I was alone, isolated. My thoughts were to open up a secure line of communication with the American Military or CIA, my being re-located would flash up on their radar. It was only a matter of time until someone came discreetly calling, I trusted the American's from the time my team and I had carried out and sensitive work for them in Iraq, Syria and across the Middle-East and Africa. So I knew it was just a case of sitting tight. The answer would reveal itself in due course. The CIA had Black Hawk helicopters landing daily, dropping off and picking up terrorists and prisoners from the CIA 'GITMO' prison facility next to Block 10.

A prisoner banged on the bars of the cell door wanting our attention, he wore traditional Afghan clothing and Kandahar head-dress. It was meal time; we were given a small bowl of rice between us, which was the meal for the day. Obviously we were on the 'forced slim fast plan'. I was asked if I was a Muslim, I answered 'no', the Afghan replied; 'none Muslims don't get meat'. He called me a 'Kafir' spat on the door and walked off. Bevan commented that the room service in here 'sucked', and that we should put in a complaint to management; we both looked at each other and laughed, not much else we could do under the circumstances. As a bonus, the bowl of rice we had been given had small stones in it, a welcome gift from the Taliban, so no way to eat it without risking breaking your teeth. This was a regular occurrence, often with the 'blessing' of the Muppet guards that were on duty handing out the food. We settled for a can of tuna we had brought with us. Luckily the guards had not taken all our food. The situation was bad but I said it could be worse, yeah they could bloody well come in here, march us outside and shoot us? I laughed at this. Dark sense of humour, every good soldier has one. We were given the daily prison bread later in the afternoon. After the green mould was broken off it was half edible, this was another of our 'welcome gifts' we were to receive. To say that the Afghans were 'accommodating' would be an understatement, 'not'! The other great point is that the bread made a good rugby ball; no way that it would ever break. The piece of bread was our supper for the evening. We were left alone until the next morning. That night I lay on the metal bed with only a flea invested blanket, looking up at the stars, it was a full moon on my first night in Pul-i-Charkhi prison. I asked Bevan his take on the first day's events. Like many times in the past and the future, we dissected the day's events and tried to make sense of what was going on. In truth we still had no idea of what was really going on, all we did know for sure with a high degree of certainty was we had both been royally fucked by the British Embassy. At least we were both alive, through keeping the 'stiff upper lip' and 'dark humour' going. In dark times it's very important to keep your sense of humour up. I had learned all those years ago in the Parachute Regiment, never let a bad or dark situation get you down. You must always 'soldier on' and keep your chin up. It's a British thing. We Brit's never give up, a bit of the old D-Day/Dunkirk spirit. It was a sleepless first night, the sobbing and screams from the other prisoners, cut through the darkness of the night; I drifted off into a restless sleep, as dawn broke and the sun rose.

I spent the next week keeping a low profile, just watching and learning how everything worked, who the main players were, what the guards were like, who the most dangerous prisoners were, this was the easy part, 'all of them'. The daily timings of life revolved around the Mosque and the Islamic lessons which were held in the Taliban and Al-Qaeda corridors. It was pretty obvious that the guards did whatever Al-Qaeda told them. Al-Qaeda ran the prison, (this was something that Saladin was later to personally confirm to Lyse Doucet in a BBC interview). Gates, cells and corridors were opened up by the guards on orders from the Al-Qaeda and Taliban Commanders. I also witnessed Taliban Commanders ordering the prison Commander out of a room because the Taliban Commander was on a cell phone to another terrorist Commander in Afghanistan. This was a little golden nugget of information that British Embassy prison mentors were completely clueless about. This would come back and haunt the FCO/BEK in the future. I have spent many years in the Middle-East, including; Saudi Arabia, Iraq, Syria, Lebanon, Kuwait and across Africa, so my understanding of the Arabic language, dialects and cultural understanding is very good. I always operate on the premise of "know your enemy like you know yourself", an old lesson I always teach the men under my Command. In Block 10 Max-Security, there were a lot of foreign terrorist fighters from several countries including; Somalia (Al-Shabab), Iraq (AQI), Saudi Arabia (AQAP), Lebanon (Hezbollah), Iraq (Hezbollah), Pakistan (Taliban) and the (Haqqani network). Pul-i-Charkhi was a modern university of terrorism on every level, Afghan prisons where also a major recruitment ground for Muslim extremists who were being brain-washed and at times forced into Islamic extremist ideology. Many prisoners I met within Pul-i-Charkhi went on to become suicide bombers, Shoiab was an example of this. The un-nerving point was that I was right in the middle of all of this 24/7. After days of just carefully listening to the other prisoners and guards, I had ascertained that I was definitely located in Block 10, supposedly Max-Security. Most of the High Value Targets (HVT's) and High ranking terrorists, were located within this Block, 80+, all located in the same place and in the same prison block. This fact had been completely over looked by Western intelligence and the British prison mentors.

Al-Qaeda had been for many months carefully arranging their men and senior fighters to be moved or transferred to Block 10. The prison Commanders were easily bribed and the odd one that could not be was threatened or killed, so there was no real resistance to anything that Al-Qaeda or the Taliban wanted to do inside British mentored Afghan prisons. An interesting point that came out over time was that a lot of the Al-Qaeda and Taliban leadership-Commanders spoke and had a good working knowledge of the English language. This was contrary to what a lot of the British and Americans' thought. I was a little taken aback when I learned that one of the senior Afghan Taliban/Al-Qaeda Commanders was educated in Hull in the United Kingdom. The Red-Cross has paid for him to do his medical training in Hull City. I found this quite alarming, due to the fact that he still kept in contact with people in the United Kingdom. The 'Doctor', as he was called by other terrorists, was interested in improving his English, so this would provide an opportunity to talk to him in the future. This was all becoming a little surreal. A British Soldier, paratrooper, was teaching senior Al-Qaeda, Pakistan Taliban, Al-Shabab, and the Haqqani network terrorists English. I saw this as an opportunity to get close to the bad guys, study them, finding out how they operated from the inside out. This was an opportunity, if done right, for a lot of good to could come out of this very dark and dangerous situation. The chance to take down active Al-Qaeda and Taliban cells from within their own networks. British and American soldiers were dying weekly, in and across Afghanistan, I had the opportunity to save British and American lives, so it was a no brainer, and I just had to tread very carefully. If the terrorists found out or even suspected what I was up to, I would be killed and beheaded in a heartbeat. Slowly-slowly catchy the monkey was the order of the day.

The cell I had been put in with Bevan was one of 16 in each corridor. There were two corridors per floor and there were two floors in block 10. The second floor, my floor was nicknamed the Al-Qaeda floor by the guards. As a 'Brucey bonus' my cell was in the Taliban corridor, which was also known as "Death Row". This gave me a nice warm fuzzy feeling all over, 'not', well I suppose it could be worse, but for acquiring information and intelligence on the terrorists I could not be better placed. At this point the British and American intelligence were not aware that a lot of terrorist HVT's were right under their noses, using false names. All hell would break loose when they were to find out in the future. The political fallout would be interesting to watch.

"Al-Qaeda and the Taliban run the inside of Pul-i-Charkhi prison"

(Above) Exclusive photographs taken by Malone inside Afghan Max Security Block 10 which housed over 100 senior Pakistan Taliban, Al-Qadea and International Terrorists.

The entire interconnected corridors and gates around Block 10 were opened at will by the terrorists, prisoners who walked around freely, there was no lockup or segregation. The Americans, during one of their short notice visits went berserk, when they found several prisoners from different corridors in one cell. One of the Americans stormed up to the prison Commanders office, screaming that the Afghan prison guard did not even know what segregation was or meant? The prison Commander came into the block an hour later shouting at the guards. Two hours later all was back to normal, the terrorists were walking around freely again. This was all part of the normal 'game' which the prison guards and Commanders played with the Americans. They agreed with everything the Americans said, they did the complete opposite when the Americans had left the prison. The prison guards also ran electric cables from the guard rooms into the Taliban and Al-Qaeda corridors, which enabled the terrorists to charge up their mobile phones and other electrical devices. These were quickly put away if the

Americans pulled up at the prison gates or an American Black Hawk military helicopter landed within the prison grounds. A message was put out over the prison guard's radio, so everyone within the prison knew that the Americans were on site. Contraband was brought in every day and sold by the prison guards and the prison Commanders. The terrorists could order whatever they wanted and it would be delivered within 24 hours. Visitors from outside the prison could come in on most mornings, even Al-Qaeda Commanders and terrorists on the terrorist 'most wanted list' just walked into the prison on visitor's day. This went on for a long time, 'years', under the full knowledge of the prison guards, until I brought this little golden nugget of information to the attention of the American military intelligence. Then all visitors were photographed. This only stopped face to face meetings, but terrorists still communicated daily via cell phone or satellite phones. When the terrorists came in on visiting days, the guards would give them VIP treatment, they were not even searched. They had already paid the guards and this was the route by which terrorists brought weapons, cell phones and new phone 'Sim' cards into the prison. The terrorists had stock piled a lot of these items around the prison, within the prison guards personal lockers. Including; ammunition, emergency phones and chargers, lockers were never searched by the Americans, or British prison mentors. In time I would also put an end to that little terrorist safety net. The guards would bring out chairs and chi-tea for the terrorist Commanders, some of them even sat in during their terrorist planning and operational meetings in the prison Commanders rose garden. To say that the terrorists had the run of the place would be a gross understatement. Another fact is that Afghan Government prosecutors and judges (that can be named) were executed in Kabul, by the terrorists on their orders from inside and outside of Afghan prisons (if the prosecutors and judges ever upset the terrorists by not following the terrorist orders or instructions). In some cases the judges asked for too much money as a bribe so the Taliban would just kill them. When an Afghan official negotiated too hard with Al-Qaeda or the Taliban he just disappeared, never to be seen again? The next official who took over the position would not make the same mistake. The turnover of the prison staff in Block 10 was unbelievable, 8 prison Commanders in two and a half years.

The British Embassy prison mentors were responsible for the mentoring of Block 10. The amount of denial and cover-up by the mentors was staggering; they knew what was going on but just buried their heads in the sand. I would challenge the Embassy on these points, which made me very unpopular, ending up in the complete lack of help and support from my own Embassy, all because the Embassy was not even doing their job properly, as written in the FCO/BEK mandate. The head of the British prison mentors at this time was 'Vicky Blakeman' who was completely clueless on every level with regards to all that was going on within Afghan prisons. She was more interested in walking around the prison in a tight blue, short sleeved t-shirt, tight black pants, and high heels. This woman was representing my country, Great Britain, she was a complete embarrassment. What the guards called her in Arabic, I will leave to the reader's imagination. I would use the words incompetence, bordering on complete stupidity. Treason is also a word I would use in the future within my official reports to British Prime Minister David Cameron, due to the mentor's actions costing the lives of British soldiers and civilians in Afghanistan.

Taliban Commander in British Mentored Afghan Max Security Prison using mobile phones to contact other Taliban Commanders across Afghanistan. Terrorist attacks were ordered by phone from within British mentored Afghan prisons. The attacks were on British and American soldiers across Afghanistan-Iraq

"One example of this is the 'Talib Jan' suicide bombing of the supermarket close to the British Embassy 2011, 12 people died. The British Embassy prison mentors and the British Embassy staff, including; John Payne, Simon Thomas, Lawrence Jenkins, and Trudy Kennedy, were fully aware that 'Talib-Jan', in block 10 was running a suicide bombing network from inside the prison for over 3 years?"

I also told Simon Thomas about the terrorist attacks on British soldiers being planned, ordered and coordinated from Block 10. This conversation was also witnessed by a Protestant Minister and two other independent witnesses (not prisoners). For 3 years the British Embassy and mentors knew about this, but nothing was done and no action was taken. "The above facts regarding 'Talib Jan' were confirmed in the report by 'Ben Farmer', in his British Daily Telegraph article. Full details, including named intelligence sources-conformation are included in this article available on the internet". Some of the British Embassy's staff in Kabul had the blood of Civilians and British soldiers on their hands? This is just one example of when Embassy politics came before saving lives. The fact which I will make now, is that the terrorist attacks ordered and planned from within Pul-i-Charkhi prison Block 10, included 100+ IED and Suicide Bomber attacks on British and American troops across Afghanistan, including, Helmand and Kandahar Provinces in Southern Afghanistan. At this point of my being in prison, I did not know to what extent terrorist activity was coming out of the prison. When I did find out, and got confirmation of the truth, I would risk my life every day to save British and American soldiers lives. In my eyes, if I was going to die or be beheaded by the terrorists, I wanted to go out fighting for what I believed in. Saving British and American lives was well worth it. I was in a bit of a precarious situation. The daily dangers were all too real, this was enough to keep a person awake at night, and it was pretty much worse case scenario. I would need all my skills, trade craft, training and cultural understanding and of course 'Lady Luck' to get me through this situation and unprecedented predicament. The British Army text book did not cover this kind of situation; neither did the CIA-The Farm, (nickname for the CIA tactical training facility). Training manuals were all out of date or obsolete, I was breaking new ground. No Westerner, British soldier, or security operator had ever been or stood where I now found myself, right in the heart of Al-Qaeda, Taliban, Commanders leadership, operations, deep within the 'War on Terror' and International Terrorism. However, elements of my 'Tradecraft' (See Glossary, tradecraft improvise-adapt-overcome) would keep me alive in the near future, through precarious and extraordinary life threatening situations. This was not exactly Disneyland I had entered. (Below) The Inner Caged area, Cell Door, Roof Hatch)

After a few days, Afghans started to talk to me and Bevan. They all thought we must have done something really bad or that we had upset someone very powerful, to end up in our present predicament. Unfortunately it was the latter. Most of the other prisoners completely blanked us, they did not want to be seen talking to foreigners. Those who did risked a beating from Al-Qaeda and the Taliban Commanders, unless they were sent by them to find out information on us. Everything we said and who we spoke too, was reported straight back to the terrorist Commanders by the other prisoners. Al-Qaeda and the Taliban were trawling us for information, the same thing as we were doing to them. For the first few months it was a 'cat-and-mouse' game, both sides knew what the other was up to, neither wanting to seem overly interested in the other. The truth was they were as interested in us as much as we were interested in them. I later found out that the reason why we were not killed straight away by Al-Qaeda and the Taliban; this important point was because the terrorists were running terrorist operations out of prison Block 10, and did not want to draw attention to that fact (the safest place really if you thought about it, no CIA drone strikes would target them in a prison?) This was a typical example of Al-Qaeda tactics; 'Hiding in plain sight'. The Al-Qaeda and Taliban were planning major escapes across Afghanistan from Afghan prisons including; Kandahar and Jalalabad. Their plan was 500+ from each prison, using carefully engineered tunnels, dug into the prisons. The terrorists did not want any un-due attention. By the grace of God I was safe for the time being. At this point I was still expecting the British Embassy to work their back door contacts and get me the hell out of 'Dodge City'. Unknown to me the British Embassy was trying to 'bury' me, to keep me quiet. I wrote several letters to the British Embassy Kabul and the Ambassador, I never received a reply. All the letters were hand delivered to the British Embassy Kabul and the Ambassadors private residences next to the Embassy. The Embassy and FCO were fully aware that my human rights had been violated and that there was epidemic of ill-treatment and corruption throughout the Afghan Justice and prison system. They could not fix the problem, so they tried to cover it up. Unknown to me this had been going on for years. Colin Berry, British national and also a former British soldier and British Intelligence operative was the first back in 2002, the FCO/BEK had covered up his ill-treatment and horrific torture; his graphic photographs had even been included within the FCO internal report. Colin was tortured by Afghan prison guards, using metal cables to whip his back repeatedly and who subjected him to horrendous electric shock torture. The FCO/BEK official response to this was to tell Colin Berry, during an official meeting with FCO senior staff London, "Not to make a fuss about the torture". I would not find out about this little gem of information for many years. (Colin Berry exclusive video, photographs, statement/evidence have been lodged with Malone legal team).

(Above) Colin Berry operating In the Afghan Desert. (Middle) In Afghan Prison Kabul. (Right) Operating in Kabul (Below) Evidence of Colin being tortured by Afghan Authorities. These photographs were included in the British FCO official file, which they would later deny. An official letter Ref (MIN/54189/2013) from the FCO to Karen Todnor (Solicitor) "The FCO has never seen any evidence of torture or ill-treatment of British nationals in Afghanistan".

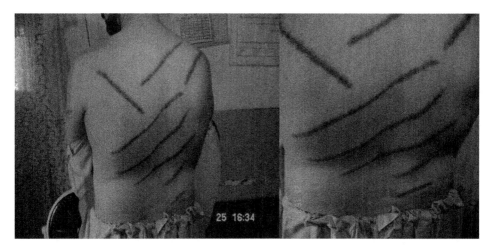

The Americans carried out VSA, (voice stress analyst) tests 'polygraph' on members of the MOJ, Afghan Ministry of Justice. Questions asked were focused on the endemic corruption throughout the Afghan Government, Justice and prison system. Over 80% of the Senior Afghans who took the test failed; a lot of the Afghan officials who did not take the VSA test called in sick that day. When later tested they also failed. So the fact was that; 80%+ of Afghan Government Officials, Judges-Prosecutors and prison Commanders and guards, had failed the test, were deemed completely corrupt, and not trust worthy (See ACP, Glossary). This must have been a 'dear diary' moment when the results of this test landed on the British Embassy's, Justice and prison mentors desk. It was no surprise that they tried covering up the shocking truth? The only problem was that the problem ran deeper and wider than Western Government officials realised. The British Embassy cover-up would cost several Civilians and British soldiers their lives in the future. When the truth about just how bad, dysfunctional and corrupt the Afghan Government really is, British officials and the FCO; will have a lot of explaining to do to a great deal of people, including the British public. How much British tax-payers money had the British Embassy Kabul-FCO wasted in Afghanistan? In a time of budget cuts, job losses and hardship suffered by the British public. The British Foreign Office and top civil servants are playing internal politics, sometimes even playing 'God' with people's lives. All while trying to safe guard their own jobs, salaries and careers? The FCO/BEK has a lot to be held accountable for. I have always said that the truth will come out in the end?

"My subject is war, and the pity of war. The poetry is in the pity... All a poet can do today is warn. That is why the true poets must be truthful"

Wilfred Owen

I had spent the past 14 unprecedented years living and operating in and across the Middle-East, Africa and Islamic countries, including several years in Iraq, Syria, Jordan, Lebanon, Turkey, Saudi Arabia, Kenya, Somalia and Ethiopia. I had spent a lot of time living with the Arab people amongst them as one of them. I knew their culture and I understood their old ways, customs and life styles. Their ways and Arab mentality was not alien to me, my time spent with the Bedu-Bedouin in the vast golden enchanting and timeless deserts of Arabia, had given me an in-depth understanding of their hard way of life and a comprehensive understanding of Islam. My previous sensitive unofficial work in the Middle East had directly and indirectly sent several Muslim terrorists to the gardens of paradise in the afterlife. 'It was, what it was' in my eyes a necessary evil which saved a lot of innocent lives. The old man upstairs, has whispered in my ear often enough when I had one of the bad guys in my sights; take him down, Anth Malone my boy. I'm a total heathen, alpha male and hunter gatherer and loving it...! JC (Jesus Christ) was dialled into my Call sign, a protestant minister (former South African military), who visited me in Pul-i-Charkhi told me I was doing God's work. I took this as divine intervention, a sign that JC was covering my '6' and back, as well as the American CIA. Nothing wrong in having a bit of extra support from the "God squad", I already had wings on my arm, British and French military parachute wings. I know that I am a tough and arrogant bastard at times, with an ego and endless aggressive optimism which comes from hard rigorous training and physical well-being. I don't take crap from anyone and I don't suffer fools gladly. I am fiercely loyal and I am willing to die for my country and the principles I believe in. I have a big heart and will put myself in harm's way to help, protect and save other people's lives. All these qualities would help me to survive Pul-i-Charkhi and the Al-Qaeda, Taliban terrorist networks and the dark beast within. In the timeless battle of good over evil, where the 'Dark Angels' fought over right & wrong, Pul-i-Charkhi with all its extreme darkness comfortably fitted into this timeless and endless battle of good over evil, which were being fought within its torture chambers and the beasts' sadistic sport and daily rituals. The epidemic torment, misery and suffering inside Pul-iCharkhi prison was the closest to modern day systematic slavery I had ever witnessed, it made the dictatorships and brutality of some third world African countries, Somalia, and the Congo, tame by comparison. I would need every ounce of my resolve, courage and solid belief system to meet this epic challenge. I still had my die hard attitude. "A man is what he stands for and what he fights for". This put me in good stead for where I now found myself.

From what I had seen and observed, most of the Afghan prisoners dressed in flowing white Arab robes and clothing, including traditional Arabian head dress. A lot of their mannerisms were Arab, not Afghan, this struck me as odd. The clothing and mannerisms of some of the Afghans and Arab Afghans was slightly off, at first I could not put my finger on it. Arab's passing themselves off as Afghans. After observing the Mosque one afternoon in the Al-Qaeda corridor the penny dropped, the style of praying was that of 'Wahabi', the sect style of Islam that Osama bin Laden and Al-Qaeda followed. This indicated to me that the Al-Qaeda network in and across Pul-i-Charkhi was vast and being very well hidden. Arab culture and mannerisms are slightly different from country to country, like the Arab language, different dialects are used in different parts of the country and provinces. I had noticed a lot of the subtle differences during my work and travels over the years through Islamic countries. I had even picked up some of the customs, ways and mannerisms, some intentionally some not. As I walked around the prison complex a lot of things started to become clearer to me. I could not believe I had over looked so many obvious things, Al-Qaeda and a large number of International terrorists were truly hiding in plain sight, just walking around under false names. It was no wonder they had fallen off the American's radar without notice. Everyone, including most Western intelligence analysts and experts, had made the assumption that they had gotten smart and had gone deep underground, within the sanctuary of their own international terrorist networks. The truth was, they had been caught, but no one had noticed. Given false names with false identification upon arrest, and with help and protection from the Afghan police and prosecutors, the Al-Qaeda and foreign terrorists had gone completely un-noticed by American and Western Intelligence. My point would be proven in dramatic fashion in the not too distant future, with an outstanding result against the terrorists plans and operational network being ran from inside the Pul-i-Charkhi prison. As I had noticed the Arab and Afghan Arab mannerisms, so too had the terrorists noticed that I had some of the same mannerisms. This confused the hell out of them. I was a foreigner, one of their enemies, who in their eyes was a lot like them. It was all the small things that threw them a curve ball. My knowledge of the Arab culture, 'cultural understanding' surprised them and my in depth knowledge of Islam and their religion surprised even the Al-Qaeda and Taliban Mullahs. I was no expert, but over the years operating within Muslim countries I had picked up and learned a lot from being around the local people. In truth I did not really notice just how much I had picked up and learned. All this put together in my present situation gave me an opening which, if I treaded carefully, would open a few doors that would normally have remained closed. I sat for hours, just talking to the older Arab and Afghan prisoners, about life, their families and children outside, their legal cases, even their political views on Afghanistan, Pakistan. I asked what they really thought about the Afghan Government and their personal views about the war raging across Afghanistan. They told me one thing in public, but a lot of these comments changed when in private. They became more open and accessible, not their normal default setting of reserved or cagey. I enquired as to what their hopes and dreams were for their future, both for themselves, families and their country. The conversations flowed over many afternoons, a lot of Afghan chi-tea was drank 'hot sweet' black tea. If you want to get an Afghan or Arab to talk, the key ingredient is lots of chi-tea and nuts and sweets. Arab men like nothing better than sitting around in a quiet corner of a room and talking about politics and their views. A lot of men like to tell War stories, it's an aspect of male ego built into their DNA. Some of these old Arabs and Afghans had some good and educational stories and points of view. I would take great pleasure debating some of the more controversial political aspects and subjects with the Arab and Afghan prisoners. These could end up in some very heated exchanges and discussions, all were very informative and telling. A lot of these prisoners knew each other on the outside, before they even came to prison. They had come from the same villages, towns and cities. Almost all were of the age, to be Muj (Mujahedin), a lot were older. They had fought the Russians back in the day.

(Right) Author with
Commander of Max Security Block 10 - Afghanistan

After a few months these conversations started to open up a little and the Arabs-Afghans started to talk more openly, it was all about trust and they were starting to feel comfortable talking about themselves. I did not really talk much, I just listened and observed. Like an Islamic Maltese falcon, the Afghan's victorious jihad against the Soviet Union was for the Muslim world 'the stuff that dreams are made of'. The Mujahedin took great pride in their past success. Their eyes would light up when talking about the Soviet jihad of old. A lot of the young 'Mujahedin', who were too young to fight in the Soviet jihad, were now inspired to fight in the modern-day Afghan Jihad against the Americans and the British military. Old Mujahedin encouraged the young ones to fight; who subsequently came to believe that killing Western troops would give them credibility as a man and a Muslim, however misguided, this was fact. This also became a major recruitment tool used and exploited by Al-Qaeda and Islamic extremists across the Middle-East and Muslim world. Prisons in Afghanistan, Pakistan, Iraq, Syria, Lebanon, Egypt, Libya, and Somalia, Kenya have become epidemic recruitment and breeding grounds for Islamic extremists.

Western Countries turning a blind eye to the torture of extremists and in some cases supporting, giving tacit unofficial approval, this has only added to exorbitantly increase the problem and in turn has made the extremists and terrorists even more utterly ruthless and extreme. These people were seething with hatred towards anything Western, "violence breeds violence". Pul-i-Charkhi was right up there close to the top of the list of prisons that Al-Qaeda was running terrorist international operations from. I had experienced and seen maybe 10% of life compared to some of these Mujahedin. Some of their stories were funny and at times very dark, killing was just a way of life for these people, and life was cheap, to the point that it was pretty much worthless. Women's rights were non-existent. Women were treated like animals. I would go as far as to say, some animals were treated much better. The stories of how some of the women within their families were treated were shocking and heart breaking, these are words that I do not use lightly or often. I was shocked at the way some of these Arab, Afghan men treated women. I was disgusted at some of the things that the men would come out with. Cutting the women if they did not do what they were told. Rape and abuse, were common place within their households. I felt sick after some of these conversations. I had personally witnessed how some of the Taliban prisoners treated their women during open prisoners visiting days; ordering their women folk around like dogs, some were too scared and scarred to even answer back. It was hard not to show any emotion when I witnessed these things and I just had to stay cold and emotionless as they were talking. Decades of war and infighting, in and across Afghanistan, had left the whole country war torn and deeply scarred beyond recognition. This fact would go some way in explaining the mentality and wide spread attitudes of a lot of Afghan men, young and old. They were truly living in the 13th century, with their routine, daily brutality, abuse, torture and thoughtless cold blooded killing. To understand Afghanistan or its precarious present day situation or future, one has to look and understand Afghanistan's past and history. Only then can a person start to make any sense of current events and the present day. The more time I spent in Afghanistan the less I understood it; this filled me with a deep need to understand Afghanistan more, on so many different levels.

Women's rights under the Taliban had been non-existent at best, this fact has already been well documented, not much had really changed over the past ten years in and across Afghanistan, outside the Capital City of Kabul, and nothing had really changed at all. Even after the Taliban were toppled from power, women's rights had not really improved. The sad thing was that everyone expected the Taliban to come back into power after the Americans and British soldiers had left Afghanistan. Women were still meant to be seen but not heard in many Afghan households. This must have been a living hell for a lot of women across Afghanistan. The Western involvement had brought a few good things to some Afghan cities and towns. These were shelters for women who had been abused. There was still only a handful of these places, but they gave hope 'Esperance' to a lot of young girls and women. In a country like Afghanistan, hope was all that some people had. Hard line members of the corrupt Afghan Government and Parliament were trying to close down the women's shelters in Kabul. Members of the Afghan Government were openly calling them un-Islamic. One of the only Afghan Member of Parliament women was now in hiding, living in one of the women shelters due to beatings and threats from her Afghan husband. Even an official MP holding a position within the Afghan parliament was not safe in her own country. Afghan law did nothing to protect or help her, under Islamic law; she had to return to her brutal abusive husband. A lot has already been written about women's rights in Islamic countries, this is an important subject, because there are no women's rights, there is generally no rule of law, which in turn leads to mass human rights abuses. Or in some cases Islamic 'Sharia law' is implemented. Before I had been illegally put in prison in Afghanistan, I had accompanied a journalist friend of mine on one of her press assignments; to report about young girls and women who had needed major hospital treatment after their families had abused and beaten them. What I saw and witnessed in a small hospital on the out skirts of Kabul that afternoon, was equally disturbing and shocking; young girls, age 12 to 14 years old had been sold to an Afghan village elder in his fifties, he had married then forced them to have brutal sex. This was just the act of rough physical sex with no love or feelings involved. The young girls had been physically abused and injured; they had suffered major internal injuries due to brutal under age sex and long term psychological damage. The hospital was treating these young girls, the sad fact was that when they were released, the girls would have to go back to the men that were responsible for such injures. That is just the way it is in Afghanistan. In any Western civilised country, the man would have been arrested and put in prison for child abuse and torture. In Afghanistan the girl would be put into prison for dishonouring the man's family name. If the girl refused to go back home she would be killed in an honour killing by her husband or family. This is the sort of abuse that girls have to put up with daily in Afghanistan and across Islamic countries. Some of the men are no more than animals. The sad thing was that these cases are not isolated, there are very common across Afghanistan and Islamic countries. I found this subject disturbing and troubling.

The Western Governments were waging a war in Afghanistan and across the Middle-East, costing billions of dollars a year and the Western Governments and mentors with all their resources could not even address the subject of women-girls human rights. The sad and alarming point and fact is even after the West has been in Afghanistan for over 12+ years, there is no political will in the Afghan Government to address this barbaric situation and problem. One can only hope that when, not if, the Taliban come back into absolute power across Afghanistan, the dark days of women being systematically abused, and becoming second rate citizens will be a thing of the past, my personal thoughts are that the abuse will be much worse. Western Government advisers will try and play this down, due to politics and this subject makes them feel uncomfortable and look bad. But the facts will speak for themselves. Women across Afghanistan hold their breath for what they already know is coming. My personal thoughts on this subject is for Western Governments to organise some kind of a program for the most serious of cases and get these women and young girls out of Afghanistan. The problem is this would be controversial and very political. There is no real political will from Western politicians to help resolve this situation. They would change their mind in a heartbeat if it was their own family or young daughters who were being abused; I think I have just made my point.

I confirmed with the hospital staff, the personal details of the man that was responsible for abusing the young girls. He had come to pick them up and the girls looked horrified when they saw him. I took some discreet photographs of him and his 4X4 vehicle 'ID' plate. Within the month the man was arrested by the American military for drug trafficking and distribution. 'There is always more than one way to skin a cat'?

Some of the Afghan prison guards made the South American "sloth" look intelligent and well mannered, hell even I looked like a 'rock star' in comparison. My future volatile and tantalizing relationship with the barbaric Afghan prison guards would be a mix of hostility, arrogance and outright distain; their uncouth default setting was one of hostility and unbridled brutality. The guards were the by-product of their war torn environment and their complete lack of education and common sense. During one of my afternoons of drinking chi-tea with the Arabs and Afghan prisoners in Pul-i-Charkhi, some of the old boys, prisoners in the 60s, were laughing and re-telling some of their old Mujahedin war stories; charging on horseback with a single hand grenade in hand, towards a Russian tank which was attacking their village in the mountains. These were the same tall tales and stories that these old boys told around their village camp fires on cold winter nights. One of the old boys stood up and lifted his shirt up; he had several scars caused by entrance and exit wounds where he had been hit by bullets from enemy fire. The Arabs laughed, they called them little love bites, the old boy turned to me and laughed too, and he smiled at me and was proud when he said the tank got him, but not before he had destroyed the Russian tank. These types of stories of bravado were common within the groups of prisoners. Different groups of prisoners tended to stay amongst themselves, I tended to mingle amongst them, drinking chi tea and catching up on the daily gossip. Some of these Arabs were worse than old women for talking; they could talk the hind legs off a donkey, which was good because I was interested in all they had to say. 'Insha Allah' is an Arabic term that is used frequently by both Arabs and Afghans, 'Insha Allah' means; 'Gods will'. You will hear this term used and put onto the end of many conversations. In the Arab world a sentence is not complete without the obligatory 'Insha'Allah' being said. It was an ongoing joke in Afghanistan, that if an Afghan man said it at the end of a sentence then it meant 'no' or at best 'maybe'. True Arabs, don't like being called Afghans, to them Afghans cannot be trusted, and they trust no one, and deceive everyone. These were the words of an Al-Qaeda Commander inside Pul-i-Charkhi prison.

There was a lot of tension between Al-Qaeda and the Taliban, inside and outside of the prison. I would later witness this tension boil over into extreme gruesome violence. Al-Qaeda would make an example of some of the Panjshiri Tribe who had joined the Taliban. The Panjshiri prisoners were being rude, singing about their dead Commander Massoud, who had been killed by Al-Qaeda days before 9/11. The Panjshiri prisoners were whipped with metal cables and chains, to within an inch of their lives by AlQaeda. The Panjshiri prisoners had learned to keep their mouths shut in prison. I had witnessed this. The blood trails along the floor and on the ceiling were a good indication, a taste of what the Panjshiri tribe could expect in the near future in Afghanistan. Al-Qaeda, Pakistan Taliban and Afghan Taliban had a lot of bad blood and history with the Panjshiri tribe, who were not even originally from Afghanistan. The Panjshiri were immigrants from Tajikistan. The Panjshiri tribe located in Northern Afghanistan were historically supported politically, financially and militarily by the Americans, but things were slowly changing. Al-Qaeda, Pakistan Taliban Leadership living in Pakistan, were just biding their time. When the Americans and British pull out of Afghanistan, old scores would be settled. I would witness the birth of groups and networks, including the 'Talib-Jan', IED and suicide bombing network, which was ran from inside the prison. The Pakistan Taliban had some of their first meetings within the prison before they became fully operational across Afghanistan and Pakistan. The Kandahar Al-Qaeda and the "Lions of Allah" were first formed within Block 10, Pul-i-Charkhi prison. These names and more extremist terrorist groups "ISIS" would show up on the West's intelligence radar over the coming years, with lethal consequences, due to their ability to launch large scale attacks, right across Afghanistan, Middle East and Internationally. I would also witness first hand Al-Qaeda talking about training, logistics, operations and attacks, on a satellite phone to Al-Shabab Commanders in Somalia and Kenya, 6 years before Western intelligence acknowledged or was fully aware that there were major operational links between Al-Qaeda and Al-Shabab (See Glossary Al-Shabab). What completely floored me personally was the high level of communication; two-way traffic coming out of Pul-i-Charkhi prison to other terrorist groups worldwide. This place was a gold mine of intelligence, both of a tactical and strategic level. At this point I had just skimmed the surface of what was going on. The overall level of activity going on was unbelievable. It was like the who's who, of the terrorist world, and more importantly, the who's who of future terrorist actions and plans. Things were starting to heat up and get interesting.

The British Embassy turned up one afternoon for an hour visit at Pul-i-Charkhi. The first I knew about this was after I had been called up to the main prison Commanders office. I had not done anything that day to piss him off, so I walked over to the office escorted by two guards. The prison Commander was well aware that I had settled in ok and that I had been making new friends and influencing people. I thought, well things could not get any worse, I was amongst Al-Qaeda and Taliban and so whatever the prison Commander had to tell me, had to be news that would be on the up-scale. I was always in the crap; it was only the level that varied daily. I just laughed at this thought, hey, maybe I would be accused of bullying Taliban prisoners, hell, I was being set up for everything else. This was one of those situations where anything could happen at any point and at any time. On approaching the Commanders office, I noticed three British Embassy B6 armoured Toyota 4X4, vehicles with the normal PSD, (Personal Security Detail) surrounding them. A few of the faces of the security staff I recognised. All the team members were former British soldiers. With a nod and a discreet 'hello', the PSD took up their firing positions around the outside of the Prison Commanders office. I was escorted up the stairs, shackles removed, and then taken into an inner office where I found Lawrence Jenkins, British Consul, and Trudy Kennedy, the British Vice-Consul at that time, sitting with the prison Commander, drinking Chi-tea. Two of the PSD were sitting off to one side. I shook their hands first, one of them I knew 'an old soldier'. I shook the hands of Trudy, Lawrence and the prison

Commander who then sat in silence through the rest of the meeting; I was shown to a seat opposite them. Trudy asked me a pretty dumb question; how was I? I thought for a moment before I answered, thinking how not to sound too flippant. I decided to give a straight answer, "I'm great, could not be better, my Al-Qaeda and Taliban fellow inmates have made me feel right at home. I've not had my head cut off yet. How's your day going, Trudy?" There was stunned silence in the room. The British security men in the room gave me a nod of approval; they had all heard of me and my situation and that the British Embassy Kabul was just procrastinating and showing face value to my situation. Trudy Kennedy went on and explained that the Embassy had not been aware that I had been moved to Pul-i-Charkhi. I asked why they did not know and why it had taken them several weeks to come and check up on me. Trudy could not give me a straight answer or look me in the eye while she spoke. I ask her why all the armed security, three armoured 4X4s, with full protection detail. Her answer was for their security. So Pul-i-Charkhi is dangerous? So why are the British Embassy allowing a British national to be kept in an Afghan run prison full of Terrorists. Trudy's words were, "Are there terrorists in here?" I laughed at this comment, if it was not so serious, it would not have been so funny. Even the prison Commander smiled at this comment. OMG, how clueless is the British Embassy. This did not give me great confidence for the rest of the meeting. Lawrence broke into the conversation. They had learned of my move after trying to visit me at Tawqeef prison Kabul. Only then did the British Embassy realise that for weeks I had been located at Pul-iCharkhi. I commented that it cannot be that hard to keep track of the British nationals in Afghan prisons because there was just one at that time, 'me'. Lawrence Jenkins quickly changed the subject. They asked if I had any update on my case, I answered 'no' and that I was waiting for the British Embassy to start investigating my officially reported miscarriage of justice. Trudy and Lawrence's faces were blank. They said that the British Embassy could not get involved in the Afghan justice system. I pointed out yet again, that the Afghan justice system was mentored by the British Embassy Kabul and that the Afghan justice system was completely corrupt and dysfunctional on every level. I had previously reported to the British Embassy staff that the Afghan Prosecutor and Judge in my case had visited me, demanding that I pay a $20,000 bribe. I had several witnesses to confirm this, and that the Afghan Prosecutor and Judge had signed into the prison to see me. I had given the names and contact details of the Afghan Prosecutor and Judge, including bank account information and their mobile cell numbers. They wanted the money paid into one of their Dubai bank accounts. If I paid, I was told they I would be released in a few days' time. I refused to pay bribes for my freedom. I made my opinion very clear, so it could not be misunderstood. I chose my words very carefully; No – Never! I would not bow down to corrupt Afghan Government officials. I had reported all this to the British Embassy verbally and in writing months before. The British Embassy had done absolutely nothing about this at all; they were trying to cover up the high level of corruption within their mentored justice prison system. Back in 2007, the British Embassy would not even admit that the Afghan Government was corrupt. The shocking, corrupt and shameful truth would come out in time. I also stated FCO 'duty of care', or lack of it in my case, and that when a miscarriage of justice is officially reported to the FCO/BEK, it is their duty to investigate and interview all concerned. This fact is written and included within their FCO/BEK official written

Government mandate. Lawrence said he would look into this. He had supposedly been looking into this for the past 6 months? To date, he never got back to me with an answer. My next of kin, Mr Dil Banerjee, pointed out the FCO/BEK current official written mandate, during one of their visits to the British Embassy in Kabul. They never investigated; over 5 years later the FCO staff in a British Court of Law, and under Oath, would admit that I had been illegally held in prison in Afghanistan with the full knowledge of the British Embassy. British FCO staff also 'claimed' that this did not happen on their shift? An senior official of FCO/BEK also confirmed in a British Court of law that during one of his very rare visits to Pul-i-Charkhi prison, he had personally witnessed; 'Taliban prisoners throwing mutilated dead bodies of other prisoners out of the prison blocks', in return for old prison bread. This barbaric act was common place within the prison. It would take 5 years for these little golden nuggets of information to come to light, until then I was left chilling out in Pul-i-Charkhi Prison with my international human rights being abused daily. I went through some of the ill-treatment that I had been subjected to, but I was very careful to word it in such a way that the prison Commander would not understand all I was saying. The prison Commander left the room for an hour. This gave me the opportunity to talk more openly, directly and to the point. My voice was calm and measured, this was the first time that I could talk to my Embassy in private. I lay everything out chronologically that had happened to me, up to that point in time. By the time I had finished the blood had drained from both the British Consulate and Vice Consulate's faces. They now knew, in no uncertain terms, that the British Embassy had really failed me in their official 'duty of care'. Unknown to them the cover-up of my situation by the British Embassy would cost them both their jobs in the future, due to internal British Embassy politics.

It is openly known about the barbaric and shocking ill-treatment of Westerners by the Afghanistan justice and prison system. This fact is why the American Government, and Embassy, will not allow its citizens to be imprisoned in Afghanistan. I put this to Lawrence Jenkins; yet again he said he would look into it?

As a British citizen, supposedly protected by the BEK/FCO; I lived through all these horrific, traumatic events and incidents during my time within Afghan prisons. I was also forced by guards to carry rotten dead decaying bodies out of prison blocks, on old flee ridden blood stained blankets and I will never forget the smell and image of this. This also caused my sleeping and eating disorders, all of which has been professionally diagnosed and documented. I associate the smells of some food with the graphic memory and smells of dead decaying bodies and my sustained torture. This came to light on my return to Britain, during my continuing PTSD Post-Traumatic Stress Disorder (PTSD) counselling. The fact that the BEK/FCO knew about all the ill-treatment and torture for years and never did anything to intervene or stop it. This was a major embarrassment to the British Government, because the Afghan Government were aware that the BEK/FCO were just turning a blind eye to everything due to politics, this only encouraged and in my personal opinion escalated this exuberant barbaric situation even further.

"For evil to triumph all it takes is for good men to do nothing"

My ill-treatment was first started by Afghan NDS (security services) who kidnapped me outside Jalalabad city, on the 22nd January 2008 at 0700hrs. (Officially reported to the British Embassy Kabul) 20 armed men (with AK47s and PKMs) in a mix of Afghan police and civilian clothing stopped me by force at gunpoint and handcuffed my hands tightly behind my back (stress position) and placed a black hood/bag over my head. I was forced into a 4X4 vehicle and driven to a remote farm house, stripped, searched and thrown into an old blood stained metal cage, guarded by several Afghan Men with Ak47s, who constantly shouted abuse and spat on me because I was British and non-Muslim (I was in fear for my life). After a period of time, of being interrogated in the cage, I was dragged out shackled and thrown into another red 4X4, I was surrounded by Afghan men in civilian clothes, all had weapons including AK47s, one of the guards in civilian clothing and wearing the black turban of the Taliban, put the barrel of his weapon to my chest, and told me if I made any trouble or shouted out in any way I would be shot and killed. I would later be handed over to the corrupt Afghan police; all were wearing the black turban of the Taliban, Al-Q. They treated me with distain because I was British. My kidnapping was officially reported to the British Embassy Kabul. Several times detailed letters were also sent from me to BEK informing them about my situation. I have never received a written official response to my letters? I brought this point up with Lawrence Jenkins and Trudy Kennedy. I gave them an overview yet again on what had happened to me, including a quick brief, due to time constraints; including the ill treatment I had witnessed.

I was dragged into an old run down police building in Kabul. There I was handcuffed to an old metal chain, fixed to the damp, bullet riddled, blood stained wall and left there for 12hrs. Guarded at gun point at all times, constantly abused by Afghan guards, who also refused to give me food, water or use of a toilet, their reason, because I was not a Muslim and an British pig and Infidel, a non-believer. I was told by official Afghan police, that if I signed a small piece of paper, that stated that I had 'not', been ill-treated, then I would be released. I read and signed, 'under duress', the small piece of paper, hand written in Farsi. I also put a thumb print of my blood, from one of my wounds received from my mistreatment, at the top left hand corner of the paper. This was so I could contest the statement at a later date. The police had lied. 'The Afghan security services where panicking, because they had kidnapped and badly ill-treated a British national and former British soldier without any due cause'. (They had been paid by corrupt Afghan officials, who were trying to cover their arse). Later I was taken and put into Kabul central jail. This jail was built to house 160 prisoners. Reality was an open prison housing 850+ Afghan prisoners, mostly Taliban and Al-Q terrorists. I was put into a room, measuring 12 feet by 12 feet with 40+ other Afghan prisoners. This was where I lived, slept, ate and washed for the next 6 months, in dangerous dark squalid conditions, with rats and spiders crawling over me as I slept. This Jail, like a lot of other Afghan jails would later be closed down by the Red-Cross and the UN because of human rights violations? The Afghan prison guards stripped searched me and made me stand naked in front of the other Afghan prisoners, while a torrent of abuse was aimed at me by the Afghan guards. They also by force, shaved my head with a blunt razor? This was done to humiliate and degrade me in front of the other Afghan prisoners. This shameful treatment also happened to other members of the Commonwealth, prison guards openly beat and whipped prisoners, on their backs and balls off their feet with long metal cables and long black rubber hoses (see witnesses and statements written by Colin Berry and Phil Young). I witnessed many people handcuffed to metal gates and repeatedly tortured almost to death by guards. 'Metal cables cut through human flesh, like a hot knife through butter'. At night, the guards used buckets of water to wash away the blood, and human body fluids, left over from the daily torture. People died on a regular basis and some prisoner's bodies even disappeared altogether, being 'Ghosted'. The Red-Cross and other people took photographs of prisoners who had been tortured. Including: Colin Berry British National, his back had been whipped with 'metal cables' repetitively by Afghan prison guards; he had also endured 'electric shock torture'. British FCO's official response to this was to tell Mr Collin Berry 'Do not make a fuss about it' (The FCO has the graphic photographs of this torture on file, evidence given to them by Collin Berry British National and former British soldier). 'Also published in Colin Berry's book Deniable Agent'. I went into as much detail as possible for two reasons (1) to make it crystal clear, my situation to the BEK/FCO. (2) I had two witnesses, independent security staff who I knew. The BEK was not aware of this fact. Everything that was said in the BEK meetings with me was passed back in great detail (sometimes even recordings of the meetings) to my official next of kin.

On several occasions I was handcuffed and painfully shackled, sharp metal cutting into my bare flesh, then dragged by prison guards up to the prison Commander's office - where a young Afghan girl had been shot and killed by the prison Commander weeks before because she would not have sex with him as payment for her husband's release from prison. A witness reported this incident to the Red-Cross, resulting in the prison Commander being demoted to second in command of the prison. The Afghan government told him not to do it again. Life and women's rights mean nothing in Afghanistan.

"Torture and Murder"

I was once handcuffed to an old wooden chair in the prison Commander's office at 'Tawqeef' prison and beaten by him and his bodyguards under his command, because I would not sign their pre-written confession in Farsi. It stated that I was working for the American Military. I refused to answer any of their questions and I did not sign anything. I would never bow down to corrupt Afghan officials or Taliban terrorists. I was informed that Afghan prison was very dangerous and I could be killed at any time because I was British and a former British soldier. Because I would not co-operate, I was dragged out of the office upon the prison Commander's orders, by his body guards and then thrown head first down the metal stairs that led from the prison Commander's office to the prison courtyard. I landed in a heap at the bottom of the stairs. The Taliban guards walked over to me and one pretended to help me get up then kicked me full force in the groin. They were wearing Old Russian army boots. I was left curled up on the floor in agony for about an hour, coughing up blood while the prison guards watched and laughed. I was thrown back into the open prison population. I was surrounded by Pakistan Taliban, Al-Q terrorists and hundreds of people who hate the west, particularly Britain and

America. On another occasion the prison guards dragged me into the outer prison courtyard, overlooked by the prison Commander's office. There without provocation or a word being said, I was firstly shackled then viciously beaten by four prison guards. One of whom had an AK47. He hit me with the butt of the weapon in the face, calling me an infidel. After a short period of time the beating stopped and I was unshackled and dragged back into the main prison courtyard and dumped in a heap on the floor.

"Daily beatings like this were a kind of sick perverse daily sport for the Afghan prison guards, who would shout and laugh during their daily beatings, torture and degrading treatment of prisoners. (See Red-Cross, UN and US State Department, official reports of ill-treatment of Afghan prisoners, by Afghan authorities)"

Mr Dil Banerjee (British National) visited me at 'Tawqeef' prison the day after one of these beatings. He witnessed the marks of the AK47 butt on my forehead. (See legal statement by Dil Banerjee British National). I repeated what had happened to me, when I first arrived at Pul-i-Charkhi prison. Unknown to the British Embassy, I was moved to the Afghan hell which is known as Pul-i-Charkhi prison, one of the most notorious and dangerous prisons in the world. This was to be my hell on earth for the next 2+ years. I thought that I would be killed in Pul-i-Charkhi Prison. I had been abandoned and betrayed by my own British Embassy (FCO), due to their internal politics. (It took the British Embassy Kabul, several weeks to find out, that I had been moved, I was still in disbelief about this troubling fact. What had happened to the BEK/FCO duty of care of a British national?) This had a profound effect on me and my whole belief system. I was surrounded by 5000+ Taliban and Al-Q terrorists, prisoners. I was singled out by prison guards and prisoners loyal to the Taliban. The prison Commander and some of the guards who were on the Al-Q and Taliban payroll, this was confirmed when I witnessed large amounts of money being handed over to the prison Commander from Taliban/Al-Q Commanders. Guards made sure that the Taliban prisoners knew that I was British and a former British soldier (paratrooper). Al-Q/Taliban later placed a bounty of $25,000 on my head later on and another prisoner 'Major Bill Shaw MBE'. This was confirmed by the British Embassy (FCO) staff and 'Saladin' an Al-Q Commander. 'The bounty would be increased by Taliban/Al-Q, at a later date'. I laid my account of the incidents, so it was explicit and crystal clear. After I had finished speaking to Trudy Kennedy and Lawrence Jenkins, in front of two witnesses, the British Consulates were dead silent, as was the room; 'you could have heard a pin drop from a hand-grenade'. I stood up, shook their hands and told them to do their job and visit me again soon when they had some good positive news for me, like my release papers. I walked towards the door, shaking the hands of the British security protection team on the way out, wishing them all the best and thanking them for taking the time to come and visit me. I asked them to please send my best regards to everyone I knew back at the base camp. I walked out the room without looking back at the British Embassy officials. I already knew that they were in deep political crap and that they did not have the shoes for it?

Major Bevan Campbell, Mr Dil Banerjee, Phil Young, Colin Berry and Major Bill Shaw MBE, and several other British and Commonwealth Nationals would also speak out about this horrendous, precarious and dangerous situation in the future.

"According to the senior judge of the European Court of Human Rights; Sleep deprivation and diet modification are classed as torture. I and other prisoners were singled out and psychologically and physically tortured daily, over a period of two years by Afghan prison guards, under the full knowledge of the British Embassy Kabul. Another form of psychological torture I had to endure was being placed on death row corridor block 10, Pul-i-Charkhi prison. Prisoners either side

Highlighted text has been repeated above from past pages, due to the nature of the conversation during the context of these pages

of my cell where dragged out of their cells by prison guards in the early morning, screaming, crying and pleading for their lives. They were dragged to the gallows within the prison grounds and hung until

dead. I witnessed this several times. The guards would smile and say I would be next? These were deeply disturbing events, which would stay with me for life"

When several senior members of Al-Q and Taliban were escaping from British mentored Pul-i-Charkhi prison. I sent an emergency SMS mobile phone message out to the British Consulate staff at the British Embassy Kabul, advising them of the escape and the situation, and that 'shots had been fired', sustained AK47 gunfire. I firstly contacted senior American military intelligence and updated them on the situation. Within a short time the Americans had acted on my report and re-captured the escaping Al-Q and Taliban terrorists within a mile of the prison. A message was passed back by the Americans to me "job well done". (An American lead investigation revealed the Taliban had paid the British mentored, Afghan prison guards $10,000 each for a copy of the keys to the gate of max-security, Block 10). The Afghan guards also walked away from their posts, which gave the terrorists a 15 minute window to escape. 'Al-Q and Taliban prisoners just walked out of the front gate, wearing Afghan prison guard uniforms? '. (See Author's personal photographs of the route Al-Qaeda used during the escape from Max-Security compound within the prison). I also wrote several letters to the FCO London and BEK, raising my grave concerns about British and Commonwealth prisoners' security and the 200+ IED, terrorist attacks and suicide bombings, being planned and ordered from within British Embassy mentored Afghan prisons. I addressed over 20 letters to; John Payne, Deputy Ambassador at that time. They never investigated, or officially interviewed myself. John Payne even cancelled a meeting with me at Pul-i-Charkhi prison. This was cancelled by mobile phone SMS message to me from the BEK staff Kabul, Simon Thomas's official British Embassy mobile phone. My Afghan personal diary, several Afghan phone 'Sim' cards, and official Afghan/American legal, and FCO/BEK letters, correspondence, reports and over 400 documents. Also a highly sensitive black note book, containing 40+ contact phone numbers and bank account details used by Taliban and Al-Q, both in Afghanistan and internationally. All this information and evidence confirms all that

I and other witnesses have said and stated in official reports and statements. I was collecting all this information and evidence at this time because I was well aware that the BEK/FCO would try and lie their way out of the situation, plus I felt that the FCO/BEK should be held accountable, so this situation would not happen to anyone else in the future. (All my highly sensitive evidence was officially lodged in by the British intelligence services. 'British Legal Chain of custody document' on my return to the UK).

I went on and described the horrific truth of what was going on inside Pul-i-Charkhi to the BEK. Another form of ill-treatment and torture I was subjected to was solitary confinement and being placed in a metal cage for hours at a time, in the hot Afghan sun, with no shade or water. My skin would painfully blister and get infected on more than one occasion. Prison guards would also throw rice at me through the metal cage bars (that was my prison food for the day). Other guards would laugh and urinate through the bars of the cage while shouting abuse at me. Raw sewage and blood would cover the floor of the cage, due to the open raw sewage pipes constantly over flowing. Rats, camel spiders and scorpions would also run freely around the cage, the guards would also throw these in with me so they could laugh at my reaction. On one fiercely, blistering hot afternoon, one of the Afghan prison guards, who took great pleasure in tormenting and torturing prisoners, I had nicknamed him 'Gargoyle', decided to wash his army boots and leave them to dry right next to the outside cage where I had been put in for the afternoon. I managed to drop a little scorpion into his boot, it stung him and it brought tears to his eyes when he put his boots back on. 'Payback is a bitch'. He was hopping mad for the rest of the day about this; obviously I denied all knowledge of how the scorpion got into his boot. 'I said it was the will of God'. This incident brought a rare smile to the faces of the other prisoners.

Prisoners would also often be handcuffed to the metal cage in 'Stress Positions' outside prison block 10 and viciously beaten by Afghan guards, with rubber hoses and metal cables. On one occasion Western prison mentors walked in, entered the block 10 prison compounds as torture was happening, the prison mentors quickly turned around and walked straight back out, without a word being said. No action was taken to stop or intervene in the torture. 'Water torture' was also used as a punishment by the Afghan guards, who would violently force a thick black rubber hose down the throat of a badly beaten handcuffed prisoner and turning the water on 'Simulated drowning'. I was forced to watch torture by the Afghan guards several times. The guards would just laugh and shout I would be next? Other forms of torture were also carried out by Afghan prison guards, prisoners being taken out of their cells at night and sexually abused. (This mainly happened to the very young Afghan prisoners who could not fight back or defend themselves, their screams, pleading and sobbing would be heard at night, throughout the prison). Other torture included the guards removing prisoner's shoes, while other guards held the prisoner down, another guard whipped the balls of his feet with a metal cable, until blood was pouring from multiple wounds and pooling with the prisoners urine across the floor. The smell of body fluids was overpowering. At night the piercing screams could be heard all over the prison. On several occasions this deliberately happened right outside my cell door, so I could see hear and smell everything. The guards all laughed and smiled and said I would be next: 'Sustained Psychological torture'? The Red-Cross took photographic evidence, and highly detailed witness statements from a large number of prisoners, regarding ill-treatment and torture, which was happening within British Embassy Mentored Afghan prisons. I worked alongside the Red-Cross, for two years; highlighting and trying to stop the culture of ill treatment and torture of prisoners in Afghan prisons. 'Mentored by the British Embassy Kabul'. When other prisoners were too scared and intimidated to speak out, for fear of being beaten or killed by the Afghan prison guards. I Anthony Malone (at great risk to myself) stood up and spoke out on their behalf.

The British Embassy's official stance on this subject was sustained denial and shameful cover-up. Neither Bevan nor I received official reply or response, not one, from all the letters, for years; we had sent over 'twenty' to the British Embassy Kabul, with relation the ill-treatment and torture of British and Commonwealth prisoners. On several occasions, the Red-Cross and their official personnel were refused entry to British Embassy mentored Afghan prisons across Afghanistan. This practice and action was a breach of both International Law and the United Nations Charter of Human Rights. Several independent witnesses can confirm the above facts, including members of the Red-Cross.

"Afghan Prison guards would come and take prisoners out in the middle of the night; their mutilated bodies were found hanged/murdered the next morning, (See Phil Young legal statement). Sometimes their bodies would just disappear altogether. Bodies were buried in unmarked graves around the back of the prison grounds. On several occasions I was forced to wash the blood off the walls, floor and ceilings, after prisoners had been tortured by other Taliban, AlQaeda prisoners and the Afghan prison guards the night before. (This was reported to the British Embassy Kabul, with no response?). The Red-Cross, United Nations and American State Department official reports confirm the ill-treatment, torture, and epidemic corruption throughout the Afghan Prison and justice system"

 The Red-Cross officially contacted the British Embassy Kabul about the situation. "The British Embassy staff told the Red-Cross to 'stop interfering in the situation. That I was a British national and the responsibility of the British Embassy'. This reply was passed back to me and Bevan, by the Red-Cross, during one of their official visits to the prison. The Red-Cross personnel were very upset by the British Embassy's response. Several members of the Red-Cross were witnesses to this. The British Embassy had also abandoned over 100 members of the Commonwealth, which they were officially responsible for. Over 100 members of the Commonwealth were just sat in an Afghan prison hell for years, without any due process or right of appeal. Their only chance of freedom was to pay the bribes to the Afghan prosecutor and judges when they visited the prison. Unofficially the British Embassy staff encouraged people to pay the bribes; it saved the Afghan Government and British Embassy embarrassment of an official investigation. This was also reported to the British Embassy, John Payne; The Deputy British Ambassador Kabul.

The General in charge of Pul-i-Charkhi called me up to his office one afternoon. The prison was in its normal chaotic state, guards running around everywhere. Taliban prisoners just sat drinking chi-tea, watching guards beat other prisoners for no apparent reason. I was lead up to the Commanders office, we shook hands and exchanged greetings in Arabic; I was amicable and polite (the Grey man) observing and taking in everything around me, it was always best to be sharp and observant at all times, nothing was ever what it first seemed in Pul-i-Charkhi. The Commanders office was large with windows at each end, framed with old dark dust covered curtains. A large old dark wooden desk, that had seen better days, was at one end and a seating area for 8 people at the other. Small wooden and glass tables were scattered around the old stained red carpeted floor. The office had the normal smell of stale cigarettes, and human body odour, but was fairly clean and orderly, a complete contrast to the rest of Pul-iCharkhi. A glass display cabinet stood off to one side, full of confiscated mobile phones 100+ and a selection of weapons, including large hunting knives some which were over 20 inches long, this was more like a trophy cabinet. Shotgun ammunition and CB radios had also been found within the prison. In the future I would point out to British Consul Jan Everleigh the knife, more like a sword, that the Taliban were going to 'use' on Bevan. The knife had been confiscated from Kandahar Taliban Commander Assadullah, in a raid carried out following my 'briefing' to American Intelligence. The Commander got straight to the point of the meeting. He admired my stand against the corruption within the Afghan Ministry of Justice and the way I had conducted myself during my time in his prison. "Then he informed me that bribes were how things got done around here, right or wrong, that was the reality of life in Afghanistan and within the Afghan Justice system". Being right does not mean anything in this corrupt society. He advised me to just pay the bribe being asked by the Afghan prosecutor and judge and walk free. There was no other way of gaining my freedom in Afghanistan. The Commander said that the whole system is completely dysfunctional, I already knew this, but my options were limited due to my wanting to make a stand against corruption and in my view paying the prosecutor and judge a bribe for my freedom within the British Embassy mentored justice and prison system was just wrong on so many levels. I thought that the British Embassy would stand up for truth and justice. I would settle for them just doing their job. I thanked the Prison Commander for his opinion on the matter and with a hand shake and a goodbye I was on my way back to Block 10. At this point the Embassy was not just trying to bury me and my situation, the standard no help or support from them was becoming pretty old hat, but now they were putting a non-official ban on the press reporting on me and my case. A lot of misinformation was coming out of the British Embassy Kabul (BEK); they were trying to discredit me on every level. One of the Embassy staff even went as far as to tell a respected journalist friend of mine that I had never served with the British Army. When I was informed of this by the journalist I was as disgusted as she was at the games the British Embassy staff where playing. Fortunately a lot of people knew me well, and were aware that some of the British Embassy official staff were lying. Not very professional conduct from British Embassy staff who were supposed to be representing my country, Great Britain, in Afghanistan. It was no wonder that the FCO has such a bad reputation amongst other British Government departments given their conduct I was experiencing in Afghanistan. Even senior British military officers did not trust them as far as they could throw them. "Snakes within the old boy network" was how one senior British military Commander "Major" described them. Kim Motley, an American lawyer, had a few other chosen words to describe them; obstructive, incompetent, disgraceful were just a few of the words she would share with me, Bevan Campbell and Bill Shaw.

"The extent of the British Embassy incompetence would only come to light in years to come. I would add the word 'treason' to the list of words I would use, with regard to some of the senior staff of the British Embassy Kabul, within my future official reports and correspondences to the British Prime Minister David Cameron and HRH Queen Elizabeth II"

See official, ill-treatment and torture statement by Anthony Malone, and Phil Young. The fact that the British Embassy Kabul had left a British national to rot and possibly die at the hands of Al-Qaeda and Taliban prisoners, within British mentored Afghan prison was a sensitive point. If I had been killed in prison in Afghanistan none of the facts and truth about my situation would have ever come out and the cover-up and lies by the BEK and FCO would never have come to light. Maybe this was what the BEK was hoping for, I'm sorry that I disappointed them...! I'm a Malone and former British paratrooper, we don't die easily.

I informed the British Embassy in writing that my Afghan lawyer had been visited at her home late one night by several members of the Taliban; Shabnama-Taliban 'night letters'(Taliban night letters are a physical warning of punishment to come). They had threatened her and her family, if she continued to represent me with my legal case. Members of her family would be killed; there would be no more warnings. I requested some help, British Embassy protection for my Afghan lawyer and her family, the British Embassy Kabul refused point blank, even after my lawyer had done work for them. My Afghan lawyer changed her job and profession due to this. She was later killed in a suicide bomb attack in Kabul, 100 meters from the British Embassy. I informed the BEK of the situation, and that I could not get any Afghan legal lawyer to represent me, due to security and the fact that the Taliban were threatening everyone who tried. The BEK was not interested and offered no assistance with this matter. I was treading water with my situation, until the Americans intervened, after witnessing the incompetence of some of the BEK staff. The Americans working out of the American Embassy Kabul were fully up to speed with the disgraceful treatment I had received from my own Embassy. I had a good rapport and reputation with the Americans which went back years and stretched over three continents that I had been operating in over the years. When the American Government officials spoke to me, the first thing they said was if I was an American I would not be in prison in Afghanistan. They already knew about my case and the true reasons for my predicament, including the sensitive matter of it all, stemming back to the fact that I had stood up to Assadullah the then corrupt Afghan Governor of Kandahar, who was a major drug dealer trafficker and who had been selling British Special Forces troop locations and the whereabouts of operational safe houses to the Taliban Command in Kandahar city? This was confirmed by an SAS Major with whom I had worked with in Kabul. Assadullah was also reported to be on the British Embassy payroll? I had attended several meetings with British SOCA (Serious Organised Crime Agency) who were locally based out of the British Embassy and villas in and around the surrounding area. I knew this to be true because some of these meetings were held at my Kabul villa and British SOCA was in attendance. I had stood up to Assadullah when he tried to use my credibility as a cover for his illegal drug operations. We had fallen out due to the fact that he did not like being called what he really was 'a corrupt Afghan drug lord'. Because the British SOCA needed Assadullah for information I was deemed expendable hence my present situation. The Americans were aware of all this and a lot more. They were disgusted at the way the BEK had treated me and basically hung me out to dry. Several senior American officials visited me to discuss my Afghan legal case. It was decided that I should have an American lawyer who could give the BEK and the corrupt Afghan Government a kick up the arse. I was told to keep this to myself at this point. The Americans wanted to set up and attend an official meeting with the BEK, to see what they were doing and to assess what progress the BEK was making to get me released. The day after this meeting took place, the Americans who had attended the meeting visited me. They handed me the official business cards they had received during their visit with the BEK. They were not impressed with the BEK? They told me everything that was said and by whom during the meeting. The Americans told me not to worry; they would get me an American lawyer ASAP. Her name was Kim Motley; she would come and see me by the end of the week. "Happy days" this proved one thing; the BEK had no intention of getting me released. Luckily the Americans were behind me. They were also aware of my close relationship with American military intelligence and all that I had done for them in the past, and still was doing for them while I was located in Pul-i-Charkhi prison. When the BEK found out I had an American lawyer they were not happy. When they broached the subject with me in the future, I told them that if they had done their job properly in the first place I would not have to have an American lawyer; this didn't go down well at all 'like a cold cup of sick'? The fact that I had an American lawyer would come back and bite the FCO and BEK on the arse a lot in the near future on every level. The situation of me having to look outside for help from the Americans was just one example of when FCO/BEK internal politics came before the wellbeing of one of their own nationals and before saving lives. The interesting facts that I was about to make and start highlighting to the British and Americans, was that attacks including; IED and suicide bombers targeting British and American soldiers across Afghanistan, including 'Helmand Province'. Where British forces were based and located in large numbers 10,000+. Terrorist attacks were being extensively planned, meticulously organised and efficiently directed from within British mentored Afghan prisons including Pul-i-Charkhi. The number of major attacks was in excess of 200. These would include the major attacks on Bagram airfield, American military base in Northern Afghanistan and 'KAF' Kandahar airfield, the joint military operations airfield on the outskirts of Kandahar City, Southern Afghanistan.

"Prime Minister David Cameron and the terrorist attack on Kandahar airfield"

One of the large and co-ordinated terrorist attacks targeted 'KAF', when the British Prime Minister was sat on a plane on the runway of KAF. In a fully fuelled British military C130 transport aircraft, 'secretly on route to visit British troops in Helmand Provence'. The order for this terrorist attack came from within Pul-i-Charkhi prison Kabul. Taliban weapons and ammunition were hidden close to the perimeter fence of KAF, two weeks before the planned Taliban attack. A little known fact is that a small number of Taliban during the attack made it as far as the runway before being neutralised. Due to a breakdown in Taliban communications the two other Taliban teams were late in getting to their planned forming up points prior to the attack. This made the three Taliban attacks uncoordinated which in turn left the Taliban attack unsuccessful. The British Prime Minister might be interested that he was targeted by terrorists from a British Embassy mentored prison. Luckily for the British Prime Minister, I was able to disrupt that attack from within Pul-i-Charkhi prison one hour before the attacks were due to start; by flooding the top floor and bottom floor of the prison block with 6 inches of water which blew all the electrics, which in turn blew and killed all the mobile phones on charge straight from the main electric cables and all homemade phone chargers and electric devices used by the terrorists to facilitate communicate and coordinate their attacks. All these were destroyed or rendered useless. 'Water and electrics don't mix well'? My destroying the whole electrics within the block, and in turn blowing all the Taliban and Al-Qaeda communications for a period of two weeks, was a good result. Obviously I managed to blame the prison guards for the flooding by kicking off about the amount of water in my cell? The stairs from the top floor to the bottom floor were more like a waterfall; it was a sight to see 'it looked great'. Al-Qaeda and the Taliban went mental about all this blaming the prison guards and calling them donkeys. I made sure that my arse was well covered, so there would be no come back on me. When I told the Americans what I had done, I got told 'well done'. The Americans paid for the whole block's electrics to be replaced. I was also told by a senior American who visited me, that if I felt the need to blow the electrics again, to disrupt and prevent future terrorist attacks, it would not be a problem. The Americans could afford to replace the electrics again if required. So Mr Cameron, British Prime Minister, I think you might want to owe me a drink, 'Gin & Tonic' please.

At this point in time I found myself in a very unprecedented situation; I was in Block 10 of a Max-Security prison, right in the middle of multiple active Al-Qaeda, Pakistan Taliban and Haqqani network operational cells, running daily terrorist operations from inside the prison. As a bonus I was also surrounded by their leaders and senior terrorist Commanders. Now that is enough to keep any person awake at night. I had to look on the funny side, there had to be a funny side somewhere. I suppose it could have been worse. I told Bevan that I had survived worse and more dangerous situations than this, Bevan said "really", I said "no, of course not, who do you think I am, bloody Rambo?" We both laughed. This was the worst situation I had ever been in and hopefully would not be my last. We both laughed at this comment too. We always tried to make fun out of our situation, if we didn't laugh we would cry. If mine and Bevan's situation was not so serious, it would not have been so funny at times.

Bevan's birthday came around quickly, something he had let it slip the night before. Early the next morning; "Happy Birthday you old bastard, how are you feeling? Older? And here I was thinking you had been 26 for the past 10 years". We will properly celebrate with a bottle of good old "Jack" when we are released, something to look forward to. Breakfast in Pul-i-Charkhi was bread and water, we had upgraded that morning with hot milky tea for Bevan's Birthday. With a hearty 'cheerio' and chill out today put your feet up and read a good book, it's only your birthday once a year, I ventured outside the prison block alone; the Taliban had invited me to play volleyball that morning. The sunlight was blinding outside, compared to the cold dark, depressing and harrowing atmosphere within Block 10. On stepping outside I was greeted with a hail of 'marHaba' hello and 'ahlan wasahlan' welcome, by the terrorists who were all sat in rows, enjoying the morning sun and reading and reciting the Quran. I replied in Arabic and placed my hand on my left chest out of respect. I received several nods of approval from the Taliban. I stood alone off to one side from the Taliban prisoners, the sun warmed my face and I closed my eyes and enjoyed a private moment facing the sun. Three little birds landed on top of the razor wire overhead, and burst into a chorus of beautiful song. It's amazing how the little things in here could make all the difference. People take so much for granted, I did, before all this, I would never make that mistake again. The little things in life are so important in there, they were a luxury, the sun light and the sounds of birds singing lifted my spirits beyond belief. These small but important things within this Afghan prison hell, helped to keep a person sane and grounded, which was a challenge in itself, given all that was going on daily within this dark location. I remember the first time I was lucky enough to see a star in the night sky, such a little thing gave me peace of mind and soul. It was absolute silent that night, the prison was dead quite, only a wild cat could be heard crying in the far distance, it could have been the wind. A stolen moment watching a star at night was a gift. It's difficult to describe just what this means to anyone who has not stood where I was at that moment in time. Priceless is a word I don't use often, but on that particular enchanting starlit night, seeing my first bright star in the clear night sky after such a long time, was just that, 'priceless'.

"Truth, Justice, Freedom, Liberty and the pursuit of all that threaten it"

A little known fact that the BEK was not aware of, and which British intelligence was trying to keep quiet, was that I had worked with and helped the American intelligence establishment for the past 12 years. I had worked with and helped American military intelligence throughout the Middle-East and Africa. I had also spent a lot of time with 101st Airborne Division (Air-Assault) in Northern Iraq during the Iraq war. I had become a friend and a work colleague with many senior high ranking military officers including; General David Petraeus (Future head of the CIA), Colonel Michael Linnington (Future Brigadier General and Commander of 'West Point' 2008), and Colonel Joe Anderson (future Brigadier General and Commanding General, 4th infantry and Fort Carson). These men were all Paratrooper's and outstanding fighting men and true military leaders. An instant bond and work ethic was forged between all of us, Colonel Linnington, radio Call-Sign 'Rock 6', was the Commander of the American Airborne Pathfinder platoon, which was located in North West Iraq at that time. I had spent a lot of time with him and his men out on the ground. Colonel Linnington always referred to me with pride as "blood brother" due to me also being a paratrooper. We had worked together when my intelligence sources pin pointed the location of HVT's (High Value Targets) in Western Iraq. A mission was launched and 28 terrorists were captured alive as they crossed over the border with Syria. 'It was a good night's work', 28 bad guys, international terrorists, were taken out of circulation. The terrorists were transported down to 'Balad' Base (See Glossary Balad). The Temporary Screening Facility (TSF) and the Joint Special Forces Operational Command (JSOC), Task Force Black and Task Force 121, as well as the American CIA operated out of 'Balad'. This was also one of the only places and locations in Iraq that you could get a good cup of coffee 'priorities in a combat zone are important'. We had both smoked a Cuban cigar after we found out the mission had been successful. The next time I spoke to General Petraeus, he told me that 'a few good men can make a difference'. During my time with the American military, we smoked a lot of Cuban cigars

- 'Victory Cigars'. One week later I went on another mission to 'Tal-al-Far', North West Iraq. Location of a terrorist safe house and Improvised Explosive Device (IED) factory, 12 terrorists were captured (See photographs taken through military night vision equipment). An interesting fact was 8 of the 12 were from Iran, confirmed by their identification. Two were from Syria and two from Lebanon, these latter two had the look and feel of being Hezbollah operating in Iraq. Later Iraq Hezbollah (IH) would be formed and openly operate within Iraq, helping to train and supply the Iraq insurgency terrorists. Another successful mission and another cigar was smoked in the back of the 'humvee' on route back to base camp, this was one of hundreds of missions I had been on in Iraq.

The Americans were as confused as I was regarding my being held in Pul-i-Charkhi prison? It was one of those strange situations that there was not a straightforward answer for. The short one was corrupt politics. The Americans were monitoring what the British Embassy was doing to help me, which was nothing. Things got interesting when Kim Motley came to visit me; she was a breath of fresh air. From day one of American intervention, she was on my legal case and more to the point onto the BEK and FCO. I would have liked to be a fly on the wall at the first meeting she had at the British Embassy. Kim informed me that the Embassy Staff were clueless about the Afghan Justice system. Kim had made a good first impression with the BEK, she had verbally kicked the door down and told them to get a grip and do their job as described in the FCO mandate. From day one the British Embassy did not like Kim Motley, because she did not take any of their political crap. She was straight and said it as she saw it. British Deputy Ambassador, John Payne, slipped up one afternoon and called Kim Motley a 'snake with tits'. John Payne said this in front of his whole PSD team who all just happened to be former British paratroopers, who coincidentally all knew me; they were disgusted at the political bullshit coming out of the BEK and John Payne relating to my situation. The BEK official personnel in Kabul were lying, trying to discredit me and telling people that I had never served in the Parachute Regiment 3 Para. It was the BEK's own PSD and bodyguard-teams that put them straight. The Embassy personnel were left with a lot of egg on their faces. I had served with members of the British Embassy PSD team; a lot were also former members of the British Parachute Regiment and in security operations across the Middle-East and Africa. Kim Motleys no nonsense approach to my case and situation was bearing fruit. Kim just wanted truth, justice and rule of law. Kim is one of the bravest people I have ever met, she is dedicated, principled and an American patriot. A lot of people admire Kim, because she is not just an exceptional human rights lawyer; she has also championed the women's rights in Afghanistan. Kim represents them and she is their voice, despite all the political pressure and threats. Kim is one of the few people who give a damn about the Afghan women, she understands their plight and being a woman, she knows how sensitive these cases are in a country like Afghanistan, which has a male dominated Government society and way of life. Kim is a shining light that gives the women of Afghanistan hope. It is no surprise that Kim (a former Miss Wisconsin, as I later discovered) would go on to do great things in the future. Kim also understood my situation well and all the nuances of the kind of work that I did in Afghanistan. We made a good solid team working together.

The BEK were feeling the pressure now that I had a good solid defence behind me 'God bless America' and all it stands for, 'Truth, Justice and Liberty'. Kim Motley was aware of all the ill-treatment that was taking place throughout the Afghan prison system; she was shocked at the level of abuse and endemic corruption. Whilst most other people would have just quit, increasingly, Kim became more and more focused, determined and increasingly tenacious. Her dedication was both admirable and inspirational. One of the questions that a lot of people had asked me many times was; why didn't I just escape from Afghan prison, given my background and experience. The simple answer is, I did not want to, because a lot of people were expecting this to be the course of action, I decided against it. I would not give the BEK or the corrupt Afghan Government the satisfaction of branding me a common criminal. My objective was to clear my name. Even being held illegally in prison would not have covered me. If I was to escape from a British Embassy mentored prison, the Embassy would also have used it against me and labelled me a common criminal. I would never give them the satisfaction either. I would stay put and clear my name. All I was looking for was an investigation into my reported miscarriage of justice and my situation. (Almost 5 years later my name was cleared and the FCO officially admitted that I had been held illegally in prison in Afghanistan).

My men, part of the Elite team who traced and tracked (under my Command) HVT terrorists including; Al-Qaeda, Taliban, Hezbollah, Al-Shabab and the Haqqani network.

"My team had meticulously planned my escape from Afghan prison"

Without my knowledge; new passports, identification-documents, transportation, helicopters (including Russian 'HIND' gunships) and specialist small arms, sniper weapons were available if required. All the routes and points were arranged. American military satellite imagery 'Falcon View',

(Above) Photograph by Author, example of Falcon view.

which the American military used to plan their military operations, was available, together with satellite photographs of every angle of the Afghan prison and surrounding area. Plan 'B' and Plan 'C' were also formulated and put in place. I had trained and taught my men well. They were very loyal and they knew that I too would 'never leave a man behind'. If one of them was being held prisoner in here; where I was, I would have moved heaven and earth to get them out, that's just the way I am. All was in place; all I had to do was give the 'green light' to go ahead. I even had members of the British Parachute Regiment and Special Forces, who offered to break me out of the Afghan prison. After a great deal of thought and a few sleepless nights, I stood my men down. They were very disappointed. They wanted payback for what the corrupt Afghan Government had done to me and wanted to leave the British Embassy with a big 'one finger salute' for their disgraceful treatment and for them abandoning me in an Afghan prison. I even had calling cards made up so I could leave them behind at key locations around the prison and Afghanistan. The calling cards were simple and just said "Elvis has left the building". I also intended to follow the time honoured tradition of escaping prisoners to send the Afghan Prison Commander of Pul-iCharkhi a postcard from my home country, saying wish you were here (This is called a home run by Second World War POW's), I wanted to keep this tradition alive. I was not just a prisoner of war; I was a prisoner at war. I must admit I 'was' tempted by the plan to get out, but I found myself in a one in a million situation. A lot of good could come out of all this, and more to the point; a lot of British and American (ISAF) soldier's lives could be saved. I decided to stay put. My men could not believe it, after great thought, and after they had come to visit me, they knew that there was more to this situation than met the eye. My men knew me well enough to know that there was a good reason behind everything I was doing. All my actions are well thought out and calculated. I'm a perfectionist in my planning and preparation before I undertake any action, task or military operation. My men suspected that something was going on and asked me if I was working for the Americans in Pul-i-Charkhi. I just smiled and told them that 'the truth always comes out in the end'. And 'not to forget that I was 'Anth Malone', at the end of the day, this was just another impossible mission to be completed. I had some good banter with my boys that afternoon, a rare opportunity for humour (as the British hero 'Black Adder' would say; ha I have danger for breakfast and death for tea? And pass me the black cap; I do love a fair trial?). In these dark times, humour was very important. I had many 'cunning plan's'. However I was not sure that infiltrating Al-Qaeda was one of them? Come to think of it one of the Afghan prison guards did look a bit like 'Baldric' from 'Black Adder'? Must have been his long lost relative from history? After a bit more light hearted banter my men told me that they were there if I needed them and support from the outside was there if it was required. I thanked them and told them to be ready for strange and epic times ahead? We would have other missions and official tasks, requests and work to undertake in the near future.

"See American Intelligence statement, transcript, UBL 'Osama Bin Laden' at rear of manuscript, Anthony Malone found OBL's location in the villa in Abbottabad
One year before the American Special Forces mission killed 'OBL' in Abbottabad Pakistan. Anthony Malone's Afghan diary, held by British intelligence since 11 September 2010, also confirms this 'chain of evidence document'. An 'Index List' of all intelligence reports handed by Anthony Malone to American Military Intelligence was given to American lawyer Kim Motley. This also confirmed the location of 'OBL' one year before the Mission to kill 'OBL'. The 'Index List' also included several other subjects which are still 'highly sensitive' and due to the 'official secrets act' cannot be named within this manuscript"

I have always been a keen sportsman; I love football, boxing and kickboxing. To my amazement, Al-Qaeda Commanders and their men also like football, and volleyball. They play whenever they have the opportunity. It's all maintaining fitness and in their words 'it helps them to fight'. I saw sport as a way into the Al-Qaeda terrorist network. Al-Qaeda is complicated, there are layers and layers and anyone who tries to move from one layer to the next is suspect. Anyone from outside their inner circle trying to move into their group is also suspect, it was a closed shop. Members had to fall within certain religious, ethnic and tribal frameworks. Al-Qaeda's OP-SEC (Operational Security) was very good. They had been betrayed in the past, and due to this they killed anyone who they suspected or seemed to pose any threat to them. You don't do anything on your own, you wait to be asked. I had been landed in this place. Call it unlucky or call it fate, I had no idea where all this was going to end, so I decided to make the most of it. I did not really want to be there, but the opportunity of infiltrating the terrorist network was too tempting. No-one had ever done what I was about to do. Many had tried and almost all had failed and been killed trying to infiltrate the terrorists networks across the Middle-East, Afghanistan and Pakistan. The amount of good that could come out of this, if I did it right, was off the scale. But the risks were also great, basically instant death by beheading, but the rewards were worth the risk; saving British and American lives. As far as I was concerned, if I was able to save one life, then I had succeeded and I had gained a small victory for myself and my country. In my eyes the risk was worth it, I have an old saying 'If you're going to do something, make sure you do it right first time'. I would only have one chance at this, so it had to be done right. I have always believed that a person can make Heaven out of Hell and Hell out of Heaven; given my present situation, I was to put this to the test. I went to work: Asset development and cultivation; Objective, gain intelligence that could be used to save soldiers' lives, and infiltrate the international terrorist network operating within Pul-i-Charkhi prison. Damn it, I had nothing better to do at this moment in time. Why not use my 22 years of military and covert operational experience and trade craft to do some good? Whatever happens, one thing was for sure, it was going to be an emotional and very rough ride.

My way of breaking down some of the cultural barriers was going to be through sport. I was not a Muslim, so my options were limited and restricted. After a few months of sport, football and volleyball for a few hours every morning; followed by an afternoon of talking, and studying, Islam with one of the Mullahs, drinking copious amounts of chi-tea and talking about general things, doors slowly started to open. At this point I never asked any questions about Al-Qaeda or the terrorist network; I didn't want to be seen asking sensitive questions, this was very important, because everything I said was always reported back to Al-Qaeda and the Taliban. The only way I could get close to these people, get to know them and build any trust, was to completely disregard my own personal safety and well-being. If I had displayed any fear or anxiety, the Afghan's and Arab's would have picked up on it. This would have also alerted them to my motives. I had adopted a pretty chilled-out attitude and approach to the whole situation. I only had two choices; (1) Hide and cower in my cell waiting for the Taliban and Al-Qaeda to come in one night and behead me. (2) Get out amongst the prisoners, make my presence known, and talk to them as if it was a natural progression. Obviously I was going for option (2) I don't cower down to anyone, especially international terrorists; my personal feelings were 'bring-it-on'. The fact that everyone knew that I had been hung out to dry by my own Embassy and that I had few visitors, due to some of the British Embassy staff advising people not to visit me only helped my credibility within the prison, and the situation regarding my tactical and strategic objective of gaining workable information and actionable intelligence on the terrorist network and the beast within.

I used all the negatives that were stacked against me and turned them into positives. My being 'blackballed' by my own British Embassy helped me to detach myself from the fact that I was British in the prison. The Al-Qaeda Commander in Pul-i-Charkhi had heard about the treatment I had received from my own Embassy and was disgusted by it. The Al-Qaeda Commander personally sent me fresh food and fruit, this was the first time I had ever heard of something like this happening. Everyone within Block 10 knew about this, even the guards, who were as surprised as I was, the Al-Qaeda Commander also sent word that the food was 'ok' to eat, just in case I thought it contained rat poison (the Taliban tried the rat poison trick on me at a later date, I would end up with two Intravenous (IV) drips in me at the same time, this nearly killed me but luckily it didn't. The Taliban were very disappointed). Because this new food was directly from Al-Qaeda and I had the Commander Saladin's word that it was ok, Bevan and I enjoyed it. The way I looked at it, if Al-Qaeda wanted me dead, they would just walk into my cell and kill me; they would not waste good food. I sent my best regards to the Al-Qaeda Commander via the prison guards who under strict instructions had brought me the food from Al-Qaeda.

I spent the next few weeks studying Islam, reading the Qur`an, playing volleyball. I got myself into a routine and remained below the radar. The CIA was keeping tabs on me from next door, over in "GitMo", so I had a little reassurance by this. I was taken to the Afghan Court a few times over the coming months, but nothing much happened. The Judge was not there and I did not have a lawyer at that point. Kim Motley was still doing the background on my case and getting the run around from the British Embassy, who repeatedly cancelled meetings with her. The British Embassy after 18 months still had no paper work or documents from the Afghanistan Government or Ministry of Justice, my official files kept on being lost? Kim did not officially take on my case until the month after we had first met and been introduced by the American's from CSSP. I was never given any notice of being summoned to court. I was just grabbed by the Afghan prison guards and shackled at gun point. I was frog marched and put onto an old prison van and at speed driven to the Afghan court house, which was located in Kabul within the market 'bazaar' area. This was a useless and futile exercise. The court also managed to lose all the so called official files and paper work on my case several times. In the first 18 months I had been sentenced to 10 months on trumped up charges which to this day I still don't have the paperwork or all official documents for. When I was dragged before a Taliban Judge for the first time and sentenced to 1 year (after already served 18 months?) this took 10 minutes from start to finish including a tea break half way through. I had no lawyer, no defence, no documents and I was not allowed to phone or speak to my Embassy. I was called a non-believer and an infidel by the Taliban Judge, he had pure hatred in his voice; he obviously detested the British and Americans. I was then quickly taken away in shackles and put back onto the prison van and taken back to Pul-i-Charkhi prison. The British Embassy Kabul was mentoring the Afghan Justice and Prison system at this point. They must have been very proud of their work. From my point of view, it was a shambles, a joke and complete waste of British tax payers money. OMG; if the British Embassy had not been mentoring the Taliban Judge, he might have sentenced me to death for being British? I spoke to the other prisoners about this; they all said this was normal. The justice system was widely known as being completely dysfunctional, corrupt and a bad joke. In my eyes the 'joke' was on the British Embassy staff for allowing it all to happen, on their watch, and under their full knowledge (ten years this had been going on for under the official mentorship programme). It was common knowledge, even the man passing on the street would say that the fact is bribes have to be paid if any prisoner wants his freedom. No cash forthcoming to the Judge or Prosecutor meant 'no' freedom. This was just part of daily life in Afghanistan. The official line coming out of the British Embassy Kabul at this point was that the Afghan Government and Justice System were not corrupt? Obviously some of the British Embassy staff must have been smoking Afghan 'heroin' on their nightly visits to the Kabul prostitute houses, 'Chinese takeaways', 250 meters from the British Embassy, to come out with such a ridiculous and incompetent comment as 'no corruption'. I sat talking to Drug Lords and War Lords about their cases. They were Taliban and Al-Qaeda, but their day job was drug dealing and weapon smuggling. The endless supply of money made from their illegal narcotics trade, financed their terrorist attacks and Jihad against the Western ISAF forces in Afghanistan and across the Middle-East and beyond. Suicide bombing, factory made IEDs from Iran, weapons, missiles and copious amounts of foreign fighters were all financed by the Afghan illegal narcotics drugs trade. The Taliban and Al-Qaeda looked upon the illegal narcotics trade as a way of fighting the Western countries by draining their resources when they tried to fight an endless and unwinnable battle against the Drug Lord's and the Taliban and Al-Qaeda network that covered the whole Middle-East and beyond. The aim of the Taliban and Al-Qaeda was to flood Western countries with Afghan heroin, from London to Paris to New York. Al-Qaeda was open about this objective; the disturbing fact is also that the Afghan illegal narcotics trade had increased almost every year since the American War on Terror in Afghanistan had started. The counter narcotics strategy and specialist teams within Afghanistan had failed, the amount of heroin coming out of Afghan in 2013 was at a high and the amount of Afghan heroin spilling over into the streets of Europe was only increasing, not decreasing (See Glossary; Hezbollah and Dubai money laundering). Al-Qaeda and the Taliban were running an International business, which was the "War on Terror". The West, Britain and America's biggest mistake is thinking that most people and Governments in the Middle-East, Afghanistan and Pakistan are our friends; the hard fact of life is that most are not? They are all too willing to take Western Governments money and funding, but as seen in Afghanistan, they are not our friends, and in some cases they are not even our true allies in the "War on Terror". As seen in October 2013 in a TV interview; President Hamid Karzai of Afghanistan, now 'openly blames' the West for the complete corruption in his 'own' dysfunctional Government? Over 447 British soldiers and in excess of 2000 American soldiers and countless others have been killed in Afghanistan supporting the incompetent Karzai Government. The question has to be asked, what has the Karzai Government achieved? Why have British and American troops stayed in Afghan for so long? No longer is anything being achieved. The Taliban are coming back into power and just liuk ehis predecessor, President Hamid Karzai, President Ashraf Ghani says talks with Taliban are solution to strife, the Taliban affirm their alliance with al-Qaida. Ghani has made peace talks with the Taliban a priority for since he was elected president last year, saying: "The negotiations are the solution, the way and this is what our nation wants, to end the bloodshed". He also thanked Mullah Mohammad Omar for endorsing the peace talks, which came after several informal contacts between the Taliban and Afghan government representatives. Meanwhile, Mullah

Akhtar Mansour, the new leader of the Afghan Taliban, who calls himself the "Commander of the Faithful," acknowledged and accepted a pledge of loyalty from the emir of al-Qaida, Ayman al-Zawahiri. This is an unusual open acknowledgement by the Taliban of its continued alliance with al-Qaida and a blatant violation of the ground rules for any political reconciliation process in Afghanistan. Mansour says victory is in sight after 14 years of war. America and its "infidel allies" have been "humiliated, disgraced, and defeated" in Afghanistan and will withdraw their last troops in 2016 in defeat. The message implies the Taliban will allow al-Qaida to operate freely in Afghanistan. As-Sahab (the media production house of al-Qaeda) has already relocated back into Afghanistan after being based in Pakistan since 2002. Osama Bin Laden's son, Hamza, reaffirmed his loyalty to the Taliban in his first ever audio tape for al-Qaida. The Haqqani network, which operates very closely with the ISI, made little secret of its support for al-Qaida. The Haqqanis have gained influence in the Taliban with Mullah Omar's departure. Mullah Mansour faces a growing challenge from supporters of the Islamic State in Afghanistan. They claim the true commander of the faithful is the Caliph Ibrahim—aka Abu Bakr al-Baghdadi. By citing al-Zawahiri's pledge of loyalty, Mullah Mansour is seeking to affirm his legitimacy by invoking the legacy of Osama bin Laden, al-Zawahiri's predecessor and the icon of all Jihadis. The ISI probably decided the bad publicity in the West was worth the gains of stronger legitimacy for its new protégé, Mullah Mansour. The terrorist threat against the West, including Britain and America is higher now than at any time since the 9/11 attacks. Islamic extremists are planning and trying to launch terrorist attacks against Western targets monthly. The politician claims that British troops being in Afghanistan for so long is 'keeping the streets of Britain and America safe' is complete 'hog-wash' and political spin? Politicians do not want to be held accountable, or face up to the true facts of the situation. On-going terrorist threats; from groups operating within Syria, Afghanistan, Pakistan and Somalia, including, Al-Shabab ordering attacks on 'named' British nationals living in Britain completely contradict British politician's official statements on the terrorist threat, or that British troops being in Afghanistan are keeping the streets of Britain safe. When an off duty British soldier is murdered, almost beheaded on the streets of London, our own public streets are not safe anymore. Global terrorism has escalated and evolved expediently over the past 10 years. So called Government Advisers, who disagree with this are playing political games and most probably have their own hidden agendas. As far as some senior military officers are concerned 'their personal view', the British military are "Lions lead by donkeys". First the fiasco of the Iraq War now the Afghan War. Government budget cuts are stripping the British military to the bone, some think beyond. Now Britain does not even have its own operational aircraft carrier. What will be next? Some of the Afghan prisoners and a lot of the men in general across Afghanistan and the Middle-East, who I spoke to; don't talk of the West in a positive way. What I was shocked about was how many despise the West. They blame us for the wars raging across their countries. They do have a point, Iraq is in turmoil, Afghanistan is not much better, Syria is war torn beyond belief, Egypt is volatile, Somalia is battling away, as it has been for the past 20+ years and Pakistan and Yemen (now in a Civil War) are not really a beaming ray of hope. In the past 14 years, the Middle-East and a lot of Islamic countries have been turned on their heads and the results are always the same; violence, war and copious killing, suffering and countless human rights abuses, nothing really positive (maybe add something on the 'refugees' flooding into Europe now – many who are linked to terrorist organisations – this was one of the 'stated aims' of the Al-Qaeda Commanders we spoke with, now it's not only 'home-grown' terrorism, but also 'infiltrated' terrorists the West has to worry about. These men/women could easily set up 'training camps/areas' to stop the radicalised Westerners from even leaving Europe, thereby making 'tracking' them harder – everything is on 'home-soil'. This equates to one BIG PROBLEM). One has to look really hard to find anything positive in any of the events that have happened there. Western Governments including British and American have haemorrhaged money, fighting foreign wars for too long and it has reached a point where the money has run out. We can hardly afford to defend this country, yet we are allowing ourselves to be bled dry by people who actually hate us with an insatiable passion. The corrupt Government officials in Afghanistan have a saying; 'In God we trust' which is also printed on the back of the American $100 bill. Corrupt Afghan Government officials take everything and give nothing, not even to their own people. The countless suitcases full of money taken out of Afghanistan and flown to places like Dubai are just an example of this. Corrupt officials are bleeding Afghanistan dry of the aid money given to them by Western Countries and organisations. Hundreds of millions of dollars of Western official aid money have been diverted and paid into corrupt Afghan official's bank accounts. Another interesting fact was regarding the National Bank of Afghanistan.

"The Kabul bank was temporally closed"

Due to the amount of money being taken out of the Kabul Bank, and the country, the Kabul Bank was temporarily closed. The bank had given criminally large loans to Afghan Government officials, whom could not afford to repay the loans, but who bought property in Dubai. All this came crashing down when the property bubble in Dubai dramatically burst. The National Bank of Afghanistan almost went bust and would have, if not for quick intervention and help from Western Governments; huge amounts of money were flown into Afghanistan. A large amount of foreigners banked at the Kabul bank, and all their money, hundreds of millions of dollars, was put in jeopardy when the Kabul bank closed. All Members of the Afghan army, police, prison and other Government employees had to be paid through the Kabul Bank, so they were not paid for several months. This situation was fully exploited by the Taliban and Al-Qaeda networks. Hundreds of Government personnel ended up being on the Taliban and Al-Qaeda payroll, for one very simple reason - these people had their families to provide for. It reached crisis point, when Government officials and employees had to sleep at their place of work, because they could not even afford to get home. I personally witnessed this within the Afghan prison and police system. The former members of the Northern Alliance, who had previously been favoured by the Karzai Government in Kabul, had taken most of the senior positions within the Afghan Government and its Departments, after the fall of the Taliban from power. The Northern Alliance had for years, persecuted the Pashtun's in the south of
Afghanistan.

Once the Taliban had gained strength and support within the Afghan Government and Parliament, the tables would be turned on the members of the former Northern Alliance even more; the Pashtuns of Southern Afghanistan would, and had started to, persecute the tribes of Northern Afghanistan. The Northern Alliance had enjoyed the support of the Americans and other Western Governments but that was no longer the case. Their day of reckoning was coming. The Taliban would not forget that the Tribes of the North, including members of the former Northern Alliance, had helped to topple the Taliban and the Pashtuns from power after the 9/11 attacks. Everyone knew that the Taliban was coming back into power; it was just a case of when. In private, the Taliban had already stated that they would deal with the corruption within the Afghan Governments. Swift justice would be delivered, it was no wonder that the corrupt Afghan officials were taking every dollar they could get their greedy claws on and fleeing the country to Dubai and European countries. The Government officials were overlooking one thing, the Taliban and Al-Qaeda have a very long reach, and even longer memories. I have extensively spoken to and interviewed many key players and people in Afghanistan. Including; Abdullah Abdullah the former Afghan Foreign Minister and 'Wali Massoud', former Afghan Ambassador to Britain and America. I have also extensively interviewed several key Taliban who hold positions within the Afghan Upper and Lower Parliament. All say the same thing; the corruption in Afghanistan is endemic and on every level. It will be interesting to see how the Taliban actually deal with this problem when the power sharing agreement with the Karzai (Ghani) Government of Afghanistan is finalised and signed. As far as the Taliban and Al-Qaeda were concerned it was just a matter of time. They knew that within a few years they would be back in power and their influence would be absolute. From what I had already seen and later learnt in meetings that I would attend within Pul-i-Charkhi prison, the Taliban, Al-Qaeda and Pakistan Taliban, had already infiltrated and wielded great power and influence over the Afghan Government and Parliament. The Taliban and Al-Qaeda were playing it out like a game of chess; they were playing the long game and in so their tactics were winning. The British Embassy was given a list of corrupt Afghan officials, including their full names and official positions within the Afghan Government and mobile phone numbers, even their bank account numbers into which their ill-gotten gains were paid into. The British Embassy Kabul did not officially respond to any of these letters. The American's were given full comprehensive lists and copies of all the data. I knew that the British Embassy would just ignore the information I had given them and not even respond. The Americans told me to give them all the evidence I had and they would action and investigate it and get back to me, which they did. Interviews and statements were taken. I was told to keep this to myself at that time; and that the British Embassy did not need to know. Afghan officials, including Afghan Prosecutors, were removed from their official positions. This was but a drop in the ocean regarding the corruption that existed within the Afghan Government.

"To mystify and mislead the enemy, has always been one of the cardinal principles of war, consequently. Ruses de Guerre of one kind or another have played a part in almost every campaign, ever since the episode of the Trojan horse, or perhaps even earlier. The game has been played for so long that it is not easy to think out new methods of disguising one's strengths or one's intentions. Moreover, meticulous care must be exercised in the planning and execution of the schemes; otherwise, far from deceiving the enemy, they merely give the show away"

Lord Ismay, forward to 'The man who never was' 1953

"First meeting with Al-Qaeda – Saladin – Taliban"

After I had been in Pul-i-Charkhi prison for about a year, the Senior Al-Qaeda and Haqqani network Commander invited me to come over to their corridor and have chi-tea. This was going to go one of two ways (1) I get beheaded, and it would be game over for me or (2) I sit down and have a pleasant cup of chi-tea and charming afternoon conversation. I would settle for a good hot brew of tea and not getting my head cut off, I kind of like it were it is. I'm no model and I know I'm an ugly bastard but this head is the only one I have so I was keen to keep it. I knew that the Head of the Al-Qaeda corridor was Commander Saladin. The prison Commander had confirmed this; when he had shown me Saladin's official prison files on his laptop computer which the prison commander had been showing off one afternoon in his office. Saladin's file was extensive and Saladin had been involved in a lot of major Al-Qaeda operations across the Middle-East. Luckily for me I never found out just how senior Saladin really was within the Al-Qaeda and Haqqani networks, until months down the line. My being a little naive at this point worked in my favour. I had watched Saladin a lot over the past year from a distance. He had done the same to me, we would play volleyball each morning, but we were always on opposite sides. We had both been weighing each other up, how we moved around the prison, who we both spoke to, how we carried ourselves, and how we handled ourselves around other prisoners, we had studied each other, and we both knew it. We had played cat and mouse with each other, the funny thing was we had both known it, and yet we still played our little game. Like chess, we had both tried to stay one step ahead of each other, he had opened the door by sending me food in the past and by doing so making a major silent statement, by doing so began paving the way to some sort of dialogue. Commander Saladin was tall, six foot and well built, he was a mountain of a man and the only way I would want to take him on in a fight would be with bloody big stick and with an 'RPG' as backup. Saladin had all the characteristics of a hardened mountain man who had been brought up in extreme conditions and the harsh unforgiving weather of the Eastern Mountains of Afghanistan. We were about the same age. I told him sometime later that he looked older but not as ugly as me. He had to work a lot harder to be as good looking and pleasantly ugly as me. We both had a similar sense of humour, which was good because we would both need it in the future. Saladin had an air of authority about him. He never raised his voice, and was professional at all times. I had also noticed that he always made sure his men were fed well and that they never went hungry. He would always eat last, after his men. I often observed that Saladin didn't eat at all; telling his men that he had eaten earlier, which in fact he had not. This to me was the sign of a good leader and Commander of men, a man who looked after his men first and himself last. For some reason I had no problem in meeting with Saladin. I would also later learn that his nickname was the 'Fox', he would laugh when he called himself or referred to this name that the American military had given him. The American military had not known who or just how significant, he, the 'Fox', really was.

The Al-Qaeda corridor in Block 10 was always dark and foreboding, even the Afghan prison guards didn't like to walk down there. It was a 'no-go' area for most people. 40+ members of the Al-Qaeda, Haqqani and Pakistan Taliban network called this corridor 'home'. A large number of Al-Qaeda were milling around their corridor, some were reading and reciting the Quran and others just sat around quietly talking. They all wore Arab drab, traditional Arabian clothing, and they had long black beards and their eyes were dark and filled with deep utter hatred, these were the real deal the real 'bad boys'. The bolt on the main gate was disengaged and slid back. I stepped inside and the Afghan prison guards quickly closed and locked the gate behind me. The sound of the metal gate being slammed behind me and the locks clattering shut echoed loudly down the corridor. I stood facing down the Al-Qaeda corridor. I remember thinking; I hope I have not misjudged this. Well I was about to find out, 'balls of British steel'. The corridor was spotless and well kept. Everything was in its place and very neat and tidy. All the Al-Qaeda fighters in the corridor stopped dead in their tracks and just stared at me when I had stepped into their corridor. I was in their domain. At this moment in time I did what any other combat veteran, who has survived endless encounters behind enemy lines, would do, I had a 'dear diary moment' combined with a little sense of humour failure (what the fuck was I doing here), not to worry, it only lasted for about a minute though. The trick was to never let anyone see your true feelings; keep them hidden, deep within you at all times. Even if you're flapping inside, Al-Qaeda and the Taliban must never see or sense it. All they should see is a cool, calm and collected individual. Being able to achieve this comes with one's own confidence and ability to deal with any situation, after all that is said and done, I am only human at the end of the day and even I get nervous sometimes, mostly though it's usually due to excitement and adrenalin.

I walked normally down the Al-Qaeda corridor towards Saladin's room; I gave respectful nods of acknowledgement to the Al-Qaeda and Taliban fighters as I passed them. They nodded silently in return, their eyes never leaving me as I continued to walk. I kept my head held high; my gait was upright and self-assured. I made a concerted effort not to rush. Saladin's room was the second from the end, next door to Al-Qaeda Saudi Arabian Commander Abdul Aziz. He was a giant of a man. If I was walking to my death, then so be it. I would go down fighting like a British Soldier, courageous 'til the end. That was my only plan of action, if they rushed me intending to kill me; I hoped to take at least two or three of the bad guys with me, before they cut off my head. I must admit this was not much of a plan, but under the circumstances it sounded like a good plan to me. I was under no illusions if Al-Qaeda wanted me dead, if they wanted my head there was not much I could do about it. I had to look at the funny side of this, it was one hell of a way to go, completely surrounded and hopelessly out numbered. I intended to go down fighting like a 'Malone' and British Paratrooper. The 'Malone' family oath, on our coat of arms is "loyalty above all else, except honour" I was living up to that oath on every level. The Malone's are made of stern stuff as my mother always said. I may have been abandoned by my own Embassy but my 'Oath of Allegiance' was uncompromising to Queen and Country. I was very proud of this fact.

As I reached the end of the corridor I turned towards the entrance to Saladin's room. I remember thinking; 'come and have a go if you think you're hard enough', for some reason this football chant seemed appropriate for my situation. A massive bear like figure stepped through the door way towards me; it was Abdul Aziz, a Saudi born Al-Qaeda, AQAP, and AQI, Commander from the Holy City of 'Medina' in Saudi Arabia. Abdul Aziz was in Block 10 for killing several American soldiers in Jalalabad. He had also beheaded several Afghan's working for the American military. Abdul Aziz was wearing flowing jet black traditional Arabian robes, with his head dress over his right shoulder (this was how some Arabs carried there headdress when not in use) He just smiled at me, with a wicked smile that I would come to know well in the future. I prayed that God and his angels were watching over me, and covering my back, nothing wrong with a little help at times like this from the 'God squad'. Abdul Aziz walked in silence into the next prison cell. A calm, deep voice, came from the inside of the room 'Ahlan Wa Sahlan' he is welcome, came from Saladin. He stood up from the back of the room, moving forward slowly to greet me, he was surrounded by ten of his best men, the cream of the Al-Qaeda fighters in Pul-i-Charkhi, all had the standard long black beards and they all wore the long traditional white Arabian dress. We greeted each other in classic Arabic. Saladin introduced me to the rest of his men, I put my hand out to shake their hands and show them respect. Al-Qaeda fighters are big on respect. A few were a little hesitant at first, but then followed the lead of the others. After traditional formal greetings, we all sat on a blanket on the floor and had chi-tea. I was positioned to the right of Saladin against the back wall. I looked back towards the door. My chances of making a run for it before things went pear shape were absolute zero. Well, I was here now, perhaps this was going to be interesting. I noticed a black flag hanging on the wall; the flag of Al-Qaeda, written on it in Arabic script was 'death to all enemies of Allah' 'God is great'. The black flag just set this chilling scene. With Al-Qaeda fighters sat beneath it sent an ice cold chill down my spine. This was the same flag I had seen on the Al-Qaeda propaganda videos on the internet, that showed Al-Qaeda fighters beheading people, this was a very sobering thought and an unwelcome escalation in my present situation (I would not recommend that anyone watch these videos. It's almost impossible to erase these images once you've seen them). In present company, I needed to keep my head and remain cool and calm. Saladin's Al-Qaeda fighters sat motionless and in absolute silence, like statues just staring at me, studying me. They were stroking their long dark beards and sat in deep thought. They looked like a right demonic mob. I was one of their sworn enemies; I was the 'Devil' as far as they were concerned. I could feel waves of animosity emanating from them. I had taught my men back in the world when I was running Security Training Courses 'hostile environment training' that when you're in a situation like the one I now found myself in, you're not going to talk your way out of a fucking thing, with these kinds of people, Islamic extremists Al-Qaeda, you shoot first, that's what they respect, it may sound strange, but a lot of the so called extremist I had encountered in the past were scared of extreme violence. The Al-Qaeda fighters I had in front of me were the extreme of the extreme; they had a macabre aura about them, like the angles of death. I felt that I was sitting in its dark presence. In the future these fighters would form their own extreme Al-Qaeda group, Kandahar Al-Qaeda, these extremists obviously thought that the normal Al-Qaeda were a little too warm and fluffy for them.

I turned to face Saladin and decided to take the initiative. I did not have an AK47 handy so my options were limited. I started to talk to him; in no way did I want them to think that I was intimidated by them. My approach took them by surprise; his men looked around at each other, not sure what to make of me. On observing Saladin's room, it was identical to my own cell with regard size and lay out, it was clean but sparse. He did not believe in worldly material belongings, he received outside visits almost every day and he received fresh food, clothing, gifts and contributions from a wide variety of people, including other terrorist Commanders and Afghan Government officials. Saladin shared everything he had or received with his men. There were two neatly folded blankets on the end of Saladin's bed, with an Islamic prayer mate placed on top, (this was large in size compared to others smaller ones I had seen. Its colours were deep blue, jet black and glimmering gold with blood red. The workmanship was unmistakable and indicated that it was obviously from Saudi Arabia), I would receive this as an honoured gift from Saladin in the future. A small wooden table sat in the corner, tea sugar and milk were placed tidily on one side and everything had its place. Saladin was professional in all things, the layout and his clean orderly room supported my opinion on this. Saladin had placed two other blankets on the concrete floor of his cell for people to sit on. A red plastic bucket was upside down under the main light. Two wires were hanging down from the protruding ceiling light to the red bucket. Three new top of the range Nokia mobile phones were on charge. Al-Qaeda had figured out a way to make homemade phone chargers and a set up to charge all the electrics including mobile phones and satellite phones. I made a mental note of this, I knew that this would be an important point in the near future.

The fact that Saladin was even willing to speak had surprised me, there was something about him that interested me, and I knew that I also intrigued him, which I knew antagonised him just a little. I had very subtly antagonised the prison guards just enough to get Al-Qaeda and Saladin's attention. Everything I had seen and witnessed with regard Saladin cried out professional soldier and Commander. I was sat in front of the enemy now. I had extensively hunted men like Saladin and his crew, 'the bad guys', all over Afghanistan, Pakistan and the Middle-East for the past 14 years. Now my life was in their hands. We spoke in Arabic, small talk first about prison life, then Saladin leaned back against the wall, he looked at me, whilst stroking his long black beard. There was a moment's silence; then Saladin leaned forward to within 6 inches of my face, he looked me in the eyes and asked about my past and who did I know in Saudi Arabia. I laid my cards on the table; I was a former member of the British Parachute Regiment, the very same people and military Regiment that Al-Qaeda and the Taliban were fighting against in Afghanistan Helmand Province. I had worked for various Governments and I had held 'Special Advisers' positions in Saudi Arabia for one of the senior Saudi families which I named. Saladin asked about my time spent in Iraq and Syria. I gave him a very brief overview. I had enjoyed travelling around the Middle-East, taking in sights, cities and culture. I left out the whole American military connection; I thought it best I kept that to myself. I mentioned that I had worked for a Private Military Company (PMC), Saladin smiled and he then pulled a piece of paper from his top left hand pocket. Saladin already knew all about me. It was all written down in Arabic on the paper he held in his hands. He knew about my military past and some of the work I had done in Afghanistan. He also had a list of my Afghan contacts, 'only the ones who were former Northern Alliance', he handed it to me; I nodded and said 'yes, these are correct'. I would later find out that one of the Afghan interpreters working for and within the British Embassy Kabul was also working for Al-Qaeda and the Taliban, feeding them information. This was how Al-Qaeda had gained some of this information on me - this was just one of the many points which I would bring up with the BEK. Saladin had asked me a straight question and I had given him a straight answer. I then asked him a question, was he really Al-Qaeda? What was Al-Qaeda? And where did they come from? Also, does he have any chi-tea and nuts? Everyone in the room laughed, Saladin addressed the room. 'He is welcome and he is a guest'. Chi-tea and nuts promptly arrived. We spent the next few hours talking about Damascus and Baghdad and the culture of the Middle-East, Saladin was intrigued that I was so knowledgeable about the Islamic world, its customs and old ways. Its little details that matter and can make a massive difference, like always standing when someone enters the room; this is a sign of respect. Always making sure everyone has chi-tea before yourself, pass nuts by hand to your guest or take the best part of food, a meat dish, and offer it to the eldest man in the room, all these things and actions are show as a sign of respect. I had followed all these customs and Al-Qaeda and the Taliban had noticed them over the past months. One of the other terrorist Commanders commented that I was more Arab than Western; did I have any Arab relatives? This comment prompted a volley of laughter from the circle of men sat in Saladin's room. The conversation was interrupted by the afternoon call to prayer. I stood up and offered my regards to everyone, thanking them for their hospitality, I promised that I would return soon to continue our conversation. I shook everyone's hand, in order of age, and stepped out of the room back into the corridor; Saladin followed and walked me down to the gate, Saladin shouted to the guards. They had changed shifts and looked very puzzled, leading to a sense of humour failure when they saw me standing in the Al-Qaeda corridor with Saladin. The guards quickly opened the metal gate; I shook Saladin's hand and thanked him for an interesting afternoon. He told me that he would organise some good food later in the week and that I should join him and his men for an evening meal. I accepted his invitation, he would just have to instruct the prison guards to come and collect me. I left the first meeting with Al-Qaeda open ended. I walked past the guard who looked at me in disbelief. I heard the gate being slammed behind me, the locks were pulled to and the echo vibrated down the corridors. I had survived the first meeting with Al-Qaeda.

I took a deep breath of relief, feeling positive about the afternoon's events. One of the most important points that came out of that first meeting and conversation, was that Al-Qaeda's intelligence gathering was very good and far reaching and that they should never be underestimated. One thing 'did' worry me though, and that was my military past, which was not common knowledge at that point in time. I walked into my cell to be greeted by Bevan's good old South African voice 'God you're still alive', we both laughed, "is everything alright he inquired". "It was proper emotional", I answered. I really needed a good cup of sweet strong coffee, we had hidden a little for emergencies and this was definitely one of those times. I could relax now. OMG; my nerves were shot; I certainly needed some chill out time. Whilst enjoying my coffee, I gave Bevan an account of all that had happened that afternoon. The fact that Saladin had acquired a hell of a lot of information on me had spoken volumes about their Operational Security (Op-Sec'), Al-Qaeda's due-diligence was very good, even from inside a Max-Security prison. The whole conversation with Saladin had been a test to see if I would be truthful. It's difficult to explain but I had gone with my gut instinct and whilst talking to Saladin my gut had told me to play it straight. By doing this I hoped to begin building bridges toward gaining their trust; something that I might be able to use to my advantage in the future. They had all thought that I would not disclose my military past, I had not, and now they weren't quite sure how to take me or deal with me. The fact I had seemed so chilled out asking for chi-tea and nuts had thrown them a 'curve ball' and in doing so had help to defuse the situation. I wanted to be unpredictable, projecting a nonchalant vibe, but it was critical that I remained focused. I appeared not to have a care in the world; otherwise I would not have made it out of the lair of the beast, the lion's den. To describe the afternoon in one word is difficult, but hey, I am used to the impossible, so I would say that it was 'challenging'. God I needed a stiff drink, where's the brandy when you need one?

Several Taliban Suicide bombers had attacked targets across Afghanistan that morning and afternoon, killing a total of 74 people. The carnage and bloodshed had become an all too frequent daily occurrence. Not just in Afghanistan, but across the whole Middle-East, including; Iraq, Syria, Africa, Somalia, Kenya, Egypt and Libya. One of the bombers had detonated his explosives in the middle of a busy market in Kandahar city, Southern Afghanistan. The target was a corrupt local Afghan politician, who had tried to stand up against the local Taliban. He and his bodyguards had been blown to pieces, but the suicide attack had also killed many innocent women and children, who had been at the market going about their normal daily business of buying and selling food and vegetables.

"Taliban Collateral Damage"

The Taliban just referenced this as collateral damage. The death and devastation of a suicide blast in such a confined area, full of people is beyond comprehension. I had personally witnessed the aftermath of many such blasts. One of them had happened in Baghdad. I had luckily missed the explosion only by a couple of minutes. I too would have been blown to pieces had I been there. The results of these attacks are almost indescribable. Blood and body parts are everywhere. Severed bloody body limbs, fused and burnt into the side of walls and surrounding buildings, due to the immense heat and force from the shockwave from the blast. It is more like a grotesque scene from a horror movie. All those innocent lives gone, lost within the blink of an eye. Women and young children barbarically murdered in the so called Taliban Afghan Jihad. It takes but a moment for a suicide bomber to push the switch that detonates the explosives attached to a suicide belt. But the loss of life lasts for an eternity. There is always a moment of silence straight after an attack, then the horrific reality of the situation becomes apparent and the gravity of the situation hits home. The piercing cries, screams and uncontrollable wailing of human suffering and helplessness fill the air. The bloody carnage becomes slowly visible. The putrid smell of burnt human flesh and clothing, hangs in the air. Injured people slowly come into view, covered in blood, faces blackened, clothes torn and limbs missing. People pleading for help, desperately shouting and screaming out to their loved ones, who were one minute next to them, the next, a bloody mass of unrecognisable, broken and smashed body parts, white bones and blood drenched shredded clothing. These horrific images come into view and could be heard and seen through the dust that started to lift from the blast and shock wave. I had witnessed these scenes all too often across the Middle-East, yet again this horrific death and carnage had come to the cities and streets of Afghanistan. Within moments of the blast, which seemed like an eternity? Emergency vehicles and loud wailing ambulances arrived up at speed. They began to ferry the dead, dying and seriously injured to the local hospital. Strangers picking up torn bloody remains of bodies and placing them un-ceremonially on the backs of old wooden horse carts, silently moving them away leaving thick trails of blood behind them. Government water trucks then arrived. The entire area was power washed, even the trees. The cold water mixing with the blood on the trees gave a horrific visual sight when the blood dripped from the branches and green leafs on the tree. It gave the appearance that the tree itself had been mortally wounded and was bleeding. The jet washes were washing away, erasing all traces of the suicide attack. 'No evidence was taken or collected' no point really, this was just one of an endless number of such murderous atrocities. Washing the area down, washing away all the blood and human body fluids and shredded internal organs is horrendous to witness. Copious amounts of blood mixing with high pressure water, sent sprays of crimson up the walls of the surrounding buildings. Government workers went to work, using stiff brooms trying to scrub away the blood stains on the concrete. The area was flooded in a blood red mist from the jet power wash. Its objective was to get rid of all traces of the attack, so daily life could return to normal, until the next time. The clean-up took just two hours. I walked over to a small tree off to one side of the blast area. A small piece of human flesh attached to a scrap of burnt cloth was hanging from a low branch. This little piece of what had once been part of a human being with dreams and a future; they had started the day full of life, but now had been violently ripped from life itself. This was the only evidence of what had happened here that day.

Several suicide attacks had been and were being planned and ordered by 'Talib-Jan' a terrorist Commander from inside Pul-i-Charkhi prison. There had been 8 suicide attacks so far that day, 32 that month and counting. This was going to be a bloody month for the Afghan people. (See Glossary; Claymore and Suicide vest). After studying Al-Qaeda within Pul-i-Charkhi and 12 years' operating against them globally, I noticed many aspects of their operations were evolving into quite a complex and effective structure. Their operational scope, due to global franchises in several countries was rapidly expanding. The multimedia and propaganda campaigns are recruiting and more disturbingly brain washing young Al-Qaeda and Islamic Jihad fighters across the Middle-East and within Western Countries. Including; Britain, America, Canada, Germany, Sweden to name but a few. Home grown terrorists are now not just a local problem, they are an increasingly serious threat to all Western Countries. The political structure within and across the Al-Qaeda and Haqqani networks are vast, complex and comprehensive. The new breed of personalities helping, supporting, fighting, funding and financing Al-Qaeda and their political objectives through 'Gunship Diplomacy' are truly on a globe scale. Including; Bankers, corrupt Politian's and Government officials, International business men, oil rich Arabs and Arab Intelligence, police and army personnel. These are the new foundations, members and political structure and complex makeup of areas of support within the Al-Qaeda International terrorist network. Add extremist Al-Qaeda ideology to this melting pot of hatred towards the West. It makes for one hell of a potent mix and a major future problematic tactical and strategic nightmare, and future ongoing problem for all Western Governments and Intelligence services. Al-Qaeda, the beast; is now a major threat not just to British National security, but also to all Western interests and assist's across the Middle-East and beyond. Examples of how the 'Global War on Terror' has evolved and escalated are the attacks of; 9/11, 7/7, 11/3, and 21/9 Kenya attack by Al-Shabab on the Westgate shopping Mall (See Glossary; 21/9 and Al-Shabab). I was now sat in the lair of the beast, right in the heart of Pul-i-Charkhi prison; my gut instinct had saved my life while In Baghdad and again while talking to Al-Qaeda Commander Saladin.

"Iraqi Insurgents"

I will always go with my gut instinct, it has never let me down, especially when my life has depended on it. In Iraq during the Iraq war I was driving point in a two vehicle civi 4X4 convoy, one day passing through some old orchards, along the banks of the Euphrates River, close to the Syrian border. We were all in local Arab dress, white and brown robes, with traditional Arabian head dress; we had gone 'native' in order to blend into our surroundings and the local population. If an Iraqi insurgent was looking at us through a spotting scope or binoculars, they would not be able to tell we were not Arabs at a distance, until we got really close then all hell would break lose. Generally with a lot of 'hot lead' being fired from AK47s in my general direction? This tactic of going and looking native had worked well and brought me a few extra seconds in a previous terrorist ambush. This enabled me to drive through and escape at speed. However, this had also caused a few tense and hairy moments with the American military, while they carefully identified me and my team. When you have 20, M4 machine guns pointing at you, with their safety catches off, being held by American soldiers with itchy trigger fingers, you tend to be very clinical and precise when answering there questions. Not to worry, all part of the fun in operating covertly within a combat zone. I always worked point, leading my men and team from the front, that's just the way I am, 'I would never ask anyone to do anything, that you would not do yourself' - that's one of my rules of Command. I was looking for bad guys (crocodile hunting, the term I had coined and used while hunting terrorists, and 'business was booming'). Al-Qaeda fighters had been spotted in the area and my American contacts had shared new intelligence with me. This was quite normal for me, intelligence was a two way street. I had achieved great results in the past months whilst working with the American military across Western Iraq and Eastern Syria. We were approaching the location of an old bridge down a long dusty track. Satellite photographs had confirmed that the bridge was intact at 0500hrs that morning. Driving down, windows open and observing my surroundings, something felt strange, not right, out of place, for a few moments I could not put my finger on it. My instinct told me that something was very wrong. About 200 meters from the bridge, trees lined each side of the track. Could this be yet another enemy ambush? No, it was something else. I pulled off the track onto some wasteland that would give us some cover from enemy fire and stopped. The second 4X4 followed in and took a holding position behind me to my right, keeping the engines running Standard Operating Procedure (SOP), I ordered my team to 'de-bus' from the vehicles, they immediately went into all round defence, with 'weapons hot' weapons at the ready, safety catches off, searching for any threat that might come our way from the tree lines that surrounded us. My Secord-in-Command (2IC) Deputy Team Leader from the other 4X4 came up beside me and crouched down. He asked me 'what's wrong', 'Bad guys' I answered, 'not sure' but my gut instinct told me something was not right, 'that's good enough for me' he replied. You have a bloody spooky sixth sense. My 2IC was also a professional soldier and seasoned security operator. We had worked together on and off for years, we enjoyed working together and had enjoyed each other's company in many jungles and deserts. He was a mad fucker, always looking for the bad guys and trouble. With him watching by back I was in good hands, the trust between us was absolute. Even though he was a 'crap hat' and not former 'Para Reg', my 2IC saw us as shining knights, agents of wrath, to bring Gods punishment on the evil wrong doers and the plague of Islamic extremists, 'not just mad fuckers who get angry and slotted people'. Personally I saw us as professional security and military operators just doing a specialized job, with a little help from the 'God squad'. British soldiers are paid and trained to fight and be aggressive, a good and necessary skill set on the battle field, but this can also be problematic when soldiers return to Civilian Street (See Glossary, and 'PTSD'). The area close to the river was still, it wasn't just quiet it was dead quiet, not even any sounds from wildlife or birds. After spending years living and observing in this part of the world, I concluded that this was very unusual. Things generally go quiet when something bad is about to happen, even the local wild life could sense it. I left my 2IC in charge of the team, I moved forward slowly, I told him to cover me and "I may be coming back in a hurry if I get engaged by the bad guys". We knew that the Iraqi insurgency, were operating in this area. I moved stealthily towards the river bank 200 metres away, using the tree line for cover. Keeping my men's firing position and arks of fire in mind. I stopped and just listened. All was still ahead of me; I noticed my 2IC moving slowly and carefully behind me. I stayed put until he was level. He whispered "Can't let you have all the fun, anyway, if anything ever happened to you, your Sam would kill me". I smiled at this comment, he was right; hell if anything happened to me Sam would kill me twice out of principle and then some. Sam was the only women I had ever listened too; she was both beautiful with her Italian model looks and intelligent, a dangerous combination for any man. But her passion for life was only matched by her fiery temper. This obviously came from the Italian blood in her. What she was doing with an old soldier like me I will never know. I must just be lucky. Sam was always supportive but hated the fact that I worked in war zones. I had left her with 'Esperance', Latin for hope, and a kiss and promise to return in one piece. That was one promise I intended on keeping. I moved along the tree line on my stomach. I slowly made my way through the under growth with no sudden movements, observing everything in great detail. The river and the bridge were in view through the bushes, my 2IC slowly moved up until he was beside me. Through small range finder binoculars I monitored the area in front. The far bank of the river was visible through the water reeds, nothing there, no visible human presence or movement. The only sound was from the fast flowing river, water lapping against the bank. The local wild life and insect population could smell fresh blood, the little fuckers, mosquitoes were biting the hell out of us, after feasting on our blood, one of the fattest, ugliest, and happiest mosquito's that I have ever seen landed on the water reeds to our front. It had gorged itself so much on our blood that it could not even fly properly. I looked past the greedy little fucker, towards the bridge; I zoomed in on the underside of the bridge. My heart suddenly skipped a beat, bloody hell; the bridge was rigged with multiple IED's. From the look of it there was enough UXO and explosives to blow the whole bridge to hell and back, including anyone who was caught on the bridge when it went up. I passed the binoculars to my 2IC, he confirmed and added a few colourful words. He passed the binoculars back and asked what I wanted to do. I paused, and then a sudden movement on the other side of the river bank grabbed my attention. Two men dressed as locals were crouched down behind some old ruins of a traditional mud building. I focused on the bridge again, this time noticing a single command wire, attached to the UXO on the bottom of the bridge and strung out through the grass and water reeds, all the way up to the position of the two men in the ruins 150 metres away. The two men were ducking down and were now out of sight again. They were waiting for an American military patrol to come along and then they would detonate the IED using the command wire, killing everyone on the bridge. It was time to get out of 'Dodge City'. We carefully, not to give our position away, silently re-tracing our steps and route back to the vehicles and my waiting fire team. We mounted up quickly then drove back up the long dusty track at speed, leaving the area in a dust cloud in my rear view mirror, guns up and at the ready, 'weapons hot', waiting for an enemy contact or ambush. I led, making my way towards the American Forward Operating Base (FOB), 5km away along the river to the East of my position. I used my satellite phone to contact the American military operations room and called in the incident. I gave the GPS location of the bridge so that all American Military units would be told to stay clear. Air assets were tasked and airstrikes quickly took out the 'bad guys'. No friendly force killed or injured, 2 enemy insurgents confirmed dead, 'Job well done'. My instinct had saved my life that day and the lives of my men. My instinct would save my life several times in the future in Iraq, Syria and Afghanistan. Including the time when I would blow up a major terrorist weapons and ammunitions storage facility in the Western deserts of Iraq, (an old Iraqi Republican Guard Facility), surrounded by insurgents. My actions stopped a large amount of weapons, munitions and UXO, being used by the terrorists and insurgency for launching attacks and IED attacks on British and American troops in Iraq and beyond. My controlled explosion could be seen 6km away. A full report was given to the American military at 'QW', their reply was 'job well done', but that is another interesting story. While in Pul-iCharkhi prison, my gut instinct would also serve me well, saving my life several times.

(Above) By Author, American Apache gunships on route to deliver fire support mission along the Iraq Syrian border.

(Above) By Author; Looking for terrorists along the Iraq Syrian Border.

I would not recommend walking down a corridor full of Al-Qaeda members, whose dreams are to kill British and American soldiers; this was a 'dear diary' moment, which was not a very sensible thing to do, at the best of times. Being in such close proximity to Al-Qaeda seriously challenges one's bravado and also plays havoc with one's nerves. However I generally find that the direct approach to a problem or situation works best. If I have a problem, I go straight to the horse's mouth. In this case, it was a notorious Al-Qaeda, Taliban Commander. I would find out much later from the infamous Taliban Commander 'Talib-Jan' that if I had not been straight with Saladin during our first meeting by admitting that I was a former British soldier, then I would have been beheaded. Obviously having my head cut off would not have been good for my health and a real game changer, so today was a good day, I'm alive.

Over the coming weeks I was frequently invited over to the Al-Qaeda corridor by Saladin, for food and to continue our conversation. I was officially Saladin's honoured guest. The prison Commander was told personally by Saladin that no harm should come to me; he had given his word. The Pashtun tribe and people take guests and hospitality very seriously. 'Pashtun-Walli' is the traditional code of honour of the Pashtun people. Even if a person, who is an 'enemy' if they turn up at asking for 'Pashtun-Walli' the enemy has to grant this and his safety is guaranteed for a period of time. A guest cannot be harmed; if they are, it is a major insult to the person or village elder who granted it. Saladin had officially granted me the status of being an honoured guest, which implies 'Pashtun-Walli'. So my back was covered from the point of Al-Qaeda and Taliban wanting to kill me. That along with the fact that Commander Saladin's name puts the fear of God into most people, even the most extreme of the extremist would not go up against Saladin, the old boy had a bit of a reputation of being a bit naughty, lobbing the heads off his enemy's and people who went up against him. So in a very strange and unexpected way Al-Qaeda was protecting me. This situation was unprecedented. To this day I don't know why I was spared and welcomed into their inner sanctum. Even as I write this manuscript, I don't know how to even try and explain the situation. I have never, ever, even heard of this kind of situation happening to another former British Soldier, whether by luck, fate or by the hand of God? I am grateful to have my head attached to my body. The difficult part was going to be keeping it there. Over the coming weeks and months, I would spend endless hours learning about Islam and brushing up on my Arabic. I would spend many an afternoon debating, and sometimes even arguing about life, politics, religion, military history and Russian military tactics (Saladin had been trained in Russia). The cities of Baghdad and Damascus, which both of us had visited in the past, often came up in our conversations; we had been to many of the same places, locations and cities. Saladin's knowledge was extensive and detailed of the history of the Middle-East, Afghanistan and Pakistan. Saladin's memory was impeccable; he could recollect places in great, and precise, detail. This would become a great tactical advantage for me in the future, when confirming important tactical and strategic locations. Saladin had no idea what I was doing or what I was using the information for. The Americans and British intelligence services had no idea what was inside or operating within and from Pul-i-Charkhi prison. My objective was not only to prove what was really going on, but to what extent, on all levels. This was going to be difficult enough in itself, because my own British Embassy staff were trying to hide the fact that I was there, and the BEK were actively preventing anything coming out that drew attention to Pul-i-Charkhi or me. This was a very strange situation, hell I was protected by Al-Qaeda and yet I was being totally screwed by the very people who are paid to help and protect me, the British Embassy. This situation was a total 'mind fuck' whichever way anyone looked at it, from whatever view point or angle, the whole situation just did not make any sense?

When talking to Al-Qaeda and the Taliban Commanders, one sentiment was very clear and unwavering; they all loathed the West and Western influences in Islamic countries. Rightly or wrongly, Western politics, morals, principles and laws are very different to those of the Muslim world. One size does not fit all, as some Western politicians like to think. Afghanistan and Iraq are prime examples of this. You cannot take a first world country's democracy and culture and place it into an Islamic country; they just do not mix. The sooner Western politicians learn this lesson, the quicker Western involvement in the wars across the Middle-East and beyond will end. Western influence is everywhere, Muslims see Western ideologies as a corrupting threat to the Islamic world and their way of life. The airport road into Kabul is lined with billboards, that might lead you to believe that Kabul and Afghanistan are becoming safe and modern and on the upswing. Advertisements for computers competing cell-phone networks, banks and big glossy, sexy posters of beach front real estate in Dubai and the cornucopia of services that the global market wants to promote, are displayed across the dry hills and deserts of Afghanistan and

Arabia. It is only when you look deeper, past all the Western money, new luxury vehicles and oversized pretentious villas along the roadsides, which hide poverty and slums, where the extremely poor live and die, that you see the reality. Only then, when seeing the faces of the normal Afghan population, did a person realise how nervous and afraid they are. An undercurrent of extreme violence and death, bubbles away just beneath the surface, which can erupt without warning at any time. This was still the 'land of lies and secrets', where survival was the only true aim of politics, the same politics which in many cases achieved its aims and objectives through fear and violence.

"Dubai – United Arab Emirates"

The 'UAE' city of Dubai came up often in conversations amongst Al-Qaeda and the Taliban members. They spat on the floor when the name Dubai was mentioned, with venom and a deep distain in their voices, the word 'Kaffir' would normally follow, with several other colourful and nondescript words in Arabic and Pashtun? Again the Al-Qaeda and the Taliban's point of view on the 'UAE' was deeply negative on most subjects and levels. They still resided in the mentality of the 13th century. I had spent a lot of time in Dubai, not just the ultra-modern part, that all the glossy holiday posters and TV advertisements like to portray, but also the old historical part. Its souks, bazaars and markets, this was in constant contrast to the clean cut image of the wealthy, modern quarter of excessive wealth, and the gluttonous, high society glitz, which portrayed extravagant, Western style glamour with all its socialite trimmings. The class divide in Dubai was just as vast as in Afghanistan. The only difference was Dubai had all the false glitz and glamour to hide just how poor and hungry some people really were. Money can blind even the most clear sighted at times. Within the Western model of Dubai, it had retained many of the quaint, folk-ways of the Arab world in the old quarter (old part of the city), young boys at makeshift stands were hawking fruit and vegetables and dispending fragrant, bitter Arab coffee in tiny porcelain cups. Outside of the city, herds of sheep would wander onto the highways, attended by shepherd boys draped in traditional Arab clothing and black flowing cloaks, as if they had fallen out of a time capsule from 300 years ago. Dubai is old meets new, Western meets Eastern society. It is a melting pot of cultures and traditions. Hidden away in its old souks and bazaars were spice merchants, fortune tellers and international black market arms dealers, a whole secret world and life that was wired into a different set of circuits and networks. Al-Qaeda's hidden world of money laundering, planning, recruitment and organising is just hidden away under the surface. Al-Qaeda has not targeted Dubai because of its geographic location, as an international transport hub, that helps facilitate terrorist's movements internationally. Also Dubai's International banking systems are very useful and at times important to the Al-Qaeda network and their war on the West. 'Talib-Jan' a Taliban Commander laughed when he spoke about Dubai women. Western style cosmetic surgery had become a leading industry in the new Dubai, a women hadn't arrived until she had her nose fixed or her breasts enhanced, it was like the Los-Angeles of the Middle-East, Dubai had taken over from Beirut in Lebanon, as the Paris of the Middle-East, and playground of the insanely wealthy, oil rich Arab's, some of which drank copious amounts of alcohol, took class 'A' drugs and womanised all night long in their private beach front villa's, along the exclusive beach front and yachting marina areas. There is an ongoing Jihadist network that passes through Dubai, safe houses, medical treatment, planning and operational meetings, logistics, 'hawala' (international money transfers), skilfully hidden and used by the Al-Qaeda leadership and their Commanders including, Al-Qaeda members from Afghanistan, Pakistan, Iraq, Syria, Lebanon, Yemen, Saudi Arabia and their African brothers, Al-Shabab from Somalia. Weapons shipments from Iran and Russia were also coming through Dubai on a monthly basis, on route to other Middle-Eastern countries and terrorist groups.

I think that secretly the British Embassy was hoping, if not praying, that I would die or be killed then no one would have ever known or found out the truth about my situation, my work, or the shambles regarding my Afghan legal case. The fact was that the British Embassy had overlooked one important fact, I was a former British Paratrooper '3 Para' and the Parachute Regiment (including some of my friends) were fighting and dying in Helmand, Southern Afghanistan.

"The Airborne brotherhood needed someone on the inside of Al-Qaeda and the Afghan/Pakistan/Iraq terrorist networks"

Author photographed by Al-Qaeda inside Max Security, Block 10 Afghanistan

Inside knowledge would help reduce and disrupt the amount of IED and Suicide attacks that Al-Qaeda and the Taliban were carrying out against British and American soldiers. British troops in Afghanistan were being hit daily with ever increasing IED attacks. So all I was doing was what any member of the Parachute Regiment would have done; stepped up and soldiered on, doing everything in my power to save British and American soldiers lives, even after the disgraceful treatment I had received from my own Embassy and FCO London. This situation now was not about me, or any one person, it was about doing the right thing and saving lives. This was now about principle. As a British man I stepped up to be counted, regardless of the consequences, which at that point in time, I must admit was not looking too good for me having a long life expectancy. 'From great sacrifice comes great opportunity'. When I took everything into consideration, my biggest concern was not being killed by Al-Qaeda or the Taliban, that threat I could cope with. My biggest concern was the British Embassy, and some of its incompetent staff, who I knew if given the chance would lie again and try to brand me as a bloody international terrorist. Now that would have been 'rude' and 'definitely not cricket'! This was a sobering thought. I had to really contemplate and think about all of this. I was very disappointed, just think if I had the full support of my own Embassy; the good that could have come out of this situation via the BEK was off the scale, the BEK could have taken the credit for such high level intelligence as discovering the location of 'Osama bin Laden' but the BEK staff's gross incompetence would have jeopardised this kind of precious information.

Not to worry, all I would have to do was adapt, improvise and overcome any problem that came my way, all at the same time as covering my back, both physically and politically. I have a lifelong curse, I always do the impossible, whether in work or combat, I do it because I'm comfortable and confident in my own ability and I know that hard tasks, missions and jobs can be done and accomplished, if the planning and preparation is done and carried out correctly. This has always been my curse, I have never failed in any operational task, 'ever', I don't know how to fail, that's just the way it is. If I ever did fail, it would be because I'm dead, which would be game over anyway. I would find out much later that my work and more importantly my great results were the reason why I had ended up being held illegally in prison in Afghanistan, and also why my position was so politically sensitive. I had embarrassed British government officials who were not doing their jobs properly. This would all come out in the future. This would also be confirmed at a later date by a senior officer serving within the British SAS, with whom I had worked in the past on tasking and hunting Al-Qaeda leader Osama bin Laden and the Taliban number one, Mullah Omar, plus several other high level International Terrorists, including Gulbuddin Hekmatyar, the leader of 'Hisbi-Islami' terrorist group. Hekmatyar had strong ties and links to several other countries including Italy and Cyprus. My '2IC' in Afghanistan, Sergeant Trevor Cooper, and I had traced Hekmatyar to one of his safe house's on the Afghan/Pakistan border. This location was given to a senior officer ("Major") of the British SAS. My comprehensive files were also passed on, together with other intelligence, by my '2IC' during a meeting with a senior Colonel at the Ministry of Defence (MOD) offices in London.

One night, after having spent the afternoon learning the Qur'an and studying Islam with Commander Saladin and his men, I was sat alone with Bevan, drinking Chi-tea and eating rice, and the remains of a meat dish which Saladin had sent over for me. Bevan's status within Pul-i-Charkhi prison was also a little strange, he was my 'guest', so in turn as Commander Saladin's 'guest', no one could kill him or harm him in any way. Bevan was obviously happy about this, he also liked keeping his head were it was. My personal status had gone up even more over the previous weeks due to my friendship with the Al-Qaeda corridor and Commander Saladin. 'From great sacrifice comes great opportunity' I hoped these words would prove right. I felt uncomfortable being so close to the Al-Qaeda members. I had begun running fitness training classes and kickboxing lessons. They took place within the Mosque area, on the second floor of Block 10. This was great because I could throw members of Al-Qaeda and the Taliban around, breaking a few of their bones along the way. I especially picked out the terrorists who had killed British and American soldiers, I would call these forward to the front of the class and use them to demonstrate on, the look of horror on their faces when I picked them out was priceless, many a member of the Taliban walked away from my kickboxing lessons with limps and bruises. When they were about to complain about being hurt, I would say "you are all hardened 'Muj' holy warriors, nothing can hurt you". This persuaded them to suffer in silence due to their ego and pride. This gave me great pleasure, their egos and pride were two of their weak points; I exploited this to the full 'it would have been rude not too'. One morning after a really good work out the day before, half of the Taliban fighters could not even get out of bed. They were stiff, bruised and in pain. Being the kind hearted person I am, I went around each of their beds 'bright eyed and bushy tailed' gave them a bit of encouragement with my foot, to get their arses out of bed and into the Mosque for the morning fitness classes. After a bit of whinging and whimpering, they were once again enjoying the health benefits of morning exercise. A few would run away to the doctor and paid him to say that they were sick. My morning kickboxing gave me great pleasure on many levels; it was my little payback on the Taliban for killing British and American soldiers. The Americans were very happy to supply me with all the sports equipment and kickboxing pads, but the prison Commander put a stop on that saying that my kickboxing lessons were 'too violent'. I laughed when the Americans told me about this, as they did, they asked me what the hell I was doing to the poor Taliban, and terrorist's inside here, I just smiled, my personal opinion was that members of the Taliban had paid the prison Commander to say 'no' to the request of my getting kickboxing pads and equipment including a boxing ring. I wanted to start inter-Block kickboxing days, a legal way of being able to beat the hell out of the Taliban, and all in the good name of sport. Not to worry, I continued with my lessons without any of the padding or safety equipment, personally I thought this was more realistic anyway. Many a good morning was had, well for me anyway. One morning I even ran my kickboxing class outside at the rear area of Block 10, this was in full view of 'Git-Mo'. I ran the Taliban ragged all morning, 'beasting' the hell out of them and shouting at them, I used the same words of encouragement, but in Arabic, that the 'Para Reg' (Parachute Regiment) staff use on new recruits. By the time they all hobbled back into the block, all they could do was fall into their beds with exhaustion. The CIA had watched all that I was doing that morning, I thought I saw a cheeky smile from one of the CIA officers the next time I saw him. I walked into my cell, only to be greeted by Bevan who handed me a nice hot cup of sweet tea, he added, 'I hope you know what you are doing'. I just smiled. If the Taliban and other terrorist were too tired to even walk, then they will not be thinking of killing us, so there was a method in the madness of running training classes. This was just one of those strange situations, and events that happened to me. You have to look at the funny side of this, a British Para 'beasting' the hell out of Al-Qaeda and Taliban terrorists. This thought always brought a smile to my face. People outside, back in the normal world would not believe it, luckily I have several witness, including two 'Majors' who thought that my actions were outstanding and typical of a British Paratrooper. As far as I was concerned, I was making the best of my time, building trust between myself and the Taliban and Al-Qaeda.

Bevan did not know the full extent of what I was doing, and the lengths I was going to, to acquire information and intelligence, but he was not stupid. Bevan had served as a 'Major' in 'Air Force Intelligence', he had already worked it out, but if things went wrong he had full 'deniability', that's the way I wanted it. Bevan was supporting me and covering my back as best he could, he also trawled the corridors for snippets of information, listening into Taliban conversations, then feeding it all back to me. Then I would very subtly go and dig a little deeper. We worked very well as a team. Bevan is also a devout Patriot and jumped at the chance of helping to save British and American soldiers lives. Prison Block 10 had just received a new block Commander. Bevan had spoken to him whilst he exercised outside the front, in one of the metal cages, or 'chicken runs' as we named them'. Bevan was not allowed to exercise or carryout any fitness training with Al-Qaeda in the volleyball area, the prison Commander could not risk both of us being killed at the same time. The BEK would have agreed if they had known about my being allowed contact with Al-Qaeda and the Taliban. "The British Government does not like two disasters in one day; it looks bad in the newspapers and puts the public off their breakfast". The new block Commander was very street wise and intelligent, a complete contrast to the other prison Commanders I had met. He had been popping into the block at strange times just walking around! He wore no rank on his uniform, so no one actually knew who he was. The new Commander was unassuming, quiet by nature, but very sharp. He already knew who the main players were within prison Block 10 and was well aware of what was going on across Afghanistan and Pakistan. Bevan soon established a rapport with the new Commander. They were both old in their ways and their outlook on life. The Commander was in his late 50s, close to Bevan's age, his demeanour and the way he carried himself was that of a professional soldier, it takes one to know one. As we had noticed him, he had noticed us. The Commanders name was Colonel Karem. He did not have a problem with Westerners. After chi-tea in his office I learned he had children at college in Britain and that he was also very well-travelled, he had received his military training in Russia, when he was a young man and later by the Americans. This last point got my attention. The Americans had been responsible for getting him the job in Block 10; this was good because he could keep an eye on me, and the situation with Al-Qaeda and the Taliban. He never asked me any questions; he just said if I need anything, at any time, all I had to do was speak to him, and only to him. I felt that he was more like my safety net if things went wrong in Pul-i-Charkhi. Col Karem's English was very good, but he never spoke English in front of his own men, he did not trust them, which spoke volumes. He always waited for his men to leave the room and then he would switch to English. If one of his men entered the room when I was there he would seamlessly switch back to classic Arabic. He was good, I had my own suspicions of what he was really doing at Block 10, I had a feeling that we were both working for the Americans, but time would tell.

The American 'prison mentors' (read: American military intelligence) started turning up shortly after. I had got people's attention and they were taking notice of what I was saying. The American CIA and Military Intelligence were in and out of 'Git-Mo' next door almost every day, so them popping in and having a quick walk around was not out of the ordinary. They were setting the ground work. The American group would split up into two teams and go off in different directions as soon as they entered Block 10. The Afghan prison guards could not keep tabs or eyes on all of the Americans. One American operator would hang back and slip in undetected to see me and Bevan, just to touch base and check up on us. This was good because this was my secure line of communication, pickup and drop off for information. It had taken its time, and after a lot of ground work, a secure line of communication and 'dead drops' had been carefully set up with American Military Intelligence and the CIA. Now things would start to get very interesting. The senior Americans, who had come to speak to me personally including; Majors, Colonels, Congressmen and very senior American Intelligence personnel, were fully aware of my connections and relationship with American military intelligence in the past. They were actually chuffed when they found out who I was. One of their 'own people', and a trusted 'Grade A' intelligence source, moving up within the Al-Qaeda and terrorists networks inside Pul-i-Charkhi and beyond. The Americans, at this, soon became aware that all was not quite as it seemed in the prison. The truth about Al-Qaeda and Taliban running the inside that Al-Qaeda had keys to the prison gates and cells. They did the obvious thing and changed the locks and keys. Within the week, Al-Qaeda received copies of all the new keys from the prison guards. I made a point of showing the Americans several Al-Qaeda mobiles and satellite phones, a bit of a 'dear diary' moment for them when they told Bevan and myself that it was 'impossible' that there were 'any' phones in Max-Security, I asked them 'not to get upset' and subsequently hauled a satellite phone and 2 mobile phones from my jocks, enough said! I was copying all the Al-Qaeda and Taliban contact phone numbers down, which the terrorists were storing on their phones. I also showed the Americans some of the copied prison keys that I had discreetly borrowed from Al-Qaeda. The Americans were completely floored when they saw this. Within a week of the new expensive locks and keys being put into the prison, they were useless and obsolete. The Americans would end up changing the locks every month, this was just a cat and mouse game between them and Al-Qaeda and the Taliban. It was a pointless exercise, but it was the 'fuck about factor' that gave Al-Qaeda a headache. The Americans were not bothered, it was just money at the end of the day, plus we were finding out who was bringing in the new copies of the keys to Al-Qaeda and where the prison guards were getting the keys cut in Kabul. This was useful because Al-Qaeda and the Taliban were using the same key cutter for a lot of their other work, including keys being copied and cut for other Afghan Government buildings and gates. American intelligence was just following the keys and the money, we were slowly mapping out parts of the Al-Qaeda and Taliban operation, and how they were running there logistics and supply networks, within the prison and Kabul. The Americans were previously unaware of this.

The Americans would turn up unexpectedly at odd hours, by Black Hawk helicopters, that were landed next door at 'Git-Mo' every day and at odd times, so when the Americans could just walked around to block 10. This made the terrorists nervous, anxious and edgy every time a helicopter went overhead or landed, the Americans could just walk in 5 minutes later 'mind games'. This gave the prison guards little or no time to get a message out to the Al-Qaeda and Taliban prisoners. This was good because it helped to disrupt some of the terrorists operations and attacks and their operational planning meetings and conference calls. I prompted a lot of these out of the blue visits. Within hours of my phone calls and SMS messages to my American intelligence contacts; the Americans were all over the prison. I just waited for the Al-Qaeda corridor to go very quiet, no one walking around, a first sign that Al-Qaeda and the Taliban were up to something and that attacks could be imminent. I would walk down, have a cup of chi-tea and a quick chat with Al-Qaeda, then I would walk back to my cell and send a message to American military intelligence about the timings and the 'players', terrorists of the Al-Qaeda and Taliban network who were involved in the planned, preparation of Taliban, Al-Qaeda attacks. Depending on who was planning and coordinating the attacks, highlighted how big the future attack was going to be and how significant the target was that Al-Qaeda and the Taliban had picked for the attack. Depending on which terrorist members were preparing, coordinating or planning operational meetings, who headed the meetings and operational conference calls to their terrorist Commanders outside the prison and across Afghanistan and Pakistan. All these details would dictate how long I had to get a message out to the American Military intelligence. After a while my timings became very accurate. I could predict how the Al-Qaeda and Taliban networks within the prison would operate. Over time my objective was to learn their full Modus Operandi (M/O) from within the Al-Qaeda and Taliban terrorist networks. The more I learned about the international terrorist networks and connections, the deeper I became involved with the groups. I profiled and submitted detailed and comprehensive written reports to the American military intelligence, on all major Al-Qaeda and Taliban Commanders and of future attacks and suicide bombers from within Pul-i-Charkhi prison and beyond, over a period of almost 2 years (See Afghan diary for precise dates of covert handovers to American military intelligence-CIA). I had walked through the gates of hell and now I was knocking on the private room of the beast himself, asking him for the keys. Well, I always say if you're going to do something, do it right first time. I was there with Al-Qaeda and International terrorists 24/7, month in/out, year in/out. The amount of knowledge and information I was acquiring was off the scale. I was right in the middle of a golden treasure trove of highly important tactical and strategic intelligence and information, some of which was extremely 'time sensitive'. I had been accepted and trusted, and was now moving up their Command and Control structure. My prime objective was to learn about and neutralise their Command and Control structure. With a little help from 'Uncle Sam', the CIA and my friends within American Military intelligence, I would hopefully be able to achieve this.

Later one night I sat with Bevan in our cell, "we're losing this war Bevan, you realise that don't you" Bevan replied "of course I do, assuming you mean the little war in Afghanistan, but we're not losing the big war, at least not yet; the one that could take down everything from London to Paris, to New York". London had been hit with the 7/7 terrorist attacks on the underground and the bus bombing. That was just one day of attacks. To get some perspective, these kinds of attacks happen almost every day in Afghanistan, Baghdad and across Syria and the Middle -East. The thought of more attacks on the UK was disturbing. I have witnessed suicide bombings and attacks. I have seen whole families wiped out in Iraq and the after effects and reprisals.

"Children murdered in the Kill House' in Mosul, Northern Iraq"

Women and young children had been executed, shot in the back of the head by terrorists. Their bodies had been in the house and extreme summer heat for days before they were discovered. An American military officer had asked me to take photographs of the crime scene. Some of her own men had tried, but the smell made them nauseous. The blood drained from their faces when they saw the bodies of small children. They did not have the stomach for it. In truth neither did I, but someone had to take the photographs. These would be used as evidence and would help identify the terrorists who were responsible for the murder of these innocent people. So I took the photographs of the bodies and the rooms. I had seen war and extreme violence on three continents, but nothing came close to what I saw that day. These vivid memories will stay with me for life, as well as the sight of the four inches of blood and bodily fluids covering the whole floor which would permanently stain my boots. The smell was horrendous, to the point that it was difficult to breath. I rubbed menthol cream under my nose to mask the sickening stench of dead decaying bodies, a little tip that I had picked up whilst working across the conflict zones in Africa. I ended up throwing away my boots and the combat clothes I wore that night. I never want to see such things on the streets and in the cities of Europe, UK in my beloved England. I told Bevan that such attacks 'would' happen in the future, they would happen across Europe. All I could do was 'disrupt and prevent' as many of them as I possibly could. By God I was going to give it a good go at stopping as many as I could, or fight and die trying.

After the extensive time I had spent in Iraq, Syria, Lebanon and Saudi Arabia and after my visit to the site of the World Trade Centre New York the location of the 9/11 attacks on the twin towers; I began reading the Arabic newspapers and visiting Mosques. I talked to Mullahs and Sheiks had real in-depth conversations and did research. The more I went into and researched the world of extremist Islam the more obvious it became, that these people hate us. They don't want to negotiate anything; they just want to kill us and destroy anything that is Western. The British, American military and intelligence services all say 'know your enemy', so I extensively studied radical Islam and Islamic extremism. In doing so only managed to scrape the surface. Where did it all begin? Was it in 2001, 9/11 or back in the days of the crusades? Who were the bad guys? Who are Al-Qaeda? What motivates them to fight and continue fighting against the West? I assume that it is not all Muslims, because I have met and know some good, kind, respectable Muslims. If it's only the misguided Muslims who hate Britain, America and Western powers, that is still a lot of Muslims. What are we going to do, kill all the bad Muslims? This is not the answer 'violence breeds violence'. The real answer lies between a fine balance of military action and skilful negotiations. Afghan President Karzai is negotiating a power sharing agreement with the Taliban in Afghanistan. A lot of people don't agree with this and they have a very good point.

Why did Western Governments and the military go into Afghanistan? Are Western Governments giving 'tacit' approval to the power sharing agreement with the Afghan Taliban? Western Governments are not officially speaking out against the Taliban power sharing agreement.

By Author, Terrorist Suspects in Iraq

"Interrogation – Water Boarding"

I have always been very patriotic and since the 9/11 and 7/7 attacks I felt even more so. The war on terror had become personal and I was even more determined to aid ongoing efforts, when and wherever I could. There is something that happens when ambition fuses with principles; it's like a chemical reaction. Add that to a person who possesses a diversity of military skills, specialist trade craft and has had over 12 years' experience in covert security, operating in and across the Islamic world. Mix all this into a person who 'gets the job done'. Put all this together and the result is someone who's knowledge and experience should be listened to. The problem is politicians don't want to know the truth, the truth does not fit into their agendas. What I have experienced both good and bad has made me a very different person, I have become more principled. In one of my meetings with General David Petraeus, he told me that 'a few good men can make a difference' in my extensive experience a few good men can make 'all the difference'. On one of my trips back to the UK, I was attending training with British Special Forces, I asked Chris a long standing friend, who had been my original Close Protection Instructor, about interrogation techniques, I was very specific. How much pressure could a person handle or take during interrogation. How long could a person under interrogation last before breaking. It could be 24hrs for some people, a lot longer for well-trained military personnel. The new political correct term for interrogation is 'interview techniques'. American intelligence use 'water boarding' (simulated drowning) to gain information and intelligence; this has been well documented in reports. The British Government do not use these kinds of 'interview techniques'. The British Government officially doesn't carry out 'Extreme Rendition' either? (See Glossary, Balad TSF and Extreme Rendition) There is a question mark regarding the British Governments involvement and knowledge of such things, after official documents were found in the old Libyan Intelligence Offices in Tripoli, Libya. Following several other incidents the British Government has made large pay outs to keep 'extreme rendition' cases out of British courts. Terrorists and terrorist suspects have human rights. Whether it's right or wrong depends on your point of view. The question is should they have rights when they have not afforded any human rights to their victims? When a terrorist has cut off the head of a soldier, or hostage, should that terrorist have any rights? In Western countries he does, but in the Middle-East, including; Afghanistan, Iraq, Syria and Saudi Arabia, the terrorist doesn't, he or she is just put to death, in some case with no human rights. Do the terrorists complain? No, they don't get the chance, an eye for an eye, as per their own Islamic law. As one senior military officer told me, 'as long as we have to play by these bullshit rules and the terrorists don't, they will win and we will lose'. This was a powerful statement, but very true. This echoes the frustration of many Western countries military Commands, who have had their hands tied by politics. This stops the military from doing their operational tasks and missions as effectively as they could, hamstrung by politics and political correctness that has gone completely mad. The term 'lions lead by donkeys' is used by British military personnel including, Senior Officers and Commanders to describe this challenging situation. Politicians are not the ones on the battlefield being shot at and blown up by IED's every day. The soldiers are the ones that die. You will never hear about a politician dying in combat operations? Maybe politicians should all live in a FOB in Helmand for a month, coming under enemy fire every day. I bet that would soon change their political outlook on things on every level, including the whole 'PC' rules gone mad. British politicians appear on the reality TV show 'Big Brother', if they want reality, Helmand Province, Afghanistan has it in abundance. Now that would be a 'real dear diary moment' I would be interested in getting peoples feedback on this point?

"Since 2003 I have studied interrogation in all its various forms and how they have been conducted throughout history and right up to the present day. My research proved a very important point. Extreme hard interrogation techniques do not work. Information and intelligence gained from the use of such techniques is too unreliable. As seen during the American intelligence process of 'waterboarding' Al-Qaeda terrorist suspects. They would say anything just to stop the torture. Physical torture does not work. The only way to gain any information, especially high value intelligence, is through the infiltration and or interception of key players and their communications, plans and resources and actions. This takes time, patience and a great deal of work and resources. I learned this over 12 years ago while working in Africa and Central America. Gathering information takes time. It is my professional opinion that hard interrogation techniques don't work and are a sure way to close down valuable sources of information and intelligence. I am also a strong believer that Western Governments should always take and hold the moral high ground. This is all that separates us from the animals"

I recalled the conversations with Chris and other military Commanders regarding ill-treatment and torture many times during my time in Afghan prisons. The amount of ill-treatment and suffering I had been subjected to and the amount of sustained interrogation and torture I had personally witnessed by the Afghan authorities was always fresh in my mind. The big difference between us and animals is that we live by certain rules and laws. When we disregard these laws, we are no better than the animals or the bad guys such as Islamic extremists. I am a strong believer in rules and laws. Our society could not function without them. Interrogation is a very hot political and controversial topic and everyone has their own point of view on this sensitive matter. It all boils down to an old adage 'do you take 1 life to save 100s'. This subject is open to endless debates and depending on which side of the fence you stand.

"Abdul Aziz an Al-Qaeda operational Commander and Islamic religious leader from Saudi Arabia"

(See Glossary Abdul Aziz AQAP-AQI)

One day at approximately 7am, I was sitting on my metal framed bed looking out of the window. The morning sun light was shimmering on the countless rows of razor wire that encompassed the outer compound and walls of Pul-i-Charkhi prison. The glimmer off the barrels of the new AK47 assault rifles caught my attention. The guards held the weapons, practicing their sighting, focusing prisoners in their sights, from the sanctuary of their reinforced concrete guard towers. The towers had been upgraded to repel RPGs from possible Taliban attacks on the prison. I noticed again that the heavy machine guns were facing into the prison and aimed at the Al-Qaeda blocks. Unnervingly most were aimed at Block 10. 'It's nice to feel loved by the guards'. The guards were more worried about the Al-Qaeda and Taliban prisoners inside the prison, than the attacks from outside. This was another example of how things are all back to front in Afghanistan. The morning was peaceful and quiet; the birds had returned and were sitting on the razor wire singing and chirping away, with not a care in the world. Bevan was awake and the smell of coffee filled the room. Coffee was like gold dust in prison, the only things that sold for a bigger premium were cell phones and laptop computers, everything else came a distant second.

I looked up at the sky; it was completely clear and bright blue, not a cloud in sight. A familiar face appeared at the cell door, it was Abdul Aziz. My first thoughts were OMG, what does Al-Qaeda want this early in the morning? He had walked past the cell door and smelled the coffee. Unbeknown to Bevan and I; Abdul Aziz had a great love for American coffee. For obvious reasons he kept this little fact a secret from the rest of Al-Qaeda. Abdul Aziz barked orders at the guards, who proceeded to open the cell door. It was nice to know who was really in charge in the prison. Abdul Aziz stepped into our cell, we told him to wipe his feet, as we had a new blanket on the floor. It was our pride and joy. We all laughed. I was being sarcastic, but he removed his black leather sandals anyway. He then came in and we had a cup of coffee and a chat. The three of us sat on the red blanket on the floor. We conversed in English and Arabic. Ten minutes later he finished his coffee, thanked us and asked that we didn't tell anyone about this. Not a problem, he could pop in any morning for a quick cup of coffee. This became a morning ritual. On any other day that might have appeared strange. An Al-Qaeda Commander sitting in our cell, talking away and drinking coffee. But this was Pul-i-Charkhi where strange was becoming the new normal. Bevan wrote about this in his diary, a true 'dear diary moment' we would have a lot of them in Pul-i-Charkhi. Abdul Aziz was in prison after being caught by the Americans, after he and his men had ambushed an American patrol in Jalalabad, in Eastern Afghanistan. Heavy casualties on both sides, Abdul Aziz had been shot three times by the Americans; he had the bullet holes in his chest to prove it. He boasted that the only reason he had been captured was because he had been hit three times by the standard American military 5.56mm bullets. Somehow he had been lost within the Afghan prison system. His official file disappeared once the Americans had handed him over to the Afghan authorities. More like Al-Qaeda had paid the Afghan Chief Prosecutor (ACP) to lose the file and produce a new one, including a name change, I would confirm this at a later date. Apart from the Jihad, Islam and American coffee, one other love in his life was his beloved football team, Manchester United? You could have picked me off the floor when he came out with this golden gem of information. Abdul Aziz could name all of the Manchester United football team, which he would regularly do; he even listened very discreetly, using headphones, to the British Premiership football results every Saturday on the BBC world service. This brought a whole new dimension to our relationship with Al-Qaeda members, Bevan was a lifelong Liverpool FC supporter, so things got very interesting when Liverpool played Manchester United, I joked with Bevan, "don't antagonize and provoke him too much if Manchester United lose". I didn't want Al-Qaeda and Abdul Aziz cutting off Bevan's head in an uncontrollable, irrepressible rage. This didn't stop us antagonizing Abdul Aziz, just a little. I was contentious during the live football matches on the radio as was Abdul Aziz, who would wear his Manchester United premier football top with absolute pride. We told him that the Manchester United goal keeper that week must be playing for the other team, 'butter fingers' and 'blind'. I even told him that 'he needs to go to spec savers to get some new glasses' this was another term that was used, Al-Qaeda did not get the joke but we did. I turned around one week and told Abdul Aziz that it was the 'will of God' that his team had lost. He was not happy about this 'the look on his face was priceless. He prayed on his Islamic prayer mat all week, luckily the next week Manchester United won. I was very much relieved.

Later that morning I was called outside, as the rest of the Al-Qaeda prisoners were going out to play volleyball. This was part of the daily routine. The CIA in their dark sunglasses conspicuously appeared one morning in the building next-door "Git-Mo", they stood on the fire escape which over looked our exercise area, watching us. Then, out of the blue, they started taking photographs using cameras with large zoom lenses. The prisoners of block 10 were not impressed. We all put our Arab head dress on 'Talib' style to cover our faces and walked off the volleyball area and straight into the prison block. The Afghan prison guards all scurried away to their little office, without a word being said. We all waved goodbye sarcastically to the American CIA as we entered our own prison block. Little games like these were often played between the CIA and Al-Qaeda. My reaction was always watched closely by Al-Qaeda and the CIA. It was a good indication for the Americans to note and assess my progress in being accepted by the Taliban prisoners and infiltrating the Al-Qaeda and Taliban networks within the prison. Sometimes these games played by both side became quite heated. There was always one constant; when any trouble started, the guards would just disappear. When Al-Qaeda or the Taliban were not happy about anything and a fight erupted, the Afghan prison guards would all run off, deserting their posts. Not just out of the prison block but out the compound as well. They would close the big blue metal doors at the main entrance, locking us in and them out. This was quite a common occurrence. The guards had absolutely no control over the inside of the prison. During these visits by the CIA, their American-Afghan translators always wore black balaclavas, so they could not be identified by Al-Qaeda. The translators did not translate everything that the Al-Qaeda prisoners were shouting at the CIA personnel. If they had the Americans would probably have called in an airstrike or drone strike on prison block 10. On one occasion things did get a little out of hand and rocks were thrown. One rock came our way, and about 100 rocks were returned, in the general direction of "Git-Mo". We got locked down by the Americans for three hours after that little incident. It helped to relieve the boredom and kill a little time. Time was something I had a lot of in Pul-i-Charkhi. I welcomed the lockdown, as I could have a little time to myself without Al-Qaeda and the Taliban being around. I needed time to switch off and relax. Being on edge and having to be switched on and alert at all times can be very tiring, both psychologically and physically. It is also extremely emotionally draining. My morning routine was blurring into a haze, the same from one day into the next. One morning we had been outside playing volleyball but had come in at midday due to the searing heat. I studied Islam in Saladin's room for about an hour. I had also become a tutor, teaching Saladin and some of his men. We used English text books, which were supplied by the Red-Cross at my request. I thought that, if certain key members of Al-Qaeda that I had contact with in prison could speak English, then the Americans would be able to talk to some of the moderate Commanders directly in future. My endeavours would be rewarded in time, with exceptional results. On one occasion, having just started our English class, cell phones started to ring.

"CIA Signature Drone strikes – Waziristan"

There were over 30 cell phones going off at the same time and their echoes could be heard all over the prison block. Something was very wrong. 'Tiab' one of the Taliban, Al-Qaeda

Commander and one of their official Afghan spokesmen, came running into Saladin's room. There had been multi American Predator Drone strikes across Waziristan, in North West Pakistan that morning. The border area, a major strong hold for the Pakistan Taliban and Al-Qaeda were the intended targets. The men, prisoners and some of the guards in Block 10, had families and friends whom still lived and operated in and across Waziristan. Most of the prisoners in Block 10 were originally from some of the villages and hamlets that had been targeted by the drone strikes. The intended target was one of the Al-Qaeda elusive chieftains, who was hiding in that area. The first reports were that there had been many civilian casualties. Updates were coming in every few minutes. Within 5 minutes of the first calls, Saladin's room was transformed into an Operations Room. Ten Al-Qaeda members were taking incoming phone messages and writing down information. Other Pakistan Taliban members were walking up and down the corridor, phoning people they knew for updates and any details regarding casualties. Hussein, who was also a prisoner and active member of the Pakistan 'ISI', Pakistan's Government Intelligence Services, was walking up and down the corridor, making phone calls to senior members of the Pakistan ISI, obtaining the latest news on the Drone strikes. The whole place was a hive of activity. I just sat watching and listening to everything that was going on. You can tell a lot about a group of people, who can operate efficiently during a crisis and when under pressure. All I was witnessing was organised and functioning, like a well-oiled machine. They all had their jobs to do and they all got on with it. When they had something to report, Saladin would be handed a piece of paper with an update of the latest information on it. The whole corridor was well organised and professional, that was very apparent. I turned to leave, feeling uneasy. I wanted to eavesdrop, but this could be dangerous. I was in close proximity with the Al-Qaeda and Taliban network, at a time when they weren't 'happy bunnies'. Saladin called me back and motioned for me to sit next to him. I sat in silence just taking in every detail of all that was happening around me. I had seen American Drones in action in Iraq and Afghanistan, during some of my earlier missions there. I had also seen a lot of 'Pred Porn', nickname given to live feed and recorded playback of Predator Drone strikes. I had viewed real time images from the video cameras located at the front of the Predator and Reaper Drones, as they had engaged, fired and neutralised HVT's and terrorist across Afghanistan, Pakistan and the Middle-East. I had also witnessed many HVT's killed in American missile strikes. The Drones had been very effective against Al-Qaeda and the Pakistan Taliban. Predator and Reaper Drones were also widely deployed across the Middle-East and Africa, including Somalia. I had seen the Drone operators working their magic while I was at one of their tactical operating base locations in 'Tikrit', Northern Iraq. During a Drone attack I had actually witnessed a CIA operator manoeuvre the joystick, he clicked the mouse and watched a HVT target disappear in a ball of fire on the screen. It looked like a scene from the 'Play Station' game 'Call of Duty - Black Op's. The computer hardware manufacturer had probably never envisioned its devices being used for that. Al-Qaeda was pretty good, but pretty good did not cut it, when they were up against 'outstanding'. In 'Tikrit' the CSA-CIA was operating out of specially modernised, white cargo containers housed in the grounds of one of Saddam Hussein's old palaces. The drone operation was slick, precise and deadly. The call-signs, names for the drones were always one or two word, names; 'Falcon, Sky-bird, Wolverine, Hawk, Pac-man and Eagle were some of the most common names chosen by the drone operators. Some were a little more creative like; Apocalypse Now, Godfather and

Rogue Warrior. The drone operators obviously had fun naming their Drones. It was all good for the morale of the American troops. One of the drone operators had named his UAV as a girl's name, Vicky. He explained that it was the name of his ex-wife, he said the name was fitting because she was also a blood sucking bitch that he could not hide from and always fucked him when he did not expect it. He added; his ex, had the same characteristics as the drone, cold and calculated. After his explanation he just smiled and went back to work. On frequent occasions intelligence or the locations of HVT's are not accurate, which ends up in a mission being a 'dry hole', meaning that the target is not found or that there is nothing there. 'Dry holes' frequently take up a lot of time and resources. Intelligence operators on every level have to have clarity of vision of the overall objective.

"Intelligence work gave operators:

Clarity of vision & action

A sense of good versus bad

Good wins Evil loses

We are guided by my own moral compass"

The Drone strikes that had gone into Pakistan and Waziristan that morning were credible and accurate.

They had found their targets resulting in death and devastation from thousands of feet above the rolling green hills, mountains and hamlets of the Al-Qaeda and Taliban strong holds of Waziristan. The Drones Hellfire missiles had made short work of Al-Qaeda HVT's. The Drones were remote controlled by a CIA operator located at an American FOB along the Afghan-Pakistan border. The biggest of these bases being 'Camp Chapman'. Al-Qaeda and the Pakistan Taliban knew of its location and were trying to infiltrate the base. Al-Qaeda had been planning attacks to try and blow up this FOB for some time. Their plan in 2008 to 2009 was to get a suicide bomber inside the CIA base, located within a secure compound inside Camp Chapman. I had heard the name Chapman in a lot of conversations between Al-Qaeda and the Pakistan Taliban, but I hadn't heard any details. I had also learnt in the same way in 2008 that the Pakistan Taliban was planning a car bomb attack on Times Square in New York. I submitted all this information in a report to American Military Intelligence. This was an indication and confirmation that the American Drone strikes were disrupting Al-Qaeda and the Pakistan Taliban's operations and movements across their areas of cross-border terrorist operations, which in turn was disrupting Taliban, Pakistan Taliban and Al-Qaeda terrorist attacks across Afghanistan, Pakistan and beyond. The bad guys were not happy about it.

President Obama, during the past several years had given Executive Orders for the number of drone strikes to be increased, against terrorist targets across the Middle-East, particularly in Pakistan and Afghanistan. This indicated a sharp increase in Drone attacks and missions 24/7, 7 days a week against the Al-Qaeda and Pakistan Taliban. The greater frequency of strikes had taken out many more training camps and other key locations. The terrorist Command and Control structure was significantly impaired. Including their ability to launch tactical and strategic missions and attacks, to the point where they were drastically reduced and just barely functioning. The pressure has got to be kept on the terrorist networks, if the Drone strikes are cut back, due to political pressure, the terrorist's leadership will be given breathing space in which to replenish their numbers. They will start building new training camps. Operational missions across the border into Afghanistan, against British and American targets, will begin all over again. Only time will tell. The personnel within the terrorist training camps are of major interest to the American and British Governments and their Intelligence Services because some of these personnel, attending these training camps are from Europe and beyond. Including; Britain and America. Another very interesting point and 'open secret' is that several Irish nationals have been discovered in numerous terrorist training camps across the Middle-East, Afghanistan, Pakistan and Africa. These Irish nationals were also reported as being former members of the 'IRA'. They were teaching members of Islamist terrorist groups including, Al-Qaeda, Pakistan Taliban, Afghan Taliban, AlShabab and Hezbollah in Iraq, Lebanon, Syria and Afghanistan. Hezbollah were also being trained extensively in unconventional warfare, including IED's, by the Iranian military Republican Guard, in Iran, Iraq and Syria. Former members of the IRA were teaching and instructing terrorists how to build and use IED's. The level of sophistication of the IED's found across Afghanistan and the Middle-East, confirmed that the Islamic extremist groups operating against Britain and America (ISAF) forces, were getting help and support in the manufacture of IED's and specialist 'factory made shape charges'. Within a few years the level of IED's had come on about three generations. This was unprecedented making them almost 100% combat effective. This rapid progression was the cause of great concern. A Senior Officer in the British SAS, who was also the former Chief of Staff based out of the British Embassy Kabul, confirmed my findings during one of the meetings at my Kabul villa. I had acquired the GPS location of one of these terrorist training camps located in Southern Pakistan, close to the border of Afghanistan, and Helmand Provence. The GPS location I had acquired from my HUMINT that covered Afghanistan and Middle-East.

"During a future unofficial meeting between the former BEK 'SAS' Chief of Staff and my operational '2IC' Sergeant, Trevor Cooper, in a coffee shop in Hereford, England, the SAS officer confirmed that my GPS location and brief had been accurate, and that 'Air Assets' had been tasked. The terrorist training camp had been destroyed by an airstrike. Two 500 pounders, were dropped on the target. Message passed back; 'happy days'. Other information was also confirmed during this meeting"

This meeting took place while I was being held illegally in prison in Afghanistan. If the British Embassy thought that keeping me locked up would stop me or my team from operating, the Embassy was very wrong. Some of the BEK senior staff's incompetence would not stop me or my team from saving British and American soldiers lives. I would frequently receive requests and intelligence updates from my team outside. I would also pass on time sensitive information to them, some of which was passed onto the American military intelligence. My team and I had a line of communication set up, which I had arranged from inside Pul-i-Charkhi, I always try to think one tactical step ahead, but I don't try to be cute about it.

It had been confirmed that drones were operating from Camp Chapman. A suicide bomber posing as an Intelligence source would later kill several members of the CIA there, including the CIA Chief of Station, during what should have been a scheduled meeting. The trusted source was supposed to hand over information on the Al-Qaeda leadership, as well as the possible locations of 'Osama bin laden' and Pakistan Taliban leader 'Hakimullah Mehsud'. It was the biggest single loss of life the CIA had suffered in 25 years. The trusted Jordanian suicide bomber was not searched on entering Camp Chapman, due to his privileged status. He had been feeding the CIA some accurate information and intelligence over time, just to build up his credibility. This trust was exploited by the bomber. Misplaced trust cost the CIA personnel stationed at Camp Chapman their lives. The Stars on the Memorial Wall at the CIA American Headquarters Langley, Virginia, are a testament to the gallant, courageous and selfless sacrifice of the CIA's personnel. I feel extremely honoured to have worked with CIA operators in the theatre of operations across the Middle-East, in the 'War on terror'. I am also very lucky to be able to call some of these outstanding and thoroughly professional people my close friends.

"Update; the CIA revenge strike 1st November 2013. Pakistan Taliban leader, Hakimullah Mehusd with a $5 million bounty on his head, his deputy and driver were all confirmed dead by the CIA following a drone strike in their compound, house and vehicle during a 'Shura' Council meeting, near Miranshah, the capital of Pakistan's restive tribal region in North Waziristan, close to the Afghanistan border. The CIA drone unleashed its hellfire missiles, which had found their targets. The CIA had held Hakimullah Mehusd responsible for the murders of the seven CIA personnel at Camp Chapman, Eastern Afghanistan in 2009 and the failed car bomb attack in Times Square, New York. American Justice had been served. History had also repeated itself. Hakimullah Mehusd's predecessor had also been killed by a CIA drone strike"

Mullah Rausak, walked into Saladin's room late in the afternoon, just hours after the Drone strike that had targeted and hit Waziristan. It was two hours after the first reports had started to come in regarding casualties. We greeted each other in Arabic. We both sat down and Saladin joined us. Saladin asked everyone else to leave the room for five minutes. 'Taib' stood at the entrance to the room, to make sure that we would not be disturbed and our conversations would remain private. The news and updates from Mullah Rausak were not good (well for them anyway). Ten people had been confirmed dead in one of the American Drone strikes and they had lost contact with one of the villages up in the mountains of Waziristan. The name Hamza, the suicide bomber whose explosives had not detonated when he tried to become a martyr came up again, Bevan and I always joked about this to him, saying that his batteries had run flat; hence his explosive suicide vest had not worked, and in future he should 'test' the vest prior to use. This was something he thought about but 2 days later came back to us and asked if he tested the vests, how was he to make sure they worked without exploding prior to deployment. We told him to 'work it out'. This was a question that was to vex him for some time until he came back and said that they had tried it but had lost someone in the process, so in future the

Suicide Bombers would just have to take their chances. Bevan and I just smiled at each other. Chalk up one for 'us'. Hamza's village had been the first one hit by an American Drone strike. His family were safe and all accounted for. The Drone had targeted and hit another house where a Pakistan Taliban and Haqqani network meeting was taking place. It was just a local meeting; no real HVT's were present. The house had been blown to pieces. The locals were still pulling dead bodies out of the rubble. It had been a great loss to the prisoners of Block 10, because some of the dead had been family members and friends. The villagers who had been out of contact, during the previous hours, touched base with Commander Saladin directly, using 'satellite' phones, cell phones were too unreliable up in the mountains of Waziristan. It was also confirmed that an American missile strike down in the valley that morning had also killed ten people. The body count was still rising. All the dead would be buried within 24 hours, according to Islamic custom. Pul-i-Charkhi prison observed three days of mourning; the black turbans of the Taliban and Al-Qaeda were worn by all Al-Qaeda and Pakistan Taliban out of respect for the dead. During a lull in activity, I walked over to my cell to bring Bevan up to speed on the situation. He sat reading and drinking chi-tea. He had known that something was going on, but he did not know what, he had just kept his head down and stayed out the way. I updated him on everything. We sat on the floor talking and drinking chi-tea when one of the prison guards came in. I had been called down stairs to see the block Commander, Col Karem. I was escorted through the block. The guards opened the gates as we walked through the labyrinth of dark corridors. We made our way along the bottom floor, to the far corridor. It was full of dirt and debris, the foul odour of captivity filled the air. I walked past several cells, all their doors were locked. Through the bars of one door, in the lurid flickering fluorescent light, I caught a glimpse of the badly beaten, swollen bloody faces of the two new prisoners. I asked the guard who they were. The guard informed me that these two men had just been brought in from NDS (The Afghanistan National Directorate of Security) in Kabul.

"Prisoners Tortured By NDS, Afghan Security Services"

The two prisoners had been beaten senseless and tortured, during their interrogations by the NDS in their dark cold prison cell and the interrogation rooms. Some filled with 3 feet of cold dirty water, under the NDS headquarters (prisoners would be beaten and tortured then thrown back into the water cells). Prisoners were forced to stand in the cells by chaining them to the walls; the cells were filled with waist high cold dirty water, accompanied by big black rats and spiders, which fed on the waste found in this dungeon. The guards made sure that the rats were ravenous when they put a prisoner into this dark hell hole. It was not uncommon for prisoners to be left in these barbaric and medieval conditions down in these cells under NDS for 48hrs at a time. This kind of psychological torture was used to break the spirit of defiant prisoners. I would later take food, water and blankets down to these two prisoners who had managed to survive. The Red-Cross had left me some spare provisions to give to prisoners who needed them. I visited them and saw the gruesome marks on their bodies. Rat bites and other injuries consistent with brutal and sustained electric shock torture. I could also see that they had been whipped with metal cables on the balls of their feet, the back of their legs and across their backs and shoulders. I tended to their wounds, making sure that they were clean and not infected. In these filthy conditions the deep open lacerations were susceptible to all kinds of infections. Some of the lacerations were 20 inches across their backs and 5 inches across the balls of their feet. These were the same kind of injuries that 'British National and former British soldier Colin Berry had received at the hands of the Afghan Authorities. The two Afghan prisoners could not move without suffering excruciating pain. They would whimper at the smallest of movement. They could not walk or put pressure on their feet for well over a week. One of them had cigarette burns and blisters where Afghan Prison guards had stubbed their cigarettes out on the back of his neck, the balls of his feet and the backs of his hands. The other prisoner had some of his finger nails missing. They had been painfully, deliberately and forcefully ripped out at the root. The prisoner whispered to me in a low trembling voice that the NDS had used pliers to get him to talk. He asked me what month it was. They had been down in the dark dungeon for two weeks, but already had lost all sense of time. To the prisoners, it must have seemed like a life time of hell. After the torture they had been subjected to, they were indeed lucky to be alive.

I got a phone message to the Red-Cross Doctor in Kabul. I expressed with extreme urgency that he visit the two prisoners and give them medical treatment they desperately needed; intravenous drips and pain relief. The Red-Cross also took statements and photographic evidence of their torture. Saladin also came down to check up on them and brought some fresh food with him. He ordered them to eat all of it, so that they could regain their strength. I helped and administered medical treatment carefully to the prisoners because it was the humane thing to do. Regardless of who they were. I would not let another human being suffer, when I had the knowledge and basic medical supplies and skills to help them. My actions were purely 'humanitarian', I wanted to make this point, because I don't want anyone thinking that I was siding with or aiding the enemy. That was definitely not the case; these people were prisoners, but they were still the enemy. I was following the rules and guidelines of the Geneva Convention and making a point to Al-Qaeda and the Taliban that Westerners are not animals, we live by rules and laws and we have ethics and principles. As a British man I stand by my actions. The overall prison Commander, followed by all of his personal security and bodyguards, came storming into the block. He demanded to know who and how the Red-Cross had been called into his prison. I told him that I was responsible for involving the Red-Cross. The two prisoners could not wait days for the prison's slow chain of Command to act. I also added that he would have done the same in my position, him being a good Muslim and all. The prison Commander was surprised by my directness. He thought for a moment and then asked if the two prisoners were alright and did they need anything. I asked for the two prisoners to be moved to a clean dry prison cell. The prison Commander looked at me then ordered his men to make it so, it was done within 5 minutes. I shook the Commander's hand thanking him for his kind actions. What else could he do? He was a Muslim and Saladin was watching him very closely. He said he had pressing business that he had to attend to. He left the Prison block with his body guards as quickly as they had arrived. Saladin had been watching this exchange between me and the prison Commander. Because the Red-Cross was involved, he kept a low profile, not getting directly involved, he could not been seen co-operating with Western organisations. Saladin had noticed everything. I mentioned to him later that my actions were purely humanitarian and I hoped that if a Westerner needed medical help, he and his men would do the right thing. They acknowledged what I said. Unknown to me, what I had said and done would influence future events and incidents not just inside Pul-i-Charkhi. Al-Qaeda would give medical assistance to people, who they would normally have killed or left to die. Saladin and his men were the 'enemy', but they had learned an important and valuable lesson that day. Even enemies can and must have rules and ethics in times of war.

"For evil to triumph, all it takes is for good men to do nothing"

I was later shown into the Prison Block Commanders office. Col Karem, looked up from his desk and motioned for me to take a seat. He finished off his writing and paper work and looked up again, and ordered the guard to bring some chi-tea. The guard quickly left the room, closing the door quietly behind him. Col Karem waited until the guard had left the room and the door was closed, we listened for the sound of the footsteps to fade as the guard made his way down the corridor. The Commander asked how I was and if everything was alright. I answered as well as can be expected under the circumstances, living one day at a time. He nodded and commented that it was pretty obvious that I was from a military background. The conversation turned to my Afghan legal case, which made no sense to him. He enquired about the politics surrounding my case, and why the British Embassy was were not working harder to get me released and out of this prison and dangerous situation. This was no place for a British national, especially a former British soldier. The Commander looked at me; you are learning Islam and Arabic, yes, from Saladin? "You do realise who he is don't you". The question hung in the air for a moment; he added he is "an Al-Qaeda Commander". This was further confirmation that Saladin was senior Al-Qaeda. Col Karem already knew that I knew that Saladin was Al-Qaeda but he played along anyway. Col Karem then enquired about my time in Afghanistan and the Middle-East. He was aware that I had stood up against the Governor of Kandahar 'Assadullah' regarding his corruption and involvement in the illegal Afghan narcotics trade. He was so corrupt that even Al-Qaeda wanted him dead. There was a personal issue between Assadullah, Al-Qaeda and the Taliban. It turned out that he had been playing both sides against each other, hence several suicide bomb attacks targeting 'Assadullah'. Al-Qaeda had already said that his day would come, even if they had to wait and kill him outside of Afghanistan. They would wait and just bide their time, patiently waiting for an opportunity to arise. Time was something that Al-Qaeda had a lot of. Assadullah and his business dealings and joint bank accounts with President Karzai's brother were also a bone of contention with Al-Qaeda, the Taliban and Western Intelligence agencies. I was interviewed by Afghan officials about Assadullah. They confirmed the information on him and his joint bank accounts, with the President's brother in Dubai. This investigation and the fact that I had spoken out against Assadullah ended in him being removed from official office as the Governor of Kandahar. However, to everyone's amazement, he was given a new official position within the Afghan Parliament. President Karzai's brother had organised this. Hence my present situation Assadullah and his cronies had lodged a complaint about me in Afghanistan. Assadullah now being a member of the Afghan Parliament had made my situation very political and the British Embassy staff at that time did not have the balls or guts to stand up to the corruption within the Afghan Government. The British Embassy staff had told me that there was not a lot of corruption in the Afghan Government. This totally floored me and basically meant that I was totally screwed. One senior American official (a Colonel) told me that Assadullah would fit right into the Afghan Parliament, with all the other corrupt Afghan officials, drug and War Lords. Col Karem asked me why I don't just pay the Judge and the prosecutor the bribe that they had asked for. It seems that everyone was aware of my case and my stand against the corruption within the British Embassy mentored Afghan Justice System. I would not pay the bribe out of principle. I had reported the situation several times to the British Embassy, Col Karem was disgusted at the actions of the British Embassy; he called the Embassy staff shameful. Col Karem could not understand why the British Embassy was cowering down to the corrupt Afghan Government? Why didn't the British Embassy just expose all the corruption, deal with it head on and put the corrupt Afghan Government officials in prison, which was the logical thing to do. Unfortunately the British Embassy has chosen to cover-up, lie and deny everything. Their shameful actions would come back and bite them on their arses in the future, costing several key Embassy staff their jobs.

Col Karem wished me luck with my case and my stand against the Afghan Government corruption. If I needed any help with anything whilst I was there, he would do his best to help. Col Karem always ended our meetings by saying this. He asked if there was anything he could get me 'I asked for a ladder' he laughed at this. He said it would have to be a pretty long one to get over the prison wall? At least we both had a good sense of humour; we would both need it over the coming months. Col Karem knew that I had no intention of leaving Pul-i-Charkhi prison until my name had been cleared. The young prison guard knocked on the door and entered the room, he served us both chi-tea and sweets and we shifted the conversation to the prison conditions. Col Karem apologised for the fact that I had to live in such squalid and dirty conditions. He stated that even dogs and animals should not have to live like this. He was sincere when he spoke, the conditions 'were' bad. I was just making the best of a very bad situation. The daily conditions were really horrendous and extremely dangerous 'the stuff of nightmares'. For the first 18 months of my being a prisoner it was hell. Eventually, because of my working closely with the Red-Cross staff, I attended more than 30 meetings and interviews. I was able to help improve the living conditions for all the prisoners. I had unintentionally become a very high profile entity in Pul-i-Charkhi prison, due to my stand on human rights. Particularly the human rights of British and Commonwealth Nationals. I had done the job of the British Embassy...! My actions had made me very unpopular with the staff from the British Embassy in Kabul, for obvious reasons. Their 'duty of care' was at best very lacking. Due to my new found celebrity status I was able to wash or have a rinse down every few days, using an old hosepipe in the exercise area 'metal chicken run'. It wasn't good, but it was the only way of staying clean in the exceptionally squalid conditions. Personal hygiene was very important to me; sadly not everyone was of the same opinion. Some of the Afghan prisoners did not wash themselves or their clothes for several months at a time. The stench from some of their bodies and cells was over whelming. There was no need to voluntarily live like that, but that was just the way some Afghans were. Al-Qaeda members did wash every day when they could; all their clothes were washed at least once a week. I finished my chi-tea and stood up and shook Col Karem's hand, thanking him for his hospitality. He wished me luck and told me to watch by back in the prison block because emotions were running high due to the American Drone strikes that morning across Waziristan. I nodded my head. I would have many such conversations with Col Karem in the future. My instinct told me that I could trust him. He called out to the guard, who was standing at the end of the corridor. He then escorted me back to the prison block.

I found Bevan reading in our cell, he looked up at me "what's new?" he enquired. I gave him a quick update on my meeting with Col Karem and the new prisoners downstairs. Events outside Pul-i-Charkhi had a great and profound impact on life within the prison. It was best to have a finger on the pulse at all times, information and knowledge was everything. Pul-i-Charkhi was dangerous, volatile and could burst into extreme violence at any time, without any warning. The Taliban were fighting with Al-Qaeda and other prison gangs were always cutting each other up, with hunting knifes. There was not a day that went by without someone being badly cut up, seriously injured or killed. For the most part, I was left alone, as I did not fit into any warring factions. I was an unknown entity, but everyone knew that I could look after myself if confronted or threatened. I just told people that if they wanted to cut me, they better make sure they kill me quick, or a world of pain would come down on them that even 'God' could not save them from. I did not have to do much; Saladin's name was the deterrent that was needed. Everyone knew the kind of temperament I had and that I wouldn't ever back down or take crap from anyone. I have to admit that I had a bit of a bad attitude, just a little attitude problem with regard to authority and the Taliban. I certainly had a problem with the Taliban prisoners who tried to bully the younger prisoners or those that could not defend themselves. An example of this was when the Taliban took food from the young prisoners. The prison food was bad and unfit for human consumption at the best of times, but for some prisoners, it was all they had. In the past I had been one of those prisoners who received little or no food for over a year. One afternoon I witnessed a Taliban Commander taking the small pieces of old prison meat from a group of young prisoners, I watched in disbelief as this unfolded before my eyes. I had seen enough of this crap happening every day, so I put my little bowl of rice down, stood up and without a word being said, walked over to the Taliban Commanders group which were sitting in a huddle at the end of the corridor. I picked up the plate of meat, what there was of it, after they had all had their paws all over it. I told the Taliban Commander that he should be ashamed of himself and that he was a bad Muslim? In the Qur'an it says that the strong should always look out for and protect the weak. I spoke in Arabic, pointing this out to him. I walked back and returned the plate of meat to the young Afghans; they looked up at me sheepishly, hesitantly, before taking the meat. I told them that it was ok. There was hell afterwards about this with the Taliban. After what I had done, had time to sink into their thick heads. I told them that if they had a problem, to come and see me later in my cell. I told them 'not to be shy, to bring a friend or two; as they would need someone to carry them out again'? Bevan said "fuck me that was subtle. Is that your idea of making friends and influencing people", I just laughed, looking on the funny side. That's another reason why the Taliban would want to kill me. Within 5 minutes of this incident with the food, Saladin knew about what I had done. He just laughed and shook his head. He told the Taliban that I was right in what I had done and said. Obviously the Taliban were well pissed off with me. Not because of the meat but because I had made them appear weak and like 'Muppets' in front of the other prisoners. I'm sure that the Taliban had lots of cruel and unusual punishments lined up for me. Not to worry, it was what it was and what will be will be. This was one crazy situation and frankly I didn't give a damn. The next afternoon the Taliban made a point of giving the young ones their food first, they watched me while they did this. I nodded in silent approval. One of my real hates in life is bullies. I can't begin to tolerate them. My being in a prison surrounded by Taliban and Al-Qaeda did not change my point of view or my principles. I did not like the attitude of the Taliban Commander anyway. We would cross swords many times in the future. Life in Pul-i-Charkhi would throw up new challenges every day. The mood within the prison was mostly dark and the anti-British and American feeling throughout the prison had put me in a very precarious and delicate position. I was British at the end of the day. I had to handle this very delicately; to describe the feeling amongst the prisoners would be hard, but sensitive, with the general feeling across the prison was that any little thing could cause the situation to explode at any moment. It was like walking on the razors edge, in the knowledge that extreme violence was coming sooner rather than later.

During a conversation with Saladin, I had learnt that the Taliban wanted to grab Bevan as a hostage; this was a 'dear diary moment'. I asked what about me, Saladin told me that I was alright and not to worry. The Taliban wanted to take all their frustration out on Bevan. I told Saladin if the Taliban tried to hurt Bevan I would step straight in and that I would fight by Bevan's side no matter what the outcome or consequences were for me. Friends don't desert each other in places like this. Saladin knew exactly where I was coming from. He also knew that I was willing to die protecting Bevan. Saladin would have done the same for any of his close friends or men. Saladin called the Taliban Commanders over to the Al-Qaeda corridor for a meeting. This testosterone fuelled meeting ended in the Taliban fighting each other. 'Talib-Jan', whom for some reason got on well with me and Bevan, had hit and dropped the main Taliban Commander, Assadullah from Kandahar, on the floor during the meeting, making an example out of him. This went down well in Block 10. The Taliban Commander had to be put in his place, but it had to be done by a fellow member of the Taliban due to internal Taliban politics. The end result was that Bevan was to be left well alone, with the threat of instant death to anyone who tried to harm him. I was happy with this outcome and obviously Bevan was extremely relieved. I went down to see 'Talib-Jan' later that afternoon about what had happened. He just said 'no problem' and smiled at me. He asked if we were still doing our kickboxing lesson the next morning. I gave him a big smile "yes, same time same place see you there". In the weeks and months that followed, Taliban Commander Assadullah and Bevan became 'good friends', to the extent that Bevan was 'trusted' by Assadullah to 'look after his phones' during searches of Block 10. This played right into our hands as we had access to all the telephone numbers on the Sim Cards, all this information being passed on to American Military Intelligence.

Bevan and I stayed up late into the night, just talking about all that had happened that day and the situation we now found ourselves in. I was right in the middle of Al-Qaeda and the Taliban. I was experiencing everything from the inside out, from the other side of the looking glass. This was like a parallel world, compared to the one I am use to or come from. This other World was seething with hatred and steeped in extreme violence, life meant nothing, words meant nothing to certain groups of people, all they seemed to understand was violence, it was survival of the strongest and fittest. This other World which I was experiencing was war torn beyond belief, its entire history was steeped in blood and killing. This was the land were the first 'assassins' came from, fighting and killing was in there 'DNA'. Some of them just lived for the kill, mix this mentality with the Al-Qaeda and Taliban extremist ideology, with endless men and women prepared to die for their faith and beliefs, and it makes for an explosive mix, all they then need is a common enemy to focus on, and to channel all there hate towards. Give the Taliban a cause to fight for and they are happy. When British and American troops pull out of Afghanistan, the Afghans and the Taliban will go back to fighting each other. Then blood will start to flow in the streets again. You have to ask yourself, what has changed? Unfortunately the West and anything that is Western has become an open target for Al-Qaeda and Islamic extremists. With countless innocent lives lost and lives shattered due to terrorist attacks. The overall casualty figures are rising monthly, with no end in sight. The future in the Middle-East doesn't look good at all. One thing is for certain, a lot more innocent blood will be spilled on all sides. Anyone who reads or researches the history of Afghanistan and the Middle-East will realise this, especially with current daily events evolving and the bloody violence and widespread unrest being visually and graphically splashed across Western TV screens nightly. Too many people and politicians are ignoring the history of Afghanistan and other Islamic countries, 'at their peril'. It seems that doing the right thing is not in some politicians best interests. Decisions are made by a lot of politicians, based upon what they want at that time for themselves or their political party. The welfare of the counties and its people they interfere with normally come second to their own agendas and objectives. The lessons which Western Governments have learned from Iraq, Afghanistan and later in Libya and Syria are bitter pills to swallow for some politicians. But none the less it's imperative that these lessons are learnt and remembered. Otherwise Western leaders will send their counties into more future foreign conflicts in Islamic countries. Western publics are tired and weary of what politicians say and all their political spin, terminology and buzz words. People just don't trust politicians anymore. The body count of military personnel in Afghanistan alone is over 450 British and in excess of 2000 American soldiers killed. Thousands have been maimed and seriously injured. These figures are still rising with every week and month that passes. In this part of the world, good local sources of information are rare and when found are like gold dust. The development and cultivation of intelligence assets and contacts, is rule 101 for any intelligence operative operating across the Middle-East, Afghanistan, Pakistan and Africa. If you don't trust your sources at some point, you just would not get anywhere. There is an old Afghan saying; 'Afghan men are only loyal until the ink dries on the money you give them'. Some are also very skilled at deception; they say one thing, then do something completely different. One important lesson for all Westerners is to remember that all Westerners are outsiders. Westerners are not them; Westerners don't belong in Afghanistan according to some Afghans. They are just visitors, one of a long line of such visitors. The Russians, then the Americans, shortly followed by the British. The Afghans see Western troops as yet another occupying army that will soon leave Afghanistan. Due to this opinion and mentality which is widespread, some Afghan men see the Western presence in Afghanistan as walking 'ATMs', cash machines for their personal gain and indulgence, profiteering and use. The level of corruption in the Afghan Government is evidence of this and is very well documented (UN and US State Department reports on Afghanistan corruption). There are a few Afghans who do not fall into this sad mentality or category and who are not corrupt, but they are few and far between. Sadly the corrupt Afghans are the ones in power? The old Afghan mentality of corruption and deceiving is just a survival mechanism. Like Afghan politics its aim is pure unadulterated survival. Due to my witnessing this so many times though, I have come to call this, 'an Afghan truth'. A lot of the extremist Muslims whom I have met and interviewed believe that it is ok to deceive Western people "because they are not Muslims". They call us 'infidels' and 'none believers'. This statement which has been said by a lot of extremist Muslims is completely flawed; because they also lie, deceive and cheat their own people who 'are' Muslims. For a country to be just below Somalia on the United Nations corruption scale and lists should be shameful, but Afghanistan wears this like a badge of honour. It is politically correct for other Western Governments to white wash over this? Because they have to be seen working with and alongside the Afghan Government and its so called officials? The former British Defence Minister said it best, calling 'Afghanistan a 13th Century broken country'. Behind closed doors of most Western Governments, officials think this, but in public they have got to be seen supporting the Afghan Government in Kabul. Western Politicians wonder why their public don't trust then. The Karzai Government in Kabul has been talking to and making secret deals with the Taliban for over seven years. Some of these secret deals were negotiated with senior Taliban leaders, and Al-Qaeda Commanders who de-badge themselves and took on the role as Taliban Commanders just for these meetings. The meetings were held in Pul-iCharkhi prison Block 10. These meetings or 'Shura' took place within the prison complex. Several senior members of the Afghan Parliament were present. During one of these meetings I was invited in by Commander Saladin. My intention was merely to observe, but I ended up talking and debating with all that were present. This meeting was a real eye opener for me on every level. Especially because of who had attended? The meeting was caught on camera phone by a member of the Al-Qaeda and Taliban network. The video footage was then sent to Al-Qaeda Commanders in Pakistan and Saudi Arabia. I would attend several more 'shura' in the future (A full written report was handed over to American Military Intelligence).

"Four British Soldiers Killed"

The next three days were quiet. The Al-Qaeda members were in the Mosque reciting the Qur'an and prayers 24/7. This was an indication that something was coming to the boil. The Mosque was the only area that I could not gain access to. I was out of the loop as far as that was concerned. On the morning of the fourth day I was awoken by the sound of jubilant shouts and cheers. Prisoners were running through and along the corridors singing and shouting "Allahu Akbar" 'God is great'. I said to Bevan "the bloody natives are restless again". I ventured out into the corridor. Taliban Commander 'Wais Hudein' came up to me and hugged me. He said "great news, 4 British soldiers have just been killed by a Taliban IED in Helmand Province, Afghanistan". This had happened less than an hour ago. More attacks had been planned for later that morning. The attacks were being co-ordinated from the very prison block that I was standing in. My first instinct was to drop him where he stood and then make my way down the corridor punishing the Taliban prisoners for what they had just done. Any British soldier would have felt the same in my position. I had to quickly pull myself together and stay calm and in control, even though my blood was boiling with rage. I had to hide any emotion or it could have led to my own death and that would have stopped me from achieving my objective, which was to 'bring down their terrorist network from within'. Every fibre of my soul and being was burning with disbelief at what had just happened. It's hard to put such a feeling into words. I had to focus and just smile at the Taliban Commander. I had a feeling that this was a test to suss me out. I spoke to him saying "have a good day". He turned and ran off down the corridor shouting to other Taliban who were also celebrating. I turned and slowly walked back into my cell. Bevan was up making morning chi-tea; he took one look at me "what the fuck is wrong"? He asked. The look on my face said it all. That was the only time in my career that I had not been able to show my true feelings. I was absolutely gutted on every level and I could do nothing to help. After I told Bevan we just sat in silence. I said to Bevan I have to get into that Mosque. Bevan reminded me that only Muslims were allowed in there. I looked at him, "I know". This one incident and the loss of British soldier's lives, made me focus on what I was going to do next. I was about to take my war against Al-Qaeda and the Taliban to a whole new level. The fight had just gotten very personal. I vowed and made it my mission in life to bring down the terrorist networks operating out of Pul-i-Charkhi prison. The strange thing was that I knew I could do it. I needed to plan this very carefully and put a few things in place. Firstly I needed a face to face meeting with senior American Military Intelligence or the CIA. I knew that the British Embassy could not be trusted; there were too many leaks and hidden agendas. The BEK cover-up of my situation had not filled me with confidence. If I was going to do what I had in mind, I would need "Top-Cover" from the people in authority, they being Senior American Intelligence or higher. I did not want the British bloody Embassy in Kabul calling me a Terrorist. I knew that they would try and spin something like that just to cover their own arses. All I had to do was feed the American machine, which was American Intelligence. That would be the easy part. Now I had to penetrate the Al-Qaeda leadership. I had already infiltrated them. Now I was looking at becoming one of them, under the full knowledge of the American Government. Once I had "Top-Cover" I would become Al-Qaeda. My referral to get me in was going to be provided by one of their top Commanders, Saladin himself. This was going to be an 'emotionally epic mission'.

The shambles that was my Afghan legal case had provided me with a good cover story for being in Pul-i-Charkhi, now I had to build on that. It was also common knowledge that the British Embassy staff in Kabul had completely screwed and abandoned the only British National in an Afghan prison at that time. The Embassy's actions had given me credibility within the prison and would now help me in what I wanted to do. I had been working covertly with American military intelligence for some time now from inside Pul-i-Charkhi prison. Now I intended to exploit my position and access to the max. In my view, my actions would be totally justified because British and American soldiers were being killed by terrorist attacks which were being planned and ordered from within Pul-i-Charkhi. My being a former British soldier and Paratrooper, had compelled me to take the whole situation very personally. Any British patriot would have felt the same way.

"Once more into the breach, dear friend"

The raw data was at my fingertips. I spent a long time thinking about the pros and cons of my chosen course of action. Although I had decided to take this to the next level, I was fully aware that it was not going to be easy. I was under no illusion; this experience was going to have a profound effect on me emotionally, mentally and physically. I expected to be killed. I just hoped that I wouldn't be killed before I was able to disrupt and dismantle the Al-Qaeda and Taliban network operating from my present location. I had accepted that I would not survive this. My acceptance and acknowledgement that I might die doing something which I had chosen to do, had allowed me a sense of inner peace and calm. I was focused, acutely aware of my situation and surroundings. All my senses were heightened. Don't get me wrong I did not have a death wish and I certainly didn't want to die. Not being scared of death is a strange feeling, but I was filled with a strange confidence. Absolute clear focus and calm towards my situation. The question that crossed my mind, time and time again, was where was all this going to lead and end up? I gave myself at best a 5% chance of getting out of this alive. I think I was being a little optimistic. Hell I was the underdog yet again, but with a lot of luck I just might pull this off, before the terrorists cottoned on to what I was up to and cut my head off, now that was a sobering thought.

My family had brought me up to always stand-up for what was right. Maintaining a good moral stance and adhering to ones principles is not always easy, but I have remained steadfast as best

I can. Most people would have taken the easy way-out, the soft option. That doesn't sit well with me. I always have and I always will 'take the road less travelled'. I have always done things the hard way, most of the time unintentionally. My path through life had just worked out that way, I thought again of Lord Alfred Tennyson and his poem.

"Forward. The light brigade!

Charge for the guns! He said.

Into the valley of Death

Rode the six hundred"

I understood the essence of his words. As I walked down the Al-Qaeda corridor again an image formed in my mind and a chill ran down my spine. Was I willingly advancing towards 'my' doom? 'Once more into the breach dear friends I went'. Again, walking on the dark side within the dark beast which was Al-Qaeda? Walking to what could end with a horrible death; I had only my knowledge and wit to protect me. When a person looks death in the face, in a volatile and hostile situation, their thought processes and their senses work quicker. They become heightened and acute, to every little aspect in their surroundings. I feel a strange calm and confidence in my being within such high pressure, high intensity and dangerous situations. I was becoming more at home in a war zone, than back in the normal world. Throughout my life I had always taken the 'road less travelled'. I liked travelling and the nomadic life style. It served my purpose. As a former soldier I liked action and adventure, living life on the edge on every level. Pul-i-Charkhi was just another chapter in my unusual life. I am what I am, not perfect by any means. But I am a good human being and I always try to make the right choices. Everything I had done and been through in my life had ended up with me standing in an Al-Qaeda corridor in the presence of the beast itself. My next action was going to be for "Queen and Country" and my fellow soldiers and brothers in arms. I hope when the dust clears and the truth is known, my actions defined me as a person, a soldier and as a British gentlemen and patriot.

I remembered the words of William Shakespeare "To be or not to be" I thought fuck it, 'To be'. It was game on as far as I was concerned. I analysed my situation through purely operational eyes now. After a little over an hour talking to Saladin and his men over Chi-tea and nuts, I called Bevan outside to the Prison block Commanders little rose garden. This was the only nice place in the whole of the prison. I had asked the Commander's permission for me and Bevan to walk for an hour, in return for tending his roses (only a true Englishman can prune and water roses correctly). Once outside I made sure Bevan and I were going to be alone and that no one would be in ear shot. Bevan came out to the garden five minutes after me. It was the safest place for us to albeit very quietly talk. He asked how it went with the Americans. I said just two words "Top-Cover" and smiled. "Well done" replied Bevan. He had a little smile creeping across his face. I shook Bevan's hand, saying the words "strength and honour" the timeless words spoken by a warrior long ago, before he went into battle. I had just been asked by the Americans to engage in battle with the enemy from the inside of their stronghold, inside Pul-i-Charkhi.

Bevan and I would stand by each other to the death, no matter what fight or horrors came our way.
'There is nothing to fear, but fear itself'. I briefed Bevan on my thoughts and my plan of action. I needed Bevan on board for certain aspects of what I was about to do. The truth was that I trusted Bevan with my life, as he did me; the trust between us was absolute. We had both been through hell and back over the past 18 months in the Afghan prison. I also knew that Bevan couldn't wait for payback on the Taliban and Al-Qaeda for the killing of British and American soldiers. Bevan was an old soldier, an officer himself and he was proud to be a member of the Commonwealth, even though he had also been abandoned by the British Embassy in Kabul. Trudy Kennedy had told me personally, that the British Embassy was not there to help the Commonwealth prisoners. I was utterly dismayed and disgusted at what she had said. Bevan and I had another thing in common; we both shared an undying love for the British Embassy staff in Kabul... 'Not'.

Author and Major Campbell inside Max-Security Prison Afghanistan)

"Sin City"

I had been well and truly in 'Dodge City' one of my nicknames for Pul-i-Charkhi prison. The Americans had nicknamed Pul-i-Charkhi prison 'Sin City' due to the lawlessness and violence.

Trudy Kennedy BEK had referred to the prison as 'Butlins'. This was just another example of how clueless the British Embassy was to the horrific reality of that place. They thought it was a bloody 'holiday camp'. That must have been why the Embassy travelled around the prison with a large heavily armed security team. Obviously Trudy Kennedy was oblivious to the prisons daily regime of ill-treatment, torture and mass human rights abuses. Bevan, like me, was well up for our new mission. We were all too aware of what and who Al-Qaeda really was. Cold blooded international terrorists who had hijacked a peaceful religion and who killed innocent men, women and children in the name of Jihad and their God. That was my opinion and nothing would ever convince me otherwise. Obviously Al-Qaeda would disagree, but I think we will agree to disagree on that one. I tasked Bevan with confirming when the Americans were due next. It was supposed to be later that afternoon. The American prison mentors 'CSSP' were also mostly American military intelligence. This was not a secret; even Al-Qaeda knew it. I had recognised some of the CSSP team from Northern Iraq, D-Main 101st Airborne Divisions Headquarters in Saddam's old palace in Mosul. CMOC was a hotel within the grounds of the palace. American prison mentors and the CIA, FBI and several other spooks including CIA military Special Forces Task Forces had operated out of this location. I had stayed there many times, at 'CMOC' and 'D-Main' during my time working with the American military throughout the Iraq war. The same faces I had seen there were now walking around "GIT-MO" next door to block 10 Pul-i-Charkhi. Within the hour a 'face to face' meet was set up between myself and senior American intelligence for that afternoon. The location was going to be the prison rose garden.

1st June 2010 - 1600hrs local time. The meeting was covertly covered by ten other Americans walking around the prison block. The Afghan guards quickly locked up Al-Qaeda and the Taliban. Due to the Americans just turning up out the blue, the guards had forgotten that I was walking alone outside in the garden. I had predicted this. The American's impromptu visit had caught everyone off guard. I had 10 minutes max to spend alone with my American intelligence contact so I got straight to the point. I wanted "Top-Cover" from the American Intelligence for my becoming a member of the Al-Qaeda network. My objective was to disrupt, dismantle and stop the terrorist networks operating out of Pul-iCharkhi and beyond. I wanted "Top-Cover" so the British Embassy could not turn around in the future and brand me an Al-Qaeda terrorist. The senior American Intelligence operator, who I already knew well, said 'no problem' you got it. He added "what else do you need, how can we help". I said just cover my arse politically with the British Government. So the decision was made. I would convert to Islam (in name only) 'Taqiyya' and infiltrate the terrorist network and work my way up their Command structure. I was tasked to gather as much information as possible on HVT's living in Pakistan. The Americans wanted 'Osama bin Laden'. Due to my position within Pul-i-Charkhi over the past year I had covertly passed highly sensitive tactical and strategic information and intelligence onto American Intelligence. All of it being highly accurate. So now I had an unofficial 'green light' for me to appear as a terrorist, but as I said, only by name. As my American friend said, 'it sounds like a plan'. We shook hands, his parting words to me were "stay safe". He moved quickly into the prison block to join up with the rest of his colleagues, who by this time were really rattling Al-Qaeda's cage. I was left standing alone in the small rose garden. It was deathly quiet, not even a sound from the birds. Not a soul in sight, the heat from the sun was stifling. The scent from the red roses was very sweet. I sat alone on the concrete path, deep in thought. Had I just sealed my own fate? I have always believed that my fate had already been written in the stars. That one man can make a difference. I was about to put my theory to the test. I hope that I was right because if not, I was totally and utterly uniquely fucked? I had gone from being a British Paratrooper to Afghan prisoner, then from prisoner to Al-Qaeda Terrorist. Then from an Al-Qaeda terrorist to, God only knows. He alone knew what the future held for me. I just had to expect the worst and hope for the best. I hoped that the words, alive and British patriot were written in the stars and in my future? (My Afghan hand written diaries 2009 -2010 are a detailed record and account of all events, timings, situations, meetings, names, dates and locations of Al-Qaeda HVTs, including Osama bin Laden. On the 1st August 2010 American Lawyer Kim Motley officially received the 'Index List' handed over by me, Anthony Malone, in front of witness Major Bevan Campbell. The 'Index List' included four pages of detailed information; listing subjects of reports handed over to American Military Intelligence by us from inside Pul-i-Charkhi 2007-2010. This 'Index List' included the physical location of Osama bin Laden being in Abbottabad, Pakistan in '2009 - 2010'. If I was killed in Pul-i-Charkhi, my diaries and copies of reports were to be given to my family by my next of kin Dil. This would put the official record straight and clear my name. Extracts from these diaries are at the rear of this manuscript.

Kabul was a company 'CIA' town in more ways than one. Most of the Special Forces types and Task Forces operating under constantly changing names were visually operating across Afghanistan and the rest of the Middle-East. To covert security operators, Afghanistan was like the old 'Wild West'. Everyone had pistols strapped to their belts. The local watering holes had enough bad whisky and more than enough working girls to go around. Afghanistan was totally lawless. This was the land that the Taliban and Al-Qaeda ruled. Due to the lawlessness and the life style, security operators loved being in country. The 'CT' (Counter Terrorism) work at the sharp end, was very rewarding. Members of my team were still in Afghan. I would use all my contacts and resources to help me accomplish my task. I had two new strings to my bow. Firstly, I could tie in with the other operations being conducted by the American Military and CIA and secondly; now that I had acquired "Top-Cover" I could source more information to help destroy, disrupt and dismantle Al-Qaeda and other terrorist operational cells, safe houses and hiding places. All within the Al-Qaeda leaderships 'Command and Control structure', and their international terrorist networks. Civilians from any walk of life have the right to walk down a street and not worry about being killed in another 9/11 or 7/7 suicide attack. I was now in a very unique position. I could hopefully help make a difference. I had no idea where this journey was about to lead me. The fact is that with a lot of blood sweat and tears, since September 11th 2001, the Americans and British have captured a whole lot more Al-Qaeda members than people realise. America and Britain have done, or given tacit approval for, all sorts of unpleasant things to get them to talk. An example is 'water boarding,' sleep deprivation and diet modification. Which everyone is indignant about? Britain does not torture people? America does not torture people? Extreme Rendition does not happen? From being on the receiving end of 'Extreme Rendition' all I will say to the British FCO is 'Bollocks', any rendition without any 'due process' is 'illegal' according to 'International Law' and the 'UN' Charter of Human Rights. It does happen, however right or wrong, but it should not be used to cover up FCO mistakes? Everyone does have their opinion on this subject. If bad people like Al-Qaeda did not do bad things, then we would not even be talking about this subject. We are at war with a ruthless and uncompromising enemy. We cannot rely on the charity or help from our so called friends and allies like the Afghan and Pakistan Governments anymore. We have accepted that Al-Qaeda and the Pakistan Taliban have infiltrated both of their governments at high levels, as well as their internal security services NDS and ISI. Britain and America need to fight our own war. Which means we need our own wide ranging unilateral and hard-hitting operations against Al-Qaeda and their affiliated groups? We have no choice. The longer we wait, many more innocent lives will be lost. In 'waging war' we have to have rules. The FCO should not be allowed to use the 'War on Terror' or 'Politics' to hide their own incompetence when they make mistakes. FCO staff needs to be held fully accountable for their actions at all times. British soldiers are always held accountable. My plan was a good one. If done right it would bear fruit. This was a war and in war you improvise. In the 'Paras' we had called this 'ABI' Airborne Initiative. I have always had a keen interest in Military history and the 'Art of War' by 'Sun-Tzu'. Tactics and military intelligence operations have always interested me on many levels. As a young child my Grandad used to tell me war stories of when he was a 'Desert Rat' fighting in Libya behind enemy lines during the Second World War. His stories always inspired me. He spoke about selfless acts of bravery and sacrifice for friends and country. We all owe our freedom today to outstanding men like him. 'They will never be forgotten'.

"They shall grow not old. As we that are left grow old. Age shall not weary them, nor the years condemn. At the going down of the sun and in the morning, we will remember them"

I have read a lot about the 'SOE' (Special Operations Executive) and 'Bletchley Park'. The wizard's war of the scientists and the double-cross system the British used to deceive the Germans by manipulating their captured agents in Britain. The British had been losing the war; our enemy was stronger and ruthless back then. Like Al-Qaeda are now in the present day. I thought how I could implement the lessons of military history into my present situation. Anything can be done if it is planned and prepared properly. The Arabs have an expression in Arabic. I had heard it spoken in Baghdad, Beirut, Damascus and now Kabul. It was 'Taqiyya'. It comes from the time of the 'prophet'. It is the lie you tell to protect yourself from the unbelievers. Al-Qaeda terrorists think all westerners are ignorant, so they think that they can tell them any lie they want. The idea of using 'Taqiyya' and turning it against the terrorists intrigued me. Using their own tactics against them. It could be done. I had played Al-Qaeda Commanders and other terrorist leaders at 'chess' many times over the years, across the Middle-East. You can assess a lot from a person by the way they play chess. Al-Qaeda and Hezbollah Commanders were good at playing the game. Planning, organising and attacking when the time was right. Al-Qaeda's Intelligence network was far reaching. It covered the whole Middle-East and well beyond, including Europe and America. Al-Qaeda had carefully placed their people like chess pieces, in key positions and at strategic locations. I had to be fully aware and mindful of Al-Qaeda's intelligence capabilities given my present situation and location. Western Governments had underestimated Al-Qaeda and their reach. The 9/11, 7/7 and 21/9 attacks were evidence of that. The West was now playing catch-up. It was now and forever the days after the 9/11 attacks that changed the world. The Al-Qaeda and other terrorist networks and groups are constantly evolving like a living organism, never making the same mistake twice. They learn from their mistakes. Their operations and movements had gone back to being very old school. Not using technology, becoming 'ghosts' to everyone including 'hunter teams' (with capture or kill orders) trying to trace track and kill them. Locating Al-Qaeda and their key players was key to any operation against Al-Qaeda. Voice Intercepts combined with drone strikes were being very effective in finding the bad guys and eliminating them, but for every one killed then two more would spring up? A full company of Special Forces could not get close to the Al-Qaeda leadership. Britain and America had been trying for years to get someone on the inside of the Al-Qaeda Command and Control structure. Many had tried and many had been killed. It had been deemed as impossible. However with my acquired knowledge a lone person could gain access if it was done correctly. I started to plan how I could achieve this.

When facing a difficult adversary it is usually best to prey upon their weaknesses, such as arrogance and pride. Lure him forward and draw him in. Like an animal they can be baited and lured in a certain direction. I needed bait that Al-Qaeda and the Taliban would go for. That was easy. What better bait for Al-Qaeda then the prospect of converting a former British Paratrooper with 22 years operational experience in fighting in combat zones all over the world. I would be the irresistible and mouth-watering bait. I knew that they would swarm around like bees to a honey pot. I did think on more than one occasion, however, that I really hoped that this bit of bait did not get eaten. 'Now that would have been rude'. The right pressure on just the right spot at the right time and the terrorist cell within the prison would collapse from within. That was what Al-Qaeda had done to the British and the Americans in Iraq and Afghanistan. But this terrorist tactic implemented with care and thought could work in reverse. Deception and stealth was the only way to penetrate the Al-Qaeda network. This was now becoming very real. I felt like a little maggot on a big fucking hook whilst the sharks were circling. This was going to be 'emotionally epic'.

"The Airborne Brotherhood – Why we do the job we do"

Many people have asked me over the years why I do the work I do. Constantly putting oneself in danger and in extreme situations; what makes a man go forward when everyone else is going back. I have even been asked by people, are soldiers some kind of war junkies? My answer is this; it is not just about the war or the combat. It's about the guy stood next to you, your best mate. It's about the man standing next to you who puts his life in your hands as you would him. You go where your friends go, your comrades and brothers in arms. You watch their back and they watch yours. It's all about trust, respect, loyalty, pride and confidence in your ability to accomplish the mission and who and what you are. Combine all this with extreme professionalism at all times. Doing the job at any time, in any conditions anywhere in the world, regardless of the risks or odds and never leaving a man behind. This is what the brotherhood is about. The words that sum up the qualities possessed by a Paratrooper, which make him one of the 'Airborne Brotherhood', were best said by Field Marshall Montgomery. When people ask me why I do my job, I recommend that they read the following words. My answer lies within.

"What Manner of Men Are These That Wear The Maroon Beret?"

They are firstly all volunteers and are toughened by physical training. As a result they have infectious optimism and that offensive eagerness which comes from well-being. They have 'jumped' from the air and by doing so have conquered fear.

Their duty lies in the vain of battle. They are proud of this honour. They have the highest standards in all things whether it be skill in battle or smartness in the execution of all peace time duties. They are in fact – men apart – every man an emperor.

Of all the factors, which make for success in battle, the spirit of the warrior is the most decisive. That spirit will be found in full measure in the men who wear the maroon beret.

Field Marshall

The Viscount Montgomery of Alamein

Those words stir the blood of any Paratrooper, young or old. There is no such thing as a former Para. It's in their blood and DNA. The spirit of a Para and soldier remains within them for life.

The next morning was the start of my 'Tasking', setting out the ground work for my deep covert infiltration of the Al-Qaeda, Pakistan Taliban and Haqqani International terrorist networks. Failure was not an option....

"Great men are forged in fire; it is lesser men who light the flame".

Anth Malone (The Rogue Warrior) Part Three

The Road Not Taken

Two roads diverged in a yellow wood,

And sorry I could not travel both

And be one traveller, long I stood

And looked down one as far as I could

To where it bent in the undergrowth.

Then took the other, as just as fair,

And having perhaps the better claim,

Because it was grassy and wanted ware;

Though as for that, the passing there

Had worn them really about the same.

And both that morning equally lay

In leaves no step had trodden black.

Oh, I kept the first for another

day! Yet knowing how way leads

on to way,

I doubted if I should ever come back.

I shall be telling this with a sigh

Somewhere ages and ages hence:

Two roads diverged in a wood, and I –

I took the one less travelled by,

And that made all the difference.

By Robert Frost

"Next morning I would begin the task that I had been given by Walter Downs,
American Military Intelligence. My brief was to locate Al-Qaeda and Taliban leaders, HVTs and
terrorists, hiding and operating within Pakistan"

My new routine was to be up, bright eyed and bushy tailed at first light, 0500hrs. Then drink
some hot, sweet, black tea and eat a few scraps of flat bread with plain yogurt; this was a
traditional, quick, Afghan breakfast. Followed by a well-timed walk up and down the corridor to
stretch my legs and carefully observe the Mosque during the first prayers of the day. I made a
mental note of the positions that Al-Qaeda, Pakistan Taliban and Afghan Taliban members took
within the Mosque. There was a strict pecking order, a structure which indicated seniority and
rank of the Terrorists. Religious rank and seniority played a big part within the cell structure of
the terrorist's groupings and networks. Like the British Army has a chain of Command, Al-Qaeda
and the Pakistan Taliban had a similar system based on religious 'ranks'. There were a large
number of 'Mullahs' located within Pul-i-Charkhi prison, over 20 of them, strategically located
and placed throughout the prison. These Mullahs had been used by the terrorists to completely
control and manipulate the other 5,000 prisoners. The Mullahs had given Al-Qaeda and the
Pakistan Taliban credibility. The whole prison was being used as a recruiting ground by the
terrorists. Young, impressionable Afghans, were being brainwashed every day, with the Al-
Qaeda doctrine of extremist ideology. The Americans and the British overlooked what was
happening, and to what extent, within Pul-i-Charkhi. Al-Qaeda was able to hide and conceal
their identities and the operations coming out of Pul-i-Charkhi. The terrorist Op-Sec,
'Operational Security', was very good, but over time I would break this down. I would walk along
the corridors with terrorist Commander Wais Hudein after he conducted the morning Mosque.
He was Pakistan Taliban with close links to the Haqqani network and Al-Qaeda. I asked him to
teach me some Afghan proverbs and jokes, some were quite funny, but his English was poor. He
would point at his torture wounds and say one of the only English words he knew 'pain'. This
always made me laugh; at least this terrorist had a sense of humour. One of the proverbs he
liked to use was, 'don't stop another man's donkey'. Which means, 'mind your own business'.
He would say this to the prison guards just to rattle their cages. He was forever abusing the
guards. Most of the guards were not intelligent enough to understand, or get a lot of the jokes,
which made the jokes even funnier.

"God son of Ayman Al-Zawaniri, the leader of the Al-Qaeda network"

I used this situation to break the ice with Wais Hudein and Hussein Laghman (God son of Ayman
AlZawaniri, the (New) leader of the Al-Qaeda network). Hussein is a member of the Pakistan ISI,
and a major player and negotiator between Al-Qaeda and the Pakistan/Afghan Taliban. He also
acts as their fixer and quartermaster. Hussein is also responsible for organising safe
transportation of known terrorists between countries, including airplane tickets, passports and
money transfers, secret hideaways in strange cities, cell phones and computers. Hussein has
also been arrested in the past for selling SAM's (Surface to Air Missiles) and other weapons to
the Taliban. The Chief prosecutor in Afghanistan (Afghan Ministry of Justice), has been paid
money by Hussein and members of the Taliban network for the changing of Taliban prisoner's

official files. From terrorist charges to narcotics/drug charges, and in doing so, a large number of known Taliban/terrorists had walked free from British mentored Afghan prisons. (See ACP and Haqqani network). Wais Hudein and Hussein Laghman were two of the Terrorist Commanders that I would have to get close to. Both were knowledgeable and possessed the kind of information I wanted, such as the Arabic names of weapons, locations and terrorist smuggling routes into Afghanistan from Pakistan and Iran. They also knew, and had access to, the contact details of hundreds of other terrorists and their Commanders across Afghanistan, the whole of the Middle-East and beyond. Wais Hudein was old school 'Mujahedeen' which means that he was one of the 'Muj' Mujahedeen who had fought the Russians back in the eighties during the Afghan Jihad. He resented the Americans and British, because in his opinion the West had invaded his country and was an occupying force. Wais Hudein was also a religious leader within the 'Muj'. He was highly respected by his own men and the Afghan elders. Even Al-Qaeda and the Pakistan Taliban showed him great respect, both as a Muslim and as a 'Muj' fighter and Commander. Some of Wais Hudein's own men were located within Pul-i-Charkhi, he often paid the guards bribes to have all of his men consolidated in Block 10. In time he would have his own fighting unit and force within the prison. Bevan and I chatted about 'targeting' these two Commanders. Bevan took up the task of instructing Hussein in English, something that would come in handy later on with the notebook full of Al-Qaeda and Taliban members and 'friends' whose names and telephone numbers were written down in English by Bevan for 'safeguarding'; I took up the task of learning the basic tenants of Islam from Wais Hudein, with whom I had another connection, that was, military tactics. He was keen to learn, but in me discussing things with him, I was able to learn their Modus Operandi. There was a lot of 'trust' from Wais Hudein side towards me, something that I used in my journey forward within the terrorist structures. One of the other die hard terrorist was Taliban Commander Wah Khile. From day one we hated each other. He was a 'Muj' and a complete psycho, who loved killing Westerners. He would incite violence towards Westerners every time he took the Mosque for Islamic prayers. His sermons were full of 'fire and brimstone'. Ordering Muslims to join the Jihad and kill the Crusaders. His choice of words included; 'End of Days' speeches of how the Western Governments of America and Britain were all evil, that it was every Muslims duty to fight in the Jihad and that it was an honour to die fighting. Wah Khile was a coward; he would send young, Afghan men out, to become suicide bombers, killing themselves and other innocent people. But the gutless Wah Khile would not do it himself. I broached this subject with him. I worded it along the lines of, 'doesn't he want to go to paradise and claim his 70 virgins'. Under my breath I added, 'do the world and humanity a favour and kill yourself'. He hated it when I out smarted him, which wasn't hard to do, he wasn't the sharpest tool in the box. He was a big fish in his own little pond. In the grand scheme of things, he was nothing more than a little tadpole. Unknown to me then, I was going to really hurt his pride in the not too distant future. Over the coming months I would set him up to take the fall for upsetting the Al-Qaeda network. Once I knew the game these 'Muppets' were playing, it was not hard to play them off against each other. Whilst they were pre-occupied with fighting each other internally, they were not planning or ordering the killing of British and American soldiers. The way I looked at it, the more headwork, chaos and mayhem I could cause within the prison, the longer I would stay alive, as long as I did not get caught. So anarchy it was.

Everything I did was aimed at disrupting the terrorist network, but at the same time enhancing my position, level of trust, and credibility within the terrorist network. The American intelligence knew what I was like, 'just point me in the direction of the enemy, then get the hell out of my way'. I had always achieved the required result at the end of the day. In Iraq I had caused havoc and destruction behind enemy lines. As one military officer had told me; I had left a road map of destruction and carnage in my wake. During the Iraq war my 2IC was close to officially reporting me as 'MIA' (Missing in Action), due to me disappearing deep behind enemy lines at classified locations, where airstrikes had hit enemy targets. I turned up days later leaving a trail of destruction behind me. I was injured and bleeding but still alive and soldiering on. Now fast forward back to Pul-i-Charkhi, I was causing complete havoc and chaos within the Al-Qaeda and Pakistan Taliban networks. I have always been a good Commander, but a nightmare to control. The good thing now was that I had become Al-Qaeda's nightmare. I was slowly building my bad arse reputation up within the prison; it was not hard to do. When one of the Taliban had tried to knife me I had taken the knife off him, disarming him in seconds, then giving him the knife back, told him to try again. The look on his face was priceless. Little incidents like this helped to build up my reputation. I found the process slightly tedious, but the terrorists loved the entertaining show of force. It brightened up their days and gave them all something to talk about over chi-tea.

I needed a name for when I falsely converted to Islam. That was going to be interesting. It would have to be a good name, something be-fitting me and what I was doing, a name that was short, to the point, and easily remembered. It had to be a strong name, known and steeped in the history of hard won battles across the Islamic world. It had to be a name which would be respected and feared.

"Allah-Odin"

"Meaning 'God' in Arabic and 'Odin' is the 'Greek God of war'"

It came to me one afternoon. I had chosen the name 'Allahodin' I also kept this out of the ordinary spelling of the classic name. My spelling meant 'God' in Arabic and 'Odin' is the 'Greek God of war'. So my Islamic name translated as 'God of war'. I thought that it would suit me very well as my cover name. Also being a British Paratrooper, I thought it very apt and summed up the way I felt, and the fact that I was to have their lives and destinies in my hands. I knew that the American military and CIA would also find the name fitting and very appropriate. A covert security operator called the 'God of War', taking the Al-Qaeda terrorist network apart from the inside, had a poetic feel to it. I also knew that my Dad would approve if he ever found out. Now that was a thought. My situation would take a hell of a lot of explaining, if I was lucky enough to survive all of this. The conversation would be; Hi Dad, how are you? By the way, don't worry, but I became a member of Al-Qaeda, how's your day going? It would be one hell of a tale to tell over brandy and cigars. Hell, if Sam ever found out about this she would kill me. She would say something along the lines of, "if Al-Qaeda doesn't kill you, I bloody well will, what were you thinking?" Sam had a direct way with words. I think this was one job that I would forget to tell her about if possible. I would never live it down if she found out I had put my life on the line again, albeit for 'Queen and Country'. First and foremost, I had to achieve my objective and get out alive. (Sam if you're reading this, 'Sorry' you can kick my arse later).

Wais Hudein was a very intelligent man and Commander in his late thirties. His battle hardened face and dark eyes gave him an evil appearance, which made him look a lot older, well beyond his years. He had started fighting in the Jihad when he was just eight years old, killing his first man when he was nine. This went some way to explaining why he was the way he was. Fighting was all he had ever known, he had grown to love it. Being one of the few terrorists who were actually very bright, he had risen up through the terrorist ranks, becoming one of the terrorist tactical planners for terrorist military operations across Eastern Afghanistan. Wais Hudein's main area of operations was the same 'AO' (Area of Operations) at that time, as that of the American military's 101st Airborne Division which were headquartered within this area? Due to my past history and personal connection with the 101st soldiers and American airborne brotherhood in Iraq, this had made Wais Hudein very important to me, both tactically and strategically. I wanted to know what he knew; his knowledge was extensive. He came from a large family; all of his brothers were fighting in the Afghan Jihad. One of his brothers was being held by the American military 'black prison' at Bagram Airbase, Northern Afghanistan. Corrupt members of the Afghan Government had been trying to get his brother released or transferred to Pul-i-Charkhi prison. The Americans were not playing ball. They knew that Wais Hudein's family were important players inside the terrorist network. The Americans had underestimated Wais Hudein, he was the oldest brother and the leader of the family's Jihad fighters. Most of the prisoners in Block 10 had been tortured by the Afghan authorities or the Americans. I would make a joke of it by saying did the terrorists like playing 'water sports', this was a reference to the American water boarding torture. I did not have a problem with the way America had treated Al-Qaeda, the way I looked at it, if Al-Qaeda had not carried out the 9/11 attacks on America, then America would not be treating Al-Qaeda with disdain. I personally condemn torture, but I could see the American's point of view. As one senior American military Colonel had told me over a cigar; 'If Al-Qaeda had not pissed in our back yard, then we would not be pissing in their's. He added; 'and we are fresh out of chlorine'? The way that a lot of Americans looked at the torturing of terrorist suspects, is very different to the general outlook from the British Government. The Americans really don't give a damn. They do what they want. They act first and worry about the consequences later. Even after all these years, a lot of Americans, especially the Military, have still got the old 'John Wayne' attitude of shoot first and ask questions later. This was questionable at times, but did get results. The Americans had this attitude with regard Pul-i-Charkhi. They knew that not telling the British Government about what I was doing would raise a few questions in the future, when the truth all came out. The Americans did not worry about this. We did not trust the Staff within the British Embassy anyway; they had more leaks than a sieve. For my own safety, the British Embassy was kept out of the loop. The less they knew the better for me and the better the odds of me getting the information and intelligence I required and making it out alive. 'So I soldiered on'.

The prisoners in Block 10 all laughed every time I brought up the term 'water boarding', the prisoners were fully aware that I had been given a hard time by the prison guards and prisoners when I had first arrived over a year ago. It was also common knowledge that I had told the guards on more than one occasion 'to go and fuck themselves'. My choice of language was harsh, but given what they had put me through, a little harsh language was in my eyes acceptable. I seem to have kept my little childhood problem with authority, well, Afghan corrupt authority anyway. One afternoon whilst sitting with the terrorists, I used the word 'Muppet', this was a term I used to describe and which I sometimes called and addressed the guards. I was asked to explain what this meant, to Wais Hudein. After my humorous explanation, he and his fellow fighters rolled around laughing. For the next week, all of them would call the guards 'Muppets'. The guards were well pissed off with me for that. Saladin just laughed when he heard this, the guards had complained to him, he had told them that it was just harmless fun. Obviously I was still making friends and influencing people. I was beginning to be accepted by the terrorists.

"Torture"

The old Block 10 Commander's name came up a lot during conversations with the terrorists. Prison block Commander Fahruk had been notorious and extremely dangerous; he was old school Afghan, brutal on every level. Fahruk was former 'Khad', Afghan secret police, who had also been trained by the Old Russian KGB. I had seen Fahruk beat prisoners to within an inch of their lives. He would just walk into the prison block with some of his men and grab a prisoner who he claimed had upset them in some small way. His favourite party piece was getting his men to hold the prisoner on the floor and two guards would force the prisoner to remain there by kneeling on his chest. Two other guards would lift the prisoner's bare feet up, then Fahruk and one of the other guards would whip the bottom of the prisoner's feet with metal cables (cat-o-nine tails), this had the same effect as slashing the bare feet with a razor blade. After about 20 strokes the guards and Fahruk would just drop the prisoner in a bloody heap on the floor and walk away. The piecing screams which came from the prisoners who were being whipped were like those of a helpless animal being slaughtered. I had washed the blood sprays off the walls and ceiling several times after such torture. The blood stains were that bad that all the prison blocks had been painted to hide the evidence of what had transpired. The prisoners who talked about Fahruk still talked about him in hushed tones. Those were the dark days I had witnessed of bloodlust, torture and death throughout Pul-i-Charkhi prison. Fahruk was one of the prison Commanders that the prisoners really feared. I had made short work of Fahruk, I had informed the head of the Red-Cross in Afghanistan of what was really going on inside the prison. Fahuk had also made the mistake of refusing access to the block by the Red-Cross, which is a breach of International Law. This, along with all the witness statements I had encouraged the other prisoners to write, had helped to get Fahruk removed from Pul-i-Charkhi prison. I had used this incident as another stepping stone towards gaining the trust of the terrorists. There were still another twenty other Prison Block Commanders in Pu-i-Charkhi, who were just as bad if not worse than Fahruk.

At least Block 10 did not have prisoners being killed or torture daily anymore. The British Embassy had been made aware of what Fahruk was doing, including the ill-treatment and torture of prisoners. But they, the Embassy, did nothing. It was only after I involved the Red-Cross officially that the daily torture of prisoners ceased. The Red-Cross staff in Afghan gave medical treatment to prisoners who had been brutally tortured. Their personnel still have copies of all the graphic photographs and detailed witness statements of what took place at that time in the British Mentored Afghan prison. In a strange kind of way, the conditions and the torture helped to bring the prisoners closer together. Not all, but most helped each other to get through those desperately challenging times. British and Commonwealth prisoners did not receive any basic supplies or food rations from the British Embassy. Although I had given the British Embassy's official representative, Lawrence Jenkins, money during one of his rare official prison visits, nothing really changed. He turned up once every three to six months. The Commonwealth prisoners didn't get visits at all. I even had a letter from the British Embassy which stated; that the British Embassy would not visit Commonwealth Nationals in prison in Afghanistan.

Luckily I kept a copy, as the British Government tried to confiscate all the documents and letters that I had received from the British Embassy, in a bid to silence me and cover the truth up. After the British Embassy's Lawrence Jenkins had taken the money that I had given him as payment for some British Army ration packs or food of any kind, Lawrence Jenkins turned up four months later and gave me back the money. He told me that the British Embassy was not able to get hold of any food for me. I was completely stunned by this revelation. The British Embassy security team that was present, were disgusted at what the British Embassy had said. The security team discreetly removed some of the British army food rations from the back of their vehicle and left them for me at the prison block. The British Embassy staff, Lawrence Jenkins, had lied again. Some of the British Embassy staff were now making a habit of lying to everyone. I was told by the Embassy security team at a later date, they had pulled Lawrence Jenkins up about his lying. Lawrence had told them to mind their own business. You could imagine what the professional British Embassy security team thought of this.

To get this into perspective, the British Embassy did not once bring any food or clean drinking water up to Pul-i-Charkhi prison, for any British or Commonwealth Nationals. The Turkish, Iranian and Pakistani Embassy had brought in fresh food including vegetables and boxes of bottled drinking water up to Pul-iCharkhi prison once a month, due to Afghanistan being 'classed as a war zone'. Their Embassies paid for, and really looked after, their nationals whilst in prison. Their actions put the British Embassy to shame. So as the facts stand from a 'human rights' point of view, the British Embassy behaved disgracefully and had been found to be under par compared to such Embassies as the Turks. An official from the Turkish Embassy even brought me, a British National, food when he was informed about the disgraceful actions, negligent and woeful behaviour of the British Embassy. He also emphatically stressed that the British Embassy in Kabul had a nerve talking about the human rights violations in Turkey. I later challenged the British Embassy staff about this point, Lawrence Jenkins the British Consulat that time told me; that Afghanistan was 'not an active war zone'. This was the kind of incompetent comment that I had grown accustomed to expect from him. Over 450 dead British soldiers would certainly disagree with Lawrence's statement from beyond their graves. It is a fact that Afghanistan has been an active war zone for many, many years. I also made a point of bringing this subject up during my official 2010 TV interview with American news station CNN from inside Pul-i-Charkhi prison. I also added that because of the actions of some of the British Embassy staff in Afghanistan, even Al-Qaeda who got to hear the actions of the British Embassy Kabul were completely disgusted at the way I had been treated. Al-Qaeda and the Pakistan Taliban, 'not my own British Embassy', organised; food, medical supplies and phone calls to my next of kin. Although very grateful I was embarrassed to say that Al-Qaeda, my sworn enemy, had done the job that the British Embassy should have done? So from a humanitarian point of view, Al-Qaeda had helped me more than the shameful British Embassy. The British Embassy was not happy about my comments. When they brought the subject up, I told them that if they had done their 'mandated job' in the first place, this would never have been an issue. I also informed them that Al-Qaeda had even used their contacts within the corrupt Afghan Government to get me copies of documents from my 'lost' Afghan case files. The British Embassy had taken over 18 months, and still they were unable to give me copies of documents from the Afghan Ministry of Justice. It was pretty obvious that the Embassy could not be bothered, it does not take 18 months, and they still could not provide me with copies of my 'so called' Official Afghan legal documents/files. This was a good indication that something was very wrong regarding the British Embassy Kabul.

The British Embassy and FCO London's treatment of any British National in any Islamic Country, including Afghanistan, is at best inadequate, at worst shocking and dark aged. The fact is that the British Embassy's actions are 'not in keeping' with their duty of care guidelines and was also 'unbecoming' considering they are supposed to be representing Great Britain internationally. In short, the Embassy was showing 'very bad form'. The large list of British and Commonwealth Nationals, who have been falsely imprisoned in Islamic Countries, is most disturbing. Abuse and torture and even death are common place, examples of this being cases of British Nationals killed whilst in police custody in Dubai, UAE. These incidents cast a long dark shadow over the out-dated 'written mandate' of the British FCO and their Embassies. Further examples are the disgraceful ill-treatment of Major Bill Shaw MBE in Afghanistan and the death later of Lee Brown in Dubai in 2011; and not forgetting the savage torture of Collin Berry also in Afghanistan. These situations and examples are now all too common and not acceptable. How many more British Nationals and members of the Commonwealth, have to be ill-treated and tortured or beaten to death before the British Embassy and FCO stop hiding behind politics and their 'self-appointed red-tape'. One day the British Embassy and FCO may have the 'guts' to stand up to some of the corrupt Governments of the Middle-East and Afghanistan. We live in hope.

By now I had exhausted every possible avenue of trying to gain my 'legal' freedom from my illegal detention. There was no help forth coming from, or via, the British Embassy in Afghanistan or the FCO in London. All that was emerging from the British Embassy, via some of their staff, was more misinformation, lies and cover-ups. Not really an ideal situation. 'It was what it was'. Not to worry, I soldiered on and continued with the work and tasking I had received from American Intelligence. I knew that the truth would come out at some point in the future. The staff in the British Embassy Kabul would eventually have to bow their heads in shame. Whilst the Embassy staff were endlessly screwing me over and leaving me to the will of Al-Qaeda and the Taliban, unbeknown to them I was saving their lives from terrorist attacks on the British Embassy that had been planned from within Pul-i-Charkhi prison. I could see the 'poetic justice' in what I have just said. It was a good job that I was a British Patriot and lucky for the British Embassy that I was a former British Paratrooper. Anyone else would probably have been killed and would not have been able to prevent and disrupt the terrorist attacks. 'Good judgment comes from experience and past 'bad' judgement', it's all part of the circle of life. I have always tried to do the right thing; I have also tried to be principled in my life. Time would tell if I had made the right choice and the decision to stay in Pul-i-Charkhi Prison.

"Hunger Strike"

One method I used to help me infiltrate the terrorist network and gain their trust was to go on hunger strike. It would also be a protest against the actions of the British Embassy and some of its staff regarding my illegal imprisonment. I knew the British Embassy would not get off there arses to help me, so I turned that negative into a positive. I was confident that the staff at the British Embassy would screw me over yet again with their lies and cover-ups. I would have been shocked if they had made any effort to assist me. In time I would be proven right, yet again. The objective of my hunger strike was purely to build my credibility within the terrorist network. The terrorists on the other hand applauded me in their misguided minds, anyone who ruffled the feathers of the British Embassy could not be all bad. I knew that I would get support from the terrorists. I put my cunning plan into action. On the 23 January 0900hrs local time, I officially started my hunger strike in Pul-i-Charkhi prison. All my actions were carefully co-ordinated with my next of kin back in the UK. Hand written letters were handed simultaneously to the prison Commander, the British Embassy Kabul and the FCO London. The letters stated that my actions were due to the complete lack of help and response with regard to my officially reported miscarriage of justice and no follow up by the British Embassy Kabul with regards to my so called Afghan case. Another important point of my letters was the disgraceful treatment I had received. I focused the actions of my hunger strike on the British Embassy. There was no point in focusing my actions on the Afghans. Everyone knows that the Afghan Government and Justice system is completely corrupt. Even though the British Embassy denied it at this time? The Prison Commander allowed me to use his phone to also inform the British Embassy of my hunger strike, I knew that the Embassy would try and deny that they had received my letter. The Embassy had mysteriously 'lost' 11 previous letters that had been hand delivered to them. A Catholic priest was one of the people who had delivered the letters. The Embassy was not happy when I accused them of lying about the letters, so who was lying, a Catholic priest, or Lawrence Jenkins from the British Embassy, to whom the letters were addressed to? I will leave the reader to decide. The prison Commander also confirmed that I had called the British Embassy and the subject of the phone call in his official prison log book. This was done to cover his arse and to make everything official. I had the full support of the prison Commander, as long as I didn't incriminate him regarding my hunger strike. Lawrence Jenkins and Trudy Kennedy, British Consul and Vice Consul, were also informed of my actions by their FCO headquarters based in

London. A copy of my letter had been delivered there as well, to counter the British Embassy in Kabul denying all knowledge. I never received any official reply from the Embassy regarding my letters. My next of kin kept copies of all my correspondence. Two weeks into my hunger strike I spoke to the International press, giving them an update on my actions and the reasons behind them. I made the point of informing the press that the British Embassy had abandoned over 160 members of the Commonwealth, who were also being additionally detained illegally (according to International Law) within Afghan prisons, which were also mentored by the British Embassy in Kabul. The press phoned the British Embassy, who as usual denied that there was a British national on hunger strike in Pul-i-Charkhi prison? The press then phoned the top Afghan prison Commander at Pul-i-Charkhi prison, who confirmed the two week on-going hunger strike and my reasons behind it. The press then phoned the British Embassy again and asked them some uncomfortable questions. I was then contacted by the British Embassy Consulate staff, demanding to know why my next of kin and I had been talking to the press. My response was very polite, I told them with all due respect, to get off their Embassy arses and do their job which is written in their FCO mandate. Sometimes the truth hurts, but they needed to be told.

That day the British Embassy staff started to put out a lot of misinformation to many people, including official members of the press, some of which, and unbeknown to the Embassy, I had known for over 12 years. So every lie the Embassy told the press, quickly got back to me. My friends and contacts who were also working within the British Embassy, were keeping me completely up to speed on all that was being said by British Consulate staff. Some of their updates were very interesting and useful. It painted a very dark and disturbing picture of the goings on inside the British Embassy Kabul - lies and cover-up, and people trying to cover their own arse politically. Three weeks into my hunger strike I began to feel the effects, I felt very tired, weak and moody, disoriented at times. This was proving to be a lot harder than I had anticipated, even so, I soldiered on. I was taking in a little water but no food. The weight was dropping off me. Luckily I had been extremely fit before I decided to take this course of action. I just had to remain focused. The terrorists were taking a keen interest in me now. They all knew my reason for my hunger strike. Many of the terrorist Commanders visited my room to wish me all the best and show their support for my actions. I was gradually achieving my objective, but I still wanted to prove a point. The longest Afghan hunger strike had been 4 weeks; I wanted to beat that record out of principle. The human body can go without food for 6 to 8 weeks depending on the conditions, as long as water is drunk at regular intervals. I was being very carefully not to damage myself, I wanted to make a point, not kill myself. To my amazement some of the Staff within the British Embassy Kabul were spending more time covering-up my hunger strike than dealing with it. My friends in the International press were keeping tabs on the Embassy's actions? They knew that the time would come for all this and the truth to come out at some point. The Al-Qaeda and Pakistan Taliban Commander looked on in disbelief at the treatment I had received from my own Embassy. They thought that I must have been a real bad boy to be treated in such a way by the British Embassy. Unbeknown to the Embassy, their actions actually helped me and my situation with Al-Qaeda. I was getting closer to the terrorists and slowly the terrorists were accepting me, all part of my plan. Al-Qaeda had also confirmed that I had been blackballed by the British Embassy, via their informants who were working inside the British Embassy as Afghan translators. That little fact got my attention. At this point in time the British Embassy and their staff were openly advising any press that made enquiries, not to report on my situation. The Embassy staff even stooped so low as to use my security as an excuse to cover-up my hunger strike. I found this funny because it was the first time that the British Embassy had actually brought up my personal security. It's a shame that the Embassy did not think about this 18 months earlier before they had allowed me to be illegally put into a prison with Al-Qaeda and Taliban terrorists.

Six weeks into my hunger strike, the press were still quizzing the British Embassy. The truth about my situation was finally emerging. I had always said that 'the truth always comes out in the end'. All this at the same time as the level of corruption within the Afghan Government was beginning to come out and be reported upon and was making the news. The cat was well and truly out the bag. Even the United Nations' official reports stated that Afghanistan and its Government were among the most corrupt Governments and countries in the world. One UN official I spoke to during his visit to Pul-i-Charkhi prison told me that if every one of the corrupt Afghan Government officials was sacked due to malpractice, there would be nobody left in the Afghan Government. That was a very thought provoking statement, why were Western Governments allowing the corrupt Afghan government to continue...! When the news story broke about the level of international aid money being stolen and taken by Afghan Government officials; who were also taking aid money out of the Country in suit cases which were being flown to Dubai and deposited into the Afghan official's personal bank accounts? This sent shock waves through Western Governments. British, American, as well as all Western publics wanted to know what the hell was going on, and why Western Embassies were allowing this to continue happening, it had been an open secret for years. The high level of corruption within the Government of Afghanistan had led to no real 'rule of law', which led to no real security, which had led to the unstable situation across Afghanistan? The worrying fact had also emerged that the Taliban were gaining power right across Southern Afghanistan due to the Afghan Government corruption. This situation had been allowed to fester for too many years, now it was irreversible. Western Embassy's and Western governments have turned a blind eye to the Afghan Government corruption for over 10 years. Many years ago they could have dealt with it, but now the problem had escalated and is so wide spread it cannot be dealt with. The fact was the Taliban were gaining ground and would come back into power at some point in the near future in Afghanistan. The Afghan people are just fed up of the Government corruption and there being no real 'rule of law'. The Afghan people also want the rapid escalation in violence to stop. A lot of Afghan people are looking to the Taliban to restore law and order and to stamp out the corruption. Desperation has driven a lot of people into the arms of the Taliban. Moderate people who would not normally have become 'Talib' have not only joined up, they have also become fighters. This is very worrying and the escalation in events should be a 'red flag' to Western Governments to act. Nothing good will come of this. This will become a future problem for Western Governments and Countries. Afghan Fighters can now be found, and have been reported, in every major war zone and conflict across the Middle East and Africa, including: Syria, Iraq, Yemen, Somalia, Libya and Egypt. The terrorist Commanders inside Pul-i-

Charkhi prison were in communication with other terrorist Commanders and leaders within these countries.

The prison Commander was worried that if I died he would be held responsible and put in jail. This was how things were in Afghan. Everything worked backwards. All the prison Guards and Prison Commanders had been in prison themselves at least once in their life. Being in prison, within Afghanistan was 'a rite of passage' for Afghan men. That fact is pretty shocking, given that the British prison mentors did not even know that fact until it was pointed out to them by Afghan prison guards. The other fact of life in Afghanistan was the old saying 'pay the bribe' to the prosecutors and Judges to obtain freedom. This was both very sad and alarming, it's pretty obvious the avenue which Afghanistan as a country and its society is heading. Back to future civil war with the Taliban in power? I was rushed to hospital just after the sixth week of my hunger strike. I arrived at the Kabul Red-Cross emergency war hospital late in the morning. The prison Commander had sent three armed guards in his personal vehicle to get me there quickly. I was shackled, thrown in the back, and quickly driven to the hospital at speed. On arrival I was taken into the emergency room. The Red-Cross staff shouted and ordered the Afghan guards to remove the shackles off me and get out. I was asked to sit on the treatment table. When the Afghan guards had left the room the Medical staff referred to them as animals. They added that the Afghan guards needed a good bath or wash; as they really smelled bad. I was glad I had my clean clothes on; I even had clean underwear on (my mother 'would' have been happy about that. She used to always say to me as a kid, 'make sure you have clean underwear on, you never know what might happen', she joked about me being hit by a bus. My point of view was even if I had clean underwear on when I was a kid, if I was hit by a bus it would not remain clean for long; anyone watching a big bloody red London bus coming towards you, about to hit you at speed, this would probably cause anyone to crap themselves. So the whole thought process about wearing clean underwear was pointless. But none the less, I always made sure I wore clean underwear). The Afghan guards did smell really bad; they were the ones who treated prisoners like animals. I laughed at this thought, who really were the animals? I commented to the Red-Cross staff present that they should come up to Pul-i-Charkhi prison and see the conditions prisoners have to live in. The staff who were from Italy just looked at me. They all said "we know". The Red-Cross had been trying to get into Pul-i-Charkhi prison to inspect and investigate the mass human rights abuses endured by the prisoners. The Red-Cross had been repeatedly blocked and even turned away by the Afghan authorities several times. That was a breach of International Law, turning away the Red-Cross. The Red-Cross should have open access to anyone needing medical help or assistance in any conflict zone. These violations had re-occurred over several years at Pul-i-Charkhi prison location and other prisons and detention centres across Afghanistan, those were also mentored by the British Embassy Kabul. This was confirmed by Red-Cross staff based in Kabul.

The Red-Cross personnel at the hospital were aware of my hunger strike and the reasons behind it prior to my arrival. Many of them supported my actions and reasons. They were confused at the complete lack of help and support by my own Embassy. My first impression of the Hospital and the Red-Cross staff was how professional they were and how clean everything was. The hospital smelled clean and sterilized. It was to the same high standards of any Western hospital I had seen in Britain and America. The walls were painted white and a recently laid blue tiled floor gave the place a new build look. I observed new medical supplies and equipment which filled the store cupboards. There were more medical supplies in one of these storage areas than in the whole of Pul-i-Charkhi prison. This was the first time I had been in a normal and safe environment for over 18months, it all seemed very surreal. I had grown accustomed to the barbaric conditions and violent daily life within Pul-i-Charkhi. Being around the Red-Cross staff who were normal, polite people, Westerners who had manners and compassion was such a relief. This was the first time in a long time that I had felt safe; it was such a nice feeling. It was good to be reacquainted with normality; it would have been too easy to lose touch with normality given the conditions in Pul-i-Charkhi. An Afghan nurse came into the room. She wore a crisp clean white uniform. Her smile was captivating and she greeted me in English. Under the directions from one of the Italian doctors, the nurse attempted to insert 'IV' intravenous drips into me. My body was in a poor state by this time. The nurse could not find a vain in one of my arms, so she switched to the other arm. After ten minutes of trying the 'IV' lines were in. My arms looked like bloody pin cushions. Not to worry, I was getting much needed fluid into my system, together with a host of other injections including; Antibiotics and vitamins. I was moved to a ward that had six other beds. White walls, new metal framed beds with mattresses and clean, crisp bed sheets. The windows overlooked a rose garden and a small hospital car park. The doctor came and spoke to me. Standard tests were carried out, my vital statistics, blood and urine. Due to the well-known bad conditions in Pul-i-Charkhi, the doctors gave me a full MOT just to make sure that I was alright. My friends in the Red-Cross had already briefed them on my unique situation and the fact that I had worked alongside other Red-Cross staff in the prison to help reduce the ill-treatment, torture and human rights violations. My friends within the Red-Cross had also remembered that before I had been illegally imprisoned in Afghanistan, I had brought a lot of much needed supplies and bags of toys for the children and sent them to the women's prison in Kabul. The conditions in that prison were equally as horrendous. Unbeknown to me at that time, I would soon be experiencing these kind of harsh and brutal conditions first hand. Buying and dropping off medical and other supplies is but a drop in the ocean of what is really needed, but every little helps. I had done similar drop offs to children's hospitals in Iraq during the war. The Red-Cross doctors had already contacted the British Embassy Kabul to inform them that I, a British National, was with them, receiving emergency medical treatment and that I would be staying in the hospital for a few days. The Afghan guards would be stationed outside the room. The doctors would not allow the Afghan prison guards into the hospital ward, as they didn't trust them. The hospital had problems with Afghan prison guards in the past few weeks; they had been trying to steal medical supplies so that they could sell them at the local market. The prison guards had tried to pull the same stunt of stealing, which they always habitually did, at the prison. The Red-Cross doctors were having none of it, so the guards were barred from the inside of the hospital. As one doctor told me, 'the bloody Afghan guards try to steal anything that is not nailed down'. The Afghan guards had no shame; this was considered normal practice in Afghanistan. In normal society, people would be arrested for stealing from a hospital. In Afghanistan it's just normal; this speaks volumes about the state of the Afghan society.

I drifted off that afternoon into a deep sleep, with the knowledge that I was safe. I woke up at 0800hrs the following morning. I had slept for well over 16hrs, completely oblivious to anything and everything that was going on around me. The doctor came and checked on me. The test results had come back, all were fine. The doctor was surprised that I was in fairly good health, given what my body had been though and the horrendous conditions that I had been subjected to. Due to my military training I had kept my body in as best shape as possible. Hygiene was very important so I had made sure that I was always clean. Given the conditions, I had done well to remain in relatively good health, without picking up any waterborne diseases or really bad knife injuries. The doctor noticed a few old scars, nothing to worry about. I told the doctor that you could not work and operate in combat zones for as long as I had, without collecting a few war wounds along the way. I still had a little internal bleeding caused by one of the beatings I had received from the guards, but my body was still gradually healing. This would just take time. All in all, I was lucky to be alive, so having my body in one piece was a bonus. The doctor asked me what I wanted to do about my hunger strike. I informed him that I would remain on my hunger strike until I had spoken to the British Embassy. The doctor understood what I was doing and my reasons behind my actions. The doctor told me to find a balance between my actions and my health. I was determined to make a point, but I did not want to cause myself any permanent damage. I knew just how much punishment my body could withstand. It had been through hell and back, as far as I was concerned it was just a case of mind over matter. I have to admit that at this point I could have killed for a steak sandwich. But it was not to be, I remained resolute.

The British Embassy turned up the next afternoon, or I should say Lawrence Jenkins and another office worker, they had no 'PSD' Personnel Security Detail. This was very odd and against Embassy protocol. They had also turned up in a normal civilian 4X4 vehicle (not armoured). The British Embassy did not even want its own security staff to know that I was in hospital in Kabul, due to the fact that I knew them personally. I watched Lawrence, through the large windows, conspicuously enter the Red-Cross hospital compound. Lawrence entered the hospital ward alone. He spoke to the duty doctor very briefly and then came over to speak to me. We shook hands, I was careful not to pull out my 'IV' lines. I motioned to a chair that was by the side of my bed; Lawrence was unshaven, something which drew my attention. He had always been clean shaven, well groomed and smart every time I had seen him in the past. Not this time, he was dressed in an open collar, badly creased white shirt, trousers and boots. He also wore a new 'North Face', all weather jacket. He sat down, commenting on the Wilbur Smith book 'Blue Horizon' on my bedside cabinet. He checked at his watch repeatedly; he seemed very self-conscious and preoccupied with the time for some reason. I asked Lawrence a straight question; what was the British Embassy Kabul doing about my case and the reported miscarriage of justice that I and my next of kin had officially informed them about? Lawrence told me that the British Embassy was looking into it. I again asked Lawrence if he and the British Embassy had obtained a copy of my so called official Afghan legal file, from the Afghan Ministry of Justice. Lawrence answered "No". I added that I had been waiting 18 months. So then, why did the British Embassy not have copies of the documents, and the reason why I was being held 'illegally' in an Afghan prison. Lawrence could not give me a straight answer, he was flustered and falling over his words, I felt like offering him some toilet paper, due to the amount of crap coming out of his mouth. The fact that he had come to see me, alone, spoke volumes. Whilst looking and observing the man in front of me, I remembered that; this was the man that had been lying and helping to keep me in prison illegally for the past 18 months at this point. He must have felt that he was dead smart, in thinking that his attempted cover-up of my situation would remain undetected forever. He would get a huge shock when he realised what was really going on. I hoped that when the truth came out he would hang his head in shame; his actions had shamed the good name of the British Embassy and FCO. I knew that day would come soon enough. The British Embassy did not, even after 18 months, have a copy of the charge sheet, or any evidence against me. I also asked another obvious question, as to why the British Embassy did not have any official documents regarding the fact that I had been illegally kidnapped by Afghan NDS, and then bundled into an Afghan prison. Again Lawrence could not look me in the eye or give me a straight answer. By the look of him and his body language he was in deep crap and he knew it. It was very obvious that Lawrence was not a former British military man; he still had his school boy look in his thirties. He looked more like a back office accountant than a front line military officer. I brought to his attention the fact that I could not get an Afghan Lawyer to help clear my name because the Taliban had previously threatened to kill any Lawyer and their families if they tried to represent me, this was because I was British. So I demanded to know what the British Embassy was going to do to help me resolve my situation. I did not even have a release date from prison. Lawrence changed the subject, asking me what it would take for me to break my hunger strike. My answer was pointed and contentious; get the British Embassy's 'rule of law' team, based within the British Embassy, to look into and investigate my case and situation. My objective was simple; to clear my name. Lawrence told me that he would talk to the British 'rule of law team'. I told him that my protest would continue until he had done it and I had received confirmation on this point. Upon me saying this he became agitated and his body language changed again. He became very twitchy. It was very obvious that he was under a lot of pressure. He went on talking for another minute or so, nothing really relevant. The Embassy was not happy about my hunger strike and I was beginning to draw a lot of attention. There was a great deal of politics involved in my case. My answer was again direct; deal with it. The politics are not my problem, they are yours. I then informed Lawrence that the Chief of Station (MI6) and the Chief of Staff, both located within the Embassy in Kabul, were fully aware of my predicament, so it was about time that they stopped trying to hide the truth and spend some time being productive. I also added that the British Embassy has abandoned over 100 members of the Commonwealth who were now also located in Pul-i-Charkhi prison, they needed urgent help and assistance. Lawrence didn't even answer me.

Lawrence stood up and left without shaking my hand. His meeting with me had lasted just under 20 minutes. His office worker, come driver, met him outside the ward opposite the windows. As Lawrence walked across the car park area he was shouting and throwing his arms in the air. Obviously his meeting with me had not gone according to plan. As far as I was concerned and from my perspective everything had gone exactly according to plan, just like clockwork. I knew what Lawrence was going to say; he tried telling me what I wanted to hear in an attempt to get me to come off my hunger strike. He had failed spectacularly. I could read Lawrence like a book. All I had done was put more pressure on him; he had now put even more pressure on himself. I knew that he was in deep political crap and he was not wearing the shoes for it. It was inevitable that my situation would cost Lawrence his current position within the British Embassy Kabul office; it was just a matter of time before his treachery caught up with him. My plan of action was working out perfectly on all levels. I was obviously a major thorn in the side of the British Embassy staff. But if they had done their job in the first place then I would not be a problem. It's pretty obvious really, the British Embassy staff should have known better than to set up, and piss off, a former British Paratrooper. I was always going to fight to clear my name and at the same time covertly work from within the Al-Qaeda and the Taliban network. All in a normal day's works for a British soldier...? If the Embassy staff wanted to shaft me, they had to be prepared to deal with the consequences. I have a golden rule 'don't say or do anything, unless you can prove it'. The big problem for the British Embassy was that I 'could' prove everything I had said. They knew that I could and wanted to keep me out of the way. I spent the next few days recovering in the Red-Cross hospital, building up my strength and my body. I had been through many challenging times during my time in the Middle-East and Afghanistan. The Pul-i-Charkhi situation had pushed my body to breaking point, but I have a very strong constitution. My belief system had been tested but remained steadfast. Principles are a very powerful force; they had kept me going through the dark times, when I did not think that I was going to live. It was all character building. The hospital staff allowed me to discreetly use one of their mobile phones. I called an old friend, who lived in Kabul. Within an hour he was on route to visit me at the hospital. An hour later the main doctor informed me that I had a visitor at the main entrance. The problem was that the British Embassy had already telephoned and informed the doctor that I was not allowed any visitors and no press or journalists were allowed to talk to me. Other hospital staff confirmed this; they had been in the room when the doctor had taken the phone call. The hospital staff were not impressed with the Embassy's actions. It was very clear that the Embassy wanted to control the situation and stop me having contact with anyone outside the hospital. The British Embassy was going to great lengths to keep me quiet. The Embassy had also informed the doctor that I was not allowed to use the phone. The doctor had been put in a very awkward position by the Embassy. I appreciated his dilemma. He thanked me for being so understanding and offered to take any messages or letters I had for my visitor. He would take them to my visitor and hand them to him personally. I told him that I would be very grateful in turn. Letters were written and full updates exchanged; these were passed on by my friend within 24hrs to my next of kin back in England. I settled down for my last night at the hospital. I made the most of its facilities, a long hot shower which felt amazing. My first hot shower in over 18 months, I was used to having to use a hose pipe in the court yard of the prison. For the first time in a year and a half I felt clean and fresh. The hospital staff had also washed my clothes so I was now looking a little more human. I must have looked completely wild when I first turned up. At least now, even if it was just for one more day I looked human. The Doctors should have returned me within 24hrs, but they had told me not to worry and they had organised for me to stay for a few more days. I really needed this little respite. It was a little snap shot of normal life, well normal life in Afghanistan anyway.

"The bloodbath of a Taliban suicide attack"

1800hrs, the peace and tranquillity of the hospital was shattered by the sound of two ambulances, their sirens wailing and lights flashing. They pulled up at speed into the emergency unloading area. There had been yet another Taliban suicide attack in Jalalabad city, east of the Capital, Kabul. Two seriously injured Afghans had been rushed straight from the horrific scene of the carnage. It had been yet another public market place full of innocent people, men, women and children that had been targeted and savagely murdered by the Taliban bomber. Two victims were quickly unloaded onto stretchers and hurried into the hospital emergency treatment rooms. Even from a distance, their injury's looked horrendous. The doctors knew that seconds could save lives in situations like this. Both of the Afghan men had multiple limbs missing, arms and legs ripped off when they had been hit by the blast from the explosion. One of the Afghan men had died in the emergency treatment room, despite the best efforts of the hospital staff, he had bled out. His internal injuries were so severe he did not have a chance. At least he would not suffer any longer, or have to live with the horror of what he had just witnessed. After sustained emergency treatment, the medical staff stabilized the condition of the remaining survivor. He was moved to the bed next to mine. Bloody stumps were all that remained of his legs and part of his left arm. They were still bleeding through the bandages and medical dressings; which seeped into the clean white bed sheets. This looked like a scene from a horror movie. The smell of burnt human flesh filled the air. Unfortunately, this was a daily scene in and across Afghanistan and the Middle-East. The Afghan in the bed next to mine was high on pain relief and had several 'IV' lines running into him. His broken voice kept on asking for his friends who had been with him at the market. The nurse whispered to me that his friends had all been killed in the suicide blast. This poor man's life and dreams had been shattered in the blink of an eye. This was another stark reminder of reality and what these terrorist are capable of. I wondered if this suicide attack had been ordered from within Pul-i-Charkhi prison, just one of the hundreds that was. Seeing this poor man lying next to me in such a state only hardened my resolve to continue my dangerous work inside the prison. Lying in my hospital bed that night, looking up across the bright star lit sky, I thought of Sam. I had last spoken to her just before the whole Afghan prison situation began. She had told me to be careful out here. Without even telling her, she would know that there would be one hell of a back story to my situation. I never really appreciated the sunshine of her smile until now. I thought of the true reason behind my hunger strike, infiltrating the Al-Qaeda terrorist network. The British and American Governments and their public have been lured into a false sense of security; distance is no longer one of their allies. Western Governments and their nationals are being targeted by terrorists in every civilised country, from Kenya to Boston and London to New York. My mind switched to battle ready mode, ready to wage war against the beast again. I drifted off to sleep that night and entered a dark realm haunted by death and carnage. After a very restless night I was returned to Pul-i-Charkhi. I would continue with my covert infiltration of the terrorist network.

Upon arriving back at Pul-i-Charkhi at 1100hrs, the first thing that stood out for me was how dark and dirty the whole prison looked. As I was driven through the main gates, under the dark shadow of the prison walls, I noticed the gaunt look on the prisoner's faces. The lost look in their eyes was one of no hope. The hellish life within the prison brought me crashing back to reality. The seriousness of what I was doing also hit home. I could be killed at any time. I had returned back to the lair of the beast and International terrorism. After a quick chat with Bevan about the state of play, I updated my diary, using the notes I had written over the past 3 days. I entered all the details of what had happened during my time in the hospital, including the visit by Lawrence Jenkins. For some reason I knew that all of these details would be very important in the future. Bevan had also kept a very detailed diary log of everything that was happening; we also arranged photocopies of all correspondence we received from the British Embassy and Afghan Government. Every month we would send all our documents and copies of our diaries out via a trusted friend who visited us. The documents were then transported to a secure location. I knew that one day all these documents would help me to clear my name. On my return to Pul-i-Charkhi, I discovered that my standing within the terrorist network and Al-Qaeda had been further enhanced. My public stand against some of the staff of the British Embassy Kabul, my refusal to pay a bribe to the Afghan judge and prosecutor and my battle against the corruption within the Afghan Government had placed me in a favourable light. My stand and actions had again gained me some interesting new ground amongst the terrorist Commanders and their men. My reputation and influence within the prison was growing. I had not intended to get a bad arse reputation within the prison; it had just worked out that way. Not to worry, it was all helping me work my way into the terrorist network and gain their trust. I had achieved the objective of my hunger strike, so at the 7 week point, I broke my fast and had some soup. It would take a week or so for my body to get used to normal food again. The prison Commander was relieved and came to see me. I told him that a British Embassy representative had visited me whilst I was in the hospital and that they were going to help me. I knew that this was bullshit, but hey! Lawrence Jenkins had lied to my face, and played me, or so he thought. But unknown to him, the reality was; I was playing him. His lies had showed him for what he really was. I had predicted the outcome of my hunger strike; my plan had worked like a dream. It had achieved all that I needed from it.

Later that day, I was invited over to the Al-Qaeda corridor. I was greeted by Saladin, all the other terrorist Commanders and their men. They all shook my hand and gave me a very warm welcome back into their domain. After a lot of handshakes and people saying well-done to me for my stand against the staff of the British Embassy, we drank chi-tea. Some of the terrorists started talking about their future planned attacks on British and American soldiers. This was the first time the terrorists had spoken so openly in front of me. This was a clear indication that I had been accepted by them. Saladin patted me on the back; he said 'welcome, we are your family'. This was another 'dear diary moment' I just smiled and said 'thank you'. My objective of infiltrating the terrorist network had been achieved, despite my almost dying and in danger of being killed several times in the process. Now I had to work on obtaining the information and intelligence that I required. After an hour of conversation and listening to the entire terrorist group talking about their future plans, I excused myself. I said that I was not feeling well, which was understandable after what I had just been through. Saladin walked me down to the gate and made sure I got back to my cell ok. He and the other terrorist Commanders sent me fresh food every day for the next week, so that I could regain my strength. I had lost 4 stone over the past 7 weeks and I was down to 8 stone. I was all skin and bone, another week on my hunger strike and my body would have started to die on me. I had taken it to the max. I had also beaten the Pul-i-Charkhi hunger strike record. It had to look genuine to Al-Qaeda and the only way to do that was to take it to the extreme. It was over now so the next chapter within the terrorist network had begun. I wanted and needed my body to get back to fighting fitness as quickly as possible. I had further objectives to achieve and terrorist attacks to sabotage. Plus, I wanted to find the most wanted international terrorist in the world 'Osama bin Laden'. Like I say to my men; 'be careful what you wish for'.

"The Hurt Locker"

The term 'Hurt Locker' has different meanings to different people. For some soldiers it means the state of mind of someone who is fighting his own internal battle in his own mind set, due to the extreme conditions and violent situations they sometimes find themselves in. (See Glossary PTSD). As soldiers, we make our living in what are at times extremely hazardous and challenging environments. Coping in these kinds of situations is what it is all about. Let's be honest, soldiers want to be in combat, it's why we join up and work in combat zones in the first place. As misguided an idea as it may be, it's generally the truth of the matter. Well, that and the pulling power of being a soldier with the ladies. Being thrown into combat is a highly dangerous experience. Watching men die violently for the first time is devastating and not something I would wish upon any young man. Some people say that combat will make a man out of you, I respectfully disagree. In reality, combat and having to fight for your life, destroys far more men than it makes. It will leave many dead or crippled for life, some with wounds you can see, but far more with wounds which you cannot. I knew all too well that the events and the unprecedented situation in Pul-i-Charkhi would scar me both physical and psychologically. I truly didn't expect to survive, so my life after Pul-i-Charkhi and my future, I had never really given a moment's thought to. I could not allow myself to be distracted by dreams of freedom. I just focused on staying alive and doing the job in hand. Unbeknown to me, I would soon find myself well and truly in the 'Hurt Locker'. I wrote the below poem during this dark and traumatic personal time.

Abandoned and Betrayed

The light of the day

Replaced by darkness absolute.

The feeling of stability shattered once again

By more political games played by the guards.

The feeling of breathing easily, replaced by a choking sensation.

My freedom and liberty yet again played with, like a cat plays with a mouse.

My impeccable record stands for nothing, I'm spoken to, as If I'm a nobody, less than that, just a number.

You follow the rules and it gets me nowhere. What's the point in trying, only to be knocked down again and again?

There is no justice here,

Punished and persecuted for doing nothing wrong, I'm British, standing up for what is right.

A dark negative cloud consumes me, my mood is dark, and everything seems pointless and meaningless.

I had more respect for the guards when they physically tortured me, that I could handle, I just soldiered on, but these mind games they play now are harder to grasp, probably because there is no reason or meaning in them. Again I'm forced to wash the blood off the walls and ceiling,

Prisoners being tortured again.

The way I deal with dark times like this,

I go within myself, shut the world out,

I cannot remember the last time I smiled or laughed,

They seem a world away; my memories seem to belong to a completely different person.

I look at the reflection in the broken window; who is this old rough stranger looking back at me.

I'm a shadow of my former self. The soldier with pride has gone, what is left is an empty shell, a void of emptiness no emotion,

Haunted by the demons, memories of past battles, lost friends and a life ripped from me.

There is nothing I can do or say, I look into the future through empty eyes, so I do the only thing I can

I soldier on, saving lives, like the countless, nameless soldiers before me...   By Anth Malone (Pul-i-Charkhi, Afghan)

"Fear"

Fear is a strange beast; it can appear at any time, regardless of who you are or what background a person comes from. It manifests itself in many different ways and forms. To some people it could be the fear of losing their job, or their partner. Some people have a fear of the dark or spiders. For a soldier it's not the dark places we fear, dark places are our friends. Some of our best work is conducted under the veil of darkness. The fear of dying has never really bothered me; it is just an occupational hazard, one which soldiers face every day in places like Afghanistan and across the Middle-East and Africa. What a soldier fears most of all is failure, the failure to complete a task or a mission. A soldier's other great fear is that he will let the side down when it really matters, under fire, on the battlefield, or when your men really depend on you. When push comes to shove, when the chips are down, when most men would buckle or break, soldiers don't, it is at this time that soldiers come into their own, we excel, some of us relish at the thought of going up against over-whelming odds. We are willing to fight to the bitter end for our fellow soldiers, our 'brothers in arms'. This is what is drummed into a soldier during their training. On the battle field you 'hold the line', because if one of the bad guys gets through he could kill someone. Our mind set that is drummed into us during intense military training is; British soldiers do not lose, ever. We push forward, regardless of the risks; we do not know how to fail. Failure to a soldier is worse than death itself. The thought of letting your team, friends or country down is not an option. When soldiers are young, we all think that we are immortal and invincible. We have to think of ourselves as being immortal just to carry out orders and tasks in battle. During this time, some of us will display remarkable courage and fortitude in the face of horrendous adversity. For me, failure to complete my tasks in Pul-i-Charkhi was not an option. It was simple, if I failed, American and British soldiers would die, period!

Back to the present;

I received no visits (duty of care) or contact from the British Embassy for well over six weeks after the last 'unofficial' visit by Lawrence Jenkins at the hospital. I call it 'unofficial' because Embassy security was not informed of the hospital visit and it had not been logged in the Embassy movement's book which is kept in their Operations Room. This little point was later confirmed by Embassy security staff when they came to visit me, without the permission of the Embassy. My next 'official' visit from the British Embassy was by Trudy Kennedy the British Vice Consul. Lawrence Jenkins was on leave at the time. Trudy had no update on any aspect of my case or situation. She said that Lawrence Jenkins was dealing with my case. Over 7 weeks later Lawrence came to visit me at Pul-i-Charkhi; he also had no update for me whatsoever. Lawrence in turn told me that Trudy Kennedy was dealing with my case. I told Lawrence that it had been over three months since his hospital visit. I told him to cut the 'bullshit' and give me a straight answer, what was he and the British Embassy doing about putting right my miscarriage of justice and was the British Embassy rule of law team officially investigating the reported miscarriage of justice. He looked at me with a completely blank expression on his face. He stumbled over his words; it was very obvious that he had lied to my face in the hospital. He had told me what I had wanted to hear to try and get me to come off my hunger strike. Once again I challenged

Lawrence about the Embassy's phone call to the hospital, ordering that I was not allowed any visitors or phone calls. Lawrence lied again and said that it never happened. What Lawrence did not know was that someone I knew was standing in the room within the Embassy when he had made that phone call? They were disgusted at his actions and behaviour. Lawrence would later be removed from his job in the consulate due to my case and high level internal British Embassy politics.

"Strictly need to know and the British Embassy did not need to know"

The Americans had been quietly observing my progress from the side lines. They knew that all my actions were well thought out and all my actions had a good reason and logic behind them. All the information and intelligence I had been covertly handing over to the Americans had been checked by their 'CT' (Counter Terrorism) experts and they deemed my intelligence totally accurate. Grade 'A' source. Nothing new there, my intelligence was always spot on. However the detail and scope of what I was handing over was unique and had gotten senior American intelligence's attention. I had hit a raw nerve somewhere. At this point my actions and Intelligence gathering had conservatively prevented and disrupted over 100 terrorist attacks on American and British soldiers across Afghanistan, Iraq and farther afield. The feedback from the Americans was good. They acted upon all the intelligence I had risked my life to get for them. Working forwards, American Intelligence and the American military were achieving great results. The daily routine which I had accustomed myself to over the past months kicked in again, I was soon back to my old self. 'Making friends and influencing people'. I had no idea that my situation was going to last another one and a half years. I should have been killed long ago, but I was still alive, kicking and going strong. I continued to work my way up the Al-Qaeda Command and control structure. The Intelligence I was acquiring was unprecedented but so were the risks. I felt that the closer I got to high level intelligence the closer I was getting to my own death. I just had to stay focused. Lives depended on my acquiring and getting this intelligence out to the Americans. The Al-Qaeda, Pakistan Taliban and Afghan Taliban had ordered a dramatic increase in the number of attacks on British and American soldiers, military and soft civilian targets across Afghanistan and the Middle-East. The daily attacks had increased tenfold. Car bombings, IED's and suicide attacks were taking place every day, hitting multiple targets. These terrorist attacks were now being coordinated and were hitting their targets simultaneously. The attacks were also becoming more detailed and worryingly, a lot better organised and effective. The Terrorist network within Pul-i-Charkhi was on overdrive, multiple terrorist attacks everyday were being planned, ordered and coordinated. These figures were staggering, as were the body counts from the attacks. I was working 24/7 just to keep up with them and the increase in all the terrorist activities. I really needed a full team with me to collate and assess all the information; the problem was there was only me. So I maximised my day, not a minute was wasted. I even started to eat over in the Al-Qaeda corridor and I only returned to my cell to sleep and write reports for the Americans. Al-Qaeda and the Pakistan Taliban actually wanted me to move over to their corridor. I told them that this would be great but that I had a duty to teach Bevan about Islam and show him the 'error' of his ways, plus I also knew that the prison Commander would not agree to this. I was relieved when my moving permanently over to the Al-Qaeda corridor was refused because I needed privacy during the few hours in the early hours of the morning 1am till 5am to sleep and write out my reports. The Americans had to visit the prison every 4 to 5 days to pick up my reports. I had been tasked as a priority pickup by American Intelligence. On many occasions I would be with the Al-Qaeda and Taliban in their corridor hurling abuse at the Americans whilst Bevan slipped the written reports to the designated person. On occasions I would have to meet with the Americans and Bevan would create a diversion, not only telling the Al-Qaeda corridor that he needed to 'chat to me', but then keeping the Afghan guards at bay as I briefed, or was tasked, by the Americans. That's what 'wingmen' are for right!

One morning after one of my reports had been covertly picked up using a 'dead drop', several Americans turned up and bomb burst all over the prison block (they all entered the block and walked off in different directions). Their Chief of party quietly stayed at the back of the group. He waited for his people to distract and take all the Afghan prison guards off in different directions. He then quietly came and spoke to me in my cell. My report from the previous pickup had checked out. It had received senior intelligence attention due to the fact I had included in-depth details of a planned Pakistan Taliban attack on America. Pakistan Taliban leader 'Hakimullah Mehsud' was planning and ordering an attempted car bombing in 'Times Square' New York, to create mayhem and death in the city - this report I had written, I had personally handed to Walter Downs American Military Intelligence. My report had been very detailed and accurate. Several other very sensitive pieces of information were also stated within the report, including new safe house locations for the Pakistan Taliban and a list of contact phone numbers. The Pakistan Taliban changed their numbers every month, so getting hold of the new ones was crucial and now deemed a priority. The phone numbers were being used in several countries. Due to my reports being accurate, I was then officially tasked (my original tasking by Walter extended) to cover and gain intelligence on Al-Qaeda and Pakistan Taliban operations in Afghanistan, Pakistan and across American 'Cent-Com' (American Central Command) the American area of operations, which covered the whole of the Middle-East. David Petraeus was the Commander of 'Cent-Com' at this time, just prior to him becoming the Director of the CIA. The Chief of party with who I was talking to, was senior American military intelligence; his rank was full Colonel. He had a lot of contacts at CIA headquarters in Langley (see Glossary Langley-CIA). He knew about the work I had done previously in Iraq for the American military. I asked him to confirm that I had 'Top-Cover', he nodded and smiled. We understood each other. He asked if I needed anything. I hadn't received any food from the outside for years, so if I started to receive food now it would be noticed by the terrorists and would look odd and make them suspicious. We agreed on this point and decided that it was not worth the risk. I thanked him for the offer but respectfully declined. The Al-Qaeda and the Taliban were banging on their cell doors because the Americans were in the prison block. The noise was deafening. The Americans left as quickly as they had arrived. I asked the guards what was going on. They were clueless as normal. After the American visit I felt a little more secure and reassured about my situation and

I knew that there would be a lot of good that would come out of all this. Even with my own British Embassy abandoning me, the Americans would not abandon me; the Americans had picked up all the slack that the British Embassy staff had left. The Americans were still in disbelief at what the staff from the British Embassy had done to me. I had been told straight, that if I had possessed a 'blue' (American) passport, I would never have been put, or left, in an Afghan prison in the first place, especially with my military history and the previous intelligence work which I had carried out. Due to the internal politics within the British Embassy Kabul and due to some staff being embarrassed because of my work and ground breaking results, some of the Embassy staff were trying to silence me? The British Embassy staff had read me and my situation very wrong. Even from within Pul-i-Charkhi I had my own network across the Middle-East at my fingertips. I now started to use all my contacts. I gave my trusted people outside, and contacts, a very brief overview of what I needed, information and intelligence. I broke it down into several areas of interest. It was like the flood gates had opened, I worked from inside Pul-i-Charkhi and from within the Al-Qaeda and the Taliban networks. My contacts and team worked on the outside. I had worked with my people and contacts across the Middle-East in the past, including operations and covert action in; Syria, Iraq, Lebanon, Saudi Arabia, Kenya and Somalia. We had all been through some emotional and dangerous times together and I trusted them all with my life, as they did me. We had all survived the hellish battle fields of Iraq. The notorious and murderous Syrian secret police in Damascus, who we had evaded, and Hezbollah terrorists in Lebanon, not forgetting, brain washed Al-Shabab fighters in Somalia and Kenya. Pul-i-Charkhi was just another chapter in my 'road less travelled life'. I utilized all my 'HumInt' (Human Intelligence) contacts and the assets that I had at my fingertips. I had cleared my using phones and calling out of Pul-i-Charkhi with the Americans, so I was not worried about voice intercepts. My doing this was also helping the Americans to trace, track and locate terrorist by 'triangulating' and locking onto their mobile phone signals. No doubt the Americans would use this intelligence to drop a few Hellfire missiles from their drones. Information was now streaming into me from several different sources, daily. It was nice to feel on top of my game again. It felt as if I had never been out of the loop at all; in reality I had been out the loop for over 18 months, but I had slotted right back into my work and network like a well-fitting leather glove. Everyone knew about my situation, that I had been screwed by my own Embassy 'plausible deniability', so everyone was all too ready and willing to help me and in some cases my contacts and my personal team, including many former American and British officers and seasoned Special Forces personnel, went well above and beyond the call of duty in helping me. With all the intelligence that was coming in to me, and my being able to access intelligence from within the Al-Qaeda and the international terrorist networks being ran from within Pul-i-Charkhi, I was able to write unprecedented intelligence reports. These included; Locations of terrorist safe houses and IED factories in several sensitive countries; locations, dates and timings of Taliban weapons and explosives shipments being smuggled from Iran into Afghanistan, to be used against British and American soldiers in Helmand; and Bank account details used by terrorists to finance terrorist operations, including suicide bombings; details of planned terrorist attacks including; where, when and how these terrorist attacks were to be carried out. I had the contact details of over 80 active international terrorists and a lot of other information which had been classified under the British Governments official secrets act. Things were moving in the right direction and the Americans were very happy with my progress and the accurate, workable intelligence that I was acquiring. I was also focusing on locating HVT's, including Osama bin Laden. I was getting closer with every month I spent in Pul-i-Charkhi.

Al-Qaeda's own 'Hum-Int' network was good and far reaching. Al-Qaeda, from within the prison, had already confirmed the British Embassy Kabul actions on my hunger strike and the fact that I had really upset the Embassy staff by my actions. Al-Qaeda still had Afghan translators working within the British Embassy on their payroll. Al-Qaeda and the Taliban were acquiring a lot of information from within the British Embassy. I had already notified the Americans about this. They would discreetly pass this on to MI6 and British intelligence. But they would never reveal the source of the information. So my arse would remain covered. I wanted to keep the loop of people who knew the truth about my activities within Pul-i-Charkhi very small. 'This was on a need to know basis and the British Embassy did not need to know'. Late one night I began to compile a comprehensive 40 page hand written report for the Americans. A pickup had been arranged for the next morning. My rule was that within 12hrs of my writing a report, it would be picked up by American intelligence. I could not risk any information being in Pul-i-Charkhi for more than 12 hours. If the guards or terrorists ever found it I would be killed, so I lessened the risk factor whenever I could. I wrote up everything from my notes between 11pm and 5 am under the cover of reading and studying Islam. The reality was I spent this time reading, analysing and writing my intelligence reports. When I had finished, I destroyed all my notes, by cutting them up then putting them into a bottle, adding hot water and shaking it. This process turns all the paper to mush and in doing so makes it impossible to retrieve the paper or the information on it. It's a very basic method but it works well. One name in particular kept on cropping up during my investigation from within the terrorist network, 'The Fox'. The Fox was everywhere and nowhere. In Radical Mosques, people would whisper his name, as if he was a phantom or a ghost. Al-Qaeda and other terrorist fighters that I had met, wrote poems about him. American Special forces had found other intelligence confirming that the Fox was a terrorist Commander. He left no trace or leads to what he really was, or his true identity. In the diffuse world of Al-Qaeda and the Pakistan Taliban, the Fox had become a true operational planner and military leader. The Fox was the man who had fused the class of terrorist 1999 from Kabul and Islamabad with the class of 2014 from Baghdad, Beirut, Damascus and Kabul. The Fox was a bridge, the link between the old terrorist's ideology and that of the new breed. The Pakistan Taliban and Al-Qaeda membership increases with every month and year that goes by. Many of the fighters within the Pakistan Taliban are Al-Qaeda but for political reasons have de-badged themselves. Many of the Afghan Taliban has also done this, again purely for appearances sake. Many male members of Fox's family and friends had been killed by American signature CIA drone strikes in Afghanistan and across Waziristan, Western Pakistan. The Fox was known to be a member of the Terrorist leadership, and in being so, his notoriety resulted in him being placed on the American 'capture or kill' list. Nobody had actually seen the Fox for years. The Americans did not even have a photograph of the man, or so they thought. Due to him falling off the American HVT radar, many had thought that he was fighting a Jihad in Iraq or Syria, even Yemen was said to be one of the countries that he was involved in, an active Jihad that was linked to the Afghan terrorist networks. The truth was far more interesting. Some of his family were also senior members of the Haqqani terrorist network which was closely interwoven with the Pakistan Taliban and Al-Qaeda. The Haqqani terrorist network which operated across Afghanistan, Pakistan and far beyond, this network and its leadership council were now a priority target for American intelligence. Al-Qaeda members and fighters often moved between groups and most of the terrorist groups operating across the Middle-East and Africa are sharing intelligence, fighters and safe houses.

"Lost American specialist weapons and equipment including; Stinger missiles, sniper rifles and 'silenced' M4 rifles, with thermal imagery and Generation 4 night vision, being used by terrorists to kill American and British troops"

Weapons were also being shared; including captured and lost American weapons; Stinger Missiles; 50 calibre sniper rifles and M4 5.56mm assault rifles which were fitted with silencers and scopes. All these weapons had been sprayed painted in a factory in America, desert 'cammo' colour, which made them stand out from the normal American M4 assault rifles. Over 180 of these weapons had been lost by the American military while they were in transit in Pakistan. The terrorists now had them. A senior Pakistan politician had bought them when they had first gone missing; he was now selling them on, for a large profit. Many of these weapons had been seen and discovered in Afghanistan, Iraq and Syria. Some of them had even found their way to Somalia. The American CIA had tried to retrieve these weapons but failed. I had acquired photographs and the serial numbers of some of them. I had passed this information onto American intelligence. A worrying fact that came to light was that some of these weapons had been found on dead Taliban fighters in Helmand, Afghanistan. Stolen specialised American weapons were now killing British and American soldiers across Afghanistan and the Middle-East. No wonder the Intelligence Services wanted to keep this quiet (See photographs of examples of stolen military equipment at rear of book). Al-Qaeda wanted the terror and killing to spread from the streets of Afghanistan, Iraq and Syria, onto the streets and within the cities of Western Countries, such as London, Paris and New York. The Fox and his men shared this sentiment. The Americans and the British had 'CT' (Counter Terrorism) analysts working on trying to locate the Fox, but with no success. Little did they know that the top American military General in Afghanistan at that time had already met him? The problem was that the General had no idea of the Fox's true identity at that time. The General had interrogated the Fox at the Black Prison, located within Bagram Air Base, in Northern Afghanistan. The General had asked the Fox where his boss, 'Osama bin Laden', was located. The Fox had just laughed at the question and said that he is everywhere and nowhere. He was behind him. The American General had shouted at the Fox and stormed out of the room. The Fox took great delight in retelling me this story many times over tea and nuts. He liked to refer to 'himself' as the Fox. He had a network of sleepers who could operate under the radar. They were able to build car bombs and IED's, put them in place and then escape. These Al-Qaeda operatives knew their stuff. They implemented surveillance and counter surveillance techniques, used stolen cars as there means of delivery and wore a wide range of disguises whilst they move around. They were known to wear gloves most the time and have been known to have worn women's clothes including the Islamic 'Burka' to avoid detection.

"Every terrorist bomb maker at some point, gets bitten by his own work"

Al-Qaeda and Pakistan Taliban IED and bomb makers also wear gloves when making and assembling their IED's and suicide bombs. This was done to prevent the Americans and ISAF from identifying who the bomb makers were by their finger prints and DNA. One important fact that I have found to be very true is, every bomb maker at some point gets bitten by his own work. Many bomb makers that I have met and seen from Syria, Lebanon, Iraq and Egypt have missing fingers or eyes. The Americans had started to collect all the fragments of exploded IEDs and ones that had been seized. A fingerprint database was now up and running (from 2006 onwards in Afghanistan). The Americans were tracking the bomb makers across Syria, Lebanon, Afghanistan, Pakistan and the whole of the Middle-East and Africa including; Egypt, Libya, Mali, Algeria, Nigeria, Somalia, Kenya and Tanzania. The new age of Al-Qaeda and international terrorism is very professional and widespread and has strong political protection in several Islamic countries. As of 2014 Western Intelligence agencies did not know the identity of the Fox, I would soon change that.

"Bedouin of Arabia and my moody camel"

I read, studied and had developed a keen interest in Middle-East history and poetry 'Rumi'. My knowledge of Persian poetry and history intrigued the terrorists. I was slowly but surely in their eyes, becoming more like them. Everything I did was aimed at building my credibility within the terrorist network. I used all my past knowledge and skills that I had learned during my time spent in and across the deserts of Arabia. The Arab Bedouin are the best navigators in the world; they can travel through deserts without maps with only the wind and the stars in the night sky to guide them. I had spent some time living with the Bedouin in and across the vast golden deserts of 'Old Arabia', talking and sharing dates, salted meats and water, around camp fires late into the cool nights of the desert. I had been a keen listener, taking in all their knowledge and wealth of experience. The lessons that I had learned from them on many subjects, including cultural understanding, were becoming invaluable given my present situation. While in Pul-i-Charkhi I retold some of my stories of life in the desert. I recalled a funny story about the time my moody camel decided to eat my food when I was not looking. The bloody wretched beast had a habit of running off in completely the opposite direction to which I wanted to travel. This became a big problem when I was sat on top of the bloody thing. After many months we eventually became a team, and after a lot of hard work, it did what I asked of it. I had also discovered that it had a sweet tooth and liked certain sweets, so often I bribed it too. The stories of my adventures across the deserts of Arabia always made the Afghan and Arab prisoners laugh, so it helped to break the ice. The more I was seen interacting with the other prisoners including the Taliban the better.

"Air Power; AC130 Combat Talon, Apache helicopter gunships and parachuting"

One cool morning when I was walking with members of Al-Qaeda in the caged area at the back of the prison block, I noticed that the American Air force was flying 'CAP's (Combat Air Patrols) over Kabul and Pul-i-Charkhi. This always happened when the fighting was close to Kabul. The Americans were carrying out refuelling of their fighter jets over Kabul and Pul-i-Charkhi. This was odd because I knew that the American Air force was not supposed to carryout mid-air refuelling over population centres. The F16s were fully loaded with missiles and bombs and were carrying extended fuel tanks. These F16s were on call for 'Air Strikes' in Pakistan and Eastern Afghanistan. The unmistakable roar of two A10s, American jet aircraft also known as the 'tank buster', came over Pul-i-Charkhi at 300 feet. The A10s always travelled and hunted in pairs, they never hunted alone. A long, high pitch sound suddenly filled the prison compound; American Apache helicopter gunships were flying at low level and playing tag between the prison blocks. I loved watching all of this. On the contrary, Al-Qaeda and the rest of the terrorists on the other hand hated it. The Americans just did it to piss the terrorists and prisons off. It was a good show of force. This also gave me a great confidence boost as a soldier doing my work within the prison and the terrorist network. Later that morning C130s, American military transport aircraft also passed over Pul-i-Charkhi at less than 300 feet. This made the whole prison block shake. I loved the sight and sound of these aircraft; all Para's love the C130 aircraft, aka 'Fat Albert', because they are the planes we, as Para's, have to jump out of most frequently. There is nothing like jumping out of a perfectly good serviceable aircraft with a parachute strapped to your back. Military parachuting is an extremely dangerous environment. Sixty-four guys crammed into the back of a C130, thirty-two each side, each man wearing a parachute weighing 55lb on his back. He also has a container, a 'Bergen rucksack' and weapon valise strapped to his legs that can weigh anything up to 160lb, your overall weight is well over 200lb. When you're standing up ready to go out the door, about to be deployed into the aircrafts slip stream by the 'PJI' (Parachute Jump Instructor) with a container hooked onto your front by two hooks situated just below your reserve chute. The hooks are released manually and the container hangs 15 feet below you, after your parachute has been deployed and you're in 'clear air', having made sure that there is no other parachutist below you. I have done well over 100 parachute jumps and still love the adrenaline rush of jumping out of a bucking aircraft at 1000 feet. Jumping at night is even more fun. The only problem is that sometimes you cannot see or judge the distance to the ground, then all of a sudden this big green thing comes out of nowhere and hits you hard. You then lay there on your back looking up at the sky for a split second, thanking God for a safe landing. My first jump had been 22 years ago whilst I was serving with 4 Para, D Company 'patrols platoon', before I joined 3 Para. My first balloon jump was also a very strange experience. I stood in a basket which was hanging beneath what resembled a Second World War barrage balloon. A large wooden box, known as the basket or cage, suspended below it. They are capable of carrying five men; four jumpers and a PJI (Parachute Jump Instructor). It's open topped with an opening at one end, with a small flimsy metal safety bar across the exit. The Balloon is tethered via a strong steel cable to a winch truck 800 feet below. When the winch has let the balloon rise to 800 feet it stops and is turned off. At this point there is an eerie stillness and silence, only the creaking of the cage and the wind can be heard. Apart from these faint noises, the world is silent. When the wind picks up the cage swings unnervingly in a rocking motion. You don't really have time to enjoy the amazing 360-degree view of the countryside below or the peace and tranquillity. The thought of throwing yourself out of the side of a balloon cage is an unnerving and daunting feeling. Anyone who likes doing this is not right in the head and it's not a normal act. God did not mean us mere mortals to fly. In the cage, the PJI moved forward to lift the safety bar at the exit. As I stood alone in the doorway with the whole world stretched out beneath me, I remember thinking 'what the fuck am I doing here'. I noticed the Red Cross painted on the roof of the ambulance 800 feet below me. If my parachute did not open I would need a lot more than a bloody ambulance, they wouldn't need a stretcher to recover me, and they would need a shovel. The PJI shouted "Red on". After weeks of training I instinctively let go of the bars on each side of the door and folded my arms across the top of my reserve chute. A second later the PJI slapped me on the left shoulder and yelled "Green on", "Go". I launched myself out of the doorway into the silent emptiness. For a split second I seemed to move forward not down, like in the cartoons when the character realises he has just fallen of a cliff edge and stands motionless, before, gravity takes over and you are hit with a rapid descent, falling sensation 200 feet in three seconds, what a rush, you look up and check that your parachute has deployed correctly. The words 'thank God' normally come out of my mouth at that glorious moment. Then it's just a case of controlling your descent towards the ground, as you're about to land, you get ground rush then the ground hits you and your training kicks in. I have to admit that there have been a few times when the Para roll has gone out the window and I have landed like a sack of shit. Luckily I have never been seriously injured, 'touch wood'. After I land, I always give my body the quick once over to make sure I have all my body parts still intact and in the right places. I have had many close calls when jumping, one of them was when I collided and went through the rigging lines of a fellow parachutist when we had collided under the back of the aircraft at 900 feet. We came down on one fully inflated parachute; we communicated on the way down and jettisoned our containers to minimize the weight and reduce the risk of both of us being killed or injured. We both had hard landings but safely walked away from the incident. This was a timely reminder that people can be killed very easily and that accidents do happen.

One of the Elite AC130 Combat Talons, the mother of all gunships and weapon platforms was the last aircraft to fly over Pul-i-Charkhi that day. It came over low level at well under 200 feet, the sound was deafening, but it looked and sounded spectacular. I knew what a Combat Talon was; I smiled as it flew at low level over my head, on route to deliver its payload onto a designated terrorist target. God help anyone who was caught on the receiving end of the life ending firepower of the AC130. I silently wished the aircraft and its crew good luck and good hunting on their mission. I had seen the AC130 gunships operating in Iraq, when they had wiped out an entire terrorist training camp in the Western desert. The rate of firepower, destruction and death, delivered by the AC130 weapons platform is awe inspiring and absolute. Basically every bad guy within 1km of the target area was wiped out. 'Happy Days', the Angel of Death had paid them a visit. I felt a great confidence and reassurance in the knowledge that AC130 weapons platforms were operating in Afghanistan and across the Middle-East.

 Russian made 'HIND' helicopter gunships are effective work horses and were the back bone of the Afghan Air force due to the fact that they were not allowed any new jet fighters by the Americans. New faster fighter jets would make the Afghan Air force independent. The Americans did not want that for obvious reasons.

The HIND's would also frequently buzz the prison blocks. The down force and vibrations of the HINDs, buzzing the blocks at 150 feet sent pots and pans flying off the walls and across rooms, on more than one occasion windows were even smashed due to the down force from the helicopter blades. I thought this was great, but the terrorists within the prison would kick right off at the guards about it. This was pointless because the prison guards were completely powerless to stop such things happening anyway, the terrorists just took their frustrations out on the guards. That was cool because during such occurrences I would not be the target of their petulance anymore. Due to the high risk from the Taliban of SAMs, 'Surface to Air' missiles being fired at aircraft over Kabul and across Afghanistan, all military aircraft were flying at low level in and out of American air bases. The Afghan Taliban via The Pakistan Taliban and Al-Qaeda had brought shipments of SAMs 'Surface to Air Missiles' into Afghanistan from Pakistan and Iran. American 'Stinger' advanced Surface to Air Missiles, were also reported to be in the hands of Taliban fighters, in and around the capital Kabul. The American and British Government had given the 'Muj' Afghan fighters in the 1980s hundreds of 'Stingers' and 'Blow pipes' Surface to Air Missiles. Years later, Western Government's missiles were being used against their own military forces. The American and British Governments had tried unsuccessfully to retrieve these weapons. The problem was the proliferation of such weapons. Western Governments including America and Britain did not want such weapons as SAMs Surface to Air missiles falling into the hands of international terrorists. I remember thinking; God forbid Al-Qaeda ever getting their hands on such weapons. If they ever did, terrorists could bring down any passenger airliner over any country in the world. So understandably, the retrieval or destruction of such weapons was imperative. I had worked with American intelligence and British Special Forces in the past to locate and track those weapons. The results of such work were very interesting; some things though are best left unsaid due to the sensitivity of what happened and the nature of such events being classified.

Two Russian built 'HIP' helicopters; (troop carriers), would also often fly low level over Pul-i-Charkhi prison. They were carrying and operated by Afghan Special Forces. The two 'HIP's were stationed at 'Camp Moorhead', a Special Forces base and training school run by the American Special Forces for the Afghan military. I had conducted a lot of live fire training on the ranges there. I would often take my team members up there to test fire my personal weapons and to conduct live fire training. I had an open invitation from the American Military to use their facility (See photographs). I had seen the two 'HIP' Russian helicopters training there many times. It was a little surreal now seeing them again flying over my head in Pul-i-Charkhi. These two 'HIP's were very distinctive because they had a special ramp built into the rear of them, this enabled equipment and quad bikes to be loaded and unloaded very quickly. This ramp also enabled troops to swiftly 'de-bus' (get off) the helicopter. This enabled the helicopter pilots to carry out fast drop-offs and pick-ups in hostile territory while under enemy fire, which in Afghanistan was always a possibility. The Turkish military had their own way of preventing the Taliban from shooting down their military Blackhawk helicopters. Their tactic was hidden in plain sight. The Turkish military had painted large Turkish flags on the sides and bottoms of all their Blackhawk helicopters. This was done so the Taliban and Al-Qaeda could spot them and tell the difference between the American and Turkish helicopters. This did not make much sense to me at first, but I was told by members of the Taliban and Al-Qaeda why the Turkish military had done such a thing. A secret deal had been brokered between the Turkish Military and the terrorists. The deal was that no helicopters bearing the Turkish flag would be shot down or targeted by the terrorists; in return the Turkish military would not kill any terrorist Commanders. I had thought the real reason was because Muslims did not want to kill other Muslims, obviously I was wrong there. This is just another example of how nothing is clean cut in Afghanistan.

One afternoon, I quietly observed a convoy of American Blackhawk helicopters flying over Pul-i-Charkhi prison. One of them had just dropped off some prisoners to 'Git-Mo', the helicopter then flew right over Block 10 at no more than 50 feet. Hussein came out and sat with me in the metal chicken run (cage). He pointed to the Blackhawk helicopters that were just flying over the prison walls; Hussein spoke one word in English as he pointed, "danger". The door gunner sitting on the side of the American Blackhawk was only about 30 meters way; the smile on his face was visible. He waved at Hussein; this made the situation even funnier. I burst out laughing. I told Hussein that he had made a new friend; the look of utter disgust on Hussein's face was absolutely priceless. The American door gunner thought that Hussein had waved to him. Hussein totally 'threw his toys out of his pram'. He stormed off into the prison block cursing in Arabic and stamping his feet. Bevan passed him on his way out. Bevan looked at me, I was laughing my head off and Bevan asked what had tickled my fancy. I told him what had happened, he too burst out laughing. The Blackhawk flew away at low level over the prison and out of sight. The next time Bevan and I saw Hussein, we pointed at him and said 'Danger', after a few days Hussein had calmed down and saw the funny side. Hussein's prison sentence was in excess of 38 years. He had been caught selling two American 'Stinger', SAM's 'Surface to Air missiles' to the Taliban. Hussein had also previously helped several Al-Qaeda member's escape from Pul-i-Charkhi in 2008. Another interesting point was that Hussein was a member of the Pakistan 'ISI' (Government Intelligence Services). His day job was acting quartermaster for the Al-Qaeda and the Taliban network in Pul-i-Charkhi prison. Hussein was their fixer and paymaster. If you wanted anything, Hussein was the terrorist to go and see. From a rocket launcher to a phone call to Al-Shabab or Al-Qaeda Commanders in Iraq and Syria, Hussein was the man to deliver. He was due to be released from prison soon. Al-Qaeda and the Pakistan

Taliban had paid the Afghan Chief Prosecutor. This was just how things worked in Afghanistan. Hussein had friends in high places.

"American soldier Bowe Bergdahl, official POW Prisoner Of War"

Members of the Taliban and Haqqani network had captured American soldier Bowe Bergdahl in 2009, South Eastern Afghanistan. The Taliban quickly handed him over to senior leaders of the Haqqani network, along the tribal belt area of Waziristan, which was situated along the Pakistan Western border. I had reported the handover from Taliban to the Haqqani network to American military intelligence. I added that the Haqqani network was, at that point, trying to move Bowe Bergahi out of Pakistan to Yemen or Somalia. Several Al-Qaeda leaders, AQAP and AQI were present at these locations at that time. Bowe Bergdahl is officially listed and reported as an American 'POW' Prisoner of War. The Haqqani network was in the process of organising with terrorist Commanders inside Pul-i-Charkhi and negotiating with the Afghan Government, a prisoner exchange. Several names of terrorists being held in Block 10 were on the list of prisoners to be exchanged. 'Hussein' was one of those named. This list had just been handed over to members of the Afghan Parliament during one of their meetings within the prison. Hussein had asked me if I wanted my name added to the list. This was a 'dear diary moment'; this was the first of many such offers. I refused his offer on the grounds of principle. The British Embassy would have had a bloody heart attack if my name had been added to that list for the Al-Qaeda and Taliban prisoner exchange. The Americans thought that the offer was quite amusing given the situation and what I was really doing in Pul-i-Charkhi. This event confirmed that I was being accepted by the leadership of the terrorist network operating from the prison. The prisoner exchange fell through on this occasion. There would be plenty more secret exchanges in the future. (Update Bow was released in a prisoner exchange which was given the green light by the American President). That afternoon I sat in the sweltering heat in the Al-Qaeda corridor with Hussein reading the Qur'an. The corridors were dark and gloomy places; there were parts of the block that never received sunlight. The inside doom and gloom was a stark contrast to the blinding bright sunlight outside. The smell that came out from within the block was over powering, when the heat of the day turned the whole of the prison block into one big sweat box. Some days it was like being in an over bearing sauna. The smell of captivity, men living on top of each other in cramped squalid conditions, was a reminder to me of how some of these Afghan men lived. Some of the corridors on the bottom floor were really bad, I walked past some of the cells when the doors were open, the stench was shocking and it smelled like animals were living in there. Some of these men had not washed for months they were grotty and stinking from head to foot. The guards made sure that all the dirty prisoners that did not want to wash were kept on the bottom floor at the end of the corridors. I was glad that I was up on the next floor, at least we were always clean and tidy. Even the big rats did not hang around in the bottom corridors, hungry prisoners would quickly make a meal out of a rat or an unlucky bird that strayed into the corridors when the windows were open. I walked past the end of the bottom corridor on my way up the stairs, a scorpion scurried past me. I thought that this is a hell of a place to be, 'Hell', being the operative word. I took a few photographs of the inside of the prison block and the corridors. I captured the harsh conditions, rotten rubbish months old piling up the walls of some of the corridors, rats and other rodents, spiders and scorpions feeding on the over flowing human waste and blood outside the prison blocks. I thought that these photographs would be good keep sakes for the future. They would also be good evidence of what the deplorable conditions were really like. I took some photographs of the spare keys that the terrorists had, for the locks and prison gates. Al-Qaeda and the Taliban were planning an escape, so for good measure I took photographs of their escape route, out of the back of the prison block and over the wall via a guard tower. I took some good shots of the compound, the gates and walls, this was max security and I was just walking around discreetly taking snap shots on my camera phone of the important areas of the prison. I knew that these photographs would come in handy in the future. If I was caught taking photographs by Al-Qaeda or the Taliban it would have been a bad day for me, probably ending with my head being cut off. Luckily I did not get caught. I would later use them to show the Americans how Al-Qaeda planned to escape. The Americans could not believe that I had images of the whole area inside maximum security (see prison photographs). I told them if you're going to do a job, do it properly. Photographs are always a handy tool to accompany my written intelligence reports. I also photographed terrorists within Block 10; these were used to identify Al-Qaeda and Pakistan Taliban members who were hiding in the prison system using false identities. An unassuming but ruthless senior Taliban Commander from Helmand, Southern Afghanistan was just one of the terrorists I identified (see photographs of terrorists using mobile phones in prison). I had tagged this particular terrorist because he was responsible for the killing of British and American soldiers in Helmand. I made sure the American intelligence had all the information they needed on this guy. Photographs and his contacts list of phone numbers across Afghanistan and Pakistan, which I copied from his mobile phone. I even acquired copies of his hand writing. I had carried out a profile of many terrorists inside Pul-i-Charkhi prison, including some of their visitors who were also active terrorists within groups such as the Pakistan Taliban. My profiles were all very comprehensive. Information included real names of their family members and other contacts, their political stance and standing between different terrorist groups, names of known enemies and Government allies within the Pakistan and Afghanistan Parliaments. What their future hopes, fears and plans were, their rank within the terrorist groups that they were affiliated to. My profiles also included their overseas connections, in several countries, including America and Europe. Their likes and dislikes were also reported. I found out whether or not they were allergic to anything and what medication some of the terrorists were on or required. People and terrorists, HVT's, can be traced by their medication requirements, especially if it's rare or in large quantities. They have to buy and obtain their medication from somewhere. The CIA had used this method with success many times in the past. All in all I made sure that my profiles were extremely detailed and had as much useful and workable information in them as possible. I knew that a good American intelligence analyst would make good use of all the information I sent them.

"This took courage, not the adrenalin fuelled blood pumping courage you need to survive combat or a fire-fight with the enemy, but 'cold courage', calculated and precise. Silent courage"

It was the week before Eid, the most holy holiday in the Muslim calendar. Muslims fast during the day the whole month before Eid, this is known as 'Ramadan'. Eid is the name of the festival which marks the end of 'Ramadan' across the Islamic world. All the Taliban and Al-Qaeda fighters and Leaders were making preparations inside Pul-i-Charkhi prison for the festival. Food and clothing was being brought into the prison my family members and friends. Taliban within the prison had ordered that there were to be no attacks ordered or co-ordinated from inside the prison during the holy month of 'Ramadan'. This was also acknowledged by the Taliban leadership in Pakistan and Southern Afghanistan. From a Muslim's spiritual point of view, Eid was very important. It is one of the most significant dates in their religious calendar. The fasting of all the Muslims had already begun. Bevan and I had fasted alongside them as a show of respect to their faith. This had met with the approval of the terrorist leadership inside Pul-iCharkhi and the terrorist Commanders outside the prison, who I had spoken to via the phones located in the Al-Qaeda corridor. It had been useful for me to talk to terrorist Commanders outside Pul-i-Charkhi; this had helped to cement my relationship with their group. I had many dear diary moments when the phone would just be handed to me by Saladin or Hussein and a Terrorist Commander would be on the other end talking from Helmand or Pakistan. The Americans found my conversations and voice on the phone very useful; as this helped to identify further HVT's. The day before the 'Eid' festival the Red Cross turned up and handed out blankets, bars of soap and red plastic bins, these were to be used as water containers. The Red Cross knew exactly what was really going on within Pul-i-Charkhi. They had investigated and found evidence of torture and extreme human rights abuses that were still happening in the prison blocks. Most of the ill-treatment had stopped within Block 10, but occasionally the guards would beat a prisoner almost to death. This was still a big improvement on what things used to be like. The Red Cross are people from all walks of life, who give their time to come to places like Afghanistan and other war zones to help people. It takes a special kind of person to work for the Red Cross; the staff I had come into contact with, were both selfless and outstanding human beings on every level. They save lives and give hope to people who find themselves in crises amid dark situations and hard times. I have nothing but absolute respect and admiration for the men and women who work within the Red Cross. I have seen first-hand what their hard work can achieve, through pure strong will, principled actions and dogged determination. It is very humbling to experience their work and kindness. The compassion I witnessed in Pul-i-Charkhi will never be forgotten.

Over the past few years I had lived and breathed, I was surrounded by extreme fundamentalists and

international terrorists, 'the real bad boys of Al-Qaeda and the Pakistan Taliban'. I had gained access to information by staying two steps ahead at all times. I had passed every test that the terrorists had thrown at me. My actions had saved lives and limited the collateral damage from terrorist's attacks. I had taken all tasking's and requests from the Americans and more. I had completed everything that the Americans had asked of me, with exceptional results, but now my gut was telling me that I had only scratched the surface of what was really going on inside Pul-i-Charkhi and within the terrorist networks within. The only way that I would be truly accepted by the terrorist leadership was if 'I converted to Islam'. I was well aware that Al-Qaeda and some of its Commanders had already tagged me as a weapons and tactics instructor and I had already been asked if I wanted to attend one of their new training camps in Pakistan or Africa. My American contacts in intelligence were totally up to speed regarding all of all of these developments. I always kept my American contacts in the loop when dealing with any new developments, regardless of how big or small, because I wanted to know that my back was covered at all times. I had made copies of many of the reports that I had handed over to American intelligence. I had sent these out via a trusted friend and they were kept in a safe country in Europe. I had done this for future reference in case I needed to cross reference any of my reports or intelligence. This also gave me a safety net if the British Embassy tried to lie and use me as a scapegoat in the future. I always kept an 'ace card' held back just in case I needed it. I was always very careful in what I kept written down in Pul-i-Charkhi, I always stuck to my 12hrs rule, 'write what needed to be written then send it out'. Al-Qaeda had paid the guards to make sure my room was never properly searched. The Americans had also told the prison block Commander that the guards were not to search my room either. So my arse was covered from both angles. When the Americans discreetly and deliberately informed the Afghan prison guards that they were on their way to search Block 10, Al-Qaeda, Afghan Taliban and Pakistan Taliban would send their mobile phones and chargers to my room so that I could keep them safe. This worked well because I had time to quickly copy all their 'Sim' cards and contact numbers on their phones. The Americans only completed their searches once I had copied everything.

The Americans would then discreetly take all the copies off me as they left. I did this at least once a month to make sure we had all the new contact numbers being used by the terrorists to communicate. For good measure I would send the British Prime Minister, David Cameron an updated copy of one of these lists, just to prove and make a point that the British Embassy Kabul and some members of FCO staff were not being open or truthful with David Cameron or his office. I was being as diplomatic as I could be. I felt that the British Prime Minister had a right to know what members of his Government were up too. Bevan and I were able to 'convince' Hussein that it would be better for him to keep all his numbers 'safely' with us, in a ring-type notebook. Bevan would write the Names and Telephone numbers down in English, so that we could 'pretend' the book belonged to Bevan, thereby keeping the numbers 'safe' from being confiscated during prisons raids, something that Hussein had fallen foul of a number of times. It became routine for Hussein to come to our cell daily and get Bevan to update the list of numbers as they 'changed', all part of the Al-Qaeda Operational Security to change out numbers on a regular basis. This was ideal for us as we were then able to ensure that we had the latest 'updated' telephone numbers, but we were also able to determine 'who' Hussein was talking to. Very interestingly, we were able to 'confirm' the intimate relationship between Al-Qaeda, Afghan and Pakistan Taliban. One of the numbers turned out to be that of a General in the ISI, whilst another turned out to be that of a Major in the ISI that was responsible for the 'free' movement of terrorists across the Afghanistan/Pakistan border. What floored us was the 'close' interaction between Afghan/Pakistan officials and the terrorists, while all the while paying 'lip-service' to being on the side of the Americans in the 'War on Terror'. Well, GCHQ and the NSA could 'confirm' who was who in the zoo with the list of numbers I handed over to American Military Intelligence/CIA.

"I accused by name, members of the 'British Foreign Office, British Embassy Kabul' of treason, they knowingly allowed indirectly, terrorist attacks and activity to continue from inside the prison for in excess of three years"

At a later date I would also send a copy of my official 'ill-treatment and torture statement', to HRH the Queen of England. HRH Queen Elizabeth II had a right to know what members of her own Government were doing to her subjects in foreign lands. In my official legal statement I accused, by name, members of the British Foreign Office of treason, for allowing the attacks on British and American soldiers to continue for over 3 years from within Pul-i-Charkhi, British mentored Afghan prison. The FCO's actions indirectly led to the deaths of several American and British 'ISAF' soldiers in Afghanistan.

The Americans were still putting increased pressure on the British Embassy by asking uncomfortable questions, this was good because I needed to keep the pressure on the British Embassy. Al-Qaeda was still receiving updates and information from their Afghan translators working within the British Embassy, so I had to appear that I was still pushing the Embassy for my release from prison. The British Embassy had broken the age old rule: 'you never leave a man behind'. My military brothers on both sides of the Atlantic were now closely monitoring what the staff of the British Embassy Kabul were doing with regard my illegal imprisonment in Afghanistan. But like all good soldiers, I soldered on, adapted, improvised and overcame every obstacle that the British Embassy and the Al-Qaeda network put in my way. 'I turned every negative into a positive'.

"'The British stiff upper lip', it's important to keep this when faced with adversity"

When I'm fighting on 'principle', I do not compromise. I do whatever is necessary. I spent the week before 'Eid' carrying out in-depth studying of Islamic books, Arabic writing and the holy Qur'an. I was planning and preparing myself for the decision I was about to make. I spoke to Bevan extensively about the decision I was about to make. He knew what my reasons were behind this action; to infiltrate the terrorist inner circle. He reminded me, that if I was caught by Al-Qaeda I would be killed on the spot. This was a sobering thought, but my mind was made up. I needed access; the only way to enter the 'inner sanctum' of the terrorists, and obtain all their inner secrets, was for me to become a Muslim and a terrorist Commander myself. I had already spoken to a Protestant minister about my 'converting by name only to Islam'. The Protestant minister had told me that I was doing 'Gods work' and my actions were saving many British and American lives. I felt better after speaking to and checking in with the Christian 'God squad'. I was born a Catholic and by God I was going to die one. I just hoped that my demise was going to be later rather than sooner. I took a walk with Bevan in the Commanders rose garden one afternoon. We discussed all aspects of the decision that I was about to make. I was about to walk through a door, with no guaranteed return. It was a serious decision but one I had to make. It was the only way of getting close to the inner circle of the terrorists and I knew that this was my one chance to nail members of the Al-Qaeda leadership, including; Osama bin Laden. My actions would save many British and American soldiers lives, so I cracked on into the unknown. I converted to Islam at 0900hrs on the first morning of the first day of the festival of Eid. Terrorist Commander Wais Hudein was the first person I told and I first said the Islamic prayer, Kalima, with him. I wanted him to take the credit for converting me. I knew that he would get great satisfaction out of this. My naming him as the Terrorist Commander who had converted me also enhanced his standing within the terrorist brotherhood. Going to Saladin would have been too obvious. Commander Wais Hudein was a good choice. My Islamic name was confirmed as, 'Allah Odin' From that moment on I was known officially to everyone inside Pul-i-Charkhi, including Bevan, as 'Allah Odin'. My 'next of kin' had already been briefed on my course of action and the Americans were also up to speed. It was game on; I was going after the big fish.

My converting to Islam was kept quiet for all of one hour. Then it spread right across Pul-i-Charkhi like wild fire. The entire Al-Qaeda corridor came over to see me and give me their best regards. Saladin just smiled and shook my hand. He gave me his prized Islamic prayer mat and a set of flowing white Arabic robes. Taliban Commander 'Talib Jan' came to see me and handed me a full set of black robes. This was the standard battle dress of the Pakistan and Afghan Taliban. My receiving these gifts from Al-Qaeda and the Pakistan and Afghan Taliban were a clear indication of their acceptance and my standing within the terrorist network. I had just stormed through the point of no return. A while later I received a large bag of nuts and fresh fruit from the Al-Qaeda corridor. Any food I received, I shared with the other Afghan prisoners in my corridor that did not get visitors, so we all had little treats for the Eid festivities. I expected to get a response, but not the overwhelming one that I actually received. Bevan just watched, observing everything that was going on. He always observed from a distance, he could learn a lot from the way people acted around me. I knew that he would always have my back no matter what. We would talk late into the night, dissecting all that we had observed and what had happened that day. We would talk to one another as we wrote everything up in our diaries. We made sure that we did not leave anything out. We worked very well as a team. We were breaking new ground and in uncharted territory. Unprecedented events would become a daily occurrence and the danger of my situation, would escalate. My world was about to get very interesting, very quickly. I had now gone past the point of no return. This would end in one of two ways; I would be successful or I would be killed, there would be no third outcome. My fate was now written in the stars and in the hands of the Gods.

"Honouring my promise to fallen friends and soldiers who gave their lives protecting America and Britain from International Terrorism"

(Above) American Airborne Soldiers from 101st Airborne Division on operations in Iraq (Combat Camera Team)

My close friends and work colleagues always said that I had taken to the Islamic culture like a duck to water. That enabled me to be good at my job. I could blend in and I revelled in the lawlessness of the desert and mountains of the Middle-East. What some people called hell, I had called home. I have always been able to adapt to my surroundings, and this situation I found myself in was no exception. The greater the danger, the greater the chance, risk of me being killed on mission, the more I pushed myself to achieve the objective or task. I did take my work to the extreme, but in my mind you needed to be extreme to catch extremists. Nothing is impossible if you want it bad enough. I did not see any point in just playing the game. I wanted to nail the game down, play it to extreme, win the game and achieve all my objectives.

"Losers always whine about giving it their best shot, winners are the ones who go home victorious and fuck the prom queen, in my mind, Osama bin Laden was the prom queen"

Terrorist had killed many of my close friends, British and American soldiers who gave their lives for their countries. My work had gotten very personal long ago. I made a promise to my fallen friends and brothers in arms, while I stood at 'Ground Zero', the sight of the 9/11 attacks on New York. The promise made: If I could ever prevent terrorist attacks, I would, and if I ever had the chance to take Osama bin Laden down, I would, regardless of the risk, even if it cost me my own life. I was fulfilling and honouring my promise to my fallen friends, they are the true heroes. Unbeknown to me, Bevan had also visited 'Ground Zero' whilst working in Afghanistan, and he too had been struck by the devastation and cruelty of the attack, this was to become something of a driving force, albeit ever so small, to obtain retribution for innocent lives lost by these terrorists. Fellow soldiers reading this will understand what a promise, a blood oath, like this means. It's about personal honour and duty.

"Osama bin Laden had made one fatal mistake; he had really pissed of a British Paratrooper 'that would be me'. Bin Laden was already dead, he just did not know it yet...!"

I knew and understood the Islamic world and how it operated beneath the surface. Everything I had done and been through, every battle I had survived and experienced in my life had brought me to this one moment in time. Life is about experiences, both good and bad, it's the experiences that shape a person into the human beings that we are. Experiences have shaped me into the person that I am; they have also helped to shape my character. One experience that I will never forget was when I held a dying young Iraqi girl in my arms that had just been caught in a suicide attack in Iraq. The innocent young girl's injuries were so severe that all my experience and medical knowledge was useless. All I could do in her last few moments of life was to hold her close and comfort her. She died silently in my arms moments later. That emotional heart wrenching event will stay with me for the rest of my life. It reinforced in my mind, the principle that the innocent need protecting. The strong have a duty to protect the weak. Without my even realising it, the events I had witnessed across the Middle-East had moulded and helped shape my inner character and the characteristics that make me the person I have evolved into. I could be very cold and calculated when required. Good when being a soldier and security operator in hostile environments, not so good back in Civvie Street.

"My actions had been responsible for the taking out of over 100 bad guys, terrorists, but on the flip side, I had also saved in excess of 100 lives, including those of British and American soldiers and nationals. To my way of thinking, good had triumphed over evil, and a balance had been struck"

The alternative was letting Islamist extremists like Al-Qaeda and the Taliban rule over Western society, implementing strict 'Sharia' law. This is what the extremists want. Do the British public want London to become another Baghdad? Having spoken to many members of the British public, they definitely do not want 'Sharia' law, and they certainly don't want the daily extreme violence of Baghdad or Kabul coming to the streets of our green and pleasant land, the Americans don't want it in 'the land of the free and home of the brave'. The question is how do we stop the Islamic extremists? Time will tell if Western leaders have made the right decisions to keep Western countries safe. Violence breeds violence and contempt. Pure hatred is the motivation behind many extremists, which is passed on to generation after generation; I have seen first-hand how violence can escalate. It never ends well; people always die in large numbers, normally the innocent ones, women and children. The one thing I am sure of is that talking saves countless lives. Opening up a dialogue with people, whether it be the enemy or terrorists, is the real way forward. Common ground can be found if there is political will, progress can sometimes be slow, and like some new experiences, they can be extremely painful, compromises have to be made by all sides. In the end negatives 'can' be turned into positives. I personally think that a few growing pains in the office or in Government board rooms and cabinet meetings would be easier to overcome than the pain of tens of thousands of deaths on the battle field. The comment that some politicians say, "we don't talk to terrorists" that is complete hogwash, political spin and bullshit. Western Governments talk to terrorist groups all the time. The power sharing agreement with the Taliban in Afghanistan 2014 is just one example. When the British Government were talking, and making secret deals, with the IRA when the troubles were at their peak in Northern Ireland, is another example. So I'm afraid political spin doesn't cut it anymore with me. Politicians should be as quick getting Western countries out of armed conflicts as they have been in the past sending us into war. The misguided war in Iraq in 2003, pushed and then justified by flawed and fabricated intelligence and political spin, is a constant reminder of how not to send Western counties to war.

"Afghanistan, a text-book example on how to lose a war"

The Afghanistan conflict is another misjudged conflict, mission creep, and over 447 British soldier's lives and in excess of 2000 American ISAF soldiers killed and thousands more seriously injured. The Taliban are coming back into power. What have we archived? Was the human cost too great for the end result? Lord Ashdown, a critic of NATO policy in the war zone, said that Britain and the rest of the alliance would be leaving Afghanistan "with our tail between our legs". He added: "History will say that we did not succeed in Afghanistan. We failed. The biggest tragedy is that this was a war we could have won". He also added that "Afghanistan was a text-book example on how to lose a war". General Sir David Richards, who was Chief of the Defence Staff until last summer, said that the ability of the Afghan Army to mount counter-insurgency operations without western support would "rapidly fall away". Hopefully the conflicts and wars in the future will be better justified, thought out and conducted by Western politicians and Governments, than they have been up until now.

"If the people one day desire life

It is inevitable that destiny grants it

It is inevitable that the darkness lifts..."

Tunisian poet. Aboul-Qacem Echebbi

All parties and sides talking around a table at the beginning of a conflict, is a hell of a lot more cost effective in lives and financial cost, than talking after 12 years of war and international conflict, like what we have seen in Afghanistan. With open minds, the positive progress that has been so elusive, can finally be found. But when all is said and done, we must never forget the real threat from International terrorist groups with their own agenda and warped view and perspective on life, politics and religion. Islamic extremism is one of the most serious threats Western society has ever had to face and confront. We must never lose focus on what the real threat is and where it comes from. The majority of Western politicians, the world's media and Hollywood film directors like to portray soldiers as some sort of cold, unfeeling, unrelenting professional assassins. A politician once said; "soldiers from Regiments like the Parachute Battalions and Special Forces should be kept in a glass case, labelled with the words 'break glass on outbreak of war".

"PM Margaret Thatcher called the Para's her Dogs of War"

Former British Prime Minister Margaret Thatcher even called the Para's her 'Dogs of War' during the Falkland's conflict. In the case of many professional soldiers and specialist security operatives this label could not be further from the truth. Although if required, we are more than capable of killing quickly, clinically and without mercy, dispatching the bad guys so only 'God' can sort them out. However, the majority of the time, professional soldiering is spent endeavouring to help and improve the lives of the local population who we come across and are in contact with in operational locations and environments. The humanitarian work that soldiers do within combat zones is rarely, if ever, reported in the press. In my experience, the press in war zones tend to focus on the negative side of war, the killing, death and destruction. Human 'feel good' stories are not a priority. As one senior press editor once told me 'war sells newspapers', human peace stories don't. That statement by the news editor highlighted the fact that in general people like reading about violence and sensationalised war zone headlines. Governments like to use the phrase 'Hearts and minds', this is how the politicians like to refer to the humanitarian side of war and conflict. It's not the politicians who came up with the phrase, it was the military themselves. The first people to come across civilians in a combat zone, sure as hell are not politicians. Soldiers are there to do a job, but they are human beings; husbands, brothers, sons, wives, sisters, daughters. Soldiers may appear cold, distant, even emotionally detached at times, this is purely the way that some soldiers deal with the horrors that they witness, sometimes on a daily basis, in war torn environments. Sometimes blocking the emotion out is the only way of coping with extremely traumatic events. Soldiers actually have feelings and emotions that run very deep; we remember everything we see. We all deal with things very differently, 'our' big release is often drinking with our fellow soldiers after operations have finished. This is when many suppressed deep feelings and emotions rise to the surface. This is also when many dark demons within us raise their ugly heads. Drink has a way of bringing out the best in a soldier, and the worse. I have heard many times from soldiers that they only drink with fellow soldiers, as civilians just don't know or understand us. How can a soldier have a conversation with a civilian who has never been to war or seen combat first hand. A civilian would probably have a mental melt down if he heard about some of the things soldiers have witnessed and sometimes discuss. Don't get me wrong, there are some people out there, civilian people, but they are few and far between. Another very essential component in a soldiers armoury is a massive sense of humour, albeit at times very dark humour. Military humour is definitely an acquired taste. Soldiers tend to laugh at things that civilians just don't find funny, in some cases civilians are horrified at what soldiers laugh at and some of the subjects they find amusing. It's not because we are sick or weird, it's just the way we cope with life and extreme, high pressure, situations that will inevitably end in our death, or that of a friend. Soldiers, past and present, are very proud of being soldiers; we have served our country with blood, sweat and tears. So to the person reading this book, don't judge a book by its cover. The next time you see a soldier, whether he is out shopping or having a drink alone down the local pub, give him a smile and take the time to shake his hand and thank him for being a soldier and helping to protect this country. I guarantee that you will make his day. Encourage him to feel proud of himself and what he has done. There is no such thing as an ex-soldier, regardless of age, once a soldier always a soldier.

"British Embassy, Consulate and Vice Consulate are removed from their jobs"

One hot, sunny afternoon, when the dry heat was stifling and no cooling breeze from the mountains, I was accosted by the guards, shackled for show and taken to the main prison

Commanders office. The Embassy security detail 'PSD', were outside in their Toyota B6 armoured vehicles, which were positioned tactically to give interlocking arcs of fire if required around the perimeter of the Commanders office inside the prison. The PSD team was well aware that Pul-i-Charkhi prison was full of terrorists, and weapons. They wore the standard dress of all PSD teams; boots and cargo pants that had large side pockets for carrying spare field dressings and tourniquets for treating injured personnel. They all wore the 5/11 shirts under their 'Diamond Back' body armour with Armoured ballistic plates. These were the plates that could stop bullets from the Russian sniper rifles and captured American weapons which the Taliban were using. Some of the team had the wrap-around Orkney sunglasses, short hair and were clean shaven. The older members of the PSD team who were a little wiser had grown their hair and beards. This enabled them to blend in with their surroundings and the general population. Anyone brandishing really short hair and being clean shaven stood out like a sore thumb, and in the eyes of the Taliban, were Western Military, and in being so were legitimate targets. I noticed that the PSD were very heavily armed. They did not just carry their normal assault rifles, which were capable of full automatic fire. Additionally some of the PSD team were carrying 'SAW' (Section Automatic Weapons), which were belt fed. The 'SAW' is a very good weapon to use, to engage the enemy and put a sustained rate of fire down on an enemy position. I had used the 'SAW' in Iraq and Somalia, and the rate of fire it could put down was good, also being belt fed meant that there was no need to change a magazine every 30 rounds. The PSD carrying several 'SAW' weapons had drawn my attention. The fact that the full team had taken up firing positions and were aiming weapons 'hot', inside the prison spoke volumes. The security situation was very bad in Pul-i-Charkhi, and across Kabul. Even with the extra firepower that the PSD team was packing, the 'TL' (Team Leader) still appeared very pensive and on edge. I knew some of the older members of the PSD team. I had worked with the boys in the past, some of them back in the day when we were serving in the British Army. The PSD team members were in disbelief that the British Embassy had not got me out. They all knew that my Afghan case was complete 'Bullshit'. Some members of the official British Embassy security team had been removed by the Embassy staff because the military boys had asked uncomfortable questions of the Embassy about my case, in a bid to try and help me. The Embassy's staff had tried every underhanded trick in the book to cover my situation up and keep it quiet. As I approached the Commanders office, a familiar face popped out from one of the PSD vehicles. It was Terry, he stepped forward and shook my hand and informed me that the Embassy had told him not to speak to me. Terry said "fuck them", they're all 'crap hats' anyway and they should all hang their heads in shame after the way I had been treated. Terry was a good man and a very professional member of the PSD team. He did not like the political bullshit that was coming out of the Embassy, or the fact that the Embassy staff knew that the reason I had been put in prison was politically motivated and yet nothing was being done to get me released. He just wanted to let me know that the military lads had not forgotten about me. Everyone back at his base camp sent their regards. The Embassy had also told the PSD team that they were not allowed to give me anything or help me. The PSD blew the Embassy off again, they said "bollocks to those Muppets". They gave me all their bottled water and fresh sandwiches that they had on them. Members of the Embassy PSD team were also in contact with my 'Next of Kin', giving him updates on what they knew about my situation. The fact that a lot of people from both military and security were helping me really pissed off the Embassy staff. At this point the shameful British Embassy staff had no idea how many people I had supporting me, or who my contacts were within the British and American Governments. I was using all my contacts to my advantage.

I walked up the stairs into the prison Commanders office. I passed another PSD member at the top of the stairs. I shook his hand, he whispered to me "everyone knows and understands why you have gone native to protect yourself, stay safe". I gave a silent nod in acknowledgement. Another member of the team, who I did not know, came over and shook my hand, pushing some money into my palm. He said "it's from the boys, stay safe". I said "thank you". The guards followed me up the stairs and took my shackles off. I was shown into the Commanders office. On entering the office I noticed Trudy Kennedy sat on the sofa with the prison Commander sat behind his desk. I walked over and shook her hand, then I shook the prison Commander's hand. The prison Commander excused himself; I was left alone with Trudy. I appreciated her taking the time to visit me again, especially considering the high security threat in and around Pul-i-Charkhi. I sat on the seat opposite her. From past conversations with her, and what other people that I know had told her about my situation and the real back story, she knew the truth. Trudy had also discreetly investigated aspects of my case which I had told her about, everything I had told her had checked out. She had also informed me in the past, that there was a lot of high level politics involved within my situation. The fact was that the Embassy and FCO would not investigate my situation because they 'did not what to upset the corrupt Afghan Government'. Even my disgraceful ill-treatment was being covered-up by the Embassy staff. Trudy went on to tell me that she had reported everything to John Payne, the then Deputy British Ambassador. John Payne had tied Trudy's hands; he had blocked every effort Trudy had attempted to help to resolve my situation. Trudy went on to give me a full overview of what really was going on behind the scenes in the British Embassy. Trudy was very tearful; she had just been informed the day before that she had been put on 'stress leave' for 6 months due to my case. Trudy was disgusted at the way she had been treated by senior Embassy Staff. I told her that I knew exactly how that felt. Trudy also informed me that Lawrence Jenkins had also been 'binned' from the position of British Consul, a position that she had subsequently been elevated to. Lawrence Jenkins now worked within the Embassy's Finance Department...! Not exactly a promotion. The British Embassy was looking for scapegoats for my situation within the Embassy. Everyone was blaming each other, as the head of the British Rule of Law Team would later say in a British court of law; 'I had been held in prison in Afghan illegally' and 'this did not happen on his shift'?

Several other key members of the British Embassy staff were quickly transferred or put on stress leave/gardening leave. The Embassy would still not investigate my situation, but they were all too willing to transfer their own staff out in an effort to silence them, and repeatedly cover up the situation. I personally found these actions shameful. There was clearly no real 'rule of law' in Afghanistan. Painting an office and giving the Afghan Ministry of Justice, British and European law books and stationary, does not give a backward corrupt country like Afghanistan 'rule of law'. Any Western officials who think differently are living in denial. The corruption being left unchecked for several years by Western Governments had led to Islamic 'Sharia' law being implemented across the Afghan Justice system, and across Afghanistan. These are just some of the points that I brought up with Trudy Kennedy. Another example of how dysfunctional the British mentored Afghan justice system really was; when a 50 year old Afghan man had raped and killed his 12 year old daughter, having admitted to the crime, he then spoke openly about it. The prison Commander had also confirmed all the details of this case. The Afghan male had served not even 6 months of his 10 year sentence when he had paid a bribe, $5,000, to the Afghan Judge and Prosecutor. The Afghan male had been released. The prison guards were disgusted at this. They had asked me why the British prison mentors, who also mentor the Afghan Justice System, don't investigate this case. When I mentioned this to Trudy Kennedy she just shook her head and said 'I know, there is nothing I can do about it'? This was just one example of how dysfunctional the British Embassies mentorship was of the Justice System in Afghanistan. I had hundreds of other examples of this. I gave The Red Cross copies of all the information and Afghan case files and numbers that I had acquired. Trudy was all too aware of how bad the problem really was.

"Members of the senior staff from the British Embassy Kabul at this point, were still saying that there was no major corruption within the Afghan Government or the Afghan Justice System and that Afghanistan was not an active war zone"

I stood up and thanked Trudy for all her efforts in trying to help me, she was a good woman who had tried her best to help me, and other prisoners. The senior staff within the British Embassy had turned on her and were using Trudy as there convenient scapegoat. I gave Trudy Kennedy a big hug and told her to take good care of herself, she was crying at this point. She had tried to help and the Embassy had turned on one of their own staff. John Payne had well and truly screwed her over. Trudy was, and had been, following his orders. I left the prison office closing the door behind me. On the way out of the building I asked the PSD team to give Trudy a few minutes to compose herself. I did not want the Afghans to see that Trudy had been crying. I told the security team to 'stay safe' on their return trip to Kabul. I returned to my cell and wrote up all the details of what had happened that afternoon. I felt deflated due to the emotional meeting with Trudy; at least now Trudy had some time off back in England. I was still in disbelief that the British Embassy had turned on their own people in an attempt to silence the situation. All this at the same time that the British Embassy senior personnel were allowing British and American soldiers to die in Helmand in terrorist attacks that could have been prevented. Attacks emanating from British mentored Afghan prisons. I wonder what the families of dead British and American soldiers would say about this.

"Update meeting with senior American Intelligence"

The next morning my American contacts came rocking up in force. They pulled 22 Afghans out of Block 10 and interviewed them about the conditions within the prison. I was number 21 to be pulled out; Talib-Jan was number 22. He just spat on the floor and at the Americans while he shouted abuse at them in his best Arabic. The Americans, three big mean looking soldiers, promptly frog marched him back to his cell. Talib-Jan was not a 'hearts and minds' kind of a guy.

Funnily enough 'my' conversation with the Americans was nothing to do with the prison conditions. The Americans interviewing prisoners was just a cover so we could meet and talk alone. We got straight down to business; we had 30 minutes before it would start to draw attention. The Americans were fully aware of the connections between the prisoners inside Pul-i-Charkhi and the Pakistan Taliban and the Al-Qaeda network. The problem was that members of the Afghan Parliament, who were either Taliban sympathisers or Taliban themselves, were protecting the terrorists within Pul-iCharkhi. Members of the Parliament were having monthly meetings in Pul-i-Charkhi, with senior Al-Qaeda and Pakistan Taliban Commanders. The Afghan Parliament was also blocking every effort by the Americans to move the terrorists to the American air base, and 'black prison', located at Bagram. Members of the Afghan Parliament were also bringing in new mobile phones and new international 'Sim cards' for the Al-Qaeda and Taliban every time they visited. The Members of Parliament were never searched when they came into the prison. These new phones were pre-programmed with all the new terrorist Commanders phone numbers for that month. The new phones enabled the terrorist Commanders in the prison to communicate freely between other terrorist Commanders across several countries including; Afghanistan, Pakistan, Iran, Iraq and Syria. The Americans were banging their heads against a wall, as they closed down one of the terrorist lines of communication, two other lines of communication would pop up. Terrorist IED and suicide attacks on American and British ISAF troops were at an all-time high. The 'bleed out' of terrorists from the Iraq and Afghan wars was on the increase. Many new groups like the Pakistan Taliban and Kandahar Al-Qaeda, the 'Lions of Allah' (Al-Qaeda's equivalent of Special Forces), all handpicked men, were making up small teams of 4 to 6 men. All specially trained and cross trained in covert and overt warfare. (What was disturbing about this was the fact that different terrorist networks and groups were now talking and communicating between themselves). They were pooling resources and finances, supporting and facilitating each other. Large amounts of F/F (Foreign Fighters) were being utilized by the terrorist networks, as were suicide bombers and IED bomb makers. Oil, weapons, drugs and kidnapping were now helping to fund a self-sustained very complex terrorist network. Even Al-Shabab and Hezbe-Islam in Somalia were now part of the bigger terrorist network. Somali pirates also provided ships and a means of transport for Al-Qaeda and the Pakistan Taliban between countries. I knew a lot about all of this and I had included it in great detail in my written reports, which I had previously given to American intelligence. I also mentioned during my meeting with the Americans, that Al-Qaeda and the Pakistan Taliban had plans to hijack oil-tankers off the coast of Somalia, pack them with explosives and UXO and then use them as suicide bombs, targeting oil refineries in Saudi Arabia, American naval bases and locations in the Red Sea and the Suez Canal. Al-Qaeda and the Pakistan Taliban were looking at both tactical and strategic targets including the sinking of several oil tankers in the Strait of Hormuz and the Gulf of Suez (see Glossary, Strait of Hormuz attacks). This would disrupt oil shipments to Western countries and in turn would dramatically affect the price of oil. Al-Qaeda planned to disrupt the economies and financial markets of the West. I needed more than 20 minutes to talk to the Americans, but time was of the essence. I would write a full in depth report for them on the subjects which we had touched upon during our meeting. I had gained access to so much information I was on over load. I had to prioritise what information was the most important or urgent. I had several areas of interest; one of them was locating terrorist leaders in Pakistan. Slowly but surely I was building a picture on how the terrorists moved and operated across their area of operations, which was basically the whole of the Middle-East.

"Iranian missiles and IED's, Improvised Explosive Devices and 'FMSC' (Factory Made Shape Charges), which were being used by terrorists to kill American and British soldiers"

The IEDs being constructed and used against British and American ISAF forces in Afghanistan and other areas of operation were becoming a huge problem. Insurgent IED attacks were killing and injuring more soldiers than any other kind of attack in Afghanistan. There were now daily IED attacks, soldiers were being killed and seriously injured at an alarming rate, (three a day). Some of the shape charges and missiles that were being deployed against American, British and ISAF forces across Afghanistan were being made in Iran, at a location given the code name 'K1'. This was the location of one of the engineering factories which was manufacturing the IEDs and shape charges. Shipments from this factory were of extreme interest to the Americans. I had located the factory and been able to establish the dates and times of the shipments and their routes from Iran into Southern Afghanistan. This information had been utilised by the American military and CIA, resulting in drone

(Right) Taken by Author during Military Operations with American Military. IED Found in Nothern Iraq

strikes on terrorist convoys crossing the border from Iran into Afghanistan. Two of the missiles found in terrorist safe houses and weapons storage locations were the Iranian 'Sagger' and 'Arash'. I had seen some of the shape charges that had been made and transported from Iran. The workmanship and engineering was very precise. These IEDs had been used against British and American armoured vehicles in Afghanistan with lethal results, and on one occasion the insurgent IED's had even disabled an American 'Abraham' main battle tank. The Iranian rockets and weapons used by insurgents had also been used to attack British and American bases, not only in Afghanistan, but also Iraq. This was not a new development; Iranian rockets and weapons had been found previously in Somalia, Syria and Iraq, being used by extreme Islamist groups. The Iranian rockets had given the terrorist the ability to launch attacks on Western locations and military bases from greater distances. The method of the terrorist attacks in Afghanistan had changed. They were no longer 'shoot-and-scoot' attacks, what had evolved was calculated, planned and co-ordinated; multiple attacks were simultaneously unleashed. The Pakistan and Afghan Taliban had evolved into an effective, unconventional, fighting force. During the meeting I handed the Americans a comprehensive 20 page hand-written report. The when, where and how of future terrorist attacks. I could not be seen talking to the Americans for very long, so my cut off time was 30 minutes. I quickly brought the meeting to an end. I stood up and shook hands with the Americans, saying 'stay safe'. I then calmly, kicked the door open, I did not intend to break the door, it just happened. I started shouting abuse at the Americans and Afghan guards. I knew that Al-Qaeda and the Taliban would be observing everything. The Americans right on cue stormed out of the building, also not happy, we exchanged insults and expressions of hatred. The Al-Qaeda and the Taliban prisoners who witnessed the farce started loudly banging and kicking on the metal cell doors in support of my outburst. The sound was deafening and echoed around the prison compound. The Afghan prison guards came running over, to try and keep me quiet. They promptly escorted me back into my cell. I should have received an 'Oscar' for my performance. Bevan just smiled knowingly; he had distracted the Afghan guards to keep them away from the room whilst I was talking to the Americans. We boiled some water for a cup of well-earned coffee. All in all, it had been a productive day. My tasking for the Americans was coming on well and my status within the prison was still on the up. The Al-Qaeda corridor sent me plates of food and fruit, so I knew that I was okay with regards the Al-Qaeda crew. My meeting with the Americans had been informative for both sides. It was a risk, but one worth taking, lives were being saved. That was the most important aspect of the exercise.

"Al-Qaeda Commander – British and American soldiers killed"

It was early afternoon and I was studying in my room, listening to the BBC world service news on the radio. The news was bad 'two more British soldiers killed in another IED attack in Southern Afghanistan'. There had been several other insurgent attacks on American forces in Eastern Afghan; casualty figures were still not confirmed. Soldiers were dying every day.

"The terrorist attacks were unnervingly relentless. This news saddened me. For every terrorist attack I was able to stop or disrupt, two more would pop up. This was so frustrating and on many occasions really got me down. I just snapped myself out of it, refocused and soldiered on, stopping the attacks that I could. For every attack that I stopped a soldier's life was saved, that was how I looked at it. A soldier returning home to his loved ones and family safely, now that fact was worth risking my life for".

I heard my name being called from the Al-Qaeda corridor. I walked out of my cell to see what was going on. I was greeted by a sea of people that stood before me. From the look on their faces, I thought that I had been sussed and caught by Al-Qaeda. I just smiled in resignation, in the knowledge that I had already stopped many terrorist attacks and saved a lot of lives. I stepped forward, surrounded by 12 members of Al-Qaeda. I just smiled, "what's going on". I have to admit that at this point in time I was having a fucking heart attack inside... Not to worry, I kept on smiling, keeping eye contact with the terrorists that surrounded me, it was important to show no fear. Saladin stepped forward and gave me a big hug, he said, "Welcome brother Allahodin, your name is strong in the history of Islam". I also received warm greetings from the rest of the terrorists around me. I was presented with gifts of new clothing and food from the other terrorist Commanders. Saladin presented me with a white turban made from silk. He placed the turban on my head; this was very significant because of the colour of the turban, and the fact that an Al-Qaeda Commander had presented me with it. Saladin and the other terrorist Commanders had just made a big statement, this being that I was now their equal. They had just made me a terrorist Commander, (by name only), I must emphasise that. This was a 'dear diary' moment. Not all the Taliban Commanders were happy about it, but Al-Qaeda and the Pakistan Taliban had made a ruling and a decision, so it stood. We all moved over to the Al-Qaeda corridor, where we spent the next hour drinking chi-tea and talking about the coming terrorist offensive in Southern Afghan that was being planned. The rest of the afternoon was spent praying and reciting different prayers from the Holy Qur'an. The prison Commander came up to show his respects to Saladin. He sat for an hour in the Al-Qaeda corridor talking and drinking chi-tea. One of the Al-Qaeda Commanders answered his mobile phone in front of the prison Commander, the prison Commander just ignored what he saw. The phone was handed to me. "The booming voice on the other end of the phone was 'Mullah Sagul'. One of the top Taliban Commanders in Kandahar and Helmand province in Afghanistan". He sent his regards to me and everyone else who was there. He said that he would come to visit me shortly in Pul-i-Charkhi. He had heard good things about me from other terrorists Commanders. He wanted to know if I needed anything. I informed him that the Al-Qaeda brothers in Kabul were looking after me. He was happy to hear this, if I needed anything or had any problems, he told me to get a message to him through the Al-Qaeda network and he would sort my problem out. I wished him and his family all the best for Eid. I handed the phone back to one of the other terrorist Commanders to continue the conversation. Abdul Aziz called me into his room; we made a 'Happy Eid' video on his new camera phone with three other members of the Al-Qaeda network. The video was then sent as an SMS attachment to Abdul Aziz's fellow Al-Qaeda Commanders in Saudi Arabia, Yemen and Iraq. The rest of the afternoon was spent in light conversation and an endless supply of chi-tea and nuts. Abdul Aziz was the cook for the evening meal that night. He was a good cook; he spent hours preparing food, chicken and fresh vegetables, enough to feed 30 people. One of the Mullahs had organised with Saladin to get all their supplies in, to feed and look after their men over the Eid festival. What struck me was even in prison the terrorists were a very tight knit group, they had kept their command and control structure, they were very united. It reminded me of the comradeship of British POW's in World War Two, in the German concentration camps. Like the British POW's back then, Al-Qaeda now saw it as their duty to survive, disrupt the guards and try to escape at every opportunity. All escape attempts had to be cleared through Al-Qaeda and Saladin, because of the dangers to the families of the terrorists, a lot of whom had been re-located by Al-Qaeda and the Pakistan Taliban, to safe locations around the Middle-East,

Pakistan and India. The Pakistan ISI, (Government Security Services) had many of its own members that supported the Taliban and Al-Qaeda leadership, and they had facilitated the movements, and safe passage, for many terrorist members and their families through Pakistan. The Pakistan Taliban even had a person working in the Pakistan Embassy in Kabul who issued passports, travel documents and visas to any terrorist network that required them. Some of these passports found their way into Pul-i-Charkhi prison and were used by terrorists, who subsequently escaped. This and several other factors proved to me that the Al-Qaeda and the Pakistan Taliban were extremely professional, thorough and well organised. This was a very different picture to the rag-tag image of terrorists that some Western Governments, and media outlets, like to portray. Some members of Al-Qaeda and Pakistan Taliban had lived in the West for many years, and some were extremely well travelled. A lot of them spoke English and understood it very well. They just never spoke English in front of other Westerners. They would just play dumb. The fact was that they understood everything that was being said. Al-Qaeda and the Pakistan Taliban and other terrorist groups have become experts in trusting no one outside their circle and deceiving everyone. 'Taqiyya' was in the terrorists DNA. I had witnessed, repeatedly, this tactic being used by terrorist groups from Baghdad to Beirut and Mogadishu to Kabul.

While drinking chi-tea with Al-Qaeda members and the Pakistan Taliban, the conversation turned to financing, Islamic charities and their franchise of terrorist groups that facilitate the movement of money between countries clandestinely. America and its Western allies had shut down all the easy ways that money could be transferred between terrorist groups. Western Governments had pressured the banking systems of Western countries to tighten up on the transfer of money between targeted countries. New money laundering laws had helped to close down many loop holes within the banking systems. This had resulted in a strangle hold being put on known terrorist groups finances. Islamic charities were still funnelling money to known terrorist front companies; some charities were even front companies themselves. The international banking structure in Dubai and Singapore were of interest to Western intelligence due to money transfers in and out of known terrorist front companies and dummy corporations. (See Glossary, Dubai money laundering)

"Hawala money changers"

The Hawala money changers throughout the world have been utilised by the terrorist networks. (See Glossary, Hawala, Dubai). There are Saudi, Pakistani, Afghan and Iraqi communities in every Western country, including America and Britain. Within these communities Hawala money transfers are set up. This gives the terrorist groups an untraceable way to transfer money between countries. Al-Qaeda and the Pakistan Taliban and other groups including AQAP, and Al-Shabab in Somalia are using the Hawala money transfer system to fund their terrorist operations. The counter measures from Western Governments had made it harder for the Jihadists to move money from one operational cell to another. Al-Qaeda needed skilled people to satisfy its demand for funds to be sent to its operational groups and franchises. The name Hussein came up yet again. It turned out that Hussein was not just the quartermaster and money handler inside Pul-i-Charkhi, he was also one of their key players in this part of the world. Hussein was also in direct contact with Zawahiri, the second in command of the Al-Qaeda network. When 'Osama bin Laden' was located and killed in the future, Zawahiri would become the Al-Qaeda Leader. It has been said that Zawahiri had always been the brains operationally behind the Al-Qaeda network.

The Al-Qaeda network had created their own supply chain, using a handful of trusted people. Al-Qaeda Commanders across the Middle-East, Europe, Africa and America had also turned to the illegal narcotics and drug trade in Afghanistan to finance their international terrorist operations. Afghanistan produces well over 80% of the world's Heroin. Al-Qaeda and the Pakistan and Afghan Taliban are now using their safest, most established smuggling routes out of Kandahar, Helmand, Nimruz, Farah and across Southern and Western Afghanistan into Pakistan and Iran, to smuggle narcotics out of Afghanistan and on into Europe, America and Africa. These narcotics operations are financing the terrorist insurgency operations, right across the Middle East, including the Jihad against the British and American forces in Afghanistan, Iraq and Somalia and later the Al-Qaeda Jihad's in Syria, Egypt and Libya. Afghan illegal narcotics have been found throughout Europe, Africa and America. Interestingly Bevan, having been 'convicted' on an alleged drug smuggling charge and therefore having been 'accepted' by those Taliban Commanders involved in the narcotics trade, had been able to verify the same route/s used for narcotics smuggling as was being used by the terrorists to get 'F/F' across the Middle East and into Afghanistan for, and/or to give 'training'. Again this showed just how inter-woven the tri-angle of Money/Terrorist/Commodity (narcotics, weapons, human trafficking, human organ/body-parts etc) was.

According to the Afghan counter narcotics opium survey 2013, Summary finding, the overall current GDP of the Afghan opium crop for 2013 is US $ 21.04 billion. The potential production of opium in 2013 was estimated at 5,500 tons. This is an increase in the figures from 2012 which put the figures at an estimated 3,700 tons. The real figures could very well be much higher. The Al-Qaeda and Taliban networks don't exactly advertise their yearly accounts. Another interesting fact is that the number of provinces affected by poppy cultivation in Afghanistan was 17 in 2012. This also increased to 19 in 2013. The eradication of the opium crop was also down by 24% on the previous year. All in all the counter narcotics measures in Afghanistan have failed or not been enforced. Opium and Heroin is flowing in major quantities from Afghan to many other countries. The price of Heroin has fallen on the streets of Western countries due to the vast amounts of Afghan Heroin and Opium which is available. The money from the expanding and constantly evolving illegal narcotics network is helping to fund and fuel Al-Qaeda and other terrorist operations on a global scale. As long as the terrorists have access to large amounts of money, they can purchases weapons, finance their foreign fighters and run their terrorist networks effectively. One of the strategies Al-Qaeda and the Pakistan Taliban talk openly about, is their tactic of flooding Western countries, including; America and Britain, with cheap illegal narcotics (heroin and opium). They want Western Governments to drain their resources trying to deal with this problem. From the state of the illegal drugs markets, their intention is proving successful. How much money have Western Governments spent, and are spending on counter narcotics operations? With just a little research, anyone can see that the money spent on trying to counter the flow of Afghan illegal narcotics into Western countries is escalating dangerously. This is a clear example of how the war on terror has many layers and is never merely black and white.

"The darker side of terrorist networks is their smuggling routes, human trafficking and human organ trafficking"

Zaranj in Nimruz Province, South Western Afghanistan, is a key location for narcotics, weapons, suicide bombers, HVT's and foreign fighters that travel to and from Iran. Many terrorist safe houses, meeting places and forming up points are located in, and around, Zaranj city. An even darker side of the terrorist networks and their smuggling routes is the human trafficking and human organ trafficking. Over the past several years this has evolved in itself into another very profitable business. Young children are kidnapped and smuggled out of Afghanistan and Pakistan, into Iran, Iraq and Turkey for their organs, which are bought by wealthy Arabs and other rich people from across the Middle-East. The children are alive when they are smuggled. One Taliban member told me that the children are easier to transport alive, which means that the organs continue to function. The Afghan and Pakistan Taliban facilitate and protect their smuggling routes with extreme prejudice. Human and organ trafficking will dramatically increase when the British and American military's conventional forces pull out of Afghanistan, the figures and statistics of all the illegal smuggling has been increasing every year, for several years in a row. When troops pull out of Afghanistan, there will be the biggest heroin, poppy crop in ten years. All these subjects were spoken about openly by the terrorist Commanders in Pul-i-Charkhi prison. Some of the subjects and things which these prisoners talked about were horrendous. This was just a reminder of the kind of people I was surrounded by on a daily basis.

"Dinner with Senior Al-Qaeda Commanders and the Pakistan Taliban"

My world had gotten very strange and surreal. I was right in the heart of the terrorist network; it was like being in a university on international terrorism. Abdul Aziz had almost finished preparing the evening meal, a chicken dinner was almost ready and the aroma coming from the cooking area was tantalizingly good and making my mouth water. I asked Saladin if I could invite Bevan to attend the evening meal with me as my guest. He agreed. I did not feel right eating a good chicken meal and Bevan not having any. The thought of Bevan eating rice and potatoes alone was not good. The chicken meal would be ready within an hour. Abdul Aziz was also in the process of finishing off the cooking and preparing the corridor floor, it had been washed and clean white sheets were put down length ways along the middle of the floor. These were the Afghan tables. Blankets were folded and put around the white sheets. These were the seating areas. Plates and pallets of fresh fruit, nuts and Afghan sweets were placed in the middle of the sheets. I went to get Bevan. I found him drinking coffee and reading one of the many books we had acquired. I told him to get ready because he was eating a chicken dinner with Al-Qaeda in an hour. He was to be my guest. Bevan rubbed his neck, and said "where is this meal" I told him it was in the Al-Qaeda corridor. Bevan said "you're kidding right" I smiled and answered "No".

Bevan addressed me as 'Allahodin' (he would do this when he was worried about something), "what are you up to". I looked at Bevan, trust me, you will be ok. Abdul Aziz is cooking and don't forget to wear the Arab clothing that you have been keeping, in case of an emergency. He asked me if I was sure about this. I answered with a smile. What is the worst that could happen, apart from being beheaded, you get a chicken dinner?

"Dinner with Al-Qaeda and Pakistan Taliban Commanders"

You have 45 minutes to get ready. Bevan, albeit reluctantly, agreed. He found it strange that I, being an accepted member of the terrorist group had invited him over to meet the rest of Al-Qaeda and other terrorist Commanders to share in their prized chicken dinner evening meal. This was just one of many situations that people outside, back in the real world, would not be able to get their head around. Bevan and I always tried to see the funny side of our precarious situations. Bevan had agreed, but added that he would come back and bloody well haunt me for life if he got beheaded. I laughed; "just think, my own personal poltergeist".

"If you always put a limit on everything you do, physical or anything else, it will spread into your work and into your life. There are no limits. There are only plateaus, and you must not stay there, you must go beyond them"

-Bruce Lee

I wore my Black flowing Afghan robes with my black waist coat, which I had received as a gift from Talib-Jan. Bevan wore his white robes. We both looked the part with our long beards. I also wore my white turban for good measure. I wanted to make a statement when I walked with Bevan by my side down the Al-Qaeda corridor. I knew that members of the Taliban who were not invited would be watching with envious eyes from the other corridor. This was one of the first times that Bevan had worn the Arab clothing. I smiled when I walked over to get him later, he looked good, we both laughed, and I said "let's be all we can be". We walked over to the Al-Qaeda corridor. The gate was opened by the guards, we walked through the metal gates and with a loud metallic crash, the guard locked the gate behind us. The guard looked at Bevan and smiled, the guards black teeth were badly stained from years of smoking. His teeth helped to frame his crooked smile. Bevan said "does he know something we don't"? Bevan's reticence was a mix of, I hope you're right about this and, fuck me what am I doing here. I 'subtly' announced our arrival; I shouted the full length of the corridor to Abdul Aziz who was right at the other end. He shouted back, "Welcome my friends". We walked down, other members of the terrorist groups came out to greet us, Al-Qaeda, Pakistan Taliban, Afghan Taliban. They all gave Bevan a warm welcome.

I introduced Bevan to everyone, respect was shown all round. Saladin came out of his room; his tall frame fitted his flowing white robes perfectly. Saladin looked like he had just come out of the 'Lawrence of Arabia' film. Saladin greeted us in traditional classic Arabic; and gave me a traditional Arabic welcome. He then spoke in English "you are welcome" greeting Bevan and shaking his hand. Saladin motioned for us to sit in the eating area. He placed me at his right hand side and Bevan sat next to Abdul Aziz, he too had changed into his best Arabian white flowing robes. This larger than life character, with his bear like frame, bald head and wild un-kempt beard, looked menacing; his dark eyes gave him a dark evil appearance, behind his eyes laid a life time of hate and extreme violence. I smiled at him. He made Bevan feel at ease, he put his arm around him and said "welcome". This was a public exhibition of friendship, so that everyone knew Bevan was a guest. I shouted over to Bevan. No-one would ever believe that he was having dinner, and chilling out, with Al-Qaeda. Bevan just smiled back. Over 20 other terrorists including Talib-Jan joined us for the meal. I wanted Bevan to talk to these people and get to know them. I also wanted the terrorists to get to know Bevan. People are less likely to kill someone who they know and like. I told Abdul Aziz to ask Bevan about the recent football results from the British Premiership from a few days before. I knew that Abdul Aziz's favourite football team Manchester United had won. Talking about football would help break the ice all round. I asked Saladin about his family, I hoped that they were all well and in good health. His family were due to visit Saladin within the next few days. He told me that his father was dealing with a little family problem back home in Pakistan. The Pakistan ISI had just arrested two of Saladin's brothers. They had been caught with weapons and explosives in their house. Their father did not know that the explosives were there. His rule was, weapons are ok, but no explosives in the family home. He was not happy that his sons had disobeyed his rule. Saladin laughed; his two younger brothers were more scared of what their father was going to do to them when they were released by the Pakistan ISI. Saladin's father was not happy and had been down to the ISI officers and told the military Commander to hold his two sons for two days then to release them. He wanted his sons to be taught a lesson. Saladin's father was an old school mountain man, hard as nails. He had also been one of the original 'Muj' who had fought the Russians. Saladin was rolling around in laughter as he told me this story. He said that his father would beat his two younger brothers, not for being caught by the Pakistan ISI, but for bringing explosives into the family home. His father would come to visit Saladin once his brothers had been released. The two brothers would have had a sense of humour failure upon being informed by the ISI military Commander that their father was personally coming to pick them up. Saladin laughed again; he did feel sorry for his siblings. Needless to say, Saladin's family was highly respected and feared by the Pakistan ISI and military. I would meet Saladin's father and family in the near future.

Back in the Al-Qaeda corridor, we were sat in two long rows of 15, facing each other with food served on plates between us. Several large plates were brought in by other prisoners and placed in the middle of the make shift table. The food dishes were a mix of Arab and Afghan dishes, spicy chicken, beef, and a host of steaming vegetables. Rice was served on three big plates; this was adorned with nuts and dried fruit. Fresh bread was piled up at one end and passed down the line. The aroma of fresh Afghan flat bread filled the air, one of the prison guards had been tasked by the Mullah to bring it in that morning. The bread was divided up equally between everyone. Fresh fruit juice was handed round and everyone filled their cups and had their fill. Abdul Aziz spoke out above everyone; his booming voice announced "enjoy brothers" everyone began to eat, Arab style. Breaking bread with their right hands and using this handful of bread to scoop up a piece of the meat dish. The left hand is never used when eating. In the Arab culture your left hand is used, when you're going to the toilet, so it is never used to break bread or to eat with. I had lived with and been surrounded by the Arab culture for many years right across the Middle-East, so I was accustomed to their ways, customs and protocol. I broke off a piece of meat and wrapped it in a small wrap of bread. I offered it to Saladin; this is a way of showing respect to your host. Little customs like that really matter and made a massive difference; most Westerners overlook this kind of detail. I have seen many Western people offend Arabs by the lack of knowledge regarding their customs. Many Westerners don't even know when they offend people. Cultural understanding is very important when building bridges within the Islamic world. Knowing the language is very beneficial, even if a person is not fluent, the Arabs respect the fact that a person has attempted to communicate in their native tongue. This can also help break the ice when people first meet. The meal that I was enjoying with Al-Qaeda and the rest of the terrorists was the best Bevan and I had had in two years. The conversation was light hearted and jovial. Eid was the Muslims equivalent of our Christmas and this was their Christmas dinner. A towel was passed around with a bowl of hot water for everyone to wash their hands. Chi-tea was promptly brought out and served, accompanied by home-made Afghan cakes with nuts and dates. Everyone was well fed and sprits were high. This was a very surreal situation to be in, given that we were all in max-security in an Afghan war zone. None the less it was a good down day for everyone; I had even been able to relax a little. The past weeks and months had been so intense I had been worried that I would burn myself out. Today had been a welcomed respite from my work. One of the Al-Qaeda members on Saladin's ok gave Bevan a pack of antibiotic tablets. These were like gold dust in Pul-i-Charkhi. I had mentioned to Saladin that Bevan needed some. The medical facilities were none existent within the prison. Prisoners had to pay for everything they needed. The Red-Cross dropped small amounts of medical supplies off each month, but the so called Afghan Doctors would sell the supplies down the local market. It was not uncommon for Prison staff and Afghan prison doctors 'butchers', not to be paid by the Afghan Government for 3 to 4 months. People had families to feed, so they would sell anything they could and make money when they could in order to feed their own families. Western Governments were paying the Afghanistan Government large sums of money each month to cover Government wages; the problem was that the corrupt Afghan Government officials were taking the money for themselves. Bevan was very happy to receive the antibiotics, at least now he could start to get his health back to normal. We stayed over in the Al-Qaeda corridor for a few hours, just talking amongst the terrorists. It was good to see Bevan interact with them. They were as inquisitive of Bevan as he was of them. I could see Bevan's mind working overtime, watching and assessing everything around him. He also watched me and how the terrorists acted around me. I had been accepted and I was being treated as an equal, this was a dear diary moment for Bevan. All our work had paid off. We were sitting in the heart of an international terrorist operational network.

"Prisoners who were not Al-Qaeda or Taliban were taxed money (protection money) every month by the guards; this stopped some prisoners from being savagely beaten by prison guards. If a person did not pay or he upset the guards in some small way, he was dragged outside to the chicken runs, the metal exercise area for prisoners. There he would be handcuffed in a stress position to the chain fence. Depending on the mood of the guard he would be beaten, on a bad day he would be whipped with metal cables and rubber hosepipes across their back or the balls of their feet. I witnessed many prisoners being beaten so badly, other prisoners had to carry them back into the prison block on blankets with blood trailing and pooling on the floor behind them. It was not uncommon for prisons to be hospitalised after such beatings"

I understood long ago that any beating is better than a bullet in the head. People disappeared or were transferred in the middle of the night, only never to be seen or heard of again. There had been too many deaths inside Afghan prisons, one of the worst being Pu-i-Charkhi. There is no time to worry about small things like ruptured kidneys, a broken jaw or internal bleeding, they were common place and regarded as trivial. This is nothing special, just daily life. The sad thing was the British Embassy knew about how bad things were and they shamefully looked the other way 'because they did not want to upset the Afghan Government'. This was just one of the lines said by the FCO London to my official 'next of kin'. Bevan and I stood up to the worst of the guards. On many occasions we both confronted guards on behalf of other prisoners. Bevan and I are both very old school, we believe that the strong should always stand up and protect the weak. Because I was part of the terrorist network and close friends with Commander Saladin, the prison guards stayed well clear of me and Bevan. The Mullah, recited the call to prayer, the sound of other calls to prayer could be heard coming from all of the other prison blocks around Pul-i-Charkhi. The Islamic call to prayer is normally 15 minutes before the prayers in the mosque start. The top end of the Al-Qaeda corridor was the area used as the mosque. The floor was always swept clean and a large section of blue carpet was placed over the rough grey concrete floor. All was in place, clean and tidy within 5 minutes. The blue carpet was the first I has seen in 2 years in Pu-i-Charkhi. Bevan always went back to our cell while the mosque and Islamic prayers were being conducted. One of the Al-Qaeda Commanders, who had been educated in Saudi Arabia, led the mosque. He had been invited to lead the prayers of the mosque by Saladin. The Mullah stood on his Islamic prayer mat out front at the head of the formation of Muslims behind him. There were several rows of Al-Qaeda and Taliban with six in each row. The position of where the prisoners stood in the rows was an indication of their rank and status within the terrorist groups. The top Al-Qaeda Commanders, including Saladin and Abdul Aziz, did not comply with this, they moved from one row to the next, checking that everyone was saying the Islamic prayers correctly. I took my place in the front of the third row, between Saladin and Abdul Aziz. The full mosque was carried out with extra prayers said at the end for the festival of Eid. I was also officially welcomed to the mosque by the Mullah. Nothing ever interrupted the Mosque, no phones were allowed and the prison guards never interrupted. Prayer times within the mosque were very strict. If anyone disrupted the mosque they would be beaten. The same went for anyone defacing the 'Quran', one Afghan tore a page out of the 'Holy Quran'. He was swiftly beaten, almost to death, and we never saw him again. Strict 'Sharia' law was implemented and upheld throughout the prison. Most Afghans had gone back to 'Sharia' law because of the level of corruption and no 'rule of law' within the Government of Afghanistan. I would spend endless afternoons talking and drinking chi-tea with the terrorists. The mornings were for my studying Islam and teaching the terrorists English. My afternoons were more relaxed, I moved around the different corridors mingling with the other prisoners and members of the Pakistan and Afghan Taliban.

"Children being groomed to fight in the Jihad"

Terrorists being held in Pul-i-Charkhi had outside visitors daily. Other terrorist Commanders would just turn up to discuss future operations. Families and friends, Afghan and Pakistan women would bring in their children, as young as seven, some were even younger. The children would run around playing at being soldiers during their family visits. Their games would one day become the real thing.

"These children were being groomed to fight in the Jihad and would become future young terrorists. There would be no greater pride in his fathers and mother's eyes than seeing their son sever the head off his first American or British soldier at the age of seventeen. By the age of twenty, would probably be involved in an attack on a Western military base and kill many more people. At twenty two they could well be running their own terrorist cell and small training camp and planting IEDs in Helmand. Then at twenty five, the Americans would hunt them down from helicopters and by the use of telephone intercepts, and like a wolf flushing him out into the open killing ground and fire rockets at him as he darts between shell craters, splattering his brains and guts all over the place. Then he will lie in a puddle of blood and his own body fluids, while staring up at the clear blue sky above him with half open, dark lifeless eyes, now nothing more than a dead rotting corpse, which the wild animals feed off. Now being an object of rotten, lifeless disgust, as lice and fly's crawled and buzzed over him and festering in his beard. I have seen so called Islamist warriors end up like this across the Middle-East; they often grow up to meet this fate. From little young cubs, that like to play at war, into wolves that are sent to the slaughter, a waste of life, depending on your point of view. The problem is for every terrorist that is killed, two more pop up to take their place. How many more innocent young boys will meet violent deaths due to their upbringing and indoctrination by the elders of their families"?

Early one evening as the sun was setting over the mountains that surrounded Pul-i-Charkhi, I lay on my bed, gazing out of the window. The mountains were only a few kilometres away and they were a glow of a thousand shades of red and deep golden blooms. The whole sky was filled with the rich warm colours of sunset. The backdrop of the mountains, framed by the sunset, was staggeringly beautiful and enchanting. I lay on my bed, contemplating life, while looking out across the vast desert plains that surrounded Pul-i-Charkhi. The shadows at the base of the mountains were moving slowly across the vast desert landscape. I remember thinking Afghanistan is the definition of 'beauty and the beast'. A country that is war torn beyond belief and yet has staggeringly amazing natural countryside. My thoughts were interrupted by Saladin's voice calling my name from the gate opposite in the Al-Qaeda corridor. The gates had been locked by the guards because the Americans had just landed by Black Hawk military helicopter next-door at 'Git-Mo'. Only the open landing of 15 feet separated us, Saladin had acquired a new mobile phone with new international prepaid 'Sim card'. It was a gift from him to me, for teaching him and his men English. Saladin had placed the phone inside a packet of pasta. He had then re-sealed it and now threw it towards me. This was when things got interesting. The bag of pasta hit the floor and stopped 6 feet away from me, on the other side of the bars. It was right in front of the main door to the prison guard's operation room for the whole of Pul-i-Charkhi. Luckily the door was closed. I looked up at Saladin, he said; 'problem'. Then he disappeared, due to the fact that he did not want to be seen by the Americans passing out mobile phones within maximum security prison. Saladin wanted to remain below the radar and liked being the 'Grey Man', unnoticed. I called Bevan to quickly bring me a broom. He came out of the cell to see what was going on, 'what's up'? I pointed at the pasta; Bevan said "no worries just bang on the wall and get one of the guards to pass it to you". I looked at Bevan; "my new phone from Saladin is in that bag of pasta". Bevan smiled, "fuck me, problem". You have to look at the funny side of this situation. The Americans could walk in at any moment; they could even be in the operations room. I did not want to have to pay the Afghan prison guards $100 to get my phone back if they found it. The guards had not been paid for over three months again, so they were all very hungry for money. With some quick work by Bevan and me, we retrieved the bag of pasta by dragging it carefully with the broom handle to our gate. The phone was safe and as a bonus we had a bag of pasta. The Afghan guards opened the operations room door and walked out into the corridor. They looked over to Bevan and me and greetings were exchanged. That was a close call. I phoned Saladin and sarcastically called him a 'good Commander'. I thanked him, we both laughed and he called himself a 'donkey'. We would laugh about this incident for days. Another funny, dear diary moment was when the Americans carried out a flash visit. All the doors and gates were open and all the Al-Qaeda and Taliban were sat in each other's cells. The guards had then locked all the cell doors so quickly that I had been locked in Saladin's small two man cell with several other members of Al-Qaeda, including; Abdul Aziz and the Mullah. OMG; I was now locked in a small prison cell with Al-Qaeda, this was turning out to be a strange day and I just looked at the funny side of it, there wasn't much else I could do. I just carried on with my English lesson.

"The Americans had walked past the cell and looked in. The look on their faces was priceless; I said
"hello" in English and introduced myself as 'Allahodin'. I went on and explained that I was conducting an English lesson. The Americans turned to the prison guards in complete disbelief and asked them how the hell had a British national had got through all the supposedly locked gates and security measures and was sitting with several Al-Qaeda terrorists, drinking Chi-tea. The Afghan guard said "no idea". The Americans continued on their walkabout. This was a dear diary moment for the Americans; the incident confirmed that I was well and truly sitting right within the heart of the terrorist network".

I do also believe that this was the first time that American military intelligence had ever seen a former British Paratrooper teaching Al-Qaeda and Pakistan Taliban, English. That fact would most unquestionably go into their written prison report. My objective in teaching the terrorists English was to improve their communication skills with people from Western countries. I achieved this, with future exceptional results. Many terrorists would be flipped, turned and would over time, end up working directly or indirectly for Western intelligence.

I spent a lot of time carefully trawling the corridors at key times of Pul-i-Charkhi, hunting for information and cultivating my terrorist contacts both inside the prison and across the whole of the Middle-East. My focus and efforts were getting results on every level. There were in excess of 5,000 prisoners located in Pul-i-Charkhi, 5,000 potential terrorists, so the odds were 5,000 to 1 not in my favour if things came on top. I liked being the underdog, but this was a little unnerving at times. 'John Hardy' the RSM Regimental Sergeant Major of 3 Para once said in Helmand; Paratroopers are supposed to be surrounded by the enemy. I was keeping this glorious tradition alive. This thought gave me great satisfaction; I was taking down Al-Qaeda and Pakistan Taliban terrorists from inside their own network. My information and intelligence was being used to kill a few terrorists along the way.

"Hunting Al-Qaeda international terrorists was the best fun you could have with your clothes on"

Hunting HVT's and known terrorists, and either directly or indirectly neutralising them with direct action or CIA drone signature strikes or apache helicopter gunship fire missions is all well and good, but getting up close and personal, face-to-face, is better and makes a point. 'The good guys will and are coming after the bad guys'. This is what the terrorists are scared of. From my personal experience, most of the so called terrorists are scared of extreme violence. I was a little taken aback when I discovered this. I found it quite funny that some 'want to be terrorists' but are scared of terror. The old saying 'live by the sword, die by the sword' comes to mind. So why do some families of the terrorists complain when drones kill them. The circle of life goes on regardless. My advice to any future bad guy is, if you don't want to die a potentially extremely violent and unpleasant death, don't become a terrorist. Forget the Hollywood movies, when you're dead you're dead, there is no comeback and forget any bravado regarding being shot. When you get hit it hurts like a bitch. I have seen many a so-called hard man and bad guy crying out for his mammy when his insides are on the outside and there is blood gushing from where his chest cavity once was. When your time is up, it's up, no God can change that. All one can do is fight till the end and go out with dignity. Me personally, I wanted to go out in a 'blaze of glory', but that is just me.

Al-Qaeda definitely had great manpower and very accurate intelligence of their own, they also had nerve. These were a formidable combination and made a worthy opponent. I had just one thing in common with the Al-Qaeda and other terrorist fighters and Commanders, I was not scared to die for what I believed in. In my case, my oath of allegiance to 'Queen and country'.

The next few months were extremely intense; this is the only way to describe it. Terrorist Commander Wais Hudein was teaching me the military tactics of both Taliban and Al-Qaeda. These were the tactics that were being employed by the terrorists against American and British forces in Afghanistan and across the Middle-East. These tactics were both tactical and strategic in nature. It was at this time that Al-Qaeda and the Taliban had just started to use several suicide bombers, supported by snipers and four man fire teams, simultaneously on the same target. This new tactic had been tried and tested in Nimruz Province, Southern Afghanistan. A large Afghan police station and Afghan Government buildings in 'Zaranj', 2km south along the river, had been destroyed. Wais Hudein's MO (Modus Operandi) was ruthless and efficient. This new strategy of multiple attacks by several different terrorist teams would soon be implemented, not just in Afghanistan, but across several Middle-East and Asian countries, including; Pakistan, Saudi Arabia, Syria and Iraq; Africa, Tunisia, and in Europe; Britain and France (most recently in Paris in November 2015). These tactics are being seen and used by Al-Qaeda in the present Syrian and Iraq civil wars. Foreign fighters from the old Soviet-Bloc countries and Saudi Arabia were being trained in terrorist training camps in and across Syria, Iraq, Southern and Western Pakistan, Afghanistan, Uzbekistan and Northern Tajikistan, in the vast untamed mountain ranges. After training, they were smuggled into Afghanistan and several other countries which have an active Jihad, through various well established smuggling routes, including the complex tunnel complexes and deserted airstrips in Northern Afghanistan.

"Taliban and Al-Qaeda narcotics smuggling routes"

I had already given American intelligence details of numerous locations. I knew that HVTs and terrorist leaders also used these locations to facilitate their movements in and out of Afghanistan. The Taliban and Al-Qaeda narcotics smuggling routes were also being heavily used in reverse to smuggle foreign fighters into Afghanistan. Terrorist safe houses were brisling with fighters who were highly trained in Guerrilla warfare, snipers and IED bomb making. A large number of Al-Qaeda and Taliban foreign fighters were channelled into the Afghan provinces of Farah, Helmand, Kandahar, Nuristan, Nangarhar, as well as Khowst and Paktika. A large amount of weapons, ammunition and equipment were also being supplied to active terrorist military units across Afghanistan by Hussein; the terrorist quartermaster located in Pul-i-Charkhi. His prison cell was more like a terrorist operational, and logistics office. Hussein's contacts over the border in Pakistan, specifically in Peshawar and Quetta, were working flat out to keep up with demand. Factory made IED's and shape charges were also coming in from Iran in growing numbers. Al-Qaeda and the Pakistan Taliban had a full on engineering factory making them. This factory was also run by the same family that facilitated the terrorist safe houses across Iran. Another interesting fact came to light; several members of the 'Osama bin Laden' family were located in one of these safe houses in Eastern Iran, I had given the code name 'K2' to this location. I had named it after the American secret military airbase in Uzbekistan. 'This was how important the locations in Iran were'.

"All terrorist foreign fighters were sanitized within the Al-Qaeda and Taliban safe house network, prior to them being deployed on terrorist missions and operations against American and British military forces across Afghanistan"

All terrorist foreign fighters were properly sanitized within the Al-Qaeda and Taliban safe house network, prior to them being sent out on terrorist missions and operations. All their personal documents, passports, foreign money, letters and family photographs were put into a large plastic envelope or bag, sealed and marked up with their name and put into a large blue plastic container which was full of other sanitized bags. No foreign fighters would carry anything on their person that could identify who they really were. After this had been completed, the foreign fighters were then handed false identification from a wide range of places. Some of the ID's used to cover terrorist movements were identification documents from the Red-Cross and other NGO's operating in and across Afghanistan. Some of the terrorists even carried false documents from 'USAID'. The forgers within the terrorist network had been busy supplying all these counterfeit documents and travel papers. Al-Qaeda and the Pakistan Taliban network have some of the best forgers in the world, from Damascus to Riyadh and from Baghdad to Kabul. Cover identities or 'funny names' as the CIA like to call them, were widely used. This enabled the terrorists to move freely and travel between countries. The number of names used by many terrorists at first, made the network look bigger than it really was. It was not uncommon for an Al-Qaeda Commander and other terrorist leaders to have seven or eight different names and sets of documents. After a while Western intelligence confirmed that the details of one terrorist that had portrayed several personas, was in fact this one individual slippery little terrorist.

"The Crusades and the age of the Assassins, Saladin and Richard the Lion Heart"

The other very important fact when assessing and understanding international terrorist networks is most networks are in some way interconnected. The connections sometimes are not the obvious ones, but if you look hard enough there are always links and cross-overs. International terrorism comes in many different layers, terrorist ideology and extremism is always at the core. Century old blood feuds and disagreements can also be found, and in many cases, manipulated. Within the Islamic culture, old feuds are as relevant today as there were 200 years ago. In some Islamic countries the locals speak of the Crusades, the age of the Assassins, Saladin, Richard the Lion Heart and Alexander the Great, as if these historical figures and events existed just yesterday. Some of the villages I have visited in the middle of the desert and up in the snow-capped mountains of the 'Hindu Kush' would tell their children stories around the campfire on cold winter nights. The stories about Alexander the Great were retold from one generation to the next, some of these isolated villages were truly living in the dark ages.

"Al-Qaeda international Terrorist network"

The Al-Qaeda intelligence network is vast and far reaching, from Afghanistan NDS (security services) to the Afghan Army 'ANA' to the Pakistan ISI and their military. Al-Qaeda has even infiltrated the police in 'UAE' in places like Dubai. Even some airport staff at Dubai International Airport are on the Al-Qaeda payroll. This would explain how Afghan illegal narcotics are sometimes shipped through Dubai international airport freight. Even a small number of baggage staff in European airports were supporting the Al-Qaeda and Pakistan Taliban cause. This was confirmed by Al-Qaeda Commanders with whom I personally spoke. Bevan and I also learned from an international drug dealer, Marius Venter, that some DHL staff in Afghanistan were involved in, and facilitated, the transportation of Afghan heroin from Afghanistan, via Dubai, and on to European and West African countries. Al-Qaeda, the Afghan and Pakistan Taliban have utilised all their international contacts to the maximum, on every level. Many of their weapons, foreign fighters and narcotics smuggling networks would overlap when required. It is fact that a lot of the Al-Qaeda and Pakistan Taliban terrorist operations are funded through the Afghan narcotics trade. The money markets of the Middle-East, Europe (Italy) and Asia including Singapore, are used to launder terrorist money. The Government owned Casino in Lebanon is also one of the places were large sums of money is laundered (American military intelligence 'J2' confirmed my findings on this point during a meeting in Basra, Southern Iraq). Exclusive hotels in Lebanon are used to launder large amounts of money. The hotels have been brought by terrorist front companies. These hotels, on paper, are kept at full occupancy all year round? In reality the hotels are empty most of the time. This is pretty obvious to see, big flash hotels built in the middle of nowhere, north of the Lebanese Capital Beirut. The Russian Mafia have got a big foothold within many of these hotels. Many Middle-Eastern black market arms deals are carried out at these hotels located in Jounieh, Byblos and Tripoli. Another interesting point is that Hezbollah are involved in the Afghan smuggling operations, both of narcotics and weapons, it's a two way street flowing through the networks, drugs go out and weapons, foreign fighters come in. Large amounts of money, weapons and drugs make for a potent mix, add international terrorism into the melting pot and I would say we have a major problem on the door step of Europe. 'It only takes 45 minutes in a speed boat from Western Lebanon and Syria to Northern and Southern Cyprus'.

"The Bank of Al-Madina, international Scandal"

The 'Bank of Madina scandal' is linked to international money laundering from Lebanon to several countries, Including Europe and America. Due to the sensitivity of the Medina Bank scandal I cannot give details at this point, but what I can say is that in the past I was personally responsible for the security of the Banks owner, and I was personally given written permission - a 'letter of authorisation' - from the Banks owner to investigate what had been going on within the Bank. This included my being the sole representative of the Bank to liaise with Governments and intelligence agencies in countries such as America, Britain, France and the 'UN' task force which was also investigating the dealings of the Medina bank. I attended several meetings with French intelligence on the Banks owner's behalf. I had advised that the Banks owner should move (for his own protection) into one of the Royal residencies in Saudi Arabia. This was due to the Russian Mafia having placed a contract on his head. I withdrew all my assistance and services to the Bank when I discovered evidence that the bank had been involved in international money laundering. I also discovered links to the Syrian Government and Saddam Hussein's Iraq. In addition, I also found proof that there was links between the Madina Bank and the Lebanese terrorist group Hezbollah and further links to money laundering in America and several other countries. There were also links to Saddam Hussein's Iraq, which I personally witnessed, as well as several other highly sensitive subjects. According to Fortune Magazine, Maher al Assad, brother of embattled Syrian president Bashar al Assad, benefited the most from the billion dollar money laundering operation at the collapsed bank. Al Madina was used to launder kickback money of Iraqi officials and their partners in the illegal gaming of the UN's oil-for-food programme. Sources put the amount transferred, and laundered, through Al-Madina at more than $1 billion, with a 25% commission going to Syrian officials and their Lebanese allies. Al-Madina president Adnan Abu Ayyash accuses General Rustom Ghazaleh and three brothers of spiriting away $72 million from the bank between 2000 and 2003, Abu Ayyash's lawyer, Jean

Azzi, said in May 19, 2005. Meanwhile, the authorities put pressure on media outlets to abstain from any reporting that hinted to the involvement of political figures in Al-Madina. In the future, all travel restrictions put on Adnan Abu Ayyash would be lifted and he would resume his international travel, including discreet trips to the south of England. The blow back of the bank scandal continues, internationally across several countries, including Britain, America and France.

"This would make for a very interesting and unnerving story for the future. The Bank of Medina, International terrorism, the Russian Mafia, Columbian Drug Cartels, and Saddam Hussein's Iraq and his son Uday's violent death. The Syrian Government and their Intelligence Services. Add money, murder, sex, power and weapon shipments with terrorist safe houses, with Afghan drugs and the Pakistan, Afghan Taliban and the Haqqani network on the side and what a potent explosive mix this makes..."

A lot of the terrorist weapons in the Middle-East come from Russia and China. Ships are the chosen means and method of transportation. The shipments are broken down at sea and moved to small boats that then make their way to locations in Pakistan, Syria, Yemen and Somalia. Other large shipments are split up and broken down, then moved over-land into Iran, Iraq and Afghanistan, then dispersed amongst terrorist groups and their safe houses. During my time, several years in Saddam's Iraq from 2002 onwards, I had found and photographed many weapons, including; Chinese land mines, Russian Rockets and French 'TOW' anti-tank missiles. French jet aircraft engines were also found. An endless supply of small arms from Russia and China littered Iraq, before, during and after the 2003 war. Al-Qaeda and other terrorist groups had acquired large amounts of these weapons from Iraq and stockpiled them at key secret locations in Eastern Syria along the Syrian and Iraqi border. I had provided American military intelligence with several such locations. Some of these weapons that came out of Iraq in 2003 are now being used against American and British forces in Afghanistan 2014. A small number of Surface-to-Air missiles were also taken out of Iraq by the Iraqi insurgency and other terrorist groups, these have not all re-surfaced yet.

"Terrorist Afghan narcotic shipments are processed in drug refineries, hidden in the Mountains of Lebanon and Black market arms deals in Beirut and Damascus"

One of the main smuggling routes used overland is from Afghanistan, through Iran, Iraq and Syria and into Lebanon. Narcotic shipments are then processed in drug refineries hidden in the Mountains of Lebanon. The narcotics are cut and processed; this quadruples the street value. They are then packed and moved down to the coast, close to the port of Tripoli, picked up by speed boats and taken to larger ships in international waters, which then disrupts the illegal narcotics worldwide? Confirmed end users are drug gangs in South America and across Europe. Marina communication equipment is used by the terrorist groups whilst they carry out their illegal activities. The Marina communication radios are the same equipment as those used by the big oil tankers moving around the shipping routes. America will not interfere with this marina communication network as it could compromise the safety of other vessels in the same area. Al-Qaeda had cottoned on to this and used it to their advantage, using this equipment on their operations and across their smuggling routes and international networks. I had used the Marina communications setup in 2003 and 2006 in Syria and Iraq, it is very affective. It's a system that was designed for ships at sea, but also works extremely well on land. My exceptional operations manager 'Sharpy' was able, in a com's test, to reach a call sign in Brazil, Southern America. The test was carried out from our operational base located in Cyprus. It was just one example of how effective the Marina com's set-up can be. Within a short time Al-Qaeda and the Pakistan Taliban had realised just how effective Marina coms could be so it was rolled out to their terrorist operations in Africa and Yemen. Al-Qaeda suppliers would meet every few months to negotiate further deals and confirm orders for future supplies of equipment. The 'Phoenicia Hotel' in down town Beirut in Lebanon was a regular meeting location. Other smaller more discreet hotels were also used along 'Hamra Street', but the Phoenicia location was one of their favourites. The excellent wine bar and restaurant on the top floor may have had something to do with their choice of venue. This restaurant has the biggest wine list in the whole of the Middle-East. I have spent many a night sampling its vast array of wines, whilst witnessing Al-Qaeda and Hezbollah black market arms negotiations and deals. The view is splendid from the top floor, out across the bay of Beirut towards Jounieh and the rugged dark backdrop of the Lebanese Mountains. The city lights dance in the sea at night, it was quite enchanting. It is very easy to forget that there were wars being fought on the other side of the mountains. I had lived in Lebanon prior to my time in Afghanistan, so I knew it well. The Al-Qaeda and Pakistan Taliban were taken aback by how much I did actually know.

"Al-Qaeda and Terrorist Funding"

An American report which was leaked to the New York Times in November 2006, estimated that the Iraq insurgency was financially self-sustaining. It was reported that between $70-$200 million a year was being raised from illegal activities, including oil smuggling, ransom from kidnaps, counterfeiting and the connivance of corrupt religious charities. The total included up to $100 million in smuggling and other criminal activity involving the oil industry, helped by corrupt and compliant officials, other estimates of the income of insurgents were even higher. Fast forward to 2011, Al-Qaeda and their Iraq, Afghan networks have joined forces. The Pakistan, Afghan Taliban and Al-Qaeda are running their illegal narcotics trade out of Afghanistan. 'AQI' (Al-Qaeda in Iraq) are now running a $200 million a year operation; they have combined their smuggling routes, safe houses, foreign fighters and resources. (See glossary Dubai money laundering and Haqqani network) Al-Qaeda and international terrorism is now self-sustained. This is made possible by Government corruption. The latest corruption perceptions index released lists Afghanistan, Iraq, Somalia, Yemen, Democratic Republic of Congo and Zimbabwe as being the most corrupt countries in the world. Al-Qaeda and radical Islam are well established in most of these countries, the Al-Qaeda foot print is clearly stamped in many corrupt Middle-East Governments. Corruption and terrorism go hand in hand in countries like Afghanistan, Iraq and Syria. Where there is no real 'rule of law', terrorism and corruption will flourish. Afghanistan is a perfect example of this fact. This example does not bode well for the British Embassy in Kabul which was responsible for the mentorship program of the Afghan Justice system. This could very well go some way in explaining why senior staff from the British Embassy Kabul covered up the level of corruption within the Afghan Justice system and the reported miscarriages of justice and ill-treatment from British and Commonwealth nationals. Afghanistan is very close to becoming a failed state as of 2014. The fact that the corrupt Afghan Government is now blaming the West, including America and Britain, for the high level of corruption within the Afghan Government is an example of how dysfunctional the Afghan Government really is. The power sharing agreement that the Afghan Government is signing with the Taliban is another example of how dysfunctional Afghanistan is. The question has got to be asked by Western Governments, what has the Afghan war achieved, when the very people who were removed from power over 12 years ago, the Taliban are now coming back into power? What has changed and what have Western Governments achieved, were the 2000+ American and 450+ British ISAF soldier's lives, which have been killed fighting in Afghanistan worth the cost? My personal view is that not one American, British or ISAF soldier's life should have been sacrificed. Western cities and streets are not safer from terrorists now following Afghan and Iraqi wars. The fact is that the threat from terrorism, the bleed out effect from Afghanistan and Iraq is worse now than it has ever been. Poverty in Afghanistan is also playing its part in the instability; another cause for the increasing poverty is that women are no longer as economically active as they were, due to security and religious reasons. Unemployment has also soared outside the cities, making the poverty stricken and lawless lands ripe recruiting grounds for the terrorist's networks. The old saying 'a man has to feed his family' is very true. The situation is exploited by extremists. Al-Qaeda and the Pakistan, Afghan Taliban are able to infiltrate Afghanistan and Pakistan at will, in order to inflict casualties on American and British ISAF forces and the civilian population. The Al-Qaeda and other terrorist networks enable its foreign fighters to come into their 'AO' Area of Operations from any angle, whether manipulating safe houses and passage through Iran, Iraq, Syria, or through several other routes via Pakistan, Tajikistan and Uzbekistan. Multiple routes into the country and multiple escape routes with protection and safe passage from within elements of corrupt Governments like the Pakistan ISI give terrorists the advantage to move almost at will, wherever they want. Al-Qaeda is growing in strength and cunning, this is contrary to what politicians will have the general public believe. The prospect of a strong, prosperous and unified Afghanistan is further away now than at any time before. The problem is when Western military forces pull out, will the infighting start and will that lead to another bloody civil war. The fact that this is a concern to Western Governments speaks volumes; the truth is that Western Governments just want to get out of Afghanistan as quickly as possible. It will not be admitted to, but Afghan is looking more like a lost cause with every month that goes by. Terrorist networks are taking full advantage of the situation. It is now just a case of when, not if, there is another major terrorist attack on a Western city, that has been ordered and planned from Afghanistan, Pakistan or the Levant. I hope that I will be proved wrong but the facts speak for themselves. Western governments cannot afford to overlook or ignore the lessons of history, a short term fix will only lead to more 'Blow Back' on the Western countries and more 'bleed out' of radical Islam. When the former British Defence Minister Fox, publicly called Afghanistan a 13th century broken country, the Afghan Government were not happy. 'Sometimes the truth hurts'. British politicians need to save face and will publicly say that things have improved in Afghanistan and that Afghanistan is not a safe haven for AlQaeda. From my perspective, after sitting within the heart of Al-Qaeda and terrorist's international operations, the Western politicians are very wrong on both counts. The sands of time will tell.

"Emeralds and Illegal mining operations"

Another little known fact is that the wealth and future of Afghanistan may very well be lying under the feet of the Afghan people. The estimated wealth of the natural resources within the geographic location of Afghanistan is millions if not trillions of dollars. Al-Qaeda and the Pakistan Taliban have been utilising these natural resources for many years to help finance international terrorism. Illegal mining operations are scattered right across Afghan, but mainly in the north. One of the biggest is within the North of the Panjshir Valley. The Panjshiri's, with the help and protection from the corrupt Afghan police force and Afghan Army, mine and transport precious stones, including large amounts of emeralds. They are then illegally smuggled out of Afghanistan to Dubai via Kabul airport. Panjshir members of the Afghan Government use their diplomatic immunity, passports and status to facilitate the smuggling routes. Hundreds of thousands of dollars' worth of Afghan emeralds are stolen, and taken out of Afghanistan every week. The Panjshiri tribe is lining their own pockets with the wealth of the Afghan people, at the expense of the poor. The Massoud family have one particular emerald; this one stone is bigger than the size of a man's fist. I arranged for experts to view this stone on the condition that if it was sold, any profit would be given to the Afghan people. The UK expert was flown into Afghan and viewed the stone. He authenticated the stone which was valued as 'priceless'. The UK expert was the same guy that authenticates and values precious stones for 'Harrods' of London. This emerald was the biggest that the expert had ever seen, let alone held in his hands. We took photographs as evidence to retain on file. This magnificent jewel deserved to be in a museum to do it justice. Muslim Hyatt, the former Afghan Defence Attaché along with his Canadian contacts had other ideas. They were attempting to sell the emerald on the black market. I had already informed the Americans about this in the past. The money that the Panjshiri's were trying to make from the illegal selling of Afghan emeralds was to be used to de-stabilise the Afghan Government. The Panjshiri's wanted their own corrupt Government to rule over Afghanistan. The Karzai Government soon put an end to their plans. Photographs of the emerald, which confirm its size, were taken and placed at a safe location in Europe. Luckily, just before I had been illegally held and put in prison in Afghanistan, I had copied my computer hard drives during a visit to Dubai. I always try to cover my back, all the documents, reports, files; photographs both professional and personal had been copied and moved to a safe place. These files would prove to be very important in clearing my name and wiping the smile off a few people's faces, who thought that all my files had been destroyed. I would never leave myself with no backup. Copies of all files have been made and are located in three different countries, including America, Europe and the Far-East. If I was killed in Pul-i-Charkhi, all my files were to be made public and all photographs were to be openly published on the internet. Like I have always said, the truth always comes out in the end...!!

Al-Qaeda, Pakistan and Afghan Taliban had also been utilising the wealth of the Afghan emeralds. Terrorist networks were trading emeralds and Afghan heroin for weapons from Russian black market arms dealers in Tajikistan and Hezbollah terrorist Commanders in Lebanon. The Panjshiri tribe were also trading emeralds with the Afghan Taliban for weapons and vice versa. All the terrorist groups operating in and across Afghanistan are interconnected, nothing is how it first may appear to be and nothing is ever clean cut. With outside influences and third parties picking the bones dry of the Afghan country's wealth, it is no wonder that anyone who has money has left Afghanistan. China and a host of other countries have moved into Afghanistan and are claiming their stake, under the shadow of so called international development. The sad point is that the majority of the wealth found in Afghanistan does not stay there and it most certainly does not find its way into the pockets of the poor Afghan people. The wealth goes to corrupt Afghan Government officials, Afghan private security companies, warlords, drug lords and foreign powers. The most dysfunctional of the corrupt Afghan Ministries within the corrupt Afghan government is the Ministry of Mines. This is the most corrupt of the corrupt. What goes on within this Afghan Government Ministry, and is authorised by the Afghan Government, is the closest thing to slave labour I have ever witnessed in the 21st Century. Afghans who try to investigate the level of corruption often end up being murdered. Even Judges have been killed. The Afghan Mafia and the Taliban prefer to kill an Afghan judge rather than have to pay the bribes that the Judge was asking for. This is life in

Afghan. More Afghan Government officials and Judges have been killed in Afghanistan in the past 5 years than in the past 25 years put together. None of them died of natural causes, well unless a bullet from an AK47 through the back of the head is now a natural cause of death in Afghanistan.

"Al-Qaeda, 'CBC' Cross Border Communications - American Military base destroyed by suicide truck bomb"

The battle between the Western military and Al-Qaeda and the Pakistan, Afghan Taliban was raging across Afghanistan while I was within Pul-i-Charkhi. The terrorist attacks on American and British ISAF forces in Afghan and Iraq were relentless; hundreds of people were dying every month. The Terrorist Commanders within Pul-i-Charkhi were receiving daily reports and updates from their men and networks outside and across Afghanistan and internationally. Data memory cards were being smuggled in by the Afghan doctors and Afghan medical staff who visited the terrorists weekly. The memory cards held images and videos taken by Al-Qaeda fighters across the Middle-East, including Helmand province, Southern Afghanistan and the tribal border areas of Waziristan and Pakistan. Some of these home-made videos showed uncut footage of Al-Qaeda, Pakistan and Afghan Taliban ambushes and IED attacks on American and British troops. I viewed many of these images with Al-Qaeda and other terrorist Commanders whilst in Pul-i-Charkhi, some of them were equally horrific and disturbing. I suspect that some of these videos were shown to me as a test to see what my reactions were; Al-Qaeda as usual studied my reactions. I remained detached, cold and emotionless throughout. If I had shown anything other than support of Al-Qaeda I would have been killed on the spot, so I just kept my emotions in check and within. The only way to describe how I really felt would be, having the fires of hell burning inside me, but I had to keep an ice cold exterior. This was not an easy thing to do. I had to look on the situation through very cold eyes. I could not save the Western soldiers in the videos, but I could save some of them that had not been attacked yet. My focus was calm but calculated. Save the ones I could. I could not help to save anyone if I was dead, so I had to keep my emotions in check and under control. Senior terrorist Commanders across Afghanistan and Pakistan would send terrorist videos into the Al-Qaeda and Taliban leaders within Pul-i-Charkhi. If Al-Qaeda Commanders agreed that the videos were ok they would be edited in Kabul or Jalalabad and then posted or couriered to the Arabic news channels across the Middle-East including; Al-Arabiya and Al-Jazeera (24 hour Arabic news channels). One of the videos that I viewed was of a terrorist attack on an American FOB, (Forward Operating Base) located in the East of Afghanistan close to the Pakistan border. The terrorist had driven a large truck carrying a suicide bomb into the American military base and detonated the explosive charge. The blast and shock wave from the suicide blast had completely destroyed the FOB. The terrorist had positioned three video cameras in a triangular configuration on the high ground, surrounding and overlooking the American FOB. The footage that I viewed was staggering; it looked like a scene from a very brutal Hollywood movie. The effects and shock wave from the suicide blast was staggering, it flattened the FOB. I confirmed later during a meeting with American intelligence that there had been a lot of fatalities during this attack. The FOB had been completely wiped out. The terrorists began using the video as a propaganda tool. I informed

American intelligence that I had seen this video and that similar terrorist attacks were being planned on America FOB's along the Afghan Pakistan border. I covertly copied data cards and videos without the terrorist's knowledge. These were very important, because the videos were the raw footage, no terrorists faces had been blocked or pixelated out. The evidence could be used to identify the perpetrators and their Commanders, locations of training facilities were also identified. I had also ascertained, that the nature of the terrorist attacks was becoming bolder, better planned, organised and conducted, with increasingly indiscrimination in their execution. The Terrorist network was at this point transiting and relocating many more foreign fighters into Helmand, Southern Afghanistan. Any activity in Helmand grabbed my attention, due to the fact that British military forces including the British Parachute Regiment (my old Regiment), were operationally deployed across the area at this time. Al-Qaeda and the Taliban were planning a large number of attacks on British troops, so I took it upon myself to disrupt and prevent as many of them as possible. Things were about to get very interesting. The British Parachute Regiment has a fierce fighting reputation. Hard won and well deserved. Even the leadership of Al-Qaeda respect the combat ability of the Para's. This was confirmed during many of my conversations with Al-Qaeda and other terrorist Commanders. My being a former member of the British Para's was well known by the terrorist network. My advice to Al-Qaeda was to leave the Para's alone, because if Al-Qaeda or any other terrorist network went up against the Para's, they would suffer very heavy casualties. The terrorist Commanders had already decided to launch sustained attacks against British forces. Al-Qaeda being full of misguided ego decided to embark on a fierce IED and suicide bombing campaign against British troops in Afghanistan. So I was working overtime to collect and assess as much intelligence as I could on the terrorist plans; when, where and how. The Americans discreetly picked up the reports as soon as I prepared them. All my intelligence was acted upon; the Americans assured me that all relevant information relating to the attacks on British soldiers and members of the Parachute Regiment would be quickly passed onto British military operational Command at Camp Bastion, Helmand. I exploited every opportunity to move deeper and closer into the Al-Qaeda and terrorist network, in my situation knowledge was power. I had to balance obtaining high level intelligence quickly and not being reckless. I would be no good to anyone if I was caught and killed by Al-Qaeda. I feared that the terrorist Commanders would wake up one morning, wipe the sleep from their eyes and realise what I was doing, but until then I would soldier on. Stopping Al-Qaeda and terrorist attacks was good, but burning down their network from the inside would be even better. I was even more determined that good would come out of all this. I would look up at the stars at night, hoping and praying that I wouldn't become compromised by Al-Qaeda. I needed a little more time to make a big difference and help British troops in Helmand. My life had never been one of simple domesticity. It has been a living cocktail, with equal parts, perfume, danger and gunpowder. Right now, it was all gunpowder and danger. I was killing from long distance, but I was risking my life to do it and I didn't target innocent people. All those that I went after had spent their lives bringing pain to others; they were all terrorists, does that make me a bad person, or am I morally on the side of right? Is the world not a better place without those terrorists in it? This is all subjective, in my world, 'it is what it is'. In my opinion, if terrorists did not kill innocent people, then people would not kill terrorists. If the terrorists did not like it, they should look for a different line of work.

"Cold Zero, resulting in a clean kill"

An old friend once told me during his military sniper operations in the Middle-East, that 'Cold Zero' was what you looked for, that sweet spot for trigger pulls that was what he was looking for before every kill. No hand tremble, no jerk of the finger, controlled breathing until you feel the kick of the weapon and your shot is away. This controlled discipline, with the bad guy crisp and clear in the middle of the crosshairs, invariably resulting in a clean kill, one less terrorist in the world. Where his face had once been was an unrecognisable bloody gaping hole. The long distance flight from a 7.62mm bullet or my beloved .50 calibre, built up astonishing kinetic energy. In fact the further the round travelled the more energy it built up, until it finally slammed into a solid object such as a human head that belonged to a terrorist player, the result was devastating. In Pul-i-Charkhi I had Al-Qaeda, Pakistan and Afghan Taliban well and truly in the centre of my cross hairs and sights. With the help of the American intelligence and military, I was taking down terrorists and making my way up the food chain. It was only a matter of time until I nailed the location of Osama bin Laden.

"Helmand Province, Southern Afghanistan"

The South of Afghanistan had been badly neglected after the fall of the Taliban in 2002. America and its allies had put most of their efforts into squeezing the life out of what remained of the Taliban and Al-Qaeda in the mountains, east of the country along the Pakistan border. From 2003, Western military and intelligence efforts had been focused and diverted into fighting the war and the insurgency in Iraq. Troops and Special Forces based in Afghanistan concentrated on targeting Taliban and Al-Qaeda Commanders and leaders. The material help that was promised after the Taliban were driven out of the major towns and cities was slow in coming to the South. Kandahar was just left simmering away, the fundamentalism remained as strong as ever, just festering beneath the surface, underground within the Mosques, surrounding villages and hamlets. Al-Qaeda and the Taliban had re-grouped and were evolving into what would be later called Kandahar Al-Qaeda and Pakistan Taliban. A new generation of terrorists has evolved and taken route. Their new main training ground would be Iraq and Syria, young insurgent fighters were becoming battle hardened very quickly, their knowledge and expertise was being harnessed by the terrorist networks across the Middle-East. Iraq and Afghanistan has evolved into one of the worse terrorist insurgency that the world has ever seen. Syria has also become one of the newest breeding and training grounds for Islamic extremists and their call for Jihad. A lot of the Taliban and Al-Qaeda fighters went to fight the Americans and Western Government forces in Iraq. After Iraq a lot of these fighters returned to fight in Afghanistan, Pakistan and Syria. Now a large number of the fighters from the Afghan Jihad are now fighting in the Syrian civil war under the flag of Al-Qaeda. Afghan and foreign fighters can also be found fighting across Africa including Somalia, Mali and Nigeria. The Syrian Jihad would over-shadow all the other Jihads in the not too distant future. Al-Qaeda would become strong enough to attack and take over whole cities across Syria and Western Iraq. The Iraqi city of Fallujah 2014 would be an example of Al-Qaeda's growing strength; this was also a clear indication of two Jihads within different countries becoming one Geographic conflict spanning multiple countries in the region.

My personal belief is that we have not seen the worst of the violence in and across the Middle-East yet, time will tell, (See Glossary, Arab Spring).

While all the fighting was taking place in Iraq, Syria and across Afghanistan, the corrupt Afghan officials were getting fat on greed and corruption. The Afghan Government officials from the North made sure that their villages and cities in the North of the country received help and support, new roads, schools and key infrastructure. Funding was plentiful. The South of the country was a stark contrast and received very little. It is no wonder that the Taliban has flourished under these circumstances, poverty breeds contempt and contempt breeds hatred. With the absence of rule of law, it's no wonder the terrorists quickly gained power and strength right across Southern Afghanistan. This feeling was mirrored within Pul-i-Charkhi. Over time, a large number of fighters involved in the Jihads in Iraq and across Africa returned home and drifted into places like Helmand and Kandahar Province, Southern Afghanistan. Kandahar was the birth place of the Afghan Taliban, unbeknown to Western Governments in 2007; Kandahar was also the birthplace of Kandahar Al-Qaeda, whose fighters would become prominent in the Syrian, Iraq conflicts.

"International Terrorism, Foreign Fighters and the Global Jihad"

The Pakistan Taliban and Al-Qaeda have de-badged themselves for political reasons. The Pakistan Taliban was first formed operationally in Waziristan, Western Pakistan. The Pakistan Taliban has been conducting international terrorist operations from 2006. The biggest to date was the New York, Times Square attempted car bombing and the Suicide bombing of the CIA base at Camp Chapman in Afghanistan. This proved that some Western intelligence so call experts had got their analysis very wrong when it came to the Pakistan Taliban, in 2006-2007 the same Western intelligence experts had said that the Pakistan Taliban does not have the capability to hit targets outside Pakistan and Afghanistan. With more terrorist operations being uncovered, the Pakistan Taliban have become a prominent international terrorist force with their fighters confirmed in every Jihad, from Somalia to Damascus and Libya to Mali. Many aspects of the Pakistan Taliban, Haqqani network and Al-Qaeda are one of the same. This point explains why the Pakistan Taliban is so far reaching and organised. The majority of the Taliban and Al-Qaeda training camps are located within Pakistan, Syria, Iran and across Africa. The size of some of these terrorist training camps confirms the massive increase of foreign fighters and foreign instructors flooding into the Middle-East, Afghanistan and Pakistan. When terrorist camps and training facilities are targeted and destroyed by the Western military using AC130 gunships and Apache helicopters, sensitive sight exploration teams, 'clean up teams', were sent in to gather evidence. Documents, travel papers from the dead terrorist bodies, note books, maps, anything that held any tactical or strategic intelligence value was photographed, then bagged and tagged. This evidence was used to stop future terrorist attacks and operations. On many occasions this was very successful. The large terrorist camp in Iraq, Code name 'Snake', is a good example of this. The operation against the terrorist camp was given the code name; 'Snake Eyes'. The 'Clean up' teams found a treasure trove of passports and other documents. This proved that the Iraq insurgency was being heavily manned by foreign fighters from countries including; Saudi Arabia, Iran, Lebanon, Egypt and Afghanistan. Evidence was found in terrorist training camps and safe houses in Pakistan when they were hit by Western Forces in 2008 – 2014. Maps of the City of London and the London underground had been found, along with plans to attack key locations across the British Capital and other cities across England. Another big problem that was uncovered was the large number of Westerners that were attending Al-Qaeda and Pakistan Taliban training courses in Pakistan. Evidence of Western nationals from America, Canada, Britain and several other European countries was uncovered; all had attended terrorist training courses. Many of these people were now back living within Western countries and Capital cities. IED bomb making and operational security, these were just two of the subjects that Western Muslims were being taught within the terrorist training camps. The skills that they had learned would later be used by Al-Qaeda sleeper cells in Western countries to launch terrorist attacks against soft targets. The links between these terrorist training camps and the new breed of home grown terrorists living within Western countries is on the increase, the large number of British and foreign fighters confirmed fighting within the ranks of Al-Qaeda groups in the Syrian Civil war, is a warning and a red flag to Western countries that when the fighting is over, these battle hardened Al-Qaeda fighters will return home to Western countries in the future. Between Afghanistan, Pakistan and Syria, the number of Western foreign fighters is conservatively put at 2000, these figures are said to be much higher from sources within Al-Qaeda. There are also thousands of Westerners fighting under the Al-Qaeda banner in and across Africa, in places like Somalia, Ethiopia, Mali, Morocco and Nigeria. There are also active Al-Qaeda cells operating in Cyprus, South Africa, Kenya, Tanzania, Zimbabwe and several other African countries. Al-Qaeda training camps and facilities can be found within most of these countries. Most travel to these countries does not draw attention, so the terrorist's networks facilitate the movements of their fighters easily and most the time all their movements fly under the radar, undetected by Western intelligence. The Al-Qaeda network flows through these countries with impunity and ruthless efficiency. The Terrorist attacks on the 'West Gate' shopping mall in Kenya by Al-Shabab has only highlighted the fact that AlQaeda has a strong operational capability in and across Africa and can use Africa as a launching platform for terrorist attacks against Europe and America. In 2003 an internal South African intelligence report stated that there would be several major future threats to South Africa and the African continent. Two of the threats were; 1) The procurement of clean drinking water and armed conflict over drinking water, and 2) Radical Islam. Already in 2014, the spread of radical Islam and Al-Qaeda has escalated across Africa. Taliban franchises have sprung up in Mali, Nigeria, Kenya and Somalia. Libya and Egypt have also witnessed a major increase in Al-Qaeda and terrorist activity. The belt of Islamic countries right across Northern Africa have all seen violent uprisings with terrorist connections and terrorist groups making their mark. The escalation of violence is still evident in news reports coming out of Africa. We hold our breath for the next major terrorist attack against innocent Westerners and Western targets and interests across Africa. The Arab spring has turned into an Arab winter and then into an Arab terror (See glossary, Arab Spring). The fact that British troops are still in Afghanistan, and Special Forces will remain there for some time, is still a very raw political subject. The British army and all its service personnel should be supported wherever and whenever they are operationally deployed. It's the politics and the flawed intelligence leading to military units being deployed that needs to be looked into carefully. After the Iraq WMD fiasco and lies, we cannot take all politicians at their word. Politicians need to learn from their mistakes from the past. In the future, politicians need to base the decision to send soldiers to war on facts, hard evidence. They should also take notice of what the public has to say. The British Government refused to use military action in Syria, which was due to the public not wanting anything to do with another ground war like Iraq and Afghanistan. If the British Government had gone against the British publics wishes; there would have been a public outcry, the likes of which have never been seen. The British Government made the right choice not to send in ground forces or attack Syria with air assets. If military force had been used, the whole situation would have escalated very quickly and the result would have been a war bigger in size and scope than the Iraq and Afghan wars combined, with the elements of Russia, Iran fighting a proxy war against America, Israel and Britain. The Shadow of the Iraq decision to go to war in 2003 still over shadows any military action Britain may take on any country in the future. The Afghan war also casts a dark shadow over Britain's politicians. Rudyard Kipling's 'Barrackroom ballads', published in 1892, contained a poem 'The young British soldier'. Which was much quoted by those predicting the dire consequences of getting mixed up with Afghanistan and Al-Qaeda, I know this poem very well. One verse ran;

"When you're wounded and left on Afghanistan's plains and the women come out to cut up what remains, just roll to your rifle and blow out your brains and go to your Gawd like a soldier"

Rudyard Kipling's 'Barrack-room ballads'

This poem was a dark warning of what was to come in Afghanistan. Before the British arrived in Helmand Province, Southern Afghanistan, there had been virtually no coalition forces presence there apart from a hundred American Special Forces. Their only concern was hunting and tracking down Taliban and Al-Qaeda leaders. The British military had been dropped, right in the middle of the Taliban and Al-Qaeda's homeland and backyard. The British politicians thoughts of not much fighting and the British mission would be mostly reconstruction went out of the window, one British politician even said that he would be happy if not one shot would be fired by British forces in Afghanistan.

"The unprecedented British High Court ruling in 2013, 'Every British soldier has a right to life in a war zone"

Using the word and term that the Americans coined all those years ago, the British mission was a 'cluster fuck' due to political naivety, nothing that the politicians had said, or predicted, happened. British soldiers were taking part in some of the most intense combat seen since the Korean War.
Military units were running dangerously low on ammunition, and Apache helicopter gunships were using their full annual quota of rockets and ammunition in just a couple of months, in air support missions to British troops fighting on the ground. British equipment was also a major problem, soldiers on the ground did not have the necessary military equipment or armoured vehicles required to protect themselves, there was also a serious shortage of operational

helicopters and shortages of body armour which are just a few examples. The British High Court ruling in 2013 confirmed that 'Every British soldier has a right to life in a war zone'. In Afghanistan, instead of reconstruction, there had been mass destruction and major loss of life on all sides. Places such as Sangin, Musa Q Alah, Lashkar Gah, Gereshk, and Kandahar were featuring more frequently and becoming common on the British daily news reports. Unfortunately they were being mentioned back home for all the wrong reasons; IED and Taliban suicide bomb attacks, beheadings and killing on a large scale. British soldiers were dying in large numbers and too many flag draped coffins were being sent home. Harsh fighting and daily military operations were a bloody reality. The Parachute Regiment had stood out to Al-Qaeda during their tours in Helmand. The professionalism and aggressive fighting spirit of the Para's had taken Al-Qaeda and the Taliban by surprise. It was the Muslim Brotherhood verses the Air Borne Brotherhood. Al-Qaeda and the Taliban had obviously met their match and they knew it. I was secretly supporting the British military and the Para's, from within the terrorist network operating from within Pul-i-Charkhi. The whole situation was always very personal for me; the Para's fighting in Helmand had just made it even more so. I knew a lot of the soldiers and officers serving in the Parachute Regiment, some of these were my close friends. So I knew that a little help from me, operating within the Al-Qaeda and Taliban terrorist network, would have been appreciated. Any Para past or present would have done the same, when its needed, you step up and help protect your fellow 'brothers in arms', regardless of the personal risk.

"Shariah law"

I often participated in debates with the terrorist Commanders during my time in Pul-i-Charkhi. Some of these debates were very interesting and gave me a deeper understanding of Islam and the Islamic world; I started debates with Al-Qaeda and the Taliban on such subjects as Shariah law and Jihad, making sure that I chose topics that I could gain something from. 'Shariah' is an Arabic word meaning 'the path to be followed', it literally means, 'the way to a watering place'. It is the path not only leading to Allah, the most high, but the path believed by all Muslims to be the path shown by Allah, the creator himself through his messenger, Prophet Muhammad (PBUH). In Islam, Allah alone is their sovereign and it is he who has the right to ordain a path for the guidance of all mankind. It is only Shariah that can liberate man from servitude to any other deity than Allah. This is the only reason why Muslims are obliged to strive for the implementation of that path and that of no other path. The problem began when people misinterpreted and manipulated Shariah law for their own personal gain, various entities or groups used Shariah law to control people, located in key population centres and geographic locations world-wide. The prime sources of the religion of Islam are the Qur'an and the Hadith. The Qur'an is the word of Allah to all Muslims. Whilst the Qur'an gives the Muslims a primary rule of life, there are many matters where guidance for practical modern living is necessary, but about which the Qur'an says nothing. In such cases the obvious thing to do is to follow the 'ancient' customs or usage of the Prophet. There are ancient customs which could be accepted in some matters. However, in some matters peculiar to the religion of Islam, there were the interpretations of the earliest believers who had been the contemporaries and companions of the Prophet. This highlights that the laws and ways of 'old' Islam are still as strong today, and influences all day to day life across the Middle East and Afghanistan and spreads across the whole Muslim world. Westerners, who have little or no contact with Islam or Muslims, are unaware that many Muslims say the same thing about Western culture. No one is right and no one is wrong, this is where the edges become blurred and get very political. Everybody has their own belief system, regardless of what country they come from, some are more beneficial to mankind than others. Many of the conversations between me and Al-Qaeda touched on such sensitive subjects and intense and thought provoking, deep topics.

"Terrorist Martyrdom Operations"

I had repeatedly asked Al-Qaeda and the Taliban Commanders about 'Martyrdom operations'. Why do men and women blow themselves to pieces with explosives strapped to them, what prompts this desire for Martyrdom? What does blowing up children's schools and Bazaars 'markets' achieve? What mind set can justify killing their own innocent people. What deep routed psychological ideology can justify the killing of children and women, how can anyone try and justify such acts of extreme violence. As per one conversation I had with a senior Al-Qaeda Commander, his thoughts on the subject were that non-believers, non-Muslims see trees, water, and their material possessions in life. The things that nonbelievers own, defines them on many levels. What they eat and drink shapes them in the physical form. They are defiled in body and spirit by bodily lust. Muslims believe that the time spent on this earth is but preparation for paradise in the afterlife, so to die for their cause is regarded as an honour. A shocking report that has come out of Afghanistan recently, was of a ten year old sister of a Taliban Commander who was arrested wearing a suicide vest. Soldiers arrested the girl named as Spozhmay, moments before she had planned to blow up local Afghan police. The girl was detained in Helmand Province and is thought to be the youngest recorded would-be suicide bomber to survive. She was arrested in a remote village called Uwshi, in the Charchino District and taken to Helmand's capital Lashkar Gah. It has emerged that Taliban insurgents in Afghanistan have also been bribing starving children as young as eight years old to plant deadly roadside booby traps, to be decoys in ambushes and even act as suicide bombers. This is a prime example of how cheap life is in Afghanistan and the barbaric mentality of groups such as the Taliban, who look at children as an expendable asset, (See Glossary, Suicide vest, IED, Shape Charge).

"Prisoners of War and Shariah law"

Another subject that I pursued in conversations with Al-Qaeda was prisoners of war and the treatment that they received. Shariah law stipulates that prisoners of war must be treated with compassion. They must not be tortured or punished. They should be afforded kindness and good care while in captivity. Provision must be made for nourishing food, necessary clothing and medical treatment. In other words, once the prisoners of war are captured, either treat them well without troubling them or release them after getting ransom. This is the reason why Muslims have proclaimed that the giving of food to prisoners is a virtuous deed. The ill-treatment of prisoners or kidnapped Westerners is well documented, and many times has led to Westerners being killed and beheaded by Al-Qaeda. This has led to disagreements within the Al-

Qaeda and Taliban network, regarding Shariah law. A little known fact is that some Al-Qaeda Commanders do follow the rules and laws that follow Shariah law, whilst others display selective adherence to the old laws. A Jihad is fought under strict conditions, under a righteous Iman, purely for the defence of faith and Allah's law. Ulterior motives are strictly forbidden, greed and gain in the form of ransom for captives, was not supposed to have a place in the Jihad movements.

Because of the shocking and terrible terrorism acts of 9/11 in America and the 7/7 attacks in London, It is excepted that these events altered our view of the world fundamentally, this extremist interpretation of Islam is gaining strength and ground via and through Islamic schools, madrassa's and extremist teachings. Islamic extremism is now the biggest modern threat to Western society. The extremist madrassa's are no more than brain washing centres for the young and impressionable, in places like Pakistan, Afghanistan and Syria. They were first established in Pakistan during the Soviet occupation of Afghanistan; the new style schools are a million miles away from the traditional Islamic madrassa's which taught students how to read the Holy Qur'an, mathematics, philosophy, law and astronomy. The new hard-line radical madrassa's created by extremists are backed and supported financially by wealthy Saudi businessmen and money from the Afghan illegal narcotics networks and corrupt Afghan Government officials. These madrassa's are protected in places like Pakistan by some members of the Pakistani ISI, security services. In Afghanistan they are protected by members of the Afghan Parliament who are active members of the Afghan Taliban. These madrassas's and their teachings of radical Islam and Jihad are not only targeting Western people and its interests, but other Muslims as well. One of the biggest madrassa's I have ever seen is located within the prison at Pul-i-Charkhi. Over 2000 people attended Islamic classes there. The hatred towards everything that is Western emanates from these places. Osama bin Laden belonged to that school of thought, as does Mullah Omar and a host of other terrorist leaders who subscribe to 'weltanschauung', the world view, philosophy of human life and the view or comprehensive conception or image of the universe and humanity's relation to it.

A part of Al-Qaeda on the other hand, subscribe to the teachings of 'Salahuddin' (otherwise known as Saladin) who promoted a historic more tolerant form of Islam. There are two schools of thought within Al-Qaeda. Certainly the hardliners; Al-Qaeda, Pakistan and Afghan Taliban leaders like the ones found within Pul-i-Charkhi, believe that they and their followers can spread from Afghanistan, into central Asia, through Turkey and Chechnya into Europe and spread Islamic fundamentalism. They are the kind of people who have hijacked the true meaning of Islam, just as they had hijacked American planes, just as they bombed innocent people on the trains, tube and buses of London and Spain. The political exploitation and manipulation of religion is used widely by Al-Qaeda in the new century, Al-Qaeda also maximise their use of the press, internet and television. Al-Qaeda invests a lot of its resources, time and money into international media campaigns and PR. Some Arab media outlets are even given notice of pending terrorist attacks. This has allowed the media to obtain video footage of terrorist attacks in real time as they happen. There is a lot of covert and overt support for Al-Qaeda and other groups by a small percentage of the Arab press. There is a very delicate balance between the press and terrorist groups. Some would say that members of the press who are aware of an attack on soldiers and capturing it on video are no more than terrorist themselves by spreading propaganda. Ethically, should the press not pass on the information of attacks, whether occurring or pending, to the American military? Opinions vary depending on peoples points of view.

President John F. Kennedy, in his inaugural address in 1961, "He who rides the back of the tiger usually ends up inside".

These words spoken a long time ago are very true. President Karzai of Afghanistan would do well to remember them.

As a former British soldier I often ask the question, 'what went wrong'. For years, people in the Islamic world, especially, but not exclusively in the Middle-East have been asking the same question. There is indeed good reason for questions and concerns and even anger. The wars in the Middle-East have become increasingly more politically hot and unpopular throughout the West. The difficulty with the Afghan war lies in defining what it 'is' and what it is 'not'. After the 9/11 attacks, the phrase, 'war on terror' was born. A lot of people distrusted this, partly for its directness, partly because it seemed too limited. Western Governments are trying to drop this line now because of the ambiguity of guidelines regarding retaliatory killing and violence. Western countries are still at war with terrorism, but the lines of who we are at war with exactly are becoming increasingly more blurred as time goes by. Politics change daily, one day you have a friend, the next, that friend can become your enemy.

"Terrorist Commander Saladin gets captured, betrayed by another Afghan"

"Have faith in Allah, but always tie your camel up" (John Noel)

One afternoon, whilst Saladin and I were sitting in the shadow of Git-Mo, he began talking about how he had been captured. I was expecting an account of some big battle. The reality was far more mundane and amusing. Saladin had been arrested at a border crossing point between Afghanistan and Pakistan. One of the men he was travelling with was from the North of Afghanistan; Saladin was just standing in the passport queue, waiting for his passport to be stamped, as he had done several times in the past few months as he travelled that route. He had travelled extensively throughout the Middle-East and Russia; and he had never been stopped or encountered any problems in the past. He normally travelled alone or with a driver, on that particular occasion the driver with Saladin was from a trusted north eastern Afghan family. Suddenly he took a very large step to his right, pointed at Saladin and shouted; "that's him". (Saladin's recollection of the incident was quite funny; the way he told the story in front of the other terrorist Commanders had them all laughing). Saladin said that he just stood there in the queue, in complete disbelief at what had just happened. Men in black uniforms with large guns jumped out from everywhere and surrounded him; everyone else had dived to the floor. Twenty machine guns were pointing at him and red laser dots were dancing on his chest. Saladin looked down at his driver who was cowering on the floor and called him a 'donkey'. Saladin then looked back at the men in black, he realised that they were Afghan NDS and Special Forces. The only word that Saladin managed to get out to them was; "hello". He was then overpowered by his assailants, who didn't give a damn about his welfare. That was Saladin's polite way of saying that they kicked the crap out of him. He could not remember how he'd wound up in the back of a 4x4, but he ended up there, bound and gagged like a hog. He was not impressed about the way he had been treated. I was rolling around laughing; the way Saladin was telling the story in Arabic with all his hand gestures was hilarious, even he laughed as he told the story. This was the only time that I had seen Saladin laugh so much and so openly. Commander Talib-Jan walked over to see what all the commotion was about, so I told him, he shook his head in disbelief, laughed and quipped "don't ever trust an Afghan, especially one from the North of Afghanistan". We spoke for the next few hours or so before praying outside. We went indoors for the evening meal that had been prepared by Abdul Aziz. I knew that the CIA had visited Git-Mo that afternoon and that they would have seen me with Saladin's group of Commanders. This would have been reported to American intelligence. This was another indication that I was on track with my tasks. Confirmations like this helped the Americans to assess my situation and confirm that I was still alive. If the Americans did not see me for a few days it would probably mean that I was dead.

"Correspondence with HRH Queen Elizabeth II and the British Royal family"

In the future 2013, I wrote a strongly worded, but respectful letter to HRH Queen Elizabeth II, I informed her that the British Embassy had abandoned members of 'Her' Commonwealth, who were very loyal subjects. I also enclosed a comprehensive report on the ill-treatment and torture of British and Commonwealth nationals in British mentored Pul-i-Charkhi prison Afghanistan. I was determined that Embassy Staff should be held accountable for their actions. I emphasised the fact that my 'Oath of Allegiance' was to 'Queen and Country' and not the British Embassy Kabul. I felt that their behaviour had tarnished the good name of Great Britain. I received several correspondences back from the British Royal family, including letters from HRH Prince Charles and Prince Harry sending their best wishes. I would also have future correspondence with HRH Queen Elizabeth II and the British Prime Minster David Cameron.

During one of my daily Arabic lessons with Saladin and other terrorist Commanders, Hussein silently entered the room and sat amongst our small group. He was waiting for a phone call from the 'Shura' meeting that was taking place in Quetta, Pakistan. 'Zawahiri' the eventual leader of the Al-Qaeda network was chairing the 'Shura'. Zawahiri, who at the time was second in Command of the Al-Qaeda network, reported directly to his boss, Osama bin Laden. The phone rang, Hussein spoke very briefly to Zawahiri and the phone call was put on speaker phone. The Al-Qaeda Jihad was gaining support internationally and he gave his blessing to the Pakistan Taliban. Hussein did all the talking; everyone else sat in silence listening attentively. The phone call was short and to the point. Afterwards Hussein jubilantly left the room to spread the good news of the phone call to everyone in the Al-Qaeda corridor. The gravity of what had just happened was both daunting and worrying in equal measure; I had just witnessed a conversation with the operational head of Al-Qaeda. The tone of the phone call had shown the upmost respect for Hussein and Saladin. The old terrorist commanders and fathers of the men I was now sat with, had stood and fought by Zawahiri's side in the old days, through previous Jihads. The bond between them all was strong and unbreakable. Laughter and shouting could be heard from the corridor, the news of Hussein's phone call lifted the spirits of the other terrorists. Hussein would receive many calls from terrorist leaders and Commanders. It was a clear indication of how high up and respected Hussein and Saladin really were.

"Al-Qaeda death match between the bad arse Scorpion and the fierce camel spider"

One day I heard shouting and laughter emanating from the Al-Qaeda corridor. Some of the foreign fighters had found a scorpion and camel spider outside. They had captured them and brought them into the prison block. This was an old game that the Al-Qaeda and Pakistan fighters played. They would stand in a circle facing inwards with their legs spread to shoulder width next to each other. The spider and scorpion would then be released from their separate boxes in the centre of the circle of terrorists. The two adversaries would immediately begin fighting each other, until one or the other died. If any of the terrorists broke the circle there would be a forfeit. This game was not just about the scorpion and spider; it was also about the courage of the terrorist fighters. When a scorpion and camel spider runs between your legs it takes guts to just stand there, not moving your feet. Being stung on the inside of your leg by a bad arse scorpion was bad enough, being bitten by a well pissed off hairy camel spider was even worse. I walked out with the other terrorist Commanders to see who would be victorious. The sea of onlookers parted as we got closer, boys will be boys. The scorpion won the battle this time, the dead spider that had put on a good show had fought till the bitter end; he was un-ceremonially scooped up and chucked in the bin. The fight was over quickly compared to some; obviously the scorpion was not in the mood to prolong the battle. The ring of terrorists had remained unbroken so no one had to face a forfeit. Al-Qaeda and the Pakistan Taliban are not allowed to bet, it is frowned upon, but I was sure that I saw money changing hands at the end of the contest, there were few unhappy faces. I had played this little game of courage in the past, I had found it quite entertaining to try and pull and push the other people into the circle in an effort to get one of them to fall on top of the scorpion and camel spider. This had ended in tears for one terrorist, for some reason I was never invited to play death match again. I was relieved really; I did not want to get nailed by a little beasty. The funny thing about the scorpion was that it kept turning up in the most unlikely of places, in people's beds and boots. Screams of absolute agony would suddenly erupt from cells in the darkness of the night. The amusing thing was that it was always the Taliban who got nailed. The Prison Commander always smiled at me the following morning after the medical staff had been called in to deal with a scorpion or spider bite. I can officially say that I 'cannot confirm or deny' that this had anything to do with me. Those exceptional pieces of covert work, kept some Taliban thinking of the scorpion bite on their arses instead of thinking about attacking American and British soldiers. A lot of the Terrorists would shake out their bed sheets and blankets before going to bed; they did not want any little nocturnal visitors.

"The world is a prison and we are the prisoners: Dig a hole in the prison wall and let yourself out!"

Masnavi 1.982

One evening the terrorist Commander Talib-Jan received the news that his father had just died in Afghanistan. He had died of natural causes. The prison block went into three days of official mourning out of respect for Talib-Jan and his family. His father would be buried within 24hrs in accordance with Islamic law. A white sheet was laid out along the centre of the corridor, plates of food, nuts, cakes and sweets were placed onto the centre of the sheet. This was a display of hospitality for people who would come and pay their last respects to Talib-Jan. Everyone from the block attended, even the head prison Commander made an appearance. The Commander sat with Talib-Jan, drinking chi-tea and eating nuts. He apologised for the fact that he could not allow him to attend the funeral due to security reasons. Talib-Jan took this news well, too well. I sat alone with him late that afternoon, just talking; he was receiving phone calls and updates from his family in Eastern Afghanistan. Other members of the Taliban had helped to organise his father's funeral. That evening Talib-Jan invited Bevan and me over for dinner with the rest of the Taliban corridor in honour of his father. By this time Bevan and Talib-Jan had become 'good' friends and could often be seeing playing chess together, a game forbidden by Al-Qaeda and the hard-line Taliban unless it was to 'strategise with Jihad in mind'. Talib-Jan used the fact that Bevan was a Westerner with military experience as an excuse to play the game. According to him, he could 'learn about Western tactics' from Bevan. What 'made' the dinner 'special; was upon Bevan and myself leaving the corridor to go back to our cell, a mid-ranking Taliban suddenly barrelled down on Bevan as he was heading for the gate, my heart stopped...was this Talib going to attack Bevan, should I block him, do I just let this play out? Then something surreal happened, as he drew close to Bevan, he held out his arms and grabbed Bevan in a bear-like hug and then proceeded to 'sniff' Bevan's shirt. He had liked the deodorant that Bevan had been wearing, and wanted to know the name so he could get some. Hell, talk about a 'dear diary' moment.

The block was very quiet over the next few days, most of the time was spent in the mosque attending prayers. Shortly, Talib-Jan would unleash his suicide bombing campaign across Afghanistan. He would also target Government buildings in Kabul with lethal consequences for the Afghan Government. He was a terrorist Commander who could float between several terrorist groups and networks, including; Al-Qaeda, Pakistan Taliban and the Afghan Taliban. He was at present running the suicide bombing network from inside Pul-i-Charkhi prison. From what I had witnessed it is not uncommon for terrorist Commanders and fighters to switch between groups and international terrorist networks, depending upon operational needs, timings and circumstances.

The Al-Qaeda network cannot be categorised as a simple off-shoot of some weird fanatical ideology with overzealous members, all eager to die for a cause, or in their minds, a righteous Jihad. I had extensively studied Al-Qaeda and international terrorism, I had also come into unprecedented contact with senior terrorist leaders and Commanders right across the Middle-East over the past 12 years, the history of the Middle-East has a key part to play in the present situations within Islamic countries and their future. I saw the profound significance of the

Iranian Revolution; its effects were evident across the whole region. Whilst it was true that in 2001 Iran was publicly hostile towards the Taliban, Saddam and Al-Qaeda, but viewing through the looking glass when it comes to anything in the Middle-East it is never black and white. Behind the scenes certain elements within the Government in Tehran were actually supporting the Taliban and elements within the Al-Qaeda network. 'The enemy of your enemy is your friend'. Strange allegiances appeared at the most unexpected of times and in the strangest of places. The hostility was centred on the Shia – Sunni divide, not on the methods or world view of either. The battle was about who would lead a reactionary movement within Islam. Key events in the Middle-East over the past 30 years have nurtured the growth of radical factions into what the West calls Al-Qaeda today. To understand its ideology, you have to understand its complicated background and the affiliated groups and international networks that enable Al-Qaeda to operate in the 21st century. One example of an affiliated group is Hezbollah, based in Lebanon. Hezbollah members and fighters help to facilitate weapon distribution and movements of Al-Qaeda members, between safe houses and operational locations. You can't begin to understand Hezbollah unless you understand the role that Iran plays, or understand Lebanon, unless you understand Syria, or understand Hamas, unless you understand the roll of both, or understand either country in its present state of flux, unless you understand the history, not just of the region, but of the religion, how it sees itself and how it has developed its own narrative.

"My reports were evolving from being just high level intelligence reports from a trusted grade 'A' source, into full on target packages, including my personal opinion on such things as military mission options and recommendations"

The Americans carried out a rolling pick up the next morning during their walk around the prison block, their walk around Block 10 took no more than 15 minutes. They obviously wanted to get the report back to Kabul and start processing the intelligence within. I felt a little more at ease when they had left and the report was no longer in Pul-i-Charkhi. I was still well aware that if any of my intelligence reports were ever found in Pul-i-Charkhi, then I would be killed by the terrorists. This was not a time for me to be complacent; I had to be on top of my game at all times. It did, however, give me satisfaction and peace of mind that the intelligence I had risked my life obtaining was being put to good use, making a difference and saving lives. I had no idea just how quickly my intelligence reports were being acted upon, I was about to find out. Within 48 hrs of the Americans picking up my latest report the news was coming through the Al-Qaeda corridor that their IED factories and a suicide bomb making factory in Jalalabad, Eastern Afghanistan had been located and hit by the American military, all had been destroyed. An Al-Qaeda safe house in Jalalabad had also been compromised, raided and terrorists captured by the Americans. Al-Qaeda and the Pakistan Taliban were very unhappy. I personally was jubilant about the news and shared it with Bevan; we could not publicly show how happy we were in front of the other prisoners so we had a cup of coffee to celebrate our victory. Everything within my report to the Americans had been acted upon very quickly, every location I had given them had been hit by the American military, today was a good day. From a credibility point of view after this, the Americans knew that I was right up there within the terrorist Command and control structure.

Following hits on an explosives factory and terrorists being captured in a safe house in Jalalabad, the head of American HUMINT (Human Intelligence) came to visit me. The Americans used the fact that I had converted to Islam as the 'cover' for the meet, and to be. Bevan sat in on the first hour of the two hour meeting. The Americans and I got straight down to business. More terrorist attacks had been planned by the network operating out of Pul-i-Charkhi, in retaliation for the Americans recent military action. The attacks were to be unleashed in five days' time. The Americans would come to pick up a report from me in four days. This was cutting it fine, but I needed the time to make sure that I hadn't missed anything. I could not afford to overlook any details of the imminent attacks. The Americans had also informed me that they had called a meeting at the British Embassy to get an update regarding my case and when I could expect to be released. If I paid a bribe I could be released by the end of the week, but I had good reason to want to stay in Pul-i-Charkhi. Al-Qaeda and the terrorist network had also offered to get me released, if I took this option I would be taken by the terrorist network to Waziristan, right in the heart of terrorist operations. This latter was worth some thought and I corresponded with American intelligence. I informed the terrorists that I would never pay a bribe for my freedom, so this gave me an excuse and time to remain in Pul-i-Charkhi and continue my mission.

"Major Bill Shaw MBE, put into an Afghan prison hell"

I phoned Dil later that afternoon, just to catch up and see what was going on back in the real world. It was strange talking about life outside Afghanistan, this was possibly the closest I would ever get to seeing or being back in the normal world. It was nice to have a normal conversation that did not include the words Al-Qaeda or killing. However, the normal conversation did not last for long. I was informed that Major Bill Shaw MBE had been arrested in Kabul, Afghanistan. Bill was the manager of G4S security, the private security company that was supplying the British Embassy with armed bodyguards and protection. Former military members of G4S had contacted my Operations Manager back in the real world asking him to get a message to me, requesting my help in protecting Bill. Bill was also a former British soldier and officer, so my team knew that I would do this unconditionally. I asked Dil and Trevor to get as much information on Bill and his situation as they could, including his present location, and I would ring back in two hours for an update. I knew that the only way for me to protect him within the Afghan prison system, was to get him brought to me and my location. If the British Embassy was not attempting to get him out, then I would have to look at this option. I informed Bevan of Bill's predicament. Bevan's response was that if the British Embassy didn't get him out quickly he would be fucked and very likely killed by terrorists within the system. Bevan was right on both counts, Al-Qaeda had already put a bounty on Bills head. I phoned my boys back on the two hour mark and received a full detailed update on Bill and his situation. Dil and Trevor had been sitting in their operational office when I had called Dil two hours earlier. That was a stroke of luck because they had both used all their contacts to ascertain the real situation regarding Bill. I spoke to Dil and Trevor; they had gathered background on him. He had served Queen and

Country in the British army for 28 years; he had a remarkable military career and spent 28 years in the Royal Military Police, working his way up the ranks from Corporal to Commissioned Officer, ending up as a Major. He had been awarded the MBE by the Queen. In 2008 Shaw had taken over the role of Senior Manager for G4S Security in Afghanistan. They were responsible for the safety and security of dozens of diplomatic personnel in Kabul, including staff from the British Embassy and the Foreign and Commonwealth Office, department for International Development and the Revenue and Customs. Bill Shaw was about to learn the same lessons as I had about 'plausible deniability'. In October 2009 the intelligence wing of Kabul's police force 'NDS' had impounded two armoured vehicles used by the British Embassy Kabul, allegedly for not having the correct number plates. This was a routine dance and shake down between the NDS and Kabul's Foreign Embassy's and Western security companies. Vehicles are seized and 'release fees' are paid to get them back. Bill Shaw was asked by his company to pay $20,000 for the release of the vehicles. He did so, signed his name on the receipt and asked for a copy for his company records. He did not receive an official receipt. In December, a second pair of vehicles was impounded. This time G4S, who were exasperated, complained to the Afghan authorities, who promised an investigation. The investigation ended in Bill Shaw's arrest by Afghan NDS. It was now alleged that the fine Bill Shaw had paid earlier to NDS was now being classed as a bribe to a public office. No Afghan official was arrested, but another G4S employee was, called 'Maiwand Limar', who was with Bill at the time had been arrested by NDS. Both of them were duly sentenced to two years in prison. I was also told that during the kangaroo court, I mean the Afghan court system, when the judgement was read out; the look on the British Consulate's face was priceless. What did they expect, truth and justice from the Afghan justice system? That would never happen. Bill Shaw had been railroaded by the Afghan prosecutor and Judge. Two years. The British Consulate had swiftly left the court room. They must have been very proud of the British mentored Afghan justice system, the penny had just dropped and the realisation that the Afghan Justice system was not fit for purpose. Talk about being slow on the uptake, it had taken them several years to work that one out. Patrick Toyne-Sewell, Corporate-Affairs Director for G4S, stated in an interview with the 'Mail on Sunday' that the charges are misconceived, as a company we don't pay bribes. Bill Shaw believed he was making a legitimate payment to a security department. He had behaved totally transparently and even asked for a receipt, when he was not given one he noted it in the company accounts. Coincidentally, Bill Shaw's trial in April took place at a time when Western Governments, including Britain, had been publicly pressuring the Afghan President, Hamid Karzai, to crack down on Afghan Government corruption. President Karzai was trying to blame Western Governments for his own Governments incompetence and corruption. The British Embassy had been totally naive in thinking that Bill Shaw's case was not politically motivated by elements inside the Afghan Government, who were trying to deflect the focus from their own incompetence and wide spread corruption.

"British SAS Hero Andy McNab would later state that Bill Shaw was an honourable man, treated in the most dishonourable way"

Major Bill Shaw MBE went from being a British citizen of high standing and impeccable character to being a convicted prisoner in Afghanistan with no human rights, within the blink of an eye. British SAS hero Andy McNab would later state that Bill Shaw was an honourable man, treated in the most dishonourable way. Bill Shaw was shocked at the complete lack of constructive help and meaningful support from the British Embassy and FCO in London. He had been let down by the very people the 'Embassy' who he had expected the most help from. The first time I ever saw Bill Shaw was when he was brought to Block 10 in Pul-i-Charkhi prison, he was unshaven, shackled and his hands were chained to his waist. Even after his recent dark, unsure times and conditions, Bill had kept his British military sense of humour; the RSM in him was coming out. Bill and I shared mutual friends; he had no idea that he had so much support and so many guys looking out for him. All the British military boys that knew Bill were doing everything in their power to help him. I had also spoken to American intelligence to make sure that Bill would be brought to me and Bevan in block 10 when he arrived at Pul-i-Charkhi prison. The British Embassy could not be relied upon to do this. I left nothing to chance, Bill was a soldier and soldiers look out for each other. Unlike the British Embassy, Bevan and I, with a little help from American intelligence and Al-Qaeda would keep Bill Shaw alive and well. Bevan and I took Bill under our wing and we protected him from day one. Especially after the British Embassy confirmed that Al-Qaeda had placed a bounty of thousands of dollars on Bill's head. I spoke to Commander Saladin and another Al-Qaeda Commander based in Saudi Arabia, I informed them that Bill Shaw was to be my guest. Being a fellow Commander (by name only) I could do this. The Taliban were told in no uncertain terms that they were not to harm Bill Shaw in any way. If they did they would be punished by death. The ground rules were set and everyone from the terrorist side knew the score. My reputation within the terrorist network was well established and I used my credibility to protect Bill.

Bevan had the same thoughts as me, we would assist Bill Shaw in any way we could. God knew he would need all the help and support he could get. We already knew that the British Embassy would do nothing to help him. They would not intervene in the corrupt AJS 'Afghan Justice System', the very Justice system that the British Embassy Kabul was supposed to also be mentoring? As it stood the British Embassy had allowed yet another former British Soldier and military officer, to be placed and confined alone into a brutal and dangerous Afghan prison, surrounded by terrorists. What was the British Embassy thinking, or more to the point they obviously weren't.

"Terrorists fighting for who controlled the inside of Pul-i-Charkhi Prison"

The week before Bill Shaw arrived at Pul-i-Charkhi prison, the Taliban had physically tried to fight Al-Qaeda inside Pul-i-Charkhi. The Taliban had lost and the Al-Qaeda fighters had ripped them apart with ruthless efficiency. The Taliban now knew to keep their heads down; their mouths shut and follow the orders of the Al-Qaeda and Pakistan Taliban network. I had stood with Al-Qaeda, it could be said that I fought on their side, but I had to make sure that I was on the winning side. Not only my life, but the lives of Bevan and Bill depended upon Al-Qaeda running the show. If the Taliban took over we would be well and truly fucked. So like I have already said, the Taliban, when it came to fighting, got their arses kicked in dramatic style. I had made it abundantly clear that Bevan would not be touched by anyone. Erring on the side of caution, I made sure that Bevan was locked in his room when the fighting broke out, just in case the Taliban tried to behead him. It took a week to clean the Taliban's blood off the walls, floor and ceiling. Saladin and the rest of his men had run the Taliban out of the blocks; they even chased them around the compound, educating the ones that they caught about the error of their ways by beating them with metal chains. Saladin had taken great delight in 'disciplining' a Taliban member, known to want to take Bevan 'out', right in front of our cell that Bevan was now locked in. The Taliban that were left in the prison block were literally cowering under their beds, hoping and praying that Al-Qaeda didn't find them. When the dust settled Saladin's crew was victorious. This was how disagreements inside Afghan prison were sorted out. The Taliban respected only one thing; power through violence. This was a painful lesson, but one that they had to learn. The distraction meant that whilst the terrorists were beating the hell out of each other, they were not planning or co-ordinating attacks against American or British troops, so it was a win, win situation as far as I was concerned.

I knew that I was pushing my status to the max within the terrorist network, but Bill Shaw was a former British soldier and it went without saying that I would watch his back. And in keeping with the time honoured tradition; regardless of rank or Regiment, British soldiers stick together 'British soldiers never leave a man behind'. The British Embassy in Kabul and FCO London should take note of what I have just said. I had already spoken to the American prison mentors and Bill's room had already been selected and organised from behind the scenes. Bevan had also spoken to the Americans to confirm that Bill would be looked after when he arrived. Upon Bill's arrival, his first words after "hello" were "you have to look at the funny side of this situation". At this point in time Bill obviously did not really know how dangerous a predicament he had been placed in by the British Embassy. Bevan and I swore that we would look out for him. Once Bill had placed his personal kit in his Pul-i-Charkhi 'penthouse', we got him unlocked and brought him over to our room; a nice cup of tea was in order. I gave him a phone so that he could send out a quick SMS to his people outside, to let them know that he had arrived and would be safe with us. Bevan was working on getting Bills i-Pod from the guards; they had never seen an i-Pod before and were a little confused as to what it was. After some quite funny explaining, Bills i-Pod was returned and Bevan made sure Bill also received the $400 that the guards had taken off him when he had arrived and been searched. We knew all the games that the guards played when new prisoners arrived and we were having none of it. After the first 24hrs Bill was up to speed on the life and how things worked in Pul-i-Charkhi prison. Bill brought his i-pod in for Bevan and I to listen to, Bill had the film sound track to 'Streets of Fire'. The song 'Tonight is what it means to be young', summed up my mood. Having music really helped to raise our moral. Bevan commented that he had not listened to music in two years. I would listen to music from the 'Streets of Fire' sound track just before going into meetings with Al-Qaeda and the other terrorists, the music put me into the right mind set for taking on the enemy. This was nothing new, I would listen to the Rolling Stones and ACDC whilst operating and flying across the hostile deserts of Western Iraq and Syria. Later that afternoon Bevan introduced Bill to the guards and prison Commander. I arranged a meeting and introduced Bill to the Al-Qaeda and Taliban Commanders.

"Afternoon tea and biscuits with Al-Qaeda and International Terrorists"

Saladin and the Mullah came into my room whilst Bill was enjoying a cup of tea; they sat down next to him and introduced themselves. The Al-Qaeda Commanders shook Bills hand and welcomed him, they also offered their assistance if Bill ever needed it. Bill was taken aback by this; obviously this was not the welcome he was expecting from the Taliban and Al-Qaeda network. The guards looked on, bewildered at what was going on, they later took him to one side and asked if he realised who Saladin was. Bill just nodded his head in affirmation. We joked with Bill that people back in our world would never believe that he had met and had tea with Al-Qaeda and international terrorists. On Bills first night, the Al-Qaeda corridor sent down some food that Abdul Aziz had cooked to welcome him. So Bill had a good meal on his first night in Pul-i-Charkhi. In his previous prison, he had been kept in solitary confinement. The Americans had demanded this for his own safety. He was now in Block 10 with us, so at least he had other Westerners to talk to. It must have been a hell of a shock to Bill, being who he was, to suddenly find himself dumped amidst all the stress, uncertainty and hostility of the Afghan prison system. He coped well and kept his chin up at all times.

After conversations with Bill he decided to go 'native' and wear traditional Afghan clothing, which is very similar to Arab clothing. Doing this would help him to blend in and maintain a low profile. Which was the objective? Now there were two British nationals and former soldiers in Pul-i-Charkhi. I wanted Bill to be the ultimate grey man, to fit into his new prison life quickly, but even so, he never went anywhere without me or Bevan being with him. I trusted Al-Qaeda, but the Taliban were still looking for any reason to kill a Westerner in Pul-i-Charkhi. Bill Shaw is a glowing example of an outstanding British gentlemen, with all the qualities, courage, steadfast principles and ethics that uphold the reputation and high standards of Britain. Bill upheld his principles and dignity at all times and it was a pleasure spending time with him. As history has shown many times in the past, British military men will adapt and overcome any hardship or challenging situation that is put before them. I am proud to say that we did this in Pul-i-Charkhi, the whole experience was emotional, challenging and character building, 'what does not kill you, only makes you stronger'. Bill quickly settled into the prison daily routine, he had a lot of support from people outside and back home, this kept him strong and focused. He also started work on his future book 'Kill Switch', (which was eventually published). Writing was a good way to keep track of all the events that happened on a daily basis. For Bill, this was a whole new world. Members of Bills Company G4S really supported him. Kev and Tim, his men and long standing friends really looked after him, fresh food and supplies arrived every few days, and Bill made sure that there was a good amount of food for all of us. Some of the food and supplies were handed out to Al-Qaeda and the Taliban prisoners, this helped to keep everyone happy and also put Bill in a good light with the other prisoners. Not everyone had food brought in, so

Bill being seen handing out food as a goodwill gesture, had been noticed by the terrorist Commanders. They also respected the fact that Bill was doing this when he did not have to. Coffee was given to Abdul Aziz and bread was given to the prison guards. This helped to keep 'everyone' sweet. Kev and Tim went above and beyond the call of duty, and like I have always said, soldiers stick together and watch out for each other. Bill was very sharp and had clocked everything going on around him. He had noticed that I was spending a lot of my time in the Al-Qaeda corridor and outside walking with the other terrorist Commanders in the Rose garden. All I said to Bill one time when we were alone was, "don't judge a book by its cover". Bill never asked questions, he was a very experienced military officer, and very perceptive, he had an idea of what was going on but kept it to himself. Bill knew that Pul-i-Charkhi was a very strange place. At first, Al-Qaeda and the other terrorists had thought that our afternoon ritual of afternoon tea was strange, but after a while they would come in and join us, the conversations were very interesting and were a real eye opener for Bill Shaw. The terrorists even started to copy us by indulging in afternoon tea and biscuits at the same time. British manners were slowly rubbing off onto them 'you can take a man out of the military, but you cannot take the military out of the man'.

"Taliban barber who cuts heads off"

Bill hadn't had a hair cut in three months, he had wanted to tidy-up his hair, us soldiers do like to look smart at all times, even in Pul-i-Charkhi. Bill had told me and Bevan what he wanted. 'You might have a problem. The barber here used to behead people for the Tangos' (terrorists). Bill questioned the wisdom of exposing his throat to such a man. Saladin and I assured him that he would not be killed, so Bill decided to risk it. The heavily bearded barber used scissors and clippers before shaving his neck with a Bic razor. He was a bit rough pushing Bill's head around, but he emerged unscathed. I had a similar experience the year before, it gives you food for thought when a member of the Taliban puts a razor to your throat and smiles at you. The best things you can do are smile back and tip him well before he starts. Bill came back into our room after his emotional experience and had a nice cup of tea to calm his nerves. Bill had begun having bad dreams at night, not surprising given where he now found himself. Bill spoke about his dreams; some did not have happy endings. The worst featured the Taliban coming for him in the darkness of the night. Long fingers or knifes would reach for him through the bars of his cell as he slept, or the barber would slip in and slice him with a cut-throat razor, or shadowy figures would seep in through the open window and try to smother him with their hands. He would wake up sweating, in the early hours, fighting off dozens of imaginary assassins. It was time for Bill to get out of here. Everybody had bad dreams in Pul-i-Charkhi. I would frequently awake in pitch darkness, surrounded by ghostly shadows. I would be shivering uncontrollably and covered in sweat. The unbearable screams from other prisoners through the darkness would bring me back into the harsh reality of where I was. I would often fall back into a dark and restless sleep until dawn.

Bill updated me on the security situation in Afghanistan and Kabul from a Western security company's perspective. Things were really bad; the daily terrorist attacks across Afghanistan were at an all-time high. The Afghan Government was targeting Western companies operating within Afghanistan and trying to close them down by any underhanded means they could, in a bid to replace them with Afghan companies. These companies were companies owned by members of the Afghan Government, or that they had a major interest in. Members of the Afghan Government were trying to push all Western security companies out. Afghan and Pakistan Taliban supported security companies were on the increase right across Afghanistan and the Middle-East.

"The body is visible, the spirit concealed, the body is like the sleeve, the spirit the arm within it. The intellect is also hidden but one can perceive both the intellect and the spirit in a person's behaviour"

Masnavi 11:3253-4

"Disrupting and stopping a terrorist IED attack and ambush on British soldiers"

A Pakistan Taliban Commander had just informed me during one of our frequent walks along the corridors, that they had planned attacks on Kabul over the next couple of days. This Pakistan Taliban Commander often spoke to me, he knew that I was close to Saladin and this Pak Talib was trying to look good and win favour with Saladin through me. I was just using the Pak Talib's ego against him. One of these planned attacks in Kabul was to be an IED attack, followed up by a coordinated ambush on a British military patrol operating out of the military base next to the airport, located off the Jalalabad road heading east out of Kabul. This attack had gotten my attention. I played it down at first in front of the Commander; I said I hope that the attack had been well thought through. He assured me that it had been well planned; he gave me the details of the planned attack. The Pakistan Taliban was to attack a British military patrol with an IED and wait for the British QRF (Quick Reaction Force) to be deployed. When they got to the location of the IED and had started to tend to the British wounded soldiers, a second IED would be remotely detonated by a terrorist observer. Terrorist sniper teams were also to be in place to pick off and kill any British survivors that survived the IED strikes. Their plan was to kill the patrol, kill the QRF and then move in and kill any survivors. All this was to be videoed and posted on the internet. My first instinct was that this was an extremely thorough and well laid plan. I wanted to find out who had planned this attack and who was going to be co-ordinating it. Something this big would have one of the Pakistan Taliban's senior Commanders behind it. The Pakistan Taliban even had three children watching the British military base. The Military called these children 'dickers'. Their job was to monitor and inform the Pak Talib of all British troop movements. They would count personnel in and out and record how long it took for the British soldiers to carry out their combat patrols along the Jalalabad road. Their routes and formations arriving and leaving the patrol base were also noted by the children. The dickers that were positioned 25 metres from the main gate of the British base posed as mobile traders, hawking and selling mobile phones, sweets and drinks. The children would use mobile and satellite phones to relay in real time the information to members of the Pakistan Taliban and other terrorist groups. The British security company G4S, Bills Company's Afghan headquarters 'Camp Anjuman' was originally named by my good friend Colonel Muslim Hayatt. Camp Anjuman was situated very close to the British military camp; the dickers also monitored their movements and activities. The Old Russian road running 1K off towards the rear of the British military camp and G4S base was to be the second location for a multiple IED attack. G4S and the American military used this road every day to transport people between the American air base at Bagram and the American military bases located along the Jalalabad road. The first junction on the Old Russian road was confirmed as the location of the IED attack. The explosives would be placed inside two large water pipes that ran under the road. Two Arab snipers were to be used as top cover for the terrorists during the IED attack; they were to be placed on the flat roof tops to the right, which directly overlooked the junction and their ambush, kill zone. The snipers job was to pick off any British survivors. The Arab snipers, with their personal weapons and several other foreign fighters were already waiting in a safe house in Kabul. This safe house had been facilitated by Hezbollah. The Pakistan Taliban had everything in place; the attack would be some time in the next 48hrs. I quickly wrote up a report and got it out to the Americans, a brief SMS message was also sent out warning them of the two intended locations to be hit. My swift action prevented those attacks, more soldiers' lives saved.

"CIA Extreme rendition protocol, Bio-metrics', retina scans, digital finger prints, voice analysis, Al-Qaeda and the Pakistan Taliban had been caught with their pants down. They had just been tangoed by the American intelligence"

A few days later, I was conducting an English lesson with Al-Qaeda and the Pakistan Taliban, when the Americans turned up in force, over thirty of them. Saladin and I looked at each other; we knew that we were in deep crap. Every prisoner was shackled in the corridor and escorted by two Americans to the prison Commanders Office and put through 'Extreme Rendition' protocol. 'Bio-metrics': retina scans, digital finger prints, voice analysis, the full works. When the Afghan prisoners realised what was going on, they really kicked off, the terrorists in Block 10, had just been caught with their pants down. They had been well and truly 'Tangoed'. The Al-Qaeda Commanders knew what was going on; their days of flying under the radar were drawing to an end and their plans to travel internationally unnoticed were over. By the end of the day, all the Bio-metrics reports would be uploaded to the American Intelligence International Data Base. All my written and reported recommendations had been carried out by the Americans, even Bio-Metric testing of all Block 10 and Block 3 Pul-i-Charkhi. It turned out that there were over 30 HVTs and terrorists hiding in plain sight within the prison system. Not anymore! A terrorist Commander called the 'Doctor Wasim' was the one who kicked off the most; he shouted and spat at the Americans. Three Americans carried him into the room, restraining him as they went in the stress position. Abdul Aziz also made his feelings known to the Americans. I suddenly had a sobering thought; I had just been tagged in Block 10 maximum security with terrorists and my details had been put on the American data base. I hoped my Top-Cover was still good, if not I was well and truly fucked; next stop for me could well be Git-Mo, Cuba. Luckily I already had my shorts and sun cream packed. To keep face with Al-Qaeda and the Pakistan Taliban I performed my own outburst about the Bio-Metrics, something I would do again when the British Embassy visited. Following the Bio-Metrics, Bevan and I were locked in our cell, as were all the prisoners in the block. We had a good chuckle as we heard the Al-Qaeda and Taliban kicking off in their corridor...oh well, time for another celebratory cup of coffee.

During the next British Embassy visit to the prison Commanders Office; I had to be seen complaining about the situation. The Embassy gave me a letter stating that the Bio-Metrics testing was an 'Afghan led initiative'. Talk about being full of crap; so the 30 strong CIA Rendition Team must have been a figment of my imagination, "yeah right". There was not a bloody Afghan in sight, well, apart from the terrorists. The response from the Embassy was typical, and not at all unexpected. Unbeknown to the clueless British Embassy, it was I who had initiated the Bio-Metrics scan by the American Intelligence. So as it stands, 30 Terrorist Commanders and international terrorists had been hiding in British Mentored Afghan prison Block 10. In addition to the hundreds of numerous other known terrorist who were found over the next month hiding within Pul-i-Charkhi, under false names. This fact proved my point, that the British Embassy prison mentors were not just clueless, but could not be trusted, hence the decision the Americans had made, not to tell the British Prison mentors about the Bio-Metrics until after they had been successfully carried out. I found myself in a very strange position; I'm British and yet I could not trust my own British Embassy. The only people I could trust were the Americans, both American Embassy personnel and military intelligence operating covertly in Pul-i-Charkhi. I found this fact very worrying. But I had taken a negative situation and turned it into a positive.

"Outside terrorist meetings being held in Pul-i-Charkhi Prison, the first of many such meetings that I would be present at"

The next morning, Saladin and his men had a personal visit outside. Ten members of Saladin's family, including his father, had travelled from Nuristan and from across the Pakistan border, tribal area of Waziristan. The elders had travelled across the mountains to be here, this was an important meeting. The prison Commander had ordered his men to clear an area inside his Rose garden and a carpet had been laid out with a table. Hot Chi-tea was served to Saladin and his guests by the prison guards. After serving, the guards had been instructed to stay away from the area that the meeting was taking place in. Three of Saladin's own men stood guard on the only gate and entrance to the garden. None of Saladin's guests were searched when they had entered the prison; the guards were too scared to even think about doing such a thing. Saladin wore his best Arab clothing as did all of his men. White flowing Arabian robes with black turbans. The whole group was well and truly flying the black flag of the Al-Qaeda terrorist network. Saladin called into my cell on his way out and asked me to join him in his meeting with his family and men; I was completely taken aback by his request, I had attended meetings with him in the past, but I knew that this was a high level meeting and members of his family would be present. This was an honour; I quickly changed into my best set of white Arabian robes, similar to what Saladin was wearing. I also wore my 'White turban' that had previously been presented to me by Saladin and the other terrorist Commanders. Saladin and I walked out of the prison block with extreme defiant confidence; we looked the part in our flowing white robes, fearlessly we stepped out. We definitely turned heads, all the guards just stood and looked on, well I was not flying under the radar now, I was walking out into a terrorist meeting 'Shura' as Commander Saladin's right hand man. My status was cemented with this open show of force and status; there was no going back now. I could hear the word Al-Qaeda being softly spoken by the prison guards as we walked past them on the way into the Rose garden. Well if the CIA were watching this from a drone or surveillance point they would have fallen off their chairs. One of their own trusted grade 'A' intelligence sources, was walking into a high level terrorist meeting. Now that is a 'real dear diary moment'. I was now walking a path that no Westerner had ever walked before; we walked into the garden and were greeted by the elders and Saladin's father and family. After greetings in traditional Arabic, we all sat down in a circle. I was placed at Saladin's right hand side. The Shura began. This was a terrorist council meeting, subjects discussed and topics spoken about, included suicide bombings, IED attacks, tactic's, supply chain's and safe houses. International connections were spoken about, including messages being passed to Al-Shabab in Somalia and Terrorist groups in Iraq and Syria. The whole meeting was a real eye opener. I stayed mostly quiet, listening tentatively. I commented that the connections between the terrorist groups across the Middle-East and Afghan and Pakistan should be firmed up. I injected this into the conversation to open the door and to bring this topic up in the hope people would start to talk about it. I needed to gain inside information on how they all communicated internationally. It worked, I steered the conversation onto subjects that I needed more intelligence and clarification on. There was another secret prisoner exchange taking place between the Taliban and the Afghan Government over the next week. I took note of this, wondering if the Americans were aware of this, probably not. The prisoner exchange had been organised by members of the Afghan Parliament, the same members that I had met and spoken to during their last meeting with Al-Qaeda and the Afghan, Pakistan Taliban in Pul-i-Charkhi prison. Narcotics came up during the meeting, Saladin did not agree with narcotics and he would not have anything to do with the narcotics trade. He knew that the illegal Afghan narcotics trade helped to finance terrorist operations, both in Afghanistan, Pakistan and also right across the Middle-East. Saladin did not approve of the drugs trade, this was a subject that clearly splits the terrorist networks, some agree it's part of the legitimate Jihad, others don't, I was of the same point of view as Saladin, drugs were dirty and I would not agree on any subject that involved narcotics. In real life I hate narcotics and the people who are responsible for pushing drugs onto Western cities and streets, so my having strong opinions on this subject were not hard to air during this meeting. I found myself in agreement with Saladin on the subject. Now that was a dear diary moment, I agreed with a terrorist Commander on something. Narcotics are still a very controversial subject within terrorist networks, but as it stands the leader of Al-Qaeda supports the narcotics trade and has openly stated that the illegal drug trade is part of the Jihad against all the Western countries who are fighting Al-Qaeda. The whole Shura and meeting was interesting, informative and chilling. It had been organised, structured and very professional, no voices were ever raised. I was sat amongst the enemy; from my point of view the terrorist networks were proficient and well controlled, financed and motivated. This was going to be a long war and it was not just going to be confined to the Islamic countries, it was very obvious that the terrorist networks were going to bring the war to the cities and streets of Western countries. Britain and America were still the devil as far as the terrorists were concerned. Al-Qaeda and other terrorist networks including the Pakistan Taliban and Al-Shabab did not recognise any international borders, law or rule of law. Their thought process of war and conflict was very old school; I would even say barbaric and dark aged. It was also ruthless and direct; terror and terrorism are one of the same, terror and fear are the tools that they use to achieve their objectives. The terrorist attacks of the future were obviously going to be bigger, with a bigger body count that followed; collateral damage was not something that Al-Qaeda and other affiliated terrorist groups were concerned about, even killing hundreds of their own innocent people was acceptable in their misguided eyes and radical ideology. I completed a full comprehensive written report for the Americans on all the meetings that I had attended with Saladin. No doubt these reports would get a lot of attention from the senior American intelligence case officers and I knew it would raise a few eye brows. I knew that my being British would also get people's attention up the American intelligence Command chain. This report also brought up some other interesting questions, one of them being, if the right Al-Qaeda or international terrorist Commander or leader could be found, could a dialogue be opened up, or even covert talks set up or take place? I had just opened up Pandora's Box. All the subjects surrounding this are very sensitive on several fronts, not least political. Western politicians cannot be seen talking openly to terrorist groups, well this is what they say anyway, but in this day and age the public don't trust anything that politicians say anyway. (The fact that the Afghan Government is negotiating terms before signing a power sharing agreement with the Taliban. So what has really been achieved in the past 14 years? Fast forward, to the 17th December 2013).

"British Prime Minister David Cameron, Mission Accomplished?"

British Prime Minister David Cameron made this comment during a BBC interview from Helmand Afghanistan "Mission Accomplished". The back-lash and criticism of it was immediate. Western politicians cringed when they heard what he had said. To be fair to the Prime Minister, when asked by the media, in front of soldiers still serving in Helmand, if British troops would be able to leave with "mission accomplished", he could hardly have said no. After 447 fatalities, thousands more injured or traumatised and an estimated £38bn of tax payer's money being spent, declaring failure was not an option. When I heard the words "mission accomplished", I thought, 'which mission'? During the 12 years of war, the narrative of what we had tried to do have changed many times. There is still total confusion today. When we sent British troops into Helmand, John Reid, and the Defence Secretary at that time, described it as a 'reconstruction mission'. He hoped that a shot would not be fired. We were soon firing millions of shots. Even then, there was no real political initiative. A British attempt to talk to the Taliban backfired spectacularly. The "Taliban" negotiator turned out to be a Pakistani shopkeeper. In 2013 opium cultivation reached record levels of 6,000 tons, 36% up on the previous year. Yuri Fedotov, head of the United Nations Office for Drugs and Crime, warned that there was a risk of Afghanistan becoming a fully-fledged narco-state. An Afghan MP from Helmand Province, where British troops are based, reported that fighting continued and attempts to cull the poppy harvest, one of Britain's aims, had failed. The phrase "Mission Accomplished" first became infamous when it was used by George W. Bush after the downfall of Saddam Hussein in May 2003. The world then saw Iraq fall into a bloody cycle of chaos and violence. In 2013 I was shocked. Iraq is practically a disaster: 9,000 people died as a result of conflict in 2013 alone, but we hardly hear about it anymore. Many incidents and deaths are not even reported anymore. Iraq is off the front pages of the newspapers, therefore no longer an issue. Our politicians want the same with Afghanistan. Afghanistan is not a victory for Western countries, how could it be. If ever there was an interview and statement that a British Prime Minister could take back, that BBC interview and the words "Mission Accomplished" would surely be the one he would want to erase. That was just another clanger dropped by a politician who had not assessed the public's mood with regards Afghanistan and wars in Islamic countries, which have cost the lives of over 447 British soldiers and thousands of American soldiers. Those who gave blood and pay taxes deserve better. British and American soldiers are still stationed, fighting and dying there. Al-Qaeda are still in Afghanistan in force, and international terrorism is at its strongest it has ever been. The war against international terrorism has evolved into a global Jihad that is expanding with every month that passes. The recent international attacks by terrorist including Al-Shabab are examples of this. We want to know why 100,000 NATO troops with the most sophisticated equipment in the world failed to defeat an estimated 15,000 to 20,000 Taliban fighters. Al-Qaeda, Pakistan Taliban operations in Afghanistan, Pakistan, Tajikistan, Iran and across the Middle-East are classed themselves, as their local area of operations, only the far reaching attacks and operations that target Western interests using Al-Qaeda affiliated terrorist groups are classed as the Al-Qaeda international operations? With the Al-Qaeda franchise on the increase across Africa and the Middle-East the overall terrorist network is growing in size, strength and operational effectiveness. The increase of Al-Qaeda and the expansion of internationally based Al-Qaeda affiliated groups planning terrorist attacks on Western countries and their interests internationally. The growth and operational capability of groups like Al-Shabab supports my opinion, (See Glossary, Al-Shabab). Eastern Iran and Peshawar in Pakistan are Al-Qaeda's logistics hubs which are used for operations in Afghanistan and Pakistan. Quetta in South West Pakistan is the home of the Al-Qaeda council. This location is also the home of the Afghan Taliban Supreme Council. Terrorist training camps are still located in Pakistan and some of the large camps that house hundreds of fighters have been moved to various locations across Africa, in a bid to keep movements and camps undetected. The exceptions are the Al-Shabab training camps in Western Somalia, close to the Ethiopian border. Some are even reported to be 'within' Ethiopia and neighbouring countries.

"An open invitation to British Muslims to come and join their Jihad and join the brothers of Al-Shabab"

Al-Shabab is one of the most feared Al-Qaeda affiliated terrorist groups. 300 newly trained terrorists have completed a six month training course within one of the Al-Shabab camps. These new recruits have been trained in subjects such as suicide bombing, explosives, IEDs, bomb making and intelligence. A fact worthy of note is that Al-Shabab has their own intelligence unit that is fully operational, both in Somalia and internationally. The 300 new recruits that have graduated from their training have been placed within specialised units, within the Al-Shabab brigades. With the Al-Qaeda leadership publicly supporting Al-Shabab and their attacks on Western targets, Al-Shabab are growing into a major threat to Western countries. Britain and America have been publicly targeted by the Al-Shabab leaders. An Al-Shabab leader and spokesman justified their terrorist attacks and actions by stating that their cause is justified in the eyes of Islam and stated that it was every Muslim's duty to fight in the Jihad, including British and American Muslims. A worrying point that was stated in the end of the Al-Shabab leader's statement, was the open invitation to British Muslims to come and join him and fight in the Jihad. With home grown terrorists and attacks on the increase, Western countries are holding their breath, fearing the next devastating terrorist attack, (See Glossary, Al-Shabab).

The Western international press had become aware of the situation regarding Bill Shaw and I being held in an Afghan prison on trumped up charges. The pressure that the press put on the British Embassy for answers was becoming greater by the day. The FCO London were also receiving official requests for information from the press to ascertain mine and Bill's status and what the British Government was doing to get us, two British nationals, released. The British Embassy was far from happy that the press were publicising our predicament across the international press and internet. The Embassy's attempt to hide the fact that there were British nationals in prison was blown out the water. They could not cover the truth up any longer. Between us; Bill, Bevan and I had conducted interviews with several international newspapers and TV stations including; The Times, The Mail on Sunday and CNN. I was happy that the press were now involved and that the truth was slowly coming out. Even my family had become involved. I had no idea of that until after they had actually taken part in the interviews. I had kept my situation under wraps concerning my family, because I had not wanted them involved, plus the fact that I did not want to be released quite yet, I still had taskings to perform and information to acquire for American intelligence. Obviously my family had no idea that I had worked with the Americans for many years across the Middle-East. I had broken all contact with my family ten years ago to keep them safe and unaware of the dangerous counter terrorism work I had undertaken and became involved in. My family had no idea what the hidden facts about my situation were, I had fallen off their radar many years ago and they didn't know why. The day would come that I would have a bit of explaining to do, hell that would be one hell of an interesting conversation. But that was for later. Unbeknown to me, my family had contacted and got an MP involved in the campaign that was on going back in the UK, to get me released. It was a bit of a shock when I learnt of this. It was the Americans that first informed me about my family's involvement. The Americans knew that I had never wanted my family involved in my situation. This was an unexpected development that we had not foreseen. There was nothing I could do about it, so my family campaigned endlessly in the Press and on TV. My local MP even posed the question of the British Prime Minister during PMQ (which was aired on BBC2). Officially PM David Cameron was asked about me, regarding what the British Government was going to do to get me out. My name and situation was well and truly now in the public domain.

My Family also started a 'Facebook' campaign and petition which attracted massive support and thousands of signatures on a petition that was given to PM David Cameron's office in 10 Downing Street, London. The actions by my family and the public support I received was humbling, overwhelming and emotional. 'Thank you to all who took part in the campaign'. I had stood up to the corrupt Afghan justice system and I had refused to pay bribes to Afghan officials. I had stood by my principles and kept my dignity at all times. All I had ever wanted was for the truth to come out and now it finally was. The future would be even more interesting when the truth came out about the work that I had carried out with the support and 'Top Cover' from American intelligence whilst I was in Afghan prison. My actions, efforts and achievements had brought a whole new dimension to my situation. It was most definitely not as it may have first appeared from an outside perspective. For me personally it was just another chapter in my far from normal existence.

"In the dark times, will there also be singing? Yes, there will also be singing, about the dark times"

Bertolt Brecht from 'Motto'

Bill Shaw's family had visited him while he was in Pul-i-Charkhi, their support and endless campaigning for his release was paying off. There was a lot of political pressure being put on the Afghan Government to release him and clear his name. Bill's wife and family had shown the same outstanding qualities as Bill had shown, steadfast determination and remarkable dignity throughout. Bill Shaw was finally released on one glorious sunny afternoon. Kim Motley turned up carrying an ironed shirt on a hanger for Bill, followed by a TV crew. He was taken to the AG office in Kabul. After the Afghans made the most of grandstanding for the TV cameras, Bill was eventually released. He had lost 128 days of his life needlessly in notorious Afghan prisons. Even after this, he still had to travel back and forth three times to the Attorney Generals (AG) to sign more Afghan paper work. The most important thing was that Bill Shaw was safe and out of the Afghan prison hell. He would soon be spending time with his family and loved ones. Bill had also made two lifelong friends in Bevan and I. Bill had come into the situation within Pul-i-Charkhi at a very dark and dangerous time. He had been a breath of fresh air for Bevan and I. Being an old soldier and RSM, Bill had reminded me of how important the work that I was doing was. Bill had no Idea what was really going on inside Pul-i-Charkhi prison, for his own safety and peace of mind Bevan and I had kept Bill in the dark. Bill's jokes and sense of humour really lifted my spirits and the extra food supplies from Kev and Tim really helped me to get back to good health, which in turn enabled me to push my work for the Americans even harder. Kim Motley was now pushing for 'my' release, so I had two options of getting out, Al-Qaeda or the Americans. I was asking advice from the Americans on how they wanted to play the situation but unbeknown to either of us the British Embassy already had other ideas. They were in full 'damage limitation' mode and covering their arses politically at any cost. The official line coming out of the Afghan Government and British Embassy was that my official legal file had been "lost" by the Afghan government. The British Embassy was also holding onto and not releasing freedom of information requests that we had put in for. It was pretty obvious that the British

Embassy was trying everything in their power to bury my situation. The security situation across the whole Middle-East and Afghan and Pakistan was getting worse. The Al-Qaeda and Afghan, Pakistan Taliban were gaining strength with every month that passed. Terrorist attacks and planned attacks were at an all-time high across the Middle-East, Afghanistan and Pakistan.

"The Escalation in Violence across the Middle-East, Europe, Afghan, Pakistan and Africa"

With all the violence erupting across the Middle-East, Syria, Yemen, Iraq and across North Africa, to name but a few countries, in flux, and going through violent destabilisation and popular uprisings against military Dictators. The lessons of Middle-East history and the present conflicts across the Islamic world must be taken into consideration when Western countries, Britain and America, involve themselves and intervene in Islamic countries affairs. An important fact to remember is that the West and Western countries will always be the outsiders in a foreign land. Some people within these lands will always see the West, rightly or wrongly, as crusaders of old. Western economics back home and the need for Western countries to obtain oil should never be the driving factors in determining armed conflicts or intervention. A balance and mixture of hard and soft power can and should be used. 'You get further with a carrot than a stick'. American reluctance to be directly involved in the Syrian and Libyan conflicts spoke volumes. In Libya, the Americans very quickly handed over the 'Command and Control' to NATO Command and their military forces. This action by America, not to lead or be directly involved in the Libyan conflict, showed just how politically sensitive the situation was. Another example of how sensitive Middle-East armed conflicts have become, is the situation within Syria; it was the Western publics from both Britain and America that spoke out, not wanting any military direct action or boots on the ground in Syria. The political actions by Western countries, just on Syria alone, proves how politically toxic, Western wars and military action is in Islamic countries. "They take everything and give nothing." The cost on every level is too high, we have our own problems back home, within our own countries, and we don't need to go looking for more trouble in Islamic countries. Western countries, including Britain and America are still dealing with the 'blow back' and 'Bleed out' effect from Iraq, Afghanistan, Syria and Somalia. The Arabs and people within the Middle-East will always fight each other, history has proven this fact. In another 10 years there will still be fighting within Middle-East countries, they like fighting each other, so why don't we just leave them to it? That is my own point of view anyway, let's face it, Western intervention in Iraq and Afghanistan has not been successful for the countries involved, was Iraq more stable before the 2003 war? In Afghanistan, the power sharing agreement with the Taliban is a controversial point, regardless of what side of the fence a person is standing. People talk about peace in Afghanistan, let's face facts, it is not going to happen, Western countries including Britain and America just want to pull their soldiers out of Afghan as quickly and quietly as possible. The whole Afghan war is politically toxic back home. It is all about trying to save as much political face as possible for Western politicians. The political spin term, "Mission Accomplished" is complete hogwash; I don't think that any self-respecting politician will be using that term again anytime soon to describe Afghanistan, Iraq or any other Middle-East country.

"God save us from the short-sighted politicisation of intelligence"

At this point in time, with all the extreme violence escalating out of control throughout the Middle-East and Africa, and Western countries being targeted by both international terrorist groups and home grown terrorists, Western nationals are being killed on our own streets and cities. The violence from Baghdad, Damascus and Kabul has been seen on our own streets. The violence from terrorism has followed our troops home from far off battle fields including Afghan, Iraq and Somalia. Can we afford 'not' to try and open up a dialogue with terrorist leaders, regardless of what groups they are from or affiliated too? A person has to stop and think of what could happen and the escalation of violence if we don't? What will be the turning point, will it be after a big terrorist attack, maybe something that could be bigger than 9/11 or the London 7/7 attacks. Politicians should take a breath and have a very long hard think about what I have just said. Politics too often gets in the way of the military and intelligence services doing their job effectively, rightly or wrongly, this is a fact. We are at war and people need to remember that terrorists don't play by the rules? Our military and intelligence services being hamstrung by politics is nothing new. "God save us from the short-sighted politicisation of intelligence" we live in 'Esperance', hope.

Western counter terrorism experts and analysts have got a lot of things wrong in the past. Not so long ago people thought that Al-Qaeda was not a threat outside the Middle-East and the Pakistan Taliban could never launch an attack on America. Then the Times Square, New York attempted car bombing. These so called Government experts know that it's only a case of when, not if, the next major terrorist attack will be successful; the only question is, what country it will be in? One of these days the bomb that goes off could very well be a dirty bomb or small yield nuclear device. That is a very sobering thought is it not? Al-Qaeda or one of its affiliated groups might be years away from having the capability to do this, but if all it takes is money, then the international terrorist networks are more than capable. With the destabilisation of many Middle-Eastern countries, and Pakistan being a breeding ground for corruption and terrorist support and activity, this should be a worry for Western countries. It should be remembered that Pakistan has nuclear weapons and that old nuclear war-heads are available on the black market from several former Soviet bloc countries. Bearing this in mind, the thought of a terrorist group acquiring a dirty bomb is not at all far-fetched. Given the facts, it's a possibility and a major worry to Western countries leaders and intelligence services. To understand Al-Qaeda, Pakistan Taliban and other affiliated international terrorist groups, one needs to understand their mind set and 'Modus Operandi'. Unfortunately, most Western so called experts and Government special advisers do not.

Political, and sometimes hidden, agendas prevent a clear overview of situations. Clear warning signs that trouble and attacks are coming are evident, the warning signs are there, you just have to know what to look for. People need to start thinking outside of the box; every problem has a solution, in the murky world of Islamic extremism within Middle-East countries, where nothing is ever black and white, if there is political will, solutions can be found to any problem. Dealing with Islamic countries throws up its own challenges, especially when the countries in question are state sponsors or supporters of terrorism, there are still more questions than answers. British Prime Minister David Cameron's visit in 2011 to Pakistan is a good example of the difficulties. David Cameron spoke openly about the "war on terror" and how certain members of the Pakistan Government and security services 'ISI' were still supporting the Taliban and insurgent groups operating in Afghanistan. David Cameron's statement was very true, but the timing saw his public speech go down like a lead balloon. The Pakistan Government were not impressed, another own goal for the British PM. Obviously the Pakistan Government is corrupted and elements within the government support Al-Qaeda and the Taliban, but they did not need to be reminded of that fact. Obviously the British PM advisers needed to do a crash course in cultural understanding; it's best not to upset your host, especially when you want to ask the host for help and support in countering a problem like terrorism. The fact that 'Osama bin Laden' was found by a British national and intelligence source and then killed by American Special Forces in Abbottabad located in Pakistan has not helped the Pakistan Governments international position.

The week before September 11th 2010, Al-Qaeda and the Pakistan Taliban were planning and preparing terrorist attacks across Afghanistan and Internationally. Everything was ticking over nicely in Pul-iCharkhi. Al-Qaeda and the Afghan, Pakistan Taliban were coordinating terrorist attacks. American intelligence was picking up intelligence reports from me twice a week and actioning them. The British Embassy were disrupting Press inquiries about me and Pul-i-Charkhi prison. Kim Motley was making slow progress with the Afghan Justice system and the British Embassy (the Embassy kept on cancelling meetings with Kim at short notice, re-scheduling them for the next week only to cancel them again). I was spending most of my time with terrorist leaders and Commanders further infiltrating their international network. It was all a bit surreal. Just when I thought that my life could not get any stranger, fate was about to deal me a new hand that neither I nor the Americans saw coming.

"The British Embassy Kabul was about to blow almost three years of covert intelligence work of a Grade 'A' source inside the international terrorist network"

On September 10th 2010 without warning, I was given 45 minutes to pack my personal things under supervision of the guards. I was being taken to Kabul. No other explanation or details were given; I requested to officially phone my Embassy to report that I was being moved and to ask if they were aware of this development. I was denied the phone call by the prison authority. I was shackled at gun point and placed on a prison van surrounded by armed guards and escort vehicles. The heavily armed Afghan prison convoy then moved off slowly through the prison grounds. At this point in time, I had no idea what was going on or where I was being taken.

*Note: Due to my on-going legal action against both the British Embassy Kabul and FCO London, I cannot give any more details of the shocking events that followed on the day in question.

"An historical first, British National Anthony Malone was the first person in history to be extradited from Afghanistan to Britain, without Habeas Corpus"

This fact was reported on the BBC news and splashed across the internet by the British Foreign office. The British Embassy had every intention of charging me with terrorism offences prior to my Rendition from Afghanistan. The situation changed dramatically once I was on the plane and flying out of Afghanistan air space. The Americans had informed the British that I was one of their NOC, (None Official Cover) intelligence sources, working from within Al-Qaeda and the international terrorist networks across the Middle-East. The British Embassy Kabul, in a bid to cover-up their own incompetence and to try to cover their arse politically, had 'Renditioned' me without 'Habeas corpus', due process and the right to appeal, which was a clear breach of several human rights articles, including International law. The British Embassy Kabul and FCO had deliberately picked the first day of Eid, the Muslim equivalent of Christmas day. All the Afghan Government was on public holiday and all Afghan Government offices were closed. My American lawyer Kim Motley had informed the British Embassy that she would not be in Afghanistan but in America for a two week period. The British Embassy had conspired to Rendition me when I had zero opportunity to do anything about it.

"Internal E-Mails between the British Embassy Kabul and FCO London confirm that the British Embassy and Rule of Law Team at FCO London was aware that my Rendition had legal consequences"

As the aeroplane took off and flew at low level over Kabul, we passed right over Pul-i-Charkhi prison. I thought to myself 'I had made it', I was alive, against all the odds. I also felt a deep sadness, as we
banked over the mountains and gained altitude. Now I knew what it felt like to go into exile. I could not escape the enchanting mystery and culture of the Islamic world; I knew that one day I would return. For now my fight against Al-Qaeda and international terrorism was over, I had done my best for 'Queen and Country'. Unbeknown to me, my life was about to become even more surreal, another fight was on the horizon, not against terrorists hell bent on doing harm to Britain or America, but one against the British Foreign and Commonwealth office. I was about to find out that British politics and some top Civil Servants were even dirtier and challenging than war itself.

"What is justice...? To put something in its correct place. What is injustice...! To put something in the wrong place"

Masnavi 1:2596

It is occasionally argued that the morality of torture is a complicated business, it is not. A democratic state should always ensure that its enemies are treated in a manner that conforms to basic standards of humanity. Few, at least in America and Britain, would argue the opposite. British Prime Minister David Cameron had stood up in British Parliament and stated that "Britain" does not carry out and is not complicit in Rendition or torture. Fast forward to

December 19th 2013; Sir Peter Gibson, former High Court Judge and Dame Janet Paraskeva, submitted an interim official report (The Detainee inquiry) to the British Prime Minister, David Cameron. The Interim Inquiry report speaks for itself. It is a rigorous, thorough and independent piece of work. It reveals more information than ever before about the workings of Government and the Agencies, on issues highlighted in the report. The inquiry was halted after the British police began investigating into claims that MI6 had helped with the rendition of two men to Libya in 2004, where they said that they were tortured.

Sir Peter said:

After examining 20,000 documents relating to 40 cases, "There are matters which deserve further investigation. There was evidence of inappropriate involvement, that is what the documents have disclosed and we explain why in our report."

In summary the report states:

"Documents indicate that Government or its Agencies may have been inappropriately involved in some cases of Rendition."

Quote from Jack Straw, former British Foreign Secretary responds to the Gibson Report "I was never in any way complicit in the unlawful rendition or detention of individuals by the US or any other states."

I, Anthony Malone, was Renditioned from Afghanistan to cover-up the truth. My fight for truth, justice and against political corruption and international terrorism continues....

"The murder of Doctor Abbas Khan, British national"

Another example of the British Foreign Office not acting to protect a British national in an Islamic country was the 18th December 2013 murder of Doctor Abbas Khan. He had travelled to Syria to work and help treat injured victims, including women and children in the refugee camps. He was arrested by Syrian Government authorities and put in prison. Abbas Khan's British family accused the British FCO of not doing enough to ensure his safety within a Syrian prison and the lack of action in securing his safe release. Abbas Khan's family during interviews accused the British FCO of treating his case with 'distain and no interest'. Letters from Abbas Khan to his family during his time in a Syrian prison describe how his human rights were being violated daily and the Syrian prison authorities savagely beat him and made him beat other prisoners for the guards' amusement. The FCO called the death of doctor Abbas Khan murder, so why didn't they get him out safely? Yet another British national, ill-treated and tortured. How many more British nationals have to die before the British FCO written mandate, that they hide behind, is re-written and brought into line with modern human rights, don't British nationals in Islamic countries have 'a right to life'.

"Confirmation of my previous report on barbaric torture and Genocide inside Syria (see Authors introduction, Syrian torture chambers) – Carter Ruck report on Syria – International war crimes"

Personal note to the reader

I have lead a colourful life. It may come as a surprise to some reading this manuscript that I was once homeless and suffering with PTSD (post-traumatic stress disorder) and past problems with drink and depression. This could well have been why intelligence services and agencies unofficially employed me to do some intelligence tasks deemed too dangerous or sensitive for their normal personnel to undertake. I had nothing to lose and was perfect for 'full plausible deniability'. If I died in some far of land or desert no one would notice or care, that was how I felt back at that time. The truth was that I could have had support from family and friends, but I was too proud to ask, so I walked a very lonely path through life. All I lived for was the next impossible mission and another chance to die and end my endless suffering, fighting my own demons. The problem was I did not die, I had become a victim of my own success; I had also become a grade 'A' intelligence source. Some dark nights, sat alone with only a bottle of whiskey to keep me company I would pray for death, only to be disappointed. At my darkest point, when I hit rock bottom, I played Russian roulette, luckily I did not lose. The bullet hole in the window was a stark reminder that I was only one empty chamber and bullet away from death. Back then I had lost respect for my own life, but I had kept my respect for other people's lives. I was not scared to die, I wanted to die in combat and this would have been an honourable death in my eyes. I looked death in the face many times, but it always passed me by. My attitude at that point in my professional life was 'full on tunnel vision', I deemed no task impossible. I took risks in my work that no other highly trained operative or person would or should ever have taken. My 'No Fear' approach and attitude enabled me to do missions and accomplish tasks that were deemed impossible. I would walk into meetings with top terrorist Commanders with a 'fuck it' attitude, what have I got to lose. In any normal theatre of covert operations this would never have been allowed or achieved safely. Even when I was brutally tortured by Afghan authorities, my die hard attitude kept me strong. In my mind, the only thing that could kill me was me, so I soldiered on. In my darkest time while I was held illegally for two years eight months in an Afghan prison hell, I kept my dignity and principles at all time. My oath of allegiance to Queen and Country kept me strong and focused me on staying alive and saving lives. When lesser men would have laid down and died, I kept going. My direct actions achieved unprecedented results and saved a lot of innocent lives. The price of my actions on me personally was extremely high, it was not the physical wounds, they can always heal over time, but the psychological effects can last a life time. Many in our line of work, soldiers, will suffer broken relationships, lose the respect and love of our kids, turn to drink or drugs and may even end up on the streets, homeless and totally alone. If this happens we will be forced to spend our remaining days searching for food, another drink and a safe place to sleep. Many of us are filled with an overwhelming feeling of loneliness and no self-worth. In combat we are highly valued; we drive tanks, helicopters and are in charge of multi million pound machinery and weapon systems. Back in Civvie Street some of us too often feel that we have no real value to anyone; we feel that we do not belong. Our nights will be spent fighting long-forgotten battles, running from endless nightmares, feelings of guilt and failure that we were unable to make it on our own. The poem by 'Theo Knell' from his book 'a hell for heroes' sums up how I once felt.

Wounded Mind

The paths I tread tonight,

hold more fear for me than any desert or jungle might.

It's fear and rage that

drive me on, alone

and with nothing, life

is just an endless

fight.

An endless search for

food, another drink, a safer

place to sleep. All these things

are foremost in my mind and

they push aside the fading

memories of the family I so

cruelly left behind.

In a shop window I catch a glimpse of a man I once was,

the claret beret

Airborne wings and DZ

flash, like long lost friends

they call me back.

But unwashed and

unshaven now it's

backbone they say I lack.

A pitiful shadow of my former self,

I duck into a doorway to escape the cold and driving rain.

Tired and wet

I slide slowly down the

wall my body racked

with pain.

Sat on the cold damp tiles

I see the fear and disgust on their faces as they hurry past.

Eager to avoid eye

contact they never

look back

and I wonder just how long their fragile peace will last.

To escape my world I close my eyes

But they're there

again, cold and empty

without smiles.

The faces of the dead,

men I have fought, drank and

laughed with; we marched a

thousand miles.

They said it was normal,

Just a passing phase,

The headaches,

Depres

sion, all

the hidden

rage.

That's when it started,

the blackouts and flashbacks, the

nightmares that just went on for

days.

Surrounded by my memories

In a place that's close to hell

I spent the early days hiding in the

shadows, around corners, just to catch

a glimpse of my wife and baby girl.

She's all grown up now with a son of her

own, that makes me a granddad, I

suppose,

But I'll never

hold him, collect

him from school,

help him to fly his

kite or watch him

as he grows.

The soup kitchen has finally arrived

and with my precious food I squat in a doorway.

In my rucksack, a medal for valour won in the heat of

the fight, my baby's socks and picture of her

mum exchanged for a short note the night I left

their lives.

Too cold to sleep

I walk alone by the river.

I feel stronger when I'm moving.

'Prepare

for action,

stand in

the door,

red on

green on

GO.'

I launch myself into space.

'Thousand and one

thousand and two

thousand three

check canopy

feet and knees together.'

But instead of the bone-jolting crash

the ground is soft

and I pass straight

through, into a

cold wet darkness.

Maybe here,

at last,

I'll find my peace

amongst the other forgotten

soldiers who've died of their

wounded minds.

From 'Theo Knell SAS' book 'A hell for heroes'

My hope for those warriors and soldiers who pick up my book is that they will feel less alone and learn that they are not the only soldiers that have and are going through difficult, challenging and sometimes painful times. The fact is many soldiers go through dark times; this effects everything around them, including their family and loved ones. I hope when people read my words that they capture something of their own joy, pain, fears, sorrow and personal survival. I hope that they can share this book with others, their families and friends, so that those they love and care for can at least develop the eyes to see and hearts to hear. I have included some extracts from Theo Knell writing within my manuscript, his use of words to describe situations and how soldiers sometimes feel was so emotionally moving and accurate, I wanted to make other people aware of his writing and poems. His book 'a hell for heroes' gave me the courage, inspiration and will to finish my own book. My writing took me back to some very dark and traumatic events and times and I had to re-live them in order to write about them in so much detail. Blood, sweat and tears went into my writing this manuscript; it was an epic emotional 12 month rollercoaster of highs and lows for me personally and my loved ones. I felt the need to tell some hard truths, my objective is for other people to learn and connect with my experiences and hopefully learn from them.

I am happy to say that my life is back on track and I have a full and happy existence. I feel that I have reconnected with the human race. I have turned a negative situation into a positive. I have my family and friends to thank; it was them who pulled me back from the dark abyss that was my old life. Now when the sun rises or I look up into the night sky and wish on a star, I am happy to be alive. Thank you for taking the time to read my manuscript, I will leave you all with the words, 'Esperance-Hope'. Take care

Anthony

Phil Young's Official Statement About Pul-i-Charkhi Prison

I am Philip Frank Young a w/m, 50 years of age and residing in Cape Town, South Africa.

Between October 2009 and May 2012 I was incarcerated in various detention facilities in Afghanistan. Approximately 2 years of that time period I spent in Pul-e-Charki prison in Kabul. While there I was imprisoned in Block 1 and later in the High Security block. During the period I was in Pul-e-Charki I was not kept separate from the other prisoners and was exposed to most of the other prisoners including the Islamic radicals who formed a large part of the prison population. While some of the radicals were held in isolation, most were imprisoned with the general population.

During my 2 year incarceration in Pul-e-Charki I was witness to various events including the beating and torture of prisoners by prison officials and assault and murder of prisoners by other inmates. In my view, the torture and beating of prisoners by prison officers was systemic and widespread. Prisoners who were not compliant were often handcuffed or chained to fences or other structures, both inside and outdoors. I regularly witnessed prisoners chained outdoors to a fence in the height of winter while wearing no more than the thin traditional garb typical to Afghan men. On many occasions prisoners were chained outside while wearing only trousers. On most occasions these prisoners were left outside with no access to water or food and were left, on some occasions, from sunrise to after sunset. While handcuffed or chained these prisoners were often beaten by prison officials. I witnessed prisoners being beaten with electrical cables and batons for refusing to eat and for "insulting" prison officials. I witnessed 2 prisoners being beaten and dragged from their cell in the early hours of the morning and then dragged, literally, out of the cell block - they were then later executed by hanging in the kitchen of the cell block. (These were the two men convicted of the Kabul Bank massacre in Jalalabad) Again, the brutal treatment of prisoners was systemic and went on with the knowledge of the British mentors. I had a good relationship with the commanders of the blocks in which I was held and they were open about the methods used to "control" prisoners and were quite unaffected by the fact that mentors were on site. While guards and prison officers tended to behave more humanely when around mentors, I witnessed mentors joking and laughing about the beating and inhumane treatment of prisoners.

While incarcerated I was able to acquire a cell phone – which I purchased from another inmate. This was very common in the prison and although regular searches were carried out and some phones confiscated, it was quite common that the phones would be replaced within a fortnight or even, in one case I witnessed, returned to the radicals by a prison official. I was approached on numerous occasions by prisoners, both radicals and "normal" prisoners, asking if I wanted to 'upgrade' my phone – for a fee of course. It was common knowledge that radicals were using the cellular phones to plan attacks, communicate with radicals outside of the prison and to control activities of their former terrorist cells from within the prison. While in the High Security wing I had a conversation with a man convicted and jailed for planning and carrying out a bombing attack – an act he seemed particularly proud of. He 'boasted' that he was more secure using his cell phone in prison to carry on with his terrorist activities than if he had been outside the prison. When I say common knowledge, I mean that the prison officials knew of it, had reported it to the mentors and Afghan security forces and intelligence officials. I was once questioned by a member of the NDS (National Directorate of Security - the Afghan intelligence service) who stated to me that they were aware of the cell phone usage for planning attacks and other terrorist activities but had to rely on the prison officials to locate and confiscate cell phones. This position was ridiculous to me as prison officials were notoriously corrupt and anything could be had - if the price was right – and that was certainly common knowledge to every Afghan in the country. They were also quite often sympathetic to the Taliban/Haqqani Network/Al Qaeda and would be the willing couriers of various contraband items, including cell phones. To assume that the western mentors and intelligence agencies were unaware of the widespread cell phone usage to plan and carry out terrorist activities would be naïve in the extreme. On two occasions (that I am aware of) the NDS orchestrated, with the assistance of prison officials, the search of cells within the High Security block. No phones were recovered the first time as we were all aware that a search was to take place – the radicals had warned us that a search was to take place. The second occasion a number of phones (5 according to one of the guards) were recovered. The phone of the radical who confessed to me that he operated with impunity within the cell block, was not recovered.

As a South African and because we had no Embassy in Afghanistan the British Foreign and Commonwealth Office (FCO) was responsible for visiting me in the prison and ensuring that I was not mistreated. Their (the FCO) mandate was limited to ensuring that I was not mistreated and that I was as comfortable as possible under the circumstances and that my basic human rights in terms of the UN charter for the treatment of prisoners was adhered to. I received irregular visits (4 in total over the 2.5 years I was incarcerated) The visits ceased when I received a letter stating that the FCO would no longer be able to support commonwealth citizens due to "time restraints". However the cessation of support from the FCO corresponded with a ban, by the prison authorities, on any vehicles entering the actual prison compound area. This would mean that the FCO staff would be required to park their vehicles (they travelled in a security convoy) outside the prison and then walk the approximately 1km distance to enter the actual 'inner perimeter' of the prison. I do not believe the timing of the cessation of support from the FCO and the vehicle entrance ban, were unrelated. Although the visits by certain members of the FCO were congenial, no member of the FCO did anything to ensure that the court processes were fair and within the bounds of the proper judicial process as laid out in the Statutes and Criminal Procedure Code and other laws and instructions pertaining to the conduct of the courts and judiciary. Visits were purely of a 'social' type with no visible attempt to ensure that British or Commonwealth citizens received the due process of law.

I confirm that the above statement is true to the best of my knowledge and belief.

.... Philip Frank Young

Glossary

Acronyms, keywords, names, abbreviations, intelligence and military terminology, synopsis of terrorist groups and Arabic glossary. Including Islamic customary prayers and phrases.

Al-Qaeda and other terrorist groups and networks operate across the globe and are involved with numerous personalities, organisations and ethnic groups, crossing all geographic boundaries. The following navigational aid is meant to assist the reader of this book-report, in maintaining focus, gain in-depth knowledge, and to use for future reference.

101st:	American 101st Airborne Division (Air-Assault) paratroopers, Commanded in Iraq 2003, by General David Petraeus, who later became the Director of the American CIA. (See Petraeus).
11/3:	March 2004, Madrid. Al-Qaeda detonated ten nearly simultaneous bombs in four packed passenger trains. Killing 191 people and wounding more that twelve hundred.
21/9:	September 21st, 2013. Al-Shabab, Somali terrorist group, with close links to Al-Qaeda, Boko Haram and Nigerian Taliban. Al-Shabab terrorists attacked the Israeli owned Westgate shopping mall in Westland's, Nairobi, Kenya. Killing 70+ and injuring 300+. Casualties included; Kenyan, British, American, Australian and Netherland nationalities. The nationality of Al-Shabab terrorists killed and captured during terrorist attacks and operations, included; European and American. The 21/9 terrorist attack in Kenya was a real game changer to the international terrorist threat from Al-Shabab, Al-Qaeda coming out of East Africa, against soft Western targets across Africa and beyond. (See AlShabab/Al-Shaab and Modern Warfare).
22nd SAS:	British Special Forces 'Special Air Service Regiment'. SAS Headquarters is based at "Stirling Lines", Hereford, United Kingdom.
2IC:	Second in Command.
3-Para:	British military, 3rd Battalion the Parachute Regiment (Elite Paratroopers). Part of 16 Air-Assault, Brigade. Based in Colchester, United Kingdom.

7/7:   July 7th 2005, terrorist attacks on the public transport system in London, United Kingdom. Casualties, 56 killed 700+ injured. (See Modern Warfare-July 7th 2005).

9/11:   September 11th 2001, Al-Qaeda, Attacks on America, including New-

York, Twin Towers, The Pentagon and Flight UA93. Casualties; 2752+ killed, thousands injured. (See September 11th 2001).

A-10:   (See Thunder bolt, Warthog).

A2:   British Army standard assault rifle, ammunition 5.56mm, previously known as the SA80. The A2 can be fitted with the standard iron open sights or the SUSAT, (Sight Unit Small Arms Trillux) the ACOG sight is also interchangeable. The A2 can be fitted with a 40mm under-barrel grenade launcher and other tactical attachments.

Abbottabad: City in North East Pakistan, home of the Pakistan military academy and location where "Osama bin Laden" was traced, tracked then killed by American Special Forces, "Seal team 6", on 2nd May 2011, under the Executive order of the President of the United States of America.

Abdul Aziz: Saudi born, educated in Medina, holy city located in Southern Saudi Arabia. Abdul Aziz is an Al-Qaeda commander-AQAP and has strong ties to the Haqqani network in Afghanistan and Pakistan. Abdul Aziz is personally responsible for killing American soldiers in Afghanistan and was also one of the top insurgent Commanders in Iraq. (See Haqqani network) (Interviewed by Anthony Malone in Afghanistan).

Abu Dhabi: Capital city of the United Arab Emirates "UAE". (See Dubai).

Abu-Yahyia-Al-Libi: Second in Command of the Al-Qaeda network/group.

AC130:   American/British Hercules aircraft, specially converted C-130-gunship also known as Spectre and Combat Talon. AC-130's are operational across the Middle-East, Afghanistan and Africa. (See Spectre).

ACP: Afghan Chief Prosecutor. The ACP works within the Afghan Ministry of Justice. From 2007 to 2014+, the ACP was personally responsible for

changing the prison files in return for money, "from terrorist convictions to drugs convictions", of a large number of Al-Qaeda and Taliban terrorists, prisoners. This resulted in a large number (50+) of
Terrorists walking free from Afghan prisons. The Afghan justice system, Afghanistan Government; is one of the most corrupt in

the world according to the United Nations. (See Haqqani network and Hussein Laghman).

Afghan:	National from Afghanistan.
Africom:	American military Africa command.
Airborne Initiative:	British Paratroopers ability to think on their feet, training, knowledge, experience and initiative, all put together in a volatile or intense situation and/or environment. The ability to stay focused and deal with any situation or potential problem, "Think outside the box". (See 3 Para).
AK-47:	Russian Kalashnikov assault rifle, fires 7.62 X 39 ammunition, named after the Soviet inventor, "favoured weapon of terrorists". The AK-47 also appears on several terrorist flags, including Lebanese Hezbollah.
Akrotiri-RAF:	British RAF base, located in Western Cyprus in the Mediterranean. British long range fighter planes and bombers, surveillance assets are located at RAF, Akrotiri. The base is also the staging location for British forces operating across the Middle-East, North Africa and is a major logistics hub for British forces being deployed internationally.
Aleppo:	Also known as Halab, second largest city in Syria. Strategically located along the ancient silk route, 300km north of Damascus, close to the geographic borders of Lebanon and Turkey.
Al-Jazeera:	Arabic news/TV channel based in Qatar (Arabic version of CNN).
Al-Manama:	Capital of Bahrain, Bahrain is also the operational home of the American 5th Naval fleet, strategically located to cover the Middle-East.
AL-Q:	Al-Qaeda -Al-Qae'da- Al-Qa'dea- Al-Qaida, originally, Arabic word meaning "The Base", (See Osama bin Laden). (Anthony Malone interviewed several members, Commanders of Al-Qaeda in Afghanistan).
Al-Shabab/Al-Shaab:	Terrorist group located in Somalia, with strong ties to Al-Qaeda and the "Haqqani", network in Pakistan-Afghanistan and Boko Haram, Nigerian Taliban. Al-Shabab receives funding and

logistics from the Al-Qaeda leadership-network, in Arabia (Al-Qaeda in the Arabian peninsula-AQAP) and the Al-Qaeda leadership-supreme council in Pakistan, Afghanistan and Yemen. High jacking shipping and kidnapping-ransoming international nationals is a major contributor to Al-Shabab funding. AlShabab facilitates Al-Qaeda weapons shipments, training camps and safe houses across Somalia and East, Western Africa. Al-Shabab claimed responsibility for the 21st September 2013 terrorist attack on the Westgate shopping mall in Nairobi, Kenya. 70+ Killed including woman and young children. Killed nationals included; Kenyan, British, American, Australian and Netherlands and over 300 injured. It is reported that

British, European, American and Canadian nationals are members of the Al-Shabab group in Somalia and British and American nationals were reported to be among the terrorists who attacked the Westgate shopping mall in Kenya. (See 21/9 White Widow, Haqqani Network). (Anthony Malone interviewed members of Al-Shabab in Lebanon and Somalia).

Amman:	Capital city of Jordan.
Ammo:	Ammunition.
AMOJ:	Afghan Ministry of justice.
ANA:	Afghan national army.
Ankara:	Capital city of Turkey.
ANP:	Afghan national police.
AO:	Area of operation.
AP:	Associated press.

Apache AH64D/AH-MK1:			American, British helicopter gunship. (The British apache AH-MK1 cost £46 million each). The Apache is the most technically advanced helicopter in the world. The AH MK1-British Army Apache attack helicopter is built by Agusta Westland, all are fitted with the longbow radar. (See Longbow), (Anthony Malone interviewed Apache pilots in Iraq and Afghanistan).
APC:			Military armoured personnel carrier.

Apostles:		Special Iraqi unit, set up by British military-Special Forces, as part of TF14 (Task Force 14). Originally formed with a dozen Iraqi's, so the unit was immediately christened the Apostles. They were used for everything from interpreting for the SBS and SAS, their Blade teams, on covert and sensitive missions and operations. Their singular advantage in all these missions was their natural ability to blend into the indigenous population and remain undetected for long periods of time. (See Task Force Black).
AQAP:		Al-Qaeda in the Arabian Peninsula, (See Strait of Hormuz).
AQI:		Al-Qaeda in Iraq. In 2013 AQI moved into Syria and became ISIS (Islamic
		State of Iraq and al-Sham) ISIS joined the fight against the Assad regime
		as part of an increasingly sectarian conflict, pitting Sunni rebels against
		an Alawite and Shia-dominated regime. (Anthony Malone interviewed
		AQI members in Iraq and Afghanistan).
AQIM:		Al-Qaeda in the Maghreb (franchise of Al-Qaeda).
Arab Afghans:		The term originally used to describe the non-Afghan Muslims who fought alongside the Afghan insurgents in the 1979-1989 Jihad. This group included not only Arabs, but also Muslims from a virtually every country in the world with a Muslim population. Estimates of the total number of Afghan Arabs are all over the map, ranging from 5,000 to 100,000. Since the Soviets withdrew in 1989, a steady flow of non Afghan Muslims, still known as Arab Afghans, Mujahedeen class, Tier 2 insurgents are trained at camps in and across Afghanistan, Pakistan. These fighters are now reported to be fighting in Syria, Iraq, Pakistan,
		Lebanon, Yemen, Philippines, Kashmir, Chechnya, Uzbekistan, Indonesia, Bangladesh, Sudan, Western China and the Balkans and Sudan, Somalia, Kenya, Libya, Algeria, Mali. 'Osama bin Laden' is the most well-known Arab fighter. (See Haqqani network).
Arab Spring:		When a young, unemployed man named Mohammed Bouazizi set fire to himself in the central Tunisian town of Sidi Bouzid in December 2010, few imagined the firestorm of change his desperate suicide would ignite across the region. Within months, the dictatorships of Egyptian President Hosni Mubarak had been overthrown in a popular uprising. Within a year, leaders of other Islamic countries, Libya and Yemen had been swept aside. Syria which also started as a peaceful uprising had become a full-scale armed insurrection, when faced with the brutal dictatorship of the Bashar Al-Assad's regime. Over the past years millions of Syrian

	people/refugees have been forced to flee their home towns and villages across Syria, fleeing to refugee camps in Turkey, Lebanon and Jordan. The refugee camp in Jordan, (Zaatari), is estimated to be housing one million Syrian refugees, Men-women-children. The Arab spring had turned into an Arab winter. The Hezbollah terrorist group based in Lebanon now openly fights on Bashar Al-Assad's regimes side in the Syrian Civil-War against the FSA, Free Syrian Army and its splinter groups including; Jabhat Al-Nusra, a group with links to the Al-Qaeda Network, these groups form the opposition to the Bashar Al-Assad's Government of Syria. With the escalation in violence on all sides of the Civil- War, 150,000+ people killed so far, the body count rises daily... and over 2 million people displaced-refugees. The UN is officially calling the Syrian conflict a Humanitarian disaster. With terrorist groups including; Hezbollah, Al-Shabab, Al-Qaeda and Haqqani network, now tactically and strategically exporting International terrorism on a Global scale. The Arab Spring has turned into an Arab winter and evolved into an Arab Terror. World leaders hold their breath for the next major terrorist attack on a Western Target, not if, but when. (See Glossary, Zaatari, CW- Chemical weapons, Al-Shabab, Hezbollah, AQAP, Haqqani Network).
Asa'ib-Ahl-Al-Haq:	Also known as "The league of the righteous", An Iraqi political and terrorist group closely linked to Lebanon Hezbollah and the Iranian revolutionary guard. Asa'ib-Ahl-Al-Haq, gained notoriety in Iraq with a string of high level attacks on American and British forces, including: shooting down a British Lynx military helicopter and a RAF Hercules. They are also responsible for the Kidnapping and murder of British nationals. (See Iraq Hezbollah).
Ashgabat:	Capital city of Turkmenistan.
Asmara:	Capital city of Eritrea.
Asmara:	Capital city of Eritrea.
A-Team:	The Standard twelve-man teams that make up Special Forces.
Atlas Mountains:	Located in Eastern Morocco. Area of interest to Western intelligence, HVT's and terrorist leaders have been known to stay in Bedu and tribal encampments, scattered across the mountains and valleys of the Atlas mountain range.
ATO:	Air tasking order; the means of distributing joint firepower assets around the battlefield in a prioritised and fair as possible method.
Atropine:	Anti-nerve agent injection used by British and American armed forces. (See Glossary, Chemical weapons).

AWT:	Annual weapons test - Yearly official certification for handling/carrying weapons.
Ayman Zawahiri:	Leader of the Al-Qaeda group and network. (See Al-Qaeda-Haqqani).
B-1/lancer:	American supersonic strategic bomber, Call/sign "Bone", used for the B1.
B-2/Spirit:	American strategic stealth bomber.
B-52:	Also known as the Stratofortress; a USAF heavy bomber.
B6 – B7:	High level of armour on a civilian 4X4 vehicle. Example: B6 armoured Toyota land cruisers, used by NGO's, Diplomatic services, and private military companies PMC's, worldwide.

Baghdad Cafe:	Isolated cafe resting point in the middle of the Syrian Desert, located between the towns of Tadmor and Del-e-Zore, only one road in area, located at the junction of the main highway that leads to Iraq and the Syrian - Iraq remote border crossing point. The Baghdad cafe is 100km from the nearest town, its isolation makes it the perfect meeting location for transiting insurgents and terrorists. The Bedu also inhabit the surrounding desert. (See Glossary, Tadmor).
Baghdad:	Ancient Capital city of Iraq, Located on the banks of the Tigris River.
Bagram Airbase:	Large American military airbase and logistics hub, located in Northern Afghanistan. Bagram is also the location of one of the American Governments, "Black prisons" used to house terrorist suspects. (See Glossary, KAF-Black prison).
Balad TSF:	Iraqi town and location North of Baghdad, American military airbase and HQ-"JSFOC", for Taskforces and Special Forces including British Taskforce Black. Balad was also the location of the TSF, (temporary screening facility) interrogation centre of terrorists, foreign fighters and insurgents captured in Iraq. American DOD, Department of Defence, Rendition flights also emanated from "Balad", airbase, to locations worldwide. (See Glossary, Extreme Rendition-Black prison).
Barnard Lewis:	A world-respected authority on Islamic and Middle-Eastern history. (See Acquired reading list).
Barrett .50 Calibre:	American .50 calibre sniper weapon, effective up to 1 mile, (depending on the skills of the shooter), for engaging enemy targets and HVT's, can also be used for stopping soft skinned

		vehicles. It is reported that Taliban and Al-Qaeda fighter's use captured .50 calibres in Afghanistan, Pakistan, Iraq, Syria and Somalia. (See Glossary, Dragonov Russian sniper weapon).
Bastion Camp:		Main British military base, headquarters and logistic hub for British
		forces operating in Helmand province, Southern Afghanistan. 10,000 British Military personnel were based out of Bastion at the height of the Afghan conflict. Bastion is also the location of the airfield that supports military operations across Helmand. (KAF is also used in a supporting role). Apache MK1 are also stationed at Bastion, used as force protection; Bastion base is the size of Reading City, England and is the biggest British military base outside of Great Britain. (See KAF).
Battle group:		A military battalion-sized fighting force.
Bedouin:		Nomad tribe, also known as the Bedou or Bedu, nomads who live, inhabit the deserts of the Arabian Peninsula and old Persia, (Syria, Iraq, Jordan, Saudi Arabia, Yemen, Iran and Afghanistan).
Beirut Marine Barracks 1983:		Lebanon 1983, suicide bomber attack on the American Marine barracks. 241 American marines killed, 75 injured. 58 French paratroopers killed and 6 civilians killed. The same year 1983, American Embassy bombing killed 17 Americans, 32 Lebanese, 14 visitors and 1 suicide bomber, 120 other people were injured. (Anthony Malone interviewed one of the terrorists responsible for the attacks in Lebanon).
Beirut unload:		A rough and ready way of firing at something without risking the life of the firer, the firer stands behind cover and places, holds the weapon"AK-47" over or around a wall and fires a full magazine of ammunition, in the rough direction of the intended target, name derived from the methods of firing Ak-47's used in Beirut, Lebanon.
Beirut:		Capital city of Lebanon. Location of many terrorist meetings, several
		prominent terrorists Commanders live in and across Lebanon (See Phoenicia Hotel).
BEK:		British Embassy Kabul.
Bekaa Valley:		Also known as Al-Biqa, Geographic location in Southern Lebanon; the terrorist group "Hezbollah" stronghold close to the Syria border. The ancient town of Baalbak is located in the Al-Biqa valley. (See Hezbollah).
Bevan Campbell		Bevan and I go 'back-a-ways'. Little did we know that we'd end up together in the hell-holes of Afghanistan doing what we "did". Bevan served in the SADF/SANDF, leaving as a Major, prior to working as a Security Consultant in Africa, Europe and Asia. He

	was "convicted" on narcotics charges, and finally "Pardoned by Pres. Hamid Karzai" and released "Unconditionally" after spending 6 years 3 months and 8 days (2292 days) – possibly the longest serving "Westerner" in an Afghan prison to date.
Bill Shaw (Major) MBE:	Bill Shaw joined the cadets at fourteen and, after enlisting in the regular

army at seventeen, saw service in many countries including Northern Ireland, Hong Kong, Bosnia, Cyprus, New Zealand, Africa, Kuwait, Iraq, Germany, Spain, Argentina and Colombia throughout his twenty-eight year career. Rising through the ranks, he was promoted to Major and awarded the MBE from the Queen before leaving the Military to protect British and foreign diplomats in Iraq and Afghanistan. Bill Shaw was wrongfully arrested and imprisoned in Afghanistan, including; Pul-iCharkhi prison for four months and five days=128 days. Bill Shaw was released when all charges against him were dropped. As Andy McNab said, "An honourable military man treated in the most dishonourable way".

Bin Laden, Osama - UBL:	UBL is the abbreviation used by the CIA for Osama bin Laden. Born in
	1957, the youngest son of Muhammed bin Laden. Educated at King,
	Abdul Azziz University, he fought in the Afghan jihad and organised the
	Al-Qaeda group to assist armed Muslim insurgents around the world. Al-
	Qaeda franchises are in several countries including; Saudi ArabiaYemen-Iraq-Pakistan-Afghanistan-Syria, and across North-West Africa.
	Following the precedent set by the medieval Muslim military leader Saladin, bin Laden declared a defensive jihad against what he called the crusaders – predominately Christian Western countries led by the
	United States-in the summer of 1996. Bin Laden was killed in Abbottabad Pakistan by American Special Forces "seal team 6" during a military operation 2rd May 2011. Bin Laden's body was buried at sea by the US Government. (See Al-Qaeda, AQAP, Haqqani network, AlShabab-Strait of Hormuz).
Biometrics:	Authentication, Identification by characteristics or traits, technology, method implemented by Intelligence agencies and law-enforcement to identify high value targets, (HVT's) and terrorist suspects. Biometrics is also used to uncover and find terrorist suspects who are trying to hide behind cover identities

		and false names. (See Glossary, Sleepers).
Black Facility:		Deniable base or military facility used for Special Operations in countries across the Globe. (See Balad TSF, Black prisons, Black op's).
Black hawk MH-60:		American military standard transport helicopter, which can be armed.
		(Also used by several other countries, including, Saudi Arabia, Turkey and Israel). (See Mogadishu Battle).
Black on Black op's:		Two countries, Black operational military teams, tasked-ordered to eliminate, (capture or kill each other). (See Black op's).
Black Op's:		Military operations/missions that are off the books, no official record. The Government's official stance if a mission goes wrong or military personnel are captured, complete" Plausible Deniability". Serial numbers of weapons used on "Black Operations" are often filed off, to stop tracing and identification. (See Glossary, Sanitise).
Black prison:		Western government's unofficial terrorist prisons-located world – wide.
Black widow:		Chechnya woman suicide bomber.
Blade teams:		British Special forces teams (SAS).
Bleed out-Blow back:		Political and Intelligence term meaning, reaction-repercussion following an event or action. (For example see 21/9 Kenya attack by Al-Shabab).
Bletchley Park:		British Second World War, code-breakers. The modern equivalent is GCHQ. (See Glossary, GCHQ).
Boko Haram:		Islamist terrorist group based in Northern Nigeria. Has close links to AlShabab and AQAP, a franchise of Al-Qaeda. Many Boko Haram fighters are trained in Somalia by Al-Shabab. (See Al-Shabab).
Bounty:		Money paid out by the American Government/CIA, for the capture or killing of HVT's, known terrorists. A bounty can also be given for information leading to the death or capture of a HVT, terrorist.
Bowe Bergdahl:		American soldier captured in Afghanistan by the Taliban in 2009. Reported to be held by the Haqqani network, along the tribal belt, area of "Waziristan", situated along the Pakistan Western border. Bowe Bergdahl is officially listed and reported as an American POW, Prisoner of War. (Would later be released and returned to America)
Broken arrow:		American military communication "Code Word" stating-American military position being over ran by the enemy.
Burka:		Full body-length clothing worn by women in the Middle-East and Islamic countries/Muslims. According to Islamic law, this is to protect their modesty.

Buzkashi:		A game in which a dead goat is placed in the centre of a field and surrounded by horsemen from two opposing teams. The object of the game is to get control of the carcass and move it to the scoring area. In some games there are no teams; every player is out for himself.
C/S:		Call-sign.
C:		Commander, historically the letter "C" is used by the head of British MI6, to sign all official correspondence.
C-130:		A 4 propeller military fixed wing transport plane used by several countries to move troops and equipment. (See AC-130).
C-17:		Boeing C-17 Globemaster III – Large US Air Force strategic/tactical transport plane.
C4:		American military grade plastic explosives. (See Semtex).
Cairo:		Capital city of Egypt. (See Muslim Brotherhood).
Calibre:		The inside diameter of the barrel of a weapon. (See M4).
Camp Bastion:		British Headquarters of military operations in Helmand, Afghanistan. (See Bastion-camp).
Camp Chapman:		American FOB (Forward Operating Base) located along the Afghanistan, Pakistan border. It is also reported American "Drones" are operated from this location. A suicide bomber posing as an Intelligence source, killed several members of the CIA within Camp Chapman during a planned meeting. This was the biggest single loss of life for the American CIA in the Afghanistan conflict (See Glossary, Pakistan Taliban).
Camp Moorhead:		American Special Forces camp, Afghan commando training school, rangers training area and LZ landing zone, located 40km outside Kabul, Afghanistan. (See Glossary, Photographs).
Camp X-Ray/Delta:		The names designated by American authorities to areas that house International Al-Qaeda terrorists, within Guantanamo bay prison, located in Eastern Cuba.
CAP:		Combat air patrol.
CAS:		Close air support.
Case Officer:		Also known as a handler, someone who oversees Hum-Int (Human Intelligence Assets). A case officer is normally a very experienced CIA/NSA/MI6, operator who cultivates and develops intelligence assets. (See Glossary, Handler-Trade craft-CIA).
Casevac:		Casualty Evacuation. (See T-1).
Cat:		Counter-Action-Team, Normally a heavily armed four man team, travelling in an armoured 4X4. Sometimes used in conjunction with a close protection team.
CBRN:		Chemical - Biological – Radiological – Nuclear.

CCT:			Combat camera team.
CCT:			Combat Controller, an Air force CAS specialist.
CDS:			Chief of defence Staff.
Cedars-Mountains:			Mountain range located in Eastern Lebanon (Home of Hezbollah training camps and safe houses).
Cell:			Small team or group of people.
Centcom:			American military-Central Command.

Chai:	Afghan green or black tea.
Chemical weapons- CW:	When dealing with Chemical weapons the important point to remember when assessing a threat is the "Delivery means" of the weapon. There are two categories, battle field chemical weapons and WMD. Are the Chemical weapons adapted to be used for; Artillery-Rockets-Mortars or Air delivery means using aircraft-helicopters? VX-nerve agent that can kill in seconds has been confirmed as part of Syrians chemical weapons stockpile. Syrin gas has been confirmed, (by Britain-America –France and the UN), as being used in 2013, by one of the sides in the Syrian civil war. It is reported and confirmed by American and Russian Government sources that Syria has over 1000 tons of chemical weapons, including VX and other deadly nerve agents-spread over 42+ sites across Syria. (See Glossary, Dirty Bomb).
Chief of station:	MI6 head of deployed country office or Embassy MI6 sub-office. (See Glossary, COS).
Chinook CH-47 /MH-47:	Large military twin-turbine, tandem-rotor heavy transport helicopter, used by British and American forces. The Chinook MH-47 is specially modified for use by "Special operations forces".
CI:		Counter insurgency,
CIA/CTC:		CTC-Counter-terrorism centre, the unit within the American CIA focused on terrorism.
CIA/NOC/OCO:		(See NOC-OCO).
CIA:		American Central Intelligence Agency "HQ Langley, Virginia" (see NOCOCO-Trade craft CIA-Camp Chapman).
CII:		Counter Iranian influence. (See Iraq Hezbollah).
CJOTF:		Combined Operations Task Force.
Classified:		A security classification given or assigned to an official British Government document-report. Other classifications include: Top-Secret and Eyes only Alpha.
Claymore:		American military anti-personnel mine, homemade IED's/claymores are used by terrorists groups, including Taliban,

—		Al-Shabab and Al-Qaeda. Also suicide bombers strap homemade claymores to their bodies, (packs of small steel ball bearings), to inflict maximum death and casualties. (See Glossary, 21/9 and IED).
Cleaner/clean-up team:		Terminology used to describe a cleaner or clean-up team, used for detailed site exploration of a specific location or target area. (Example Captured terrorist training camp or safe house) Information, evidence is collected to be assessed, analysed for intelligence.
Cluster fuck:		Military term used to describe a messed up situation, made famous by the American actor, Clint Eastwood in the war movie "heartbreak ridge".
C-Mock/Nineveh:		Hotel used as CIA location Mosul Iraq "Nineveh", Located within the grounds of one of Saddam Hussein's old palaces. (See Task Force 121).
CN:		Counter narcotics.
CO:		Commanding Officer, found in a military unit-Lieutenant Colonel in charge of a Regiment, Battalion.
Coalition:		National military forces working together as one force. (See ISAF).
COB:		Contingency operating base.
COBRA:		Cabinet office briefing room "A", The British Government "Cobra", meetings are called in times of national emergency or domestic, foreign crises.
COK:		Capture or kill-order given as part of military briefings in relation to HVT's/known terrorists.
Collateral Damage:		Military / Political term used to describe damage or fallout – Civilian casualties, during military action and operations. (See Modern Warfare).

Comanche: American military RAH-66 stealth helicopter. (Similar to the Military helicopters used in the mission to kill Osama bin Laden 2nd May 2011).

Command wire: Method used by terrorists to detonate an explosive charge or IED (Improvised Explosive Device). This method of detonation was used by the IRA or PIRA in Northern Ireland during the troubles. Former IRA bomb makers/instructors have been reported in terrorist training camps around the world, including, Lebanon Hezbollah, Al-Qaeda in Iraq, Afghan-Taliban, Pakistan-Taliban and Kandahar-Al-Qaeda. Former IRA, personnel have also been reported instructing the Al-Shabab terrorist group in Somalia and Jabhat Al-Nusra in Syria.

Comms:	Communications.
Compartmentalise:	Isolated-independent units within a network-breaking down a network into independent cells that do not have contact with each other. Compartmentalise is a security tactic, used by Western Intelligence agencies and terrorist groups to keep the whole-overall information on a subject or operation secret.
Coord:	Coordinate/coordination.
COS:	Chief of Staff "British military".
Counter-Intel:	Counter Intelligence.
Coup d'état:	A sudden violent overthrow of a Government. (Example Egypt 2013).
Cover Identities:	CIA: officers call "funny Names", false names used by intelligence personnel-sources, during operations to protect their true identity. (See Glossary, Trade craft-CIA).
Covert Op:	Clandestine military action/tasking or intelligence operation. (See NOC and Special Forces).
Cow:	Taliban-Al-Qaeda slang for the British-American military Chinook helicopter.
Coy:	Company.
CP:	Check point.
CP:	Counter Proliferation.
CPO:	Close protection officer.
CQB:	Close quarter battle.
CQMS:	Company quartermaster sergeant.
Crap-Hat:	To be elite requires someone to be crap, in the eyes of the ultras of the British Parachute Regiment that designation applies to everyone else in uniform. The phrase "Crap-Hat" is used for all in uniform who do not belong to the British elite Parachute Regiment. Para's have an aggressive attitude of superiority, which comes from physical wellbeing, due to their training. Al-Qaeda -Taliban fear the soldiers from the Parachute

		Regiment-confirmed by "Saladin" and other senior Taliban- Al-Qaeda Commanders.
Crocodile hunting:		Term used by security operatives to hunt HVT's, terrorists. Throughout the Middle-East and Africa. (See Glossary, Bounty-CIA).
Cruise missile:		Ballistic-long range missile. Examples; Tomahawk (US)-Storm Shadow (UK). Cruise missiles have been used in Pre-emptive strikes against enemy/terrorist targets across the Middle-East and Africa. TLAM, Tomahawk land attack missile, a subsonic cruise missile that attacks targets on land, and can be fitted with a conventional unitary warhead, (TLAM\C), a nuclear warhead, (TLAM\N), or a sub-munition dispenser (TLAM\D).
Crypo:		Cryptographic-Secure codes which enable encoded secure communication.
CSA:		American central support agency.

CSSP:		American prison mentors located in Afghanistan. Most members of the CSSP team are former or serving members of American military intelligence.
CT:		Counter-Terrorism.
CTC:		Counter-terrorism command, the UK police unit leading the domestic counter-terrorism effort, created in 2002.
CTR:		Close target reconnaissance.
Damage limitation:		Political-intelligence-military term "containment" of a damaging situation after it has happened. Controlling the flow of outgoing information relating to a given situation or incident. Objective to minimise the damage-potential fallout, caused by the incident-situation.
Damascus:		Ancient Capital city of Syria. Damascus is the oldest continually inhabited city in the world. (See Syria).
Dasht-e-Margo:		"Desert of death", located in Southern Afghanistan.
DAT:		Defence attaché.
David Ignatius:		A prize-winning columnist for the Washington Post has covered the Middle-East and the CIA for more than twenty-five years. David Ignatius is one of the Authors who inspired Anthony Malone to write his manuscript. (See Reading list).
David Petraeus (General):		American military 4 star general and paratrooper. Also former head of CENT-COM (American Military Central Command) and former Director of the American CIA. (See Glossary, for overview

		see Petraeus).
De Oppresso Liber:		Latin for "Free the Oppressed"; the creed of the U.S. Army Special Forces, the Green Berets.
DEA:		American drug enforcement agency.
Dead drop:		One way static drop location point for information and important messages. (See Trade craft).
De-Brief:		Official briefing "post" evaluation of an operation/mission or tasking. Comprehensive statement of account-actions-information and intelligence gained. De-briefs can be given written or orally.
Del-e-Zore/Deir ez-Zur:		Town, located in central Syria, strategically placed on the banks of the Euphrates River, the town has two bridges and a small airport-airfield. Al-Qaeda-terrorist training camps and safe houses are located close to the town. Strategical geographic location, the town is used by Al-Qaeda leaders and other terrorist group commanders, for tactical, strategic and operational planning of covert meetings. Del-e-Zore is on one of the main routes used by Al-Qaeda groups to transport weapons and fighters between Lebanon, Iraq, Iran, Afghanistan and Pakistan. (See TadmorPalmyra).
Delta:		American Special Forces "Delta force" (1st Special Forces Operational Detachment-Delta).
Dems:		Demolitions.
Denied area of operations:		An operational area either behind enemy lines or in hostile country, were the operation is unauthorised and without permission (See Glossary, Black Op's and Covert Operations).
Desert Hawk:		Small British UAV-Drone.
Det:		Detachment.
DFID:		British department of international development.
DG:		Director general, the head of MI5, the UK's domestic security service.
DGSE:		General Directorate of external security, (French; Direction Generale De La securite exterieure), French foreign intelligence service.
DHS:		American, department of homeland security.
DIA:		Defence Intelligence Agency, the U.S. military's CIA.
Diego-Garcia (DG):		American naval support facility and USAF base, located on "DG" island

in the Indian Ocean. American strategic B1-B2-bombers have launched tactical and strategic raids-missions across the Middle-East and Afghanistan from "DG". Rendition flights also go through this location. (See B2).

Diplomacy: Handling of international relations. (See Gunship diplomacy).

Dirty bomb:	WMD, connected to components-conventional explosives, objective of a dirty bomb is to disperse a selection of WMD material over a tactical or strategic area. Example: City or population area. Al-Qaeda- Jabhat AlNusra and other terrorist groups in Syria, Iraq, Afghanistan, Pakistan, and Sudan have tried to acquire dirty bomb "radioactive" material. Chemical weapons could also be used as components in a dirty bomb. (It is reported that Syria has "VX" nerve agent amongst its large stock pile of chemical weapons. It is also reported that Syria has the world's biggest stock pile of chemical and biological weapons. 1000 tons of CW, over 42+ sites across Syria. Confirmed-agreed figures by the American and Russian Governments. Western Governments including Britain, France, America, and their intelligence services are rightly worried and concerned that terrorist groups operating in and across Syria are trying to acquire CW to export out of Syria to be used against Europe, American and Israeli targets. (See Glossary, Chemical weapons and Jabhat Al-Nusra).
DIS:	British Defence Intelligence Staff, intelligence unit of the UK Ministry of Defence, functioning similarly to the American DIA.
Dish dash:	Loose Kaftan-style outfit worn by many Afghan and Arab men.
Diwan:	"Arabic" room set aside for the use of gentlemen wishing to chew "Khat" (See Glossary, Khat).
Diyah:	"Arabic" blood money.
DNA:	Deoxyribonucleic-Acid, a substance storing genetic information. DNA testing and profiling is used to locate and positively identify terrorist suspects (See Glossary, Nucleic acid).
Doha:	Capital city of Qatar.
Double tap:	Military tactic, of firing two rounds from a weapon in quick secession into an enemy's head or body to kill or immobilise the target.
Dragunov:	Russian sniper rifle-used by Taliban, Al-Shabab and Al-Qaeda fighters across the Middle-East, Afghanistan-Pakistan and Africa. Terrorist sniper teams normally operate in twos, one sniper and one spotter, similar, MO (Modus operandi) to British and American military forces snipers.

Drone (UAV):	Unmanned aerial vehicle-aircraft "Predator, Rapture or Reaper", remotely piloted by an operator (sometimes in a different country) can be armed with hellfire missiles. Used widely for reconnaissance and surveillance.
Drone strike-CIA:	CIA signature drone strike, also known as airstrikes on HVT's, high value targets, and terrorists. Drone strikes have been carried out in countries including: Somalia, Yemen, Iraq, Afghanistan, Pakistan, Sudan and Syria.
Dry hole:	Location-person, viewed-monitored-searched, no useable intelligence found. Also has the meaning of an empty location, nobody found.
DU:	Depleted Uranium.
Dubai-UAE:	Dubai, in the UAE (United Arab Emirates) is an oil rich ultra-modern city which has risen from the deserts of the UAE. Dubai is a banking and financial hub for international business, with an appointed "Trade free zone" in the heart of the city. Dubai has mixed old with new, with the old "souks" markets, establishing themselves as tourist's attractions. There is also an indoor ski centre and international airport, which act as a major attraction and transport hub for travellers across the Middle-East and beyond. Dubai has been called the playground for the oil rich Arabs. The Dubai Banking sector is also the destination of choice for major money transfers, cash deposits, (suitcases full of money) out of Afghanistan, Iraq, and Pakistan. Many Islamic "NGO's" bank in Dubai and money transfers are facilitated to many known terrorist front companies around the globe. (See Glossary, Madrasah).
Dushanbe:	Capital city of Tajikistan.
Dushka:	Nickname of the DShK-Soviet built Anti-aircraft machine gun-12.7mm, (equivalent to the American .50cal) and common amongst terrorist groups across the Middle-East and Africa.
Duty of care:	Official term used to describe the responsibility towards an intelligence source or an individual who comes under their official responsibility. Duty of care also applies to "Hum-Int" (Human Intelligence Sources) or assets operating behind enemy lines or in hostile environments. Duty of care-includes, keeping

	the source safe and relocation after source extraction. (See Glossary, Wit-Sec).
DZ:	Parachute Drop Zone.
ECHR:	European Court of Human Rights.
EF:	Enemy Forces.
EIJ or Al-Jihad:	Egyptian Islamic - jihad Islamic movement, the group has a strong presence in the Persian Gulf, Yemen, United Kingdom, Pakistan, Afghanistan and Europe. The EIJ has also developed a cadre of excellent insurgent commanders across the Middle-East, Islamic world Jihad's. The EIJ has very strong links to the Al-Qaeda leadership and network. (See Glossary, Haqqani Network).
ELZ:	Emergency landing zone for helicopters or aircraft.
Empta:	O-Ethyl Methylphosphonothioic acid, a dual-use chemical used for pesticides and as a precursor in the synthesis of nerve agent. (See Glossary, VX-nerve agent-Chemical Weapons).
EOD:	Explosive Ordnance Disposal.
EQT:	Equipment.
ESB:	External Security Bureau, Sudan's intelligence service.
ETA/ETD:	Estimated Time of Arrival – Estimated Time of Departure.
EUCOM:	European Command.
E-Vac:	Emergency medical evacuation.
Extreme rendition:	Transfer of prisoners between countries without "Habeas Corpus" legal due-process. (See Glossary, Balad TSF).
Eyes on-mark one eye ball:	Term used to describe or referring to a clear line of sight on a person or target.
F/F:	Foreign Fighter, brought into a country to fight for Al-Qaeda, Taliban, Haqqani network and Al-Shabab. (See Haqqani network).

F3 Classification:	Official British Military intelligence classification, given to a "Hum-Int", source, to protect the sources personal identity. (See Glossary, grade "A" sources).
FAC:	Forward Air Controller.
Falcon view:	Classified American military satellite imagery.
Farm:	Nickname for the CIA American-tactical and strategic training facility. (See Glossary, Trade craft-CIA).
Farsi:	Language of Northern Afghanistan.
FBI:	American "Federal Bureau of Investigation".
FCO:	British Foreign and Commonwealth Office "HQ London England".
FIBUA:	Fighting In Built Up Areas.
Firm:	Nickname referring to the British Intelligence Service "SIS", "MI6".
FO:	Forward Observer.
FOB:	Forward Operating Base.
Force 84:	British Special Forces Task Force, operating in Afghanistan.
Fox:	The Fox is the codename for Saladin, an Al-Qaeda, Taliban Commander, originally from Eastern Afghanistan. (Interviewed by Anthony Malone in Afghanistan).
Friendly fire:	Also known as "Blue on Blue" when your own military or friendly forces open fire on their own side by mistake.
Front company:	Legitimate legal companies set up for ML (Money laundering) and moving assets and money around the world. Used by terrorist groups and drug cartels to hide their proceeds of illegal activity. Also used to apply for travelling visas, this facilitates the movement of HVT's and terrorists between countries. (See Glossary, Dubai).
FSA:	Free Syrian army. Armed opposition group, made up of several factions- Fighting against the Government of President Assad of Syria. (See Syria).
FSB:	Russian Secret Service, previously known as the KGB.

G1:	Senior American military intelligence officer.
Gaza Strip/West Bank:	Palestinian territories within the disputed country borders of Israel. AlQaeda and other affiliated terrorist groups operate within the Gaza Strip and the West Bank. The Rafah crossing point is the only public crossing point to and from Egypt from the Gaza Strip. Smuggling tunnels are scattered across the Egyptian, Gaza border, these are used to transport weapons and other black market material into Gaza. (See Glossary, AQAP).
Gazelle:	British reconnaissance military helicopter.
GCHQ:	British Headquarters for gathering electronic intercepts from all over the world and electronic intelligence analysis (SIS). A modern version on the British World War Two, Bletchley Park "code breakers". SIS and MI5 staff work alongside GCHQ linguists who are there to translate interpret, "Sigint" (Signal Intelligence).
GHQ:	General Headquarters, British Army.
Gitmo:	The American military abbreviation for Guantanamo bay prison Cuba.
Glock:	9mm pistol, favoured by American DEA, intelligence agencies, law enforcement and close protection teams. Can be fitted with silencer, noise suppresser (A Glock 23, can chamber a .40mm round/bullet, this gives it more stopping power).
GMG:	Grenade Machine Gun.
GMLRS:	Guided Multiple Launch Rocket System.
GMT:	Greenwich Mean Time.
GOI:	Globalisation of Intelligence.
Going Native/Deep Cover:	Term to describe a person who has immersed themselves in the local culture and population. He or she looks, speaks, acts like a local. More local than the locals, can blend in to the local environment without drawing any undue attention. The term is used to describe undercover intelligence operatives working across the middle-east to infiltrate terrorist groups and networks. (See Glossary, Trade craft-CIA).
Golan Heights:	Disputed geographic area of land between Syria and Israel. The town of

Katzrin is the capital of Golan.

GPMG: General Purpose Machine Gun.

GPS: Global Positioning System.

Grade "A" Source: In intelligence source deemed by the British and American
                         intelligence services to be an impeccable source of accurate
                         actionable intelligence, information from an grade "A", source
                         can be actioned without authenticating, if deemed time
                         sensitive and of extreme high value.

Grey man: Term used to describe a person who blends into their
                         environment and surroundings, without drawing any un-due
                         attention. A person who does not stand out in a crowd.

Grey Fox:	Codename for the American military special forces/CIA operations team/unit. Trained to dispose of, assassinate enemy personnel, during the Vietnam War. (See task Force 121-363 Afghanistan).
Guantanamo:	Official terrorist prison ran by America Government, located in Cuba.
GUB:	Guided bomb unit-Smart bomb.
Guerrilla warfare:	Unconventional warfare; a hit-and-run method of warfare used to inflict maximum damage with a minimum of weaponry and manpower. (See also UW-unconventional warfare).
Gun run:	A military term for a fighter plane or helicopter gunship, diving close to the ground and using its cannon and machine guns to strafe the enemy position on the ground.
Gunship Diplomacy:	Seeking diplomacy through the threat of direct or indirect force.
GWOT:	Global War on Terror, the abbreviated term given to President George Bush's post-9/11 strategy for countering Al-Qaeda.
Habeas Corpus:	The right to a legal hearing and legal due-process. (See Rendition).
Hamas:	Palestinian organisation based in the Garza strip and West bank. Fiercely opposed to Israel.
Handler:	Intelligence officer, CIA/NSA/MI6, case officer who handles human assets' and "Hum-Int" (Human Intelligence). A good handler cultivates and develops intelligence sources. (See Glossary, Trade craft-CIA).
Haqqani network:	International terrorist network, many of its members and fighters are drawn from Afghan Taliban-Pakistan Taliban-Kandahar Al-Qaeda and the old Haqqani resistance network based in Khost

	Eastern Afghanistan. The Haqqani network has strong ties to the Al-Qaeda network, Afghan Taliban, Pakistan Taliban and Lebanese Hezbollah. Haqqani network fighters have been reported in Syria, Iraq, Afghanistan, Pakistan, Yemen, and Somalia, training Al-Shabab and across North Africa. (Members interviewed by Anthony Malone in Afghanistan) (See Glossary, Hussein Laghman).
Haqqani-Jalauddin:	A major Afghan insurgent Commander and Pashtun tribal leader, who had close ties to Osama bin Laden and continues to have very strong ties to the Al-Qaeda network. Haqqani also has very strong links to the Pakistan Taliban and the Pakistan ISI. At one time Haqqani was the Taliban's Minister of tribal affairs. (See Glossary, Saladin-Haqqani network).
Hassake:	City located in North East Syria. Mainly Arab-Kurdish influenced. Stopover point for known insurgents, terrorists travelling from PakistanAfghanistan-Iran-Iraq, to Lebanon. (See Hezbollah and Haqqani network).
Hawala:	Un-official, Islamic money transfer money system, used throughout the Middle-east, Africa, and Europe. Also used extensively by Terrorist groups to transfer money between countries without a trace or accountability. (See Glossary, Dubai).
HE:	High Explosive (ammunition).
Heat:	High Explosive Anti-Tank (ammunition).
Heckler & Koch/H&K:	German weapons Production Company, who manufacture a wide variety of specialist weapons, including the MP5k submachine gun designed for close quarter battle, used by clandestine operators and Special Forces. (See Photographs).
Hekmatyar-Gulbuddin:	An Afghan Pashtun leader of the "Hisbi Islami", Islamist group. Exceptionally talented political opportunist, attracting funding from Iran and Saudi Arabia. Has very close ties to the Pakistan Taliban and the Afghan Taliban. It is reported that he also has major ties and unofficial support for the Pakistan ISI. The American CIA gave funding to Hekmatyar during the Soviet Jihad in Afghanistan. (See Glossary, Haqqani network).
Hellfire Missiles:	AGM-114k Sal (semi-active laser) hellfire II, is a laser-guided hellfire missile fitted to the Apache and UAV-Predator drone.
Helio:	Military slang for "helicopter". Also chopper, Huey, hawk, bird, Slick.
Heroin:	Narcotic mass produced in Afghanistan. A powerful, addictive drug narcotic farmed and produced by Taliban and Warlords across Afghanistan. The illegal narcotics trade helps fund the Taliban and AlQaeda terrorist operations across the Middle-East and beyond.

	(See Glossary, Hezbollah).
Hezbollah-Hizballah:	Lebanon based terrorist group, backed by Iran, with links to Al-Qaeda. Its fighters are involved in terrorist activity and operations across the Middle-East, Including: Lebanon, Syria, Iraq, Afghanistan, Pakistan and North Africa. Hezbollah training camps have been found in Syria, Iraq, Pakistan, Afghanistan. Hezbollah were the first terrorist group to use IED's in the Middle-East, "against Israel". Hezbollah have exported their IED knowledge to other terrorist groups including the Afghan, Pakistan Taliban and Al-Qaeda in Iraq. Hezbollah facilitate and run terrorist training camps in the mountains of Eastern Lebanon-sponsored by Iran. Iranian Republican Guard/Iranian Special Forces have been seen teaching and instructing within the Hezbollah training camps. It is reported that elements within the Hezbollah originally facilitated Taliban and Al-Qaeda illegal narcotics Laboratories in the mountains of North Eastern Lebanon. The product-narcotics (Afghan Heroin) is transported from Afghanistan, through the Taliban Al-Qaeda network of safe houses and established routes from Afghan, Iran, Iraq, Syria and Lebanon, then distributed by Land, Sea and air, to international locations including Europe and America. There are also links between Hezbollah and Al-Shabab in Somalia. (See IH-Iraq Hezbollah) (Members interviewed by Anthony Malone in Cyprus-Lebanon-Syria-Iraq and Afghanistan).
Hind/MIL-Mi24:	Russian made heavily armed helicopter gunship, used by several Middle-East countries, including; Syria, Iraq, Afghanistan and Iran. The MIL-Mi24 is also in active military service across several African countries.
Hindu Kush:	Mountain range-located in Northern Afghanistan.

Hisbi Islami:	(See Hekmatyar-Gulbuddin).
HMG:	Her Majesty's Government (Great Britain) reference to the Government of the United Kingdom.
Home grown:	Term used to describe home grown terrorists, who are born in places like Britain, American, Canada and France, who become terrorists against their own Government and country.
HUM-INT:	Human intelligence-sources. (See Handler).
Hum-vee	Also known as "hummer", American military 4X4, used extensively

	by the American military throughout the Middle-East. Can be heavily armoured and mounted with heavy machine guns and "TOW" anti-tank missiles (normally houses a four man crew, one riding top cover).
Hussien Laghman:	God son of Ayman Al-Zawaniri, the leader of the Al-Qaeda network. Hussein is a member of the Pakistan ISI and major player/negotiator between Al-Qaeda and the Taliban. He also acts as their fixer and quartermaster. Hussein is also responsible for organizing safe transportation of known terrorists between countries, including airplane tickets, passports and money transfers, secret hideaways in strange cities, cell phones and computers. Hassien has also been arrested in the past for selling SAM's (Surface to Air Missiles) and other weapons to the Pakistan, Afghan Taliban. The Chief prosecutor in Afghanistan (Afghan Ministry of Justice) has been paid money by Hussein and members of the Taliban network, for the changing of Taliban prisoner's official files, from terrorist charges to narcotics/drug charges and in doing so a large number of known Taliban terrorists have walked free from British mentored Afghan prisons. (See ACP and Haqqani network) (Interviewed by Anthony Malone in Afghanistan).
HVT:	High Value Target- The target indication of a terrorist's standing/value.
I.L.:	"Index list" Document-list of content of intelligence-source reports.
I.R.	Illum, Infer-red illumination.

IA:	Intelligence Analyst.
Ibrahim Al-Asiri:	Saudi born chief bomb maker for Al-Qaeda in the Arabian peninsula, "AQAP". Reported to be operating in Syria, Yemen, Afghanistan, Pakistan and Somalia. (See AQI and Jabhat Al-Nusra).
Ideology:	Ideas that form the basis of a political or economic theory, Al-Qaeda and Islamic fundamentalist ideology is a major modern threat to Western countries national security. (See Modern Warfare, Al-Shabab).
IDF:	Israeli defence force. (See Mossad).
IED:	Improvised explosive device. (See Ibrahim Al-Asiri- Command wireshape charge).
IH:	Iraqi Hezbollah; Hezbollah have exported their fighting experience, fighters, and knowledge of IED's and guerrilla warfare-GW, to terrorist training camps in Iraq-Syria-Afghanistan-Pakistan.

	Hezbollah facilitate terrorist safe houses in several countries including; Iraq-LebanonCyprus-Afghanistan-Pakistan. (See Glossary, Hezbollah/Asa'ib Ahl-Al Haq).
Iman:	"Arabic", a Muslim who leads prayers in a mosque and a person of authority in the Muslim community.
IMAO:	Improvise-Modify-Adapt-Overcome (See Glossary, Trade craft-CIA).
Infidels-Kufr:	Term used by some Muslims to describe none Muslims.
INMARSAT:	International maritime satellite telephone/radio.
Intel:	Intelligence. (See hum-int).
Interpol:	International European police headquarters, located in Lyon, France.
Intifada:	Palestinian uprising against Israel.
IRA:	Irish republican army (see Glossary, PIRA).

IRBM:	Intermediate-Range Ballistic Missiles.
IRG:	Iranian Revolutionary Guard.
IRT:	Immediate Response Team.
ISAF:	The UN-mandated International Security Assistance force, based in Kabul, Afghanistan. Members include: America, Britain, Canada, Germany, France, Turkey, Italy and many others.
ISI:	Pakistani Inter-Service Intelligence agency, vicious enemies of the Afghan Northern Alliance and Pakistan's version of the Russian old KGB or modern FSB. The Pakistan ISI has reported strong links to the AfghanTaliban, Pakistan-Taliban and Al-Qaeda. Some elements within the Pakistan ISI openly support the Taliban. Members of the Pakistan ISI are in prison in Afghanistan-due to them trying to sell "Surface to Air" missiles to the Taliban, (See Haqqani network). (Anthony Malone interviewed members of ISI, operating in Afghanistan).
Islam:	The Muslim religion.
Islamabad:	Capital city of Pakistan.
ISOF:	Iraqi Special Operations Force (See Glossary, Apostles).
ISOFAC:	Isolation facility where Special Forces teams prepare for combat missions and remain until they deploy.
Istanbul:	Strategically located city in Turkey. Previously known as, "Constantinople". Also known as the gateway to the West.
ISTAR:	Intelligence, signals (surveillance) target acquisition and reconnaissance.
J1 – J2:	American military intelligence officer, also used as intelligence liaison officer between friendly country's military units (See Glossary S1-G1RSO).
Jabhat Al – Nusra:	Syrian based terrorist group, with strong links to Al-Qaeda-Pakistan

	Taliban and the Haqqani network. Jabhat Al – Nusra, are logistically and financially supported by Al-Qaeda in Iraq "AQI" which in turn are supported by the Al-Qaeda supreme council in Pakistan. Europeans include: Commonwealth nationals; British, Canadian, Sweden also German nationals have been reported fighting for Jabhat Al-Nusra in Syria (See Glossary, AQAP, AQI and Iraq).
Jalalabad-Jbad:	Provincial capital city located in Jalalabad province, Eastern Afghanistan. Geographic location close to the border of Pakistan, and close to the volatile and turbulent tribal area of Waziristan (Western Pakistan). Jalalabad is historically on the major trade-transit route from Pakistan to Afghanistan. In modern times this route is used by the Taliban and the insurgency to transport fighters and weapons between Pakistan and Afghanistan. These Taliban fighters launch attacks against British and American (ISAF) soldiers across Afghanistan. Taliban safe houses and training camps are also located on the outskirts of Jalalabad city and the border area. The city and the area have a reputation for being "Lawless" the "Wild West" with corrupt Afghan Government officials. (You can rent an Afghan, but you cannot buy one) is an old saying used by local Afghan's (See Glossary, Haqqani network).
Jambia:	"Arabic" curved dagger much favoured by Yemenis and the tribes of Arabia. (See Glossary, AQAP).
Janes:	Janes military books, CD and reports, give comprehensive, highly detailed, technical background information on all aspects of modern warfare.
JDAM:	Joint Direct Attack Munitions; an upgrade kit that turns conventional bombs into GPS-navigated bombs with an INS (internal navigation system) kit that is retrofitted to the bombs. JDAM-equipment bombs can navigate to a target over fifteen miles away, regardless of weather conditions.
Jebel:	General Arabic word for mountains.
Jerusalem:	Capital city of Israel.

JFACC: Joint Forces Air Component Command.

JIC: Joint Intelligence Committee, the UK Government committee wherein intelligence gathered by the intelligence agencies is pooled.

Jihad: Islamic holy war against "infidels" declared by Islamic fundamentalists.

Jihadists: Fighters in a Jihad, "Islamic holy war".

JOC: Joint Operational Command.

JSFOC:	Joint Special Force Operational Command.
JSOC:	Joint Special Operations Command. (See Glossary, Balad).
JTAC:	Joint Tactical Air Controller.
JTAC:	Joint Terrorism Analysis Centre, the UK multi-agency "clearing house" for terrorism-related intelligence.
July 7th 2005:	United Kingdom-London, home grown, Al-Qaeda inspired suicide bomber attacks on the London public transport system, one bus and four underground stations. 56 killed and 700+ injured. Al-Qaeda leader Zawahire, then Osama bin Laden's deputy claimed credit for the attacks (See 7/7 and Haqqani network Pakistan).
K2:	American ultra-secret Special Forces operations and staging base. Located in Uzbekistan, close to the Turkmenistan border. K2 has played an important role in the "War on terror". Tactical and strategic military operations and missions have been launched from this location across the Middle-East and Afghanistan. (See Glossary, Task forces 121-323).
Kabul:	Capital city of Afghanistan.
KAF:	Kandahar airfield "American and British operational military airbase, located in Southern Afghanistan" close to the historic city of Kandahar.
Kaftan:	Loose Dish dash-style outfit worn by many Afghan and Arab men.

Kalima Tayyab	'La Ilaha Ill Allah Muhammadur Rasool Allah' (There is no god only Allah, Muhammad is the Rasool (Messenger) of Allah) is also known as Kalima Tayyab. Kalima Tayyab is the testification of faith in Islam. A person cannot be considered to be a Muslim if he/she does not believe in the words of this Kalima.
Kandahar Al-Qaeda:	Extremist group within the Al-Qaeda network. (See LOA).
Kandahar/Qandahar:	Historic Afghan City located in Southern Afghanistan, is also the spiritual home of the Taliban.
Karachi-Pakistan:	Major city-transport hub located on the coast in Southern Pakistan. It is also a known transit route for Taliban and International terrorist suspects in and out of Pakistan-Afghanistan.
Kefraya red:	Red wine produced in the Bekkaa valley Lebanon. (See Hezbollah).

Kerman:	City located in Southeast Iran. Key location on the Taliban and Al-Qaeda smuggling routes from Afghanistan to Iraq, Syria and the West. Also the location of the compound that houses members of the "Bin laden" family. Iranian factory made IED's and explosive shape charges are made, transported into Afghanistan to be used against British and American (ISAF) forces. (See Glossary, IED-Shape charge).
Kevlar:	Bullet resistant material, offering different degrees of ballistic protection against projectiles/bullets. Used in body armour and ballistic plating. (See Glossary, B6-B7).
KGB:	The committee for State Security, (Russian; Komitet Gosudarstvennoy Benzopasnosti) foreign-intelligence service of the Soviet Union, created in 1954, disbanded in 1991.
Khartoum:	Capital city of Sudan.
Khat:	Mildly narcotic leaf which can be chewed, popular in Yemen and Somalia.
KIA:	Killed in action; to be killed on the battlefield.
Killing House:	Live firing training area and location, used by Special Forces to practice CQB, close quarter battle and hostage release.
Kuwait city:	Capital city of Kuwait, oil rich, modern Muslim country. With borders to Iraq-Saudi Arabia and the Persian Gulf.

Langley-CIA:	Langley, Virginia. The headquarters of the American CIA (See Farm).
Lase:	To highlight or "Paint" a laser signature on a target, so that a laserguided bomb may use its guidance system to home in on it. (See Glossary, Smart bomb).
Lashkargah:	Provincial Capital city of Helmand province Southern Afghanistan.
LAV:	Light armoured vehicle.
Leakers:	Terrorists-insurgents, that are attempting to escape, (Leak), from the target area.
Lilly white:	Disposable, untraceable "pay as go" mobile phone. (See Trade craftCIA).
Little bird:	American military Kiowa helicopter can be heavily armed with a wide verity of heavy machine guns and rockets /missiles. (See Night Stalkers).
LN:	Local National.
LOA:	Lions of Allah: Al-Qaeda, special operations team (See Kandahar Al-Q).
Locstats:	Location Status.
LOE:	Limit of Exploitation.
Lone wolf:	Completely independent fighter, operator (Plan's their own missions).
Lonely Planet books:	Impeccably researched and published books that specialize in

	travelling across the Middle-East and worldwide. A wealth of information required for day to day travelling in foreign countries (See Acquired reading list).
Long:	Assault rifle or long barrelled weapon (A "short" would be a pistol).
Longbow-Apache:	The Longbow radar is the Apache helicopter, fire control radar, it looks like a large Swiss cheese and sits on top of the main rotor system. (See Glossary, Apache Helicopter).

Loya Jirga:	Islamic council of tribal representatives, meeting to discuss political and tribal issues.
M/L:	Money Laundering (See Dubai-Front companies).
M/O:	"Latin" Modus operandi.
M-4A1:	A shorter version of the M-16A2 assault rifle, with a collapsible stock and a heavier barrel, favoured by Special Forces, Security operators and vehicle crews. Includes a removable carrying handle and rails for mounting scopes and night-vision devices. Often includes an underbarrel 40mm M203 grenade launcher or shotgun (See Photographs).
Madrasah:	An Islamic school house used for "Educating", Taliban and A-Qaeda, in fundamentalist Islamic practices-Common throughout Pakistan. A large number of Madrasah's are funded from Saudi Arabia, and NGO's who operate out of Dubai (See Dubai and Money laundering).
Man-pad:	Any man-portable, surface to air missile, including the Soviet SA-7 and the US military stinger missile. (See SAM).
Mark Urban:	Highly respected British TV reporter-journalist and author. Mark Urban's writing and books are impeccably researched, his writing inspired Anthony Malone to write his manuscript (See acquired reading list).
Massoud:	Ahmad Shah Massoud-Former Commander of the Afghan Northern Alliance. Was killed by Al-Qaeda on the 8th September 2001, by a suicide bomber posing as part of a TV camera crew, 3 days before 9/11. Anthony Malone interviewed in Afghanistan Wali Massoud, former Afghanistan Ambassador to Britain and America (See Northern Alliance).
Mecca or Makkah:	City in Saudi Arabia, and religious capital for the Sunni Muslims and place of pilgrimage.
Medevac:	Medical Evacuation.
Medina:	Islamic holy city in Saudi Arabia.
Mercenary:	A person who is paid to fight and kill for money (See PMC).

Mert:	Medical emergency response team.
MIA:	Missing in Action.
Michael Scheuer:	Former American CIA intelligence operative, veteran of 22 years; and former head of "Alec Station" (1996-99) appointed head of "Islamic Extremist Branch", of the counter terrorism centre CTC- "Osama bin Laden" unit. Michael Scheuer is academically qualified and trained as a historian. Michael Scherer's book, "Through our Enemies eyes" inspired Anthony Malone to infiltrate the Al-Qaeda network, to stop terrorist attacks and later to write his manuscript in order to pass on his knowledge (See Glossary, acquired reading list).
Millbank:	Term used to describe MI5 headquarters location. Located along Millbank road, London United Kingdom.
MOB:	Main Operating Base (See Glossary, Bastion camp).
MOD:	British Ministry of Defence.

Modern Warfare-Urban Siege: Terrorism-Modern Warfare-Urban Siege, Examples: Syria-Hamma, Mumbai-India, 7/7 attacks-London, Westgate Mall-Kenya. It is now and forever the day after September 11th 2001, 9/11 terrorist attacks. Modern warfare has evolved like a living organism, into the modern age. Wars and battles are not fought on the battlefields, open deserts or rolling hillsides with clear enemy lines. The modern and next generation of warfare is being fought (urban warfare), amongst our homes, city streets and shopping malls. Suicide bombers and armed Islamic insurgents-terrorists groups storming public buildings, killing unarmed civilians, women and children, off duty soldiers in Capital cities. "Urban Siege" is the new terrorist tactic, hostage taking and summary executions of none Muslim men, women and children. Suicide bombers detonating during morning rush hour, in busy Western city coffee shops, boutiques, and during sporting events, covered by live TV broadcasts and cameras. The horrific images beamed live across the

Globe in full uncut graphic colour. People watching the aftermath of Chemical Weapon attacks on TV over their lunch time meal. The modern internet-tweeter-multi-media gives terrorism a 24/7, global platform of extensive coverage on the world stage. Extreme violence, death and horrific carnage are just a mouse click away. I.T, computers and multi-media are the new weapons, tools used by terrorist groups and organisations, bringing violence and terrorist ideology into our homes, offices and lives. Children and young adults have access to the internet, unlimited violence, beheadings, Al-Qaeda propaganda videos that glorify the Islamic Jihad, and the killing of none Muslims. Children and adults are being desensitized, nightly news programs show violent Jihad almost every night, no one is surprised at yet another foreign terrorist attack or suicide bombing, 10 dead, 50 dead, 100 dead and these are just the empty numbers to the faceless viewer. It's only when the local shopping mall disappears in a fireball or local bus or train is running late, due to a suicide bomber blowing themselves up, making modern warfare/terrorism's horrific scenes of death a shocking reality, and not just on the TV screens or laptops. Terror is the fundamental core of terrorism, when families are too scared to go to the local shopping mall, cinema, or train station. This should give us all pause for thought. It's been just over 12 years since the 9/11 terrorist attacks on America. What will the next 12 years in modern warfare/terrorism evolve into? Chemical weapon, VX nerve agent attacks, Dirty Bombs, whole Western cities disappearing due to a terrorist attack. All makes for one hell of a potent bedtime story and an ongoing troubling concern for Western Governments and leaders (See Glossary, Arab Spring Unconventional Warfare, Al-Shabab 21/9 attacks).

Mog or Mogadishu:	Capital city of Somalia. Location of the 3rd – 4th October 1993 battle for Mogadishu "Black Hawk Down". Casualties: 18 American soldiers killed, 80 injured and estimated three thousand Somalian guerrillas killed.
MOG:	Mobile operations group.
Mohammed Naim:	Official spokesman for the Taliban, from their new offices in Qatar.
Mosquito:	Taliban and Al-Qaeda slang for the British-American, Apache attack

helicopter. (See Apache).

Mossad:	Israeli intelligence services headquarters located, Tel-Aviv (Mossad are one of the best intelligence services in the world).
Moukhabarat:	Jordanian secret police or intelligence services/headquarters located in in Amman city.
MP:	Member of Parliament.
MSST:	Military Stabilisation Support Team.
Mujahideen-Muj:	Afghan opposition groups fought the Soviets during the Soviet invasion and each other in the Afghan civil War-plural for the word

	Mujahid meaning "Struggler or Fighter". Anthony Malone interviewed key Mujahedeen Commanders and leaders across the Middle-East and Afghanistan (See Glossary, Massoud).
Mullah Omar:	Spiritual leader of the Afghan Taliban (See Taliban).
Muscat or Masqat:	Capital city of Oman.
Muslim Brotherhood:	Egyptian political group/organisation, with strong links to Al-Qaeda and other extremist groups across the Middle-East, Afghanistan, Pakistan and Iraq. The political arm of the Brotherhood is called, "freedom and Justice" (See Glossary, EIJ).
Napalm:	A highly flammable form of petrol used in military munitions-firebombs.
Narghilehs:	Arabic, "smoker's water pipe" flavours of tobacco include, apple, orange and grape.
NATO:	North Atlantic Treaty Organisation.
NBCW:	Nuclear-Biological-Chemical-Warfare.
NDS:	Afghanistan National Directorate of Security-Afghan Security Services.
Net:	Military radio network.

Network:	Inter-connected groups, teams or cells of International terrorists. Many networks are International-global.
NGO:	None Government Organisation.
Nicosia:	Capital city of Cyprus.
Nigerian Taliban:	Franchise of the Pakistan Taliban, close links to "Boko Haram", the Islamist terrorist group operating across Northern Nigeria (See AQIM).
Nightstalkers:	Nickname of the 160th Special Operations Aviation Regiment (SOAR), the air transportation and support component to the American Special Forces (See Glossary, Special Forces-Delta).
Nimrod MR2:	British RAF reconnaissance aircraft-jet, used as a spy/surveillance plane.
NOC-CIA:	None Official Cover Operative-no diplomatic immunity. Full official deniability (See Glossary, Black Op's, and Trade Craft-CIA).
Noor:	Arabic word for "light".
Northern Alliance:	Officially titled the "United front military forces", the Mujahedeen or freedom fighters of Northern Afghanistan (See Glossary, Panjshir valley, Massoud).
NSA:	American National security agency. The American agency for gathering electronic and "signals" intelligence, surveillance; equivalent of the UK's GCHQ, based in Cheltenham.
Nucleic Acid:	Either of two, substances, DNA or RNA, present in all living cells. (DNA is used to positively identify bodies of HVT's-terrorists suspects after airstrikes, and military operations-missions (See DNA and field craftCIA).

N-U-T-S:	Second World War, American Paratroopers response, when asked to surrender by a German officer, who had the Paratroopers surrounded. N-U-T-S; was the official written response to the Germans. (Paratroopers never surrender...They fight till the last man and then
	some). N-U-T-S; was the same responses that Anthony Malone (former Paratrooper) gave the Taliban/Afghan authorities when they tried torturing him to sign a confession, that said he was working for the American military intelligence. Anthony Malone's response was N-U-T-S... he was not a prisoner of war; he was a prisoner at war. Anthony Malone also gave the answer "Donald Duck" when asked by his interrogators who he worked for; this made him laugh, but got him another beating. (See Ill-treatment Statement by Anthony Malone).
NVG:	Night Vision Goggles-Night sights that are magnify light by 40.000 times.
OCO-CIA:	Official Cover Operative, covered with diplomatic immunity.
ODA:	Operational Detachment Alpha; Another term used in place of "ATeam", to describe the Special Forces, standard twelve-man team (See Glossary, A-Team).
OEF:	Operation Enduring Freedom.
OP:	Observation Post.
Op's:	Operations room, Op's officer, or literally a military operation.
Operator:	Highly experienced security or intelligence personnel.
Op-sec:	Operational security.
OSCT:	Office for security and counter-terrorism in the UK home office department, coordinating all UK counter-terrorism activity.
Osprey MV22A:	American Military aircraft, used for combat and rescue operations in Iraq-Libya-Afghanistan-West Africa. The CV22-B is the Special Forces variant. (See Glossary, Nightstalkers).
Palmyra:	(See Glossary, Tadmor).
Panic/Strong room:	Emergency armoured room within a building or structure. Used as a last resort if building is being overrun by terrorist/insurgents. Normally fitted out with Emergency rations; food, water, spare weapons,
	ammunition, medical supplies and communication equipment. Strong rooms are also fitted in residences of VIP's and can be found within the super structures of oil tankers.
Panjshir Valley:	Afghan valley, located north of the Afghan capital Kabul. Formerly the strong hold of Ahmad Shah Massoud, Northern Alliance Commander. (See Photographs).

Para:	Term used to describe a member or soldier of the British military's elite Parachute Regiment. (See 3 Para).
Pashtun:	Tribe, language of Southern Afghanistan and the Western border area of Pakistan.
Pashtun-Walli:	Pashtun honour code.
Pax:	Person.
P-Company:	Pegasus company, gruelling fitness tests used by the British military's Parachute Regiment to test suitable candidates for Parachute training and Airborne Forces. (See Glossary, 3 Para).
Persona Non Grata:	Latin-unwelcome person.
Peshawar:	City in Western Pakistan, often referred to as a lawless border town because of its proximity to the Afghanistan border. Peshawar is a major re-supply location on the route used by jihadists who fight British and American (ISAF) forces across Afghanistan (See Haqqani network).
Peshmerga:	Kurdish militia group, very well trained and equipped, located in Kurdistan- Northern Iraq. Peshmerga are fighting in Northern Syria to protect Kurdish people, towns and villages in the Syrian civil war. (Anthony Malone interviewed Peshmerga Commanders in Syria, Kurdistan and Iraq).
Petra:	Ancient Roman city, secreted away in a hidden valley and carved out of rock in eternal perfection. Located in Southern Jordan.

Petraeus-General:	General David Petraeus; American 4 Star military Commander, Petraeus Commanded the 101st Airborne Division (Air-Assault) paratroopers, in Iraq 2003. Highly regarded and respected by the men who serve under him, gained the reputation as a soldiers General. (Petraeus would never ask his men to do anything that he would not do himself), he spent most of his time on the ground, looking after the men under his Command. Petraeus believed that a good Commander always leads from the front, and was always first out of the door. Petraeus is credited for writing the counter insurgency strategy template for the American military and formulating the "Surge" in Iraq; part of the counter insurgency strategy. Petraeus's plans on dealing with the increasing Iraqi insurgency would become part of the overall American tactical and strategic plan on dealing with "unconventional warfare" in Iraq and the insurgency. Petraeus later became the Commander of "Centcom", American Centre Command and would also hold the prestigious post of Director of the American CIA. Petraeus has political aspirations and with his extensive knowledge and a wealth of experience, will excel in the future. Petraeus has been awarded 44 separate military awards.

	General David Petraeus told Anthony Malone in Iraq "That a few good men can make a difference..." (See photographs).
Phoenicia –Beirut:	Luxury hotel on the Beirut water front, overlooking the bay to Jounieh, popular location for International Press/Journalists and rich Arab's. Has been known as a meeting place for top Hezbollah and Al-Qaeda members, who book rooms or meet on the top floor wine bar and restaurant. (See Glossary, Hezbollah).
Phy-Ops:	Psychological operations/ Psychological warfare.
PI:	Politicalisation of intelligence. (See plausible deniability).
PID:	Positively identify.
Pilgrim:	Serving or former member of the British Special Forces (SAS) 22rd Regiment.
PIRA:	(See Glossary, IRA).

PKM:	Soviet-made light machine gun, fitted with bipod 7.62mm (Belt fed). Used throughout the Middle-East, Iran, Afghanistan, Pakistan and across Africa by terrorist groups.
Plausible deniability:	Term used by politicians and intelligence services, "denied operations", to give top-cover, political protection to top civil-servants and politicians.
PLO:	Palestine Liberation Organisation.
Plutonium:	A radioactive metallic element used in nuclear weapons and reactors. (See Glossary, CW-Dirty bomb).
PM:	Prime Minister.
PMC:	Private military company, private corporate businesses who employ former professional soldiers and members of the Special Forces. Working on military style contracts, implementing their skills and field craft acquired during their official military service. PMC's are also licensed to carry firearms. But because they are private they do not come under military law.
Political spin doctor:	Politicians and top civil servants who "Lie and manipulate true facts and information" for their own political agendas and/or personal gain. Example; Tony Blair's WMD in Iraq. The reason why Britain went to war in 2003...! (See plausible deniability and politicisation of intelligence).
Porton Down:	British Military, Nuclear-Biological and Chemical warfare weapons training and research facility. (See Glossary, Chemical warfare-CW).
Post-One:	First Military check point outside American Embassies. Normally manned by American Marines.
PPIED:	Pressure-Plate Improvised Explosive Device. Tactic used by Al-Qaeda in Iraq and by the Taliban and Al-Qaeda in Afghanistan to kill British and American 'ISAF' soldiers (See Glossary, IED).
Profiling:	Comprehensive detailing of personal information and habits,

	enabling

for a physiological pro-file to be formulated. This is a tactic used by Intelligence agencies to build strategies and tactics against terrorist groups and their international networks (See Glossary, Trade craft-CIA).

PSD: Personal security detail.

Pul-i -Charkhi/Pul-e-Charrkhi: Russian built prison in Afghanistan, houses thousands of Taliban and AlQaeda prisoners. One of the world's most notorious and dangerous prisons. Al-Qaeda and Taliban prisoners run the inside of the prison under strict Islamic 'Sharia law'. Ill-treatment, torture and murder is common place. (See separate comprehensive report on ill-treatment and torture, written by Anthony Malone).

Qamishle: Syrian-Turkish, border town, located in North East Syria. Kurdish influenced. Known meeting location (Islamic Mosque's), transit point and over-night stop location for insurgents and terrorists from PakistanAfghanistan-Iraq-Lebanon-Saudi Arabia. (See Hassake).

QRF: Quick-reaction force.

Quetta: City in South Western Pakistan, located close to the Afghanistan border and in close proximity to the Afghan city of Kandahar. Quetta is also the base for the Taliban and Al-Qaeda supreme councils.

Qur`an: Islamic holy book.

R&R: Rest and recuperation.

RAF-British: British Royal Air force.

Raw-Intel: Information-intelligence, prior to it being analysed and receiving an official security classification. (See Glossary, Classification).

Recce: Reconnaissance.

Rendition: Kidnapping a suspect and transporting the suspect between countries without "Habeas Corpus", legal due process, also known as "Extreme Rendition" (See Glossary, Balad TSF).

Right to Life:	British High Court ruling in 2013, which stated-every British soldier has a right to life while serving in Afghanistan and on operational tours.
Riyadh:	Capital city of Saudi Arabia.
RMP:	Royal Military Police (See Glossary, Bill Shaw MBE).
RO:	Radio Operator.
Robert Fisk:	Respected international journalist and author, an authority on writing about the Middle-East. Robert Fisk has also interviewed Osama bin Laden and several other high profile political subjects and terroristsfreedom fighters (See acquired reading list).
ROE-Rules of engagement:	Legal rules which military and Government personnel can use to engage the enemy and legally return fire to eliminate the enemy threat (See Glossary, Modern Warfare).
RPG:	Soviet designed rocket propelled grenade/shoulder launch rocket with a powerful grenade warhead fitted to the front. Widely used by terrorist groups across the globe. Including the Afghan, Pakistan Taliban, AlQaeda and Al-Shabab.
RSM:	Regimental Sergeant Major.
RSO:	American Regional security officer, posted within the American Embassies world-wide, The RSO oversees all Intelligence in the region and reports information and Intelligence back to Washington DC, Pentagon and liaisons with other American intelligence agencies, including; CIA-NSA-DIA-DEA-FBI.
RST:	Residential security team, works in conjunction with a close protection team/close protection officer.
RTI:	Resistance to interrogation. Training carried out by all Special Operations Forces who operate in hostile countries and behind enemy lines (See Glossary, SERE).

RV:	Rendezvous-Pre-arranged meeting or meeting place.
RW:	"Rogue Warrior" Call sign, the name given to Anthony Malone by "elite team" members in 2006 during Special Forces training.
S/B:	Suicide bomber (See Glossary, UW -Unconventional warfare).

S-10:	British Military respirator issued to the British Military as part of PPE- Personal Protection Equipment, as protection against nuclear-biologicalchemical warfare (See Glossary, Porton Down).
S-2:	American military Command Staff, intelligence section.
SA:	Situation Awareness.
SA7/14:	Soviet-designed surface to air missiles, man-pads. (See Glossary, SAM, Stinger Missile).
Sabre:	The tactical operators in the SAS, so avoiding confusion with medical, administrative or other military personnel (See Task Force Black).
SADM:	Special Atomic Demolition Munition; Also known as a "Backpack nuke". (See Glossary, Dirty bomb).
SAF:	Small Arms Fire.
Safe house:	Term to describe a safe location or safe haven. (See Al-ShababHezbollah).
Saladin:	Historical Islamic military commander-Sultan Salahud bin Ayubi. (See Fox/Saladin, present day, Al-Qaeda Commander).
Salvo:	A simultaneous discharge of guns; a sudden series of aggressive statements or acts.
SAM:	Surface to air missile.
Sana/Sanaa:	Capital city of Yemen.

Sanitize:	Military reference to removing any identification that could "ID" a person by name, place, military unit or country of birth. Sometimes Special Forces are sanitized, prior to deployment on operations, so if captured by the enemy they are carrying no identifying or incriminating evidence. Al-Qaeda and some Taliban foreign fighters are sanitized before they carry out terrorist operations and attacks. Sanitized covert military teams or covert security operators give governments/politicians full "plausible deniability" (See Glossary, Black Op's-Trade craft CIA and Zeranjee).
SAP:	Security Advance Party.
SAS:	British Special Forces "Special Air Service" Regiment (See 22rd SAS).
Sat-Com:	Satellite Communications.
Sat-Nav:	Satellite Navigation.
Sayyid:	Arabic ruling class in Yemen, a title given to tribal or religious leaders who claim descent from the "Prophet Muhammad".
SBS:	British Special Forces "Special Boat Service".

Seal:	Sea, Air, Land; The American navy/marine Corps clandestine forces. (See Glossary, Delta Force).
Semtex:	Military grade plastic explosives, made in the Czech Republic, common throughout the old Soviet bloc countries. Libya was supplying the IRAPIRA with Semtex during the troubles in Northern Ireland. It is reported that Al-Qaeda has acquired large amounts of Semtex from several sources; including old Libyan weapons stores. (See IED-Shape charge).
September 11th 2001:	Al-Qaeda terrorist attacks on America, passenger airliners hijacked, including AA11 and UA175 were flown by Al-Qaeda terrorists into the Twin Towers, North and South, New York City. AA77 was hijacked and flown into the Pentagon. United American passenger airliner, UA93 came down in a field in Shanksville, Pennsylvania, when the passengers bravely fought back against the terrorist hijackers. The estimated
	casualties for 9/11 is 2752 people killed, thousands injured. (More people died in the 9/11 terrorist attacks than the number of people and American service personnel who died in the Second World War, Japanese attack on Pearl Harbour). This fact gives pause for thought. (See glossary, July 7th 2005, Al-Qaeda attacks on the United Kingdom).
SERE:	Survive-Evade-Resist and Extract, part of Special Forces Training. (See Glossary, Trade craft-RTI).
SF:	Special Forces.
SFC-SAS:	Special Forces Communicator-Military Communications and Signals Specialist.
Shabnama:	Night letters-Taliban propaganda leaflets distributed under the cover of darkness, typically slid under peoples doors. Threatening death, torture and public beheading.
Shape-charge:	Specialist explosive charge, used to breach or gain access to a building through a wall or reinforced entrance. The explosive charge is shaped so when detonated the blast penetrates a specific targeted area. The Taliban in Afghanistan are also using shape-charges within their improvised explosive devices, IEDs. To penetrate British and American armoured vehicles (See Glossary, IED).
Sharia:	Arabic law, practiced and observed by the Prophet Muhammad in his lifetime, enforced in certain countries in the Muslim world (See Glossary, Al-Shabab).

Sheikh:	Arab chief. (Anthony Malone body-guarded and interviewed Sheikh's in Iraq and Saudi Arabia).
Shia:	Minority branch of Islam, centred around Iran.
Shmac:	Arabic scarf, Arabs also wear as a head dress.
Shura:	Arabic for consultation.

Side arm:	Military-security terminology for a "pistol".
Sig:	Sig Sauer 9mm pistol, Sig Sauer are issued to British Special Forces and are used by intelligence agencies and PMC's world-wide.
Sig-Int:	Signal Intelligence, intelligence gained from radio, telephone, text and e-mail intercepts (See Glossary, GCHQ-NSA).
Sinai:	Largely desert peninsular between Israel and Egypt, a lawless area of desert inhabited by local tribes and Bedu (See Glossary, Bedu).
SIS:	British Secret Intelligence Service, MI6, the UK's foreign intelligence service.
Sit-Rep:	Situation Report.
Slap & tickle:	Interrogation or torture.
Sleeper:	Terrorist operative laying low in Western society, hiding for months or years. Waiting undercover for orders to fulfil their mission.
Slush fund:	Unofficial or official sanctioned pool of money, sometimes located hidden in off-shore bank accounts, used to finance and support covert weapon purchases and covert military operations (See Glossary, Black Op's and Special adviser).
Small Arms:	Infantry light weapons/pistols, rifles and machine guns, weapons capable of being fired by a foot soldier on the move.
Snake-operation:	12 June 2003; American forces/Special forces, raided and destroyed a base for non-Iraqi mujahedin at Rawah, 20km north of the Euphrates River western Iraq, about 40km from the Syrian border. The attack killed more than eighty foreign Muslims in Iraq to fight the US-led occupation. Among the dead were Saudi's, Yemenis, Syrians, Afghans, Lebanese- Hezbollah and Sudanese. American Apache helicopter gunships and AC-130 Spectre gunship were on station during the operation (See photographs).

Snatch: Lightly armoured British military Land rover. Used in operations in Northern Ireland-Iraq-Afghanistan-Africa. Snatch Land rovers have little protection against the Taliban IED's, as seen in Afghanistan. (See Right to life and IED).

SO19:   British police specialist firearms unit.

SOAR: American, 160th Special Operations Aviation Regiment, (See Glossary, Nightstalkers).

SOCA: British police, Serious Organised Crime Agency.

SOE: Special operations executive. Exceptional British Second World War
                     Special operations unit. Members operated behind enemy lines,
                     working with résistance groups (See Glossary, unconventional
                     warfare).

SOP: Standard Operating Procedure.

Special adviser: Term used to describe covert military-intelligence personnel,
                     working or being assigned to a friendly group or official
                     organisation, as a special adviser on subjects including:
                     unconventional warfare (See OCO-CIA).

Spectre: AC-130 Hercules military aircraft gunship, fitted with specialist
                     armaments and weapons, can fly and fight in all weather
                     conditions.

Spetsnaz: Russian Military Special Forces. (See Hezbollah training camps Lebanon).

Spooks: Term use to describe spies and intelligence operatives, (CIA-NSA-MI5-
                     MI6).

SRR: Special Reconnaissance Regiment, an independent Special Forces unit of
                     the British army, specialising in close target reconnaissance (See
                     Glossary, 22nd SAS).

Standby-Standby: Warning call to watch out for something, action or movement is
                     imminent.

State sponsored terrorism: Terrorist groups and networks sponsored and supported,
                     logistically and financially, by rogue Countries and
                     Governments. Example; Iran backing

                     the Lebanese Terrorist group Hezbollah.

Stinger:	American Surface to Air Missile (see SAM, man-pad).
Strait of Hormuz:	Geographic-strategic, an ocean location between the Arabian Sea and the Gulf of Oman. 60km wide, a bottle neck for shipping-oil tankers. AlQaeda has targeted this location several times to date, including 2010, Japanese oil tanker the "M-Star", attacked-blast failed to breach the double hull of the oil tanker. Al-Qaeda's plan was to hijack and sink the oil tanker in the Strait of Hormuz, resulting in the world-wide disruption of shipping/carrying oil to Western countries, in doing so would have caused an

	environmental disaster. (See Glossary, Al-Qaeda, AQAP).
Suicide belt –vest:	Clothing worn by a suicide bomber incorporating explosives and detonators. Some suicide vests are detonated by remote control or mobile phone signal. The first recorded Suicide Bomber was during the Palestine - Israeli conflict (See Glossary, UW-Unconventional Warfare).
Sun Tzu:	Chinese strategist, "Art of War", wrote; "know your enemy and you will know yourself" (See Glossary, UW-Unconventional Warfare).
Sunni:	Majority branch of Islam.
Sun-ray:	Radio code word/keyword for British Military Commander-Commanding officer, during Military operations.
SWAT:	Special Weapons and Tactics (See Glossary, Trade craft-CIA).
Syria:	"The Land of Sham", strategically located Middle-Eastern country. Capital is Damascus; the country has been ruled-dictatorship by the Assad family for over 40 years. Syria borders, Iraq-Jordan-LebanonTurkey-Israel and the Mediterranean Sea. Russia has a naval base on the coast of Western Syria at Tartus. The Assad Government is backed by Iran and Russia, who supply large shipments of weapons, missiles, aircraft-helicopters and T72 main battle tanks. Syria has over 1000 tons of chemical weapons, the biggest stockpile in the world, including VXnerve agent. The Syria Government and Assad also backs and supports the Lebanese terrorist group Hezbollah, who fight under the flag of
	Assad and the Syrian Government, During the Syrian Civil War the opposition group formed against the Assad Government is the FSA, Free Syrian army, an umbrella organisation with several splinter groups including; Jabhat Al-Nusra, a group with links to the Al-Qaeda network (See Glossary, Hezbollah-FSA-AQI).
T.E. Lawrence:	"Lawrence of Arabia" Author of "Seven pillars of wisdom", which is now acquired reading for British and American military officers at Sandhurst and West-point prior to being deployed to Islamic countries across the Middle-East, Afghanistan-Pakistan and North-Africa. The lessons of cultural understanding and unconventional warfare in Arabia are as valid today as when they were written by T.E. Lawrence over 60 years ago (See acquired reading list by Anthony Malone).
T-1:	Triage casualty code 1, needs to be in an operating theatre within an hour to be saved.
T-2:	Triage casualty code 2, needs to be in an operating theatre quickly before they become T-1.
T-3:	Triage casualty code 3, injured and needs medical help.

T-4:	Triage casualty code 4, dead.
T62-T72:	Russian main battle tank, used by many Middle-Eastern countries including; Iran, Iraq and Syria.
Tadmor-Palmyra:	Ancient city located South Eastern Syria. Location of past Al-Qaeda safe houses and covert operational meetings between Hezbollah and the Pakistan Taliban, Haqqani network, AQI and Al-Qaeda in Iraq. Tadmor is in close proximity to the border of Iraq. (See Glossary, Del-e Zore).
Talib:	Term used to describe a Taliban fighter or members of the Taliban.
Taliban:	Meaning "Students". Extreme Afghan, Islamic fundamentalist group, with close links to Al-Qaeda-Pakistan Taliban and the Haqqani network. "Mullah Omar" is the spiritual leader of the Taliban. The Taliban supreme council is located in Quetta-city, Pakistan. (See Haqqani network-Pakistan Taliban). (Anthony Malone interviewed Taliban members and Commanders in Afghanistan-Iraq).
Tango:	Term used by Author to describe Taliban and Al-Qaeda terrorists in Puli-Charkhi prison Afghanistan.
Taqiyya:	Arabic – Means lie, deceive, secrets, a tactic used by Middle-Eastern Muslim terrorist groups.
Task Force Black:	British Special Forces taskforce in Iraq, who's mission was to hunt, capture or kill Al-Qaeda and members of other terrorist groups and networks operating within Iraq. (See Glossary, Task force 121-323).
Taskforce-121-145-323-626:	Examples of Military Taskforces; joint British and American specialist Taskforces, made up of personnel from diverse and specialist backgrounds: including-CIA-NSA-MI6-SAS-SBS-Delt-Seals. Area of operations: Middle-East, Afghanistan and Pakistan. Task force codename '121' was set up in such a way that Delta and other elements of JSOC, could switch between Afghanistan and Iraq as required. (See Task force 84). (Anthony Malone interviewed and worked with members of the Task Forces in Iraq-Lebanon-Afghanistan).
Tasking-order:	An order or specific objective within an operation or mission.
Tawqeef:	Notorious and dangerous prison, housing 650+ Afghan Pakistan Taliban, Al-Qaeda prisoners, in the centre of Kabul, Afghanistan (See Glossary, Pul-i-Charkhi).
Tehran:	Capital city of Iran.
Terp:	Interpreter.
TF:	Task Force.
Thames House:	Location of British MI5, Intelligence services headquarters in London.
The Company:	Term use to describe the American "CIA".

Theatre:	Country or area in which troops are conducting operations.

Thermo baric:	Enhanced blast Hellfire missiles-Thermo baric means heat and pressure. (See Hellfire-Apache).
Thobe:	Arabic robe worn in the highlands of the Yemen and in Saudi Arabia.
TL:	Team leader.
TOC:	Tactical Operations Centre (See Op's room).
Top-cover:	Terminology used to describe military/political support-protection from senior Government officials.
Tornado GR4:	Royal Air Force, multi-roll strike warplane. GR4-Ground reconnaissance. ADV (F3)-Air Defence variants. IDS-Ground attack.
Tracer-Bullets:	Bullets that burn with a red, orange or green glow from 110m to 1.110m, so they can be seen, used for target indication and judging distances.
Tradecraft:	Term used to describe security and intelligence operators skills-training for operations and missions into hostile environments and countries. (See Glossary, Trade craft-CIA).
Tradecraft-CIA	Subjects included within tradecraft; Asset cultivation and development Physiological assessing-Deception-Profiling-Surveillance and counter surveillance-Communications-languages-Cultural understanding Weapons SWAT-Advance driving-Interrogation- Resistance to interrogation, and several other classified specialist subjects. (See Farm).
Transjorden:	Original name for the State of Jordan.
Trawling:	Searching an area for intelligence and information. (See Tradecraft-CIA).
Tusk:	Military call-sign for the American A10 Warthog-Thunderbolt, used for close air support, supporting combat troops on the ground and for destroying Taliban-insurgents, tunnel complexes across the areas of operation, or the theatre of war (See Glossary, A10).

UAE: United Arab Emirates.

UBL: The American CIA's abbreviation used by the agency for "Osama bin Laden".

UCO: Undercover operative. (See NON-CIA).

Uday & Qusay: Saddam Hussein's sons. Quay, Saddam's youngest son, was controlling Iraqi resistance and organising the Iraqi insurgency across Iraq prior to both brothers being located and killed by American forces in Mosul, Northern Iraq 2003. A black brief case found at the scene of their deaths confirmed that they were co-ordinating the insurgency in its infancy across Iraq. Plans, maps, money '$', bank information and several other countries passports, including; Syria and Lebanon were also found in the brief case, along with other highly sensitive intelligence, including planned attacks on American soldiers and General Petraeus. Uday and Qusay were also responsible for the Kidnapping, raping, torture, killing and murder of hundreds of their own people (See photographs of the fire fight when they were killed by American forces, also photographs of Udays & Qusay's gold plated AK-47 and MP-5).

UN HQ Iraq 2003 Bombing:	Suicide truck bombing of the Headquarters of the United Nations in Baghdad, Iraq. 22 Killed and over 100 injured.
UN:	United Nations.
Uranium:	A radioactive metallic element used as fuel in nuclear reactors. (See Glossary, Dirty Bomb-CW).
USAF:	United State Air force.
USAID:	United States Agency for International Development.
USSR:	Union of the Soviet Socialist Republics, the Soviet Union, disbanded in 1991.
Utrinque-Paratus:	Latin, "ready for anything", motto of the British Parachute Regiment. (See Glossary, 3 Para).

UW:	Unconventional Warfare, "guerrilla warfare".
UXO:	Unexploded Ordinance.
Vauxhall Cross:	Term used to describe MI6 Headquarters location, London-England.
VBD:	Vehicle Born Device (IED) car-bomb.
VCP:	Vehicle Check Point.
VR:	Vibration Reduction.
VX-nerve agent:	(See Glossary, chemical weapons).
Wadi:	Arabic, a riverbed, dry except in the rainy season (when it is a river).
Wahabi:	Muslim movement-tribe in Saudi Arabia. (Conservative reform of Islam), Osama bin Laden followed Wahabi beliefs, and teachings (Anthony

	Malone Interviewed Wahabi followers in Afghanistan-Saudi Arabia).
Wais Hudein:	Taliban military Commander-strong ties to Al-Qaeda, operates in Afghanistan, Pakistan and Somalia. (Interviewed by Anthony Malone in Afghanistan).
Walk-In's:	Un-announced-Unplanned "walk-in" meeting between a potential intelligence source and official authorities-intelligence personnel.
Warthog:	American A-10 fighter jet, ground attack aircraft, also known as the Thunderbolt-Tank buster. Fitted with the GAU8, Gatling gun.
Water boarding:	Term used to describe the use of water during terrorist suspect interviews-interrogation. "Simulated drowning", controversial tactic used by the American Government-intelligence agencies during interrogation sessions.
Waziristan:	Geographic area along the Western Pakistan border area to Afghanistan. Waziristan is also a Taliban and Al-Qaeda stronghold, cross-border Afghan attacks by the insurgency/terrorists are planned, prepared and launched from this location.

Wet-work:	Intelligence or mercenary terminology used as reference to eliminating or killing (See Glossary, PMC).
WGP:	Weapons Grade Plutonium.
White Widow:	British National; Samantha Luthwate, Al-Shabab Commander and wife of 7/7 suicide bomber Jermaine Lindsey (See Glossary, 21/9, Al-Shabab).
Wilfred Thesiger:	British gentlemen – epic explorer and traveller. Author of "Arabian Sands", the lessons of cultural understanding and travelling across the deserts of Arabia are as valid today as when they were written by Wilfred Thesiger over 60 years ago. The book "Arabian Sands" is now acquired reading for British and American military officers at Sandhurst and West-Point, prior to being deployed to Islamic countries across the Middle-East, Afghanistan-Pakistan and North-Africa (See acquired reading list by Anthony Malone).
WIT-SEC:	Witness Security protection program.
Wizard:	Military radio call-sign for the British Nimrod MR2 spy plane.
WMD:	Weapons of mass destruction (See Glossary, chemical weapons).
Yak:	Large animal, indigenous to the mountains of the Hindu Kush and the Himalayan.
Zaatari:	Refugee camp in Jordan, North of the capital, Amman, built to house Syrian displaced people/refugees fleeing the civil war in Syria. United Nations estimates that over one million people alone are in this refugee camp. People and children trafficking is a major problem within the camp. Child brides are also being sold to wealthy, Saudi men, who just use the young girls for sex then

	discard them, other human rights abuses "including rape", have been reported within the camp and to the Red-Cross.
Zahedan:	Iranian city located 50km from the Afghanistan-Pakistan border. Notorious for being on the smuggling-people, children-trafficking, human organ route from Afghanistan and Pakistan.
Zarqa:	Small town in Northern Jordan, close to the Syrian border. Zarqa mosque is a known meeting place for terrorists-insurgents from Iraq and Syria.
Zeranjee:	Provincial capital city in Nimruz province, Southern Afghanistan. Location for several Taliban, Al-Qaeda safe houses. Location of fighters moving from Iran, Iraq and Syria. Zeranjee is notorious for being on the smuggling people, children trafficking, human organ route from Afghanistan to Iran-Iraq-Syria-Turkey-Europe. These routes are also used to transport and smuggle HVT's (High Value Targets) "Terrorists" Taliban-Al-Qaeda leaders, between countries. These routes also facilitate the illegal narcotics trade "Drug Trade, Heroin" from and through Afghanistan-Pakistan-Iran-Iraq-Syria and Turkey and then internationally across the globe (See Haqqani network and Hezbollah).
ZPU-"Zeus":	Soviet, anti-aircraft gun, 14.5mm-Zpu 1 is single-barrelled, ZPU 2 has twin barrels and the ZPU 4 has quadruple barrels. The ZPU, are also called "Zeus", nickname given to them by Afghan and Arab fighters insurgents. Commonly seen being fixed onto the back of Toyota 4x4's by terrorist groups and freedom fighters across the Middle East, Afghanistan, Pakistan and Africa (See Glossary, Modern Warfare, AlShabab, Haqqani Network, and Taliban).

Examples of Middle-East, Afghanistan, Pakistan and African terrorist groups; Including Geographical areas of known active operations.

Afghanistan Taliban: (Afghanistan-Pakistan).

Pakistan Taliban: (Pakistan-Global).

Hezbe-Islami: (Afghanistan-Pakistan).

Hezbe-Islami-Nigeria franchise: (Nigeria-Somalia-Kenya).

Al-Shabab/Al-Shaab: (Somalia-Kenya-Ethiopia-Yemen-Global).

Al-Qaeda: (Middle East-Afghanistan-Pakistan-Africa-Global).

Kandahar Al-Qaeda: (Middle East-Afghanistan-Pakistan-Africa-Global).

(AQI) Al-Qaeda in Iraq: (Middle East-Afghanistan-Pakistan-Africa-Turkey).

(AQAP)   Al-Qaeda in the Arabian Peninsula: (Middle East-Afghanistan-Africa-
Global).

Nigerian Taliban: (Africa, including; Somalia-Mai and Yemen).

Boko Haram: (Africa-Nigeria-Mali).

Lions of Allah: (Middle East-Afghanistan-Pakistan-Africa-Europe). Sword of

Allah: (Middle East-Iran-Africa).

Hezbollah: (Middle East-Afghanistan-Pakistan-Iran-Africa-and
Europe-Global).

(IH) Iraq Hezbollah: (Iraq -Syria-Iran-Afghanistan-Pakistan-Somalia).

ISIS/ IS Islamic State   (HQ in Northern Syria, operates World-Wide)

Hamas: (Middle East-Gaza Strip-West Bank).

Muslim Brotherhood: (Middle East-Africa-Afghanistan-Pakistan-Global).

Jabat Al-Nusra: (Middle East (Syria)-Afghanistan-Pakistan-Africa).

Asa'ib-Ahl-Al-Haq: (Middle East (Iraq).

Arabic Glossary

Fatwa   A legal Islamic verdict or ruling (pl fatawa).

Fitna   trial and tribulation.

Hadith   A narration recording a saying, action, tacit approval, habit or
physical description of the Prophet (pl.
Ahadith).

Halal   That which is permissible, lawful in Islam.

Haram That which is impermissible, forbidden, unlawful in Islam. Iblis   Satan, the devil, by his

proper noun, equivalent to Diablo.

Jihad	Jihad can be manifested entirely peacefully as well as military-depending upon circumstance (See Jihad in main Glossary).
Jihadi	One who goes to extremes in the concept of Jihad, is excessively enthusiastic about it and holds a distorted idea of it that is more akin to terrorism, (Anglicised=Jihadist).
Jinn	A demon, spirit-like being created from smokeless fire.
Kufr	Disbelief, infidelity.
Kuffar	Non-Muslim, disbelievers, infidels (sing kafir).
Mujahid	One engaged in Jihad (pl.mujahidun-mujahidin).
Quran	(Pronounced=qur`an) Lit, the recital. The Holy book of Islam.
Shari`a-Shari`ah	The divine legislation of Islam (See Sharia main Glossary).
Sunni	An orthodox Muslim, one who adheres to the Prophets Sunna.
Shura	Council meeting of local elders.
Sura	Any one of the 114 chapters of the Qur'an.
Takfir	To accuse someone of major Kufr or disbelief = To eject a Muslim from the fold of Islam.
Takfiri	One who goes to extremes in performing Takfir.
Umma	The Muslim world community.

(Arabic key words and phrases are cross-referenced within the main Glossary)

Islamic Customary Prayers and Praises

'La ilaha ill-Allah, Muhammad-ur-rasool-ullah':

There is no God but God, and Muhammad is his prophet, this is the spoken declaration of faith, the words that make a Muslim a Muslim.

'Allah u Akhbar':

God is greatest, thanks for the God.

'Sal-Allahu 'Alayhi Wa Sallam`:

May Allah send (heavenly salutations of) peace and blessings upon him, 'said after mention of the Prophet Muhammad'.

Alayhi As-Salami:

'Upon him be the peace (of Allah)' After mentioning any Prophet of God`.

Radhi Allahu 'Anhu:

'Allah be pleased with him, after the mention of a companion of the Prophet`.

These prayers and praises have been given in their Arabic forms so as not to clutter the text with lengthy Latin transliteration and also to maintain flow for non-Muslims.

Acknowledgements

There are so many people to be eternally grateful to for their concern and invaluable support during my incarceration and during operations. It would be impossible to name them all. If I have inadvertently omitted anyone, I can only apologise profusely.

Special acknowledgements go to Maria, who kindly agreed to help with the writing and editing of the early drafts, without her help this would not have been possible. My incredible and supportive family, Patrick, Veronica and Maria, all of whom campaigned endlessly and with great dignity, I am extremely proud of their efforts and their fight for justice. Pat and Ian, Karen and Family, also Sami, for all their support and encouragement, 'Esperance'. Nicki (Big Smiles) keep on going after the bad guys. J & R thank you for all your support and advice.

Dil Banerjee and J, whose friendship and loyalty has inspired me, thank you for standing by me through all the dark, dangerous and challenging times, you are fellow brothers in arms.

Trevor Cooper, Graham H (SBS), Mike (Para Reg) and Brian D, thanks for everything boys. (Once a soldier always a soldier) hold yours heads high boys, we made a difference.

My Best Regards to Paul D in Oz. we kicked ass in Iraq and Syria, hope you liked the Puma Extraction! Have a beer mate, you helped save lives.

A special thank you to Alissa Everett for covering my ass and saving my life in Syria. Thank you. I hope this book answers some of your questions! I will always class you as a good friend, (a ray of sunshine).

Kim Motley, my American defence, she remained steadfast throughout and would not rest until justice was finally served, keep up the great work for women's rights in Afghanistan.

I am indebted to my friends in Afghanistan, Peter Jouvenal and Major Bill Shaw MBE, who supported me through some dark times. Also Kevin Stainburn and Tim Ward for their kindness, support and much needed food supplies.

Bevan Campbell, who without his help, friendship and advice, I could well have been killed many times in Pul-i-Charkhi prison. You are an incredible human being and I am proud to call you not just my friend, but a True Brother. We did something Very Special in there....!! (Remember the pale horse in 'The Book'...)

Werner (RIP) and Hannelie, whose support made all the difference, I knew that I was doing God's work, thank you for all your prayers, I know you're at peace up in heaven with your two children, you are all in my prayers, I will never forget....!!

Sophie Barry who kept us in supplies when we were getting no food – even with the guards "taxing" it – it still meant that we could at least eat a little better.

Ursula Campbell, thank you also for all your kind words and support for my family and I.

Phil Young, who shared his horrific experiences of his time in Pul-i-Charkhi prison and backed it up with detailed statements, I wish you all the best for the future.

Tanya, whose kindness and prayers helped me see the light, keep your chin up, you're one in a million Doll.

Amanda Lindhout, you're still an action girl who I admire and I always will. Keep up the great and important work you're doing in Somalia, one woman can make a difference. I am proud to have met you and call you a friend. Thank you for your support.

Paula Daly, you're one of the team, thank you for everything, you're a rock star. (Forces for Their Future) Veterans Charity.

I would also like to thank MP Colonel Bob Stuart and Colonel Dave Reynolds for their concern and help. Sir Peter Gibson OBE, MP Colonel Patrick Mercer MBE and MP Alex Cunningham, for their support and advice. Sir David Richards GCB, CBE, DSO, ADC, Gen, (former chief of the defence staff), thank you for your support and advice. Bob Morrison (Rox) C&S for their help, support and messages of encouragement.

I would also like to thank HRH Queen Elizabeth II, HRH Prince's Charles, Harry and William, for their correspondences and best wishes. Also the Right Honourable David Cameron, MP, The Prime Minister, for his responses to my correspondence. I would also like to thank the Chief of Staff of the British Army for his advice and best wishes.

A special thank you to 'Sharpy' my operations manager in Cyprus, who told me that "failure was not an option", well mate, I helped to take down Osama bin Laden and stopped in excess of 100 terrorist attacks, saving hundreds of lives, I hope I did you proud. Big thanks to Julian in Lebanon, Daz and Jane (British military Cyprus) thank you for your friendship, enjoy retirement in the Northeast of England. I would also like to thank the soldiers and officers from 101st Airborne Division who served in Iraq and Afghanistan, thank you for all of your letters of support, it was an honour working alongside you all.

My special thanks to General David Petraeus, Brigadier General Michael Linnington and Brigadier General Joe Anderson, these men are all Paratrooper's and outstanding fighting men and true military leaders, it was an honour spending time with you in Iraq, stay safe gentlemen. David, remember "one man came make a difference", we did.
Malcolm in Lebanon, Sami in Jordan Intelligence, Colonel Hayatt (Afghanistan), Wali Massoud (Afghanistan), Hayatt (France-Baghdad), for all your help and support.

Members of the British Army, Parachute Regiment, Troy Holden, 3 Para and Special Forces SAS/SBS, for all their help, support and best wishes, your messages of encouragement kept me going.

CIA, Jane and all the operators and personnel, RSO's who I had dealings with and operated with across the Middle-East, Afghanistan. Keep up the good work (Stay Safe).

Ken, Walter, John and the rest of the CSSP team, thank you for covering my back when the political crap started, "We did make a difference", American, British, Canadian ISAF lives were saved, you should all be very proud of what we did.

All the Red Cross staff and personnel, Martin, who I met in Pul-iCharkhi, Afghanistan and across the Middle-East and Africa, you are all amazing people who do a job that save lives every day, I owe you my life as do countless others, thank you.

Members of the International press, Nadine (Mail on Sunday), Travis (Afghanistan), Deborah Haynes (Times), Solomon (New York Times), Abraham (CNN), Adam Nathan (Sunday Times) for your help on the Iraq task.

British Legal team, Karen Todner, Alison Walker, for all their support, help and advice, through some very challenging times. FTI (Fair Trials International), Rachel for all her work, help and advice while I was in Afghanistan. Trudy Kennedy, FCO, thank you for trying to help me in Pul-i-Charkhi, I wish you the best for the future. A very special thank-you to Jan Everleigh, FCO, who was the one person at the UK Embassy (Kabul) to really make a "difference" for ALL UK and Commonwealth Nationals – if only there were more of you out there.

Mitch Albert (Canadian), thank you for all your help, support, guidance and faith, stay safe my friend.

My Best regards to Paul Jenkins, thank you for all your help advice on the Documentary, the next bottle of red wine is on me!

To anybody else who helped in any small way with the campaign, added a name to the petition, sent a message, letter, or made the effort to come and visit me, I truly appreciate your support. I could never have got through this without you.

Stay safe

Anthony Malone

Bibliography

References and details from the below publications have been used within my manuscript to ensure my writing is as accurate and as detailed as possible for the reader. References from news articles have been used within my manuscript and reports, the sources of these articles were: The Guardian, New York Times, Sunday Times and American CNN. I would like to thank them all for helping me to ensure that my manuscript was as accurate and detailed as possible.

3 Para – Patrick Bishop

A hell for heroes – Theo Knell

An ordinary soldier – Doug Beattie

Apache - Ed Macy

Arabian Sands – Wilfred Thesiger

Body of Lies – David Ignatius

Bush at war – Bob Woodward

Genghis Khan – Ata-Malik Juvaini

Helmand – Diaries of front-line soldiers

In the company of soldiers – Rick Atkinson

Kill Switch – Major Bill Shaw MBE

Military Intelligence Blunders – Colonel John Hughes Wilson

Sand Strom – Lindsey Hilsum

Seven pillars of Wisdom – T. E. Lawrence

Tajikistan – Bradt

Task Force Black – Mark Urban

Task Force Dagger – Robin Moore

The Assassins' Gate – George Packer

The fall of Baghdad – Jon – Lee Anderson

The Forgotten Palestinians – Ilan Pappe

The Great war of Civilisation – Robert Fisk

The Middle-East – Bernard Lewis

The occupation of Iraq – Ali a Allawi

The war against Saddam – John Simpson

Through our enemy eyes – Michael Scheuer

Exclusive: Future publications by Anthony Malone

Honour Bound - Rogue Warrior Photography Collection

-

Tracking and locating Osama bin Laden UBL (The target package)

-

The Syrian and Iraq conflicts (Operating behind enemy lines)

-

International Terrorism (Exclusive perspective from within the International terrorist networks)

-

Extreme Rendition (The political cover-up)

Synopsis of Anthony Malone's deep covert infiltration of the Al-Qaeda and Taliban, Pakistan Taliban networks from within Afghanistan (Continuation of counter-terrorism and intelligence work carried out between 2002-2007)

A)   Between 2007 and 2010 Anthony Malone infiltrated the Al-Qaeda and Pakistan Taliban terrorist networks up to leadership level and their trusted inner circles. This task was requested and ordered by senior American military intelligence stationed in Afghanistan. American senior officers also confirmed that Anthony had top-cover from the American Military/Government. This was for future protection against the British Foreign Office, who at a later date would try and accuse Anthony of being a terrorist and member of the Al-Qaeda, Pakistan Taliban terrorist network.

B)   Conservatively over 150 international terrorist attacks were stopped and disrupted by Anthony covertly feeding intelligence back to American military intelligence (Walter Downs CSSP/American Military intelligence and Col Ken McKellar) Major Campbell can confirm this fact in interview.

C)   Infiltrating the "Talib Jan" (he ordered the bombing of the "Finest" shopping centre, just across the road from the UK Embassy) suicide bombing network being coordinated from within Pul-i-Charkhi Prison Afghanistan, Anthony stopped over 100 suicide and IED attacks on ISAF American and British soldiers in Afghanistan by infiltrating and disrupting the terrorist network. Senior Afghan NDS Security Service officers confirmed information on Talib Jan and the terrorist network operating out of Pul-i-Charkhi prison. The story also printed in the British Daily Telegraph newspaper.

D)   Disrupting and stopping of terrorist attacks also included; the disruption of attacks in several county's including, America, Saudi Arabia, Iraq, Yemen, Somalia, UAE, Europe and Cyprus.

E)   Anthony identified, while under deep cover within the Al-Qaeda, Pakistan Taliban terrorist network:

- Weapons and explosives shipments.
- Hostage locations.
- HVT and safe house locations.
- Terrorist leaders travel plans and routes.
- International terrorist financing systems, including "bank account numbers" and names of front companies used for money laundering.
- Intelligence concerning the identification and location of IED factories and international terrorists involved in bomb making across the Middle-East and the terrorist areas of operations.

F)   Anthony worked closely with the British SAS Chief of Staff and his Blade Teams, resulting in several terrorist training camps being located in Afghanistan and Pakistan. This intelligence resulted in Air strikes on the camps, a large number of terrorists killed and future terrorist attacks on America and Britain stopped. (Confirmed in meeting between Sergeant Trevor Cooper (Anthony's operations manager) and SAS Major in Hereford UK). Other task's received from SAS COS included updates and reports of locations of other HVT's and terrorist leaders including, Mullah Omar. (Copy of original reports available, Sergeant Trevor Cooper and members of Special Forces are also available to be discreetly interviewed).

G)   Anthony's deep infiltration also uncovered the Pakistan Taliban plans to detonate a large car bomb in Times Square New York. Intelligence covertly passed back to American Military Intelligence helped stop the 4x4 car bomb, parked in Time Square, before it detonated in a heavily populated area in New York City.

H)   Al-Qaeda plans to attack HRH Queen Elizabeth, and members of the British Royal Family at Buckingham Palace, were intercepted and passed onto British SOCA/NCA in Afghanistan; Anthony gave this information to SOCA/NCA employee Troy Heldon, long term SOCA/NCA contact and professional contact. Troy had passed training with Anthony for the Parachute

Regiment 15 years earlier. Troy had also previously driven Anthony, covertly, to meetings within military bases with SOCA/NCA in Afghanistan. (Troy Heldon is a witness to the above facts and information, interview also available).

I)   Al-Qaeda operational note book containing hundreds of real names and contact phone numbers used within the Al-Qaeda, Pakistan Taliban international terrorist network. A copy of this critically important note book was sent by Anthony to British Prime Minister David Cameron at 10 Downing Street London. A copy of the note book was also sent to the Director of MI6 at that time. (Copy of photographs of notebook and other exclusive photographs of inside Afghan Pul-i-Charkhi Maximum security prison are available) Important note; The original note book belonged to AKA Hussien Laghmani, the god-son of 2011 Al-Qaeda leader Al-Z, Hussien was the Quartermaster for AL-Qaeda, Pakistan Taliban and Lashkar e-Taiba operations, including the procurement of Stolen American Stinger missiles. Hussein was responsible for organising the ordinance for Lashkar e-Taiba, used in the Mumbai attack.

J)   Anthony's covert intelligence reports were shown to Col Bob Stewart (MP) by Sergeant Trevor Cooper and Dil Banerjee. Within 15 minutes of reading the reports, Col Bob Stewart arranged for the reports to be taken into an official meeting at MOD HQ Whitehall London with senior MOD officials (all the above were present at the meeting) Copy of reports available. Report included photographs, names, car registration numbers and contact numbers of Pakistani Taliban suicide bombers living in London, UK.

K)   During Anthony's deep infiltration of the Al-Qaeda network within the Prison environment, over several years, he was officially tasked by American Military Intelligence ("Major" Walter Downs). Tasking's included the tracing, tracking and locating of Al-Qaeda leaders hiding in Pakistan, several Senior Al-Qaeda Commanders were located, including Al-Qaeda No 1 HVT, UBL. This comprehensive target package was personally handed to American Military Intelligence, Walter Downs, by Anthony. This included; Location of UBL villa in Abbottabad, Pakistan:

- UBL was also living and slept on the 3rd floor with one of his wives.
- Other sensitive information and intelligence including military mission options and recommendations.
- Phone numbers of trusted couriers used by the terrorist network between Afghanistan and Pakistan.
-

Anthony and Major Campbell's Personal Diaries confirm the date and location of UBL 8 months before UBL was targeted and killed by American Seal Team 6 at the above location). An "Index List" given to an American lawyer, also confirmed the Location of UBL, as well as a list of intelligence reports handed by Anthony to American Military Intelligence. Major Campbell was witness to the "Index List" being handed over personally by Anthony to the lawyer. The America lawyer confirmed that she personally handed the "Index List" to Walter Downs, senior American Military Intelligence. (Chain of evidence for locating UBL). "Jeff" (pseudonym) the CIA Head of Humint (Human intelligence), based out of the American Embassy (Kabul), was also updated during a covert brief between Anthony and Jeff, which took place in Pul-i-Charkhi Prison. Major Campbell was witness to this meeting as well. Anthony personally updated Jeff on the location of UBL being located in a villa in Abbottabad Pakistan, this was 8 months before UBL was killed by American Special Forces, Seal Team 6.

L)   Major terrorist attack on Kandahar Air Field (KAF) was disrupted from within Pul-i-Charkhi Prison. Hours before the attack, Anthony shorted the electric mains box in the prison block, this while the Al-Qaeda and Taliban were charging their mobile phone, Sat-Com's/phones and laptop computers, all of which were being used to help coordinate the attack. This resulted in reducing the terrorist Command and Control ability, which resulted in a failed terrorist attack, having the overall effect of leaving the attack disorganised and disjointed. Following the attack, intelligence "confirmed" that the British PM, David Cameron, was sitting on-board a fully fuelled military C130 transport aircraft, a mere 400 meters from one of the terrorist attacks which managed to infiltrate the airfield, and made their way to the runway.

M)   Anthony identified and located the main terrorist IED factory and terrorist safe house at Al-Hatera Western Iraq. After an American military Special Forces mission against the target, attacks of American troops diminished within this area.

N)   Malone used his extensive international terrorist network within Pul-i-Charkhi prison, and beyond, to trace and track American Stinger missiles and other SAMs (Surface to Air Missiles). Other military hardware including weapons grade plutonium and other material that terrorist groups were trying to obtain for dirty bombs also became a priority for Anthony and his team, who were directly involved in the counter proliferation of such material. (See report of meeting with American Major set up by Tim SAS Special Forces Operations liaison officer, Bagram Air base Afghanistan).

O)   GPS co-ordinates, and other terrorist Commanders tactical and strategic information was passed by Anthony to Dil, who in turn passed information directly to Col Ken (American Military Intelligence). Col Ken also acknowledged the risk of this task and telephoned Dil to thank him for passing on such critically time-sensitive information, which had saved American and British lives. (SMS correspondence available).

P)   Anthony ascertained the date and time of a high number of terrorist attacks planned on American soldiers. An example of this was the planned multiple IED attack and sniper ambush on American soldiers (Senior American Intelligence Operatives) visiting Pul-i-Charkhi prison. The attack had been planned and put in place for 1500hrs, location; the Bridge just off Jalalabad Road backing onto the ISAF American base. The attack was disrupted; the American patrol and prison visit were rescheduled. Again American lives were saved. Within the week Anthony had identified a major IED factory, located in shipping-container company on the Jalalabad Road. This terrorist IED factory was poised to launch several attacks on British and American soldiers patrolling along the Jalalabad road from their Forward Operating Bases (FOB). They also planned to use some of these IED's to attack soldiers from the American 101st Airborne

Division, based in Eastern Afghanistan. The attacks were stopped, IED factory located and destroyed by American Special Forces. Message passed back to Anthony from American military "Job Well Done".

Q)   Anthony was tasked by American Military Intelligence and Senior British SAS officers and handed over material on several other highly sensitive subjects; this material is confidential due to on going military and international intelligence operations.

Statement and interview with Major Campbell, ex-SAAF Intelligence, confirming the above points is also available.

Major Bill Shaw MBE can also confirm Al-Qaeda-Pakistan Taliban attacks planned, coordinated and commanded from within Pul-i-Charkhi Prison Afghanistan. (See Legal Statement).

American Military Commanders overseeing intelligence from Anthony 2007-2010

1)   Col Ken XXXXX CSSP/American Military Intelligence.

2)   Senior Intelligence officer Walter Downs/American Military Intelligence.

3)   Jeff Head of American HumInt (Human Intelligence) operating out of American Embassy Kabul, under the Command of Greg RSO (Regional Security Officer, CIA Station head). 2015 Greg is now Head of the CIA "Clandestine Unit" Based at CIA HQ.

4)   Brigadier General XXXXXX, Commander of "ISAF" Forces in Afghanistan.

5)   XXXXX XXXXX, Commander American Central Command (CENTCOM) & Head of the American CIA (Central Intelligence Agency).

Senior British SAS Officers

Major,XXXXXXXX Military SAS Chief of Staff British Embassy Kabul and A&B Blade Team Commander Afghanistan.

Confidential Contact numbers are available for all the above.

Anthony Malone: Date:

During 2006 and 2007 I worked with Anthony Malone in Kabul, Afghanistan as his Operations Manager my responsibilities where to meet with clients, plan assignments and ensure the safety of the team and client.

During this period I was heavily involved with attending meeting at Baghram airport (US BASE) just outside Kabul, on several occasions I attended meeting with high ranking US officers with regards to weapon buy back projects that we took part in, during my time with Anthony Afghanistan I wrote several reports detailing weapons, equipment (vehicles, communications, Helicopter part, surface to air missile systems) that had been located in various locations in Afghanistan.

Along with this information we obtained information on suicide bombers who were to be deployed to the UK to carry out attacks I attempted to meet with the British Ambassador in Afghanistan to relate this information back to the UK, he was not interested at this time.

I was then tasked by Anthony Malone to return to the UK and hand over the information that we had to the relevant agencies, this proved somewhat impossible to get a meeting I then contact Lt Col Bob Stewart with this information, who assisted with setting up a meeting with MOD Whitehall, where the following attended the meeting TREVOR COOPER – GRAHAM HILLIARD – DILIP BANERJEE – LT COL BOB STEWART and Lt Col Richards, in the meeting where several other high ranking officers from the MOD from the rank of Colonel and above, Both Graham and myself spent several hours being interviewed by the MOD, my report was taken away and acted on.

Several weeks after I returned from Afghanistan I noticed a black Range rover sitting outside my house, this had happened for two consecutive days, on the morning of the second day I approached the vehicle to see two men sitting inside reading the New York Times and USA today, I asked why they was watching me and following me around, they asked me if I thought that Anthony Malone had gone over the Taliban and if they proved it would I take him down as I could get close enough, I told them that he had not turned and referred them back to General David Petraeus who was the Head of CIA. These men never returned.

I met with Eddy H former Chief of staff British SAS Afghanistan. SAS Chief of Staff he confirm GPS of the terrorist training camp in Pakistan was good that Anthony Malone had passed on during covert intelligence Tasking's in Afghanistan/Pakistan was accurate.

SAS Chief of Staff also confirmed American/British airstrikes had destroyed the terrorist camp.

Also Chief of Staff personal opinion was: "the way that the Elite team and Anthony had been treated by the British Embassy in Kabul due to politics was disgraceful".

Trevor Cooper

William Shaw MBE

To whom it may concern

2

REFERENCE – ANTHONY MALONE

I am William Shaw, formerly a senior manager in G4S Risk Management, Afghanistan and am currently on a sabbatical. I served in the British Army for 28 years and retired with exemplary service in the rank of Major. Between March and July 2010 I was held by the Afghan judicial system, sentenced to two years imprisonment and released on acquittal on 8 July 2010. Whilst being held I was transferred to Pol-e-Chaki Prison late May 2010, where I was placed in Maximum Security for my own protection. This was initially arranged by the British Embassy, Kabul in consultation with the prison governor due to a $10,000 bounty being placed on my head by Al Qaida and Taleban prisoners. My lawyer, Ms Kimberely Motley could testify to this.

It was well known that a bounty had been placed and the wing I was held in also housed Al Qaida and Taleban fighters. On arrival at the wing I was introduced to Anthony Malone who advised me of the daily routine and pointed out the numerous inmates who were potentially dangerous to my well being. I believe that he had suffered and witnessed numerous incidents during his detention. When allowed out for exercise in the small garden, Anthony made sure that I was kept safe and would often converse with the other inmates in order that they left me alone and no harm would come to me. He went out of his way to keep the peace and although I was treated with derision by some of the prison staff, Al Qaida and Taleban, I am aware that he spent many hours in their corridors holding meetings and discussing my safety. This in itself was a potentially dangerous situation for Anthony, but I am convinced that due to his personable approach and people skills he succeeded in protecting me until the day I was released.

I did notice whilst inside the prison that the Taleban appeared to control daily routine and even openly walked around with mobile telephones, something that was against prison rules. Information was relayed to the British Embassy staff on their visits, however nothing seemed to happen and the British prison mentors may have had their hands tied due to internal Afghan politics.

I do hope that this letter goes some way to show that Anthony is a man of principles who has suffered whilst in Pol-e-Chaki. He would help anyone in a difficult and potentially life threatening situation and should be praised for his efforts in exposing any wrongdoings.

Yours faithfully,

AFFIDAVIT

I, the undersigned

BEVAN CAMPBELL

(ID number: xxxxxxxxxx)

do, hereby, make an oath and state:-

- I am an adult male of South African nationality.

- The facts contained herein are true and correct, and within my personal knowledge.

imprisonment

- I was arrested on 04 August 2007 in Kabul, Afghanistan, on alleged drug-smuggling charges, and was imprisoned with Anthony Malone during the period from 2007-2009. During this time we were always allocated to the same rooms/cells as we were amongst the few "Western foreigners" held by the Afghan authorities.

DEPRAVATIONS SUFFERED BY ANTHONY MALONE AND MYSELF

- We were often denied food by the prison authorities and the "Boshi" (prisoner elected by the prison authorities to 'oversee/supervise the prisoners, and activities related to the prison). The average daily meal consisted of: 1x Loaf of Bread in the mornings; rice was dished up at midday with either beans/chickpeas/carrots/ turnips/cauliflower/tomato + onion, all forming part of a very 'watery soup' to go over the rice; whilst at night we had a piece of "meat", alternating with beans/chickpeas/ carrots/turnips/cauliflower/tomato + onion every alternate day. Tea was served with every meal. More often than not, Anthony and I were:-

    - Served bread that was stale (rock-hard), having to 'forfeit' "our fresh bread" to the prison guards to take home as part of "our tax to them"; or bread that had been urinated on/had rodent droppings in/on it. This due to the prison facilities being rodent infested, and the fact that we were regarded as "infidels";

    - Denied an adequate amount of food – something we had to fight on a daily basis. Portions were "minimal" to say the least. Generally each of us was served a ladle (average coffee mug) full of cooked rice, with a "splash" of the 'accompanying soup/sauce'. It must be noted that we were more often than not denied meat (buffalo, camel and/or mutton) due to the fact that neither of us was Muslim. This is something that was encouraged by the prison guards, who subsequently took our rations for themselves. On the rare occasions that we were given "meat", this would consist of fat and/or bone, again with the encouragement of the prison guards !!

    - We made numerous representations to the prison authorities about the issues surrounding the quality and quantity of food, but were "laughed off" (literally) as we were "foreigners". This did change for the better after Jan Eveleigh (the UK Emb Consul) took the matter up with the Pul-i-Charki prison commander (Genl. Barki), but the situation would always "slide back" and revert to what it had been in the past.

    - It should be noted that a means of getting "extra food" was always possible if one bribed the prison authorities, or had an outsider bring food "in" for you – something that was always subject to a "tax" by the guards – normally One Third to Half of what was being brought "in" for one had to be handed over to the Block Commander and the guards. Another point of interest was that at both "Nazarat Khona" and Taquif" we had to "buy" (10 Afs) our hot water for tea – this was a way for the Commanders to make extra money for themselves.

- Health issues were a continuous problem with a complete lack of medical facilities, although the various prisons "flouted" their respective "stocked sickbays" to visiting dignitaries, the prisoners were unable to get the necessary medicines and were forced to purchase medicines from the prison authority "doctors", who allegedly brought the medication "in" from the outside, when in fact they were selling off medicines donated by the Red Cross and other NGO organisations, all at exorbitant prices. As "foreigners" we were denied access to medical staff, such as they were, and had to rely on the Red Cross medical staff (in particular Dr Andre – an Italian doctor) for medicines. I was to suffer with a broken, and rotting, wisdom tooth for close to one year until Jan Eveleigh (the UK Emb Consul) was able to get me to a private dental clinic (Roshan Clinic) – which was for my personal account. This was NOT only the medical costs, BUT also the cost of the fuel for the 'official' vehicle, the "daily rate" of the guards/driver who accompanied me, as well as lunch for all involved in taking me to the clinic. Again, anything was possible "for the right price".

- Amenities (bath/shower and toilet) were also denied to us at various stages during our incarceration. By way of example: At all Court Proceedings, we, as "foreigners" were denied access to toilet facilities, whilst the local Afghans were allowed to make use of the facilities, using the "need for ablution before prayer" as justification for their use of the facilities but denying us the use. Another example, was a time when Anthony had an upset stomach, but went outside for the One Hour long "exercise period" we were allowed, otherwise he would have been cooped up for a 48hr period straight, but when he requested to be allowed to make use of the toilet facilities, the guards just laughed at him and refused to let him go, saying he "wanted to go, so had to stay out for the full hour". Needless to say the 'end result' was not particularly 'savoury'. We, as "foreigners", were only allowed to bathe at the 'discretion' of the prison facility commanders, in both, "Nazarat Khona" and "Taquif" – sometimes, as in my case, going without bathing for a period of 26 days straight at "Nazarat Khona". At Pul-i-Charki this changed as our respective cells had its own shower (although we often had the water to our bathroom 'turned off' to "save water" – all the while the rest of the prisoners were allowed 24hr access to water as "being Muslim, they were required to do ablution before prayers – not so foreigners").

- The lights were kept on 24 hours a day in all the prisons that we were held at, but was specifically 'enforced' at the High Security Block we were held in at Pul-i-Charki. If we dared to switch the lights off we were punished, which could mean that we forfeit our following days exercise, a meal etc. It is worth noting that whilst Anthony and I were held at the High Security Block in Pul-i-Charki "for our own safety", this was the Block that held all the Taliban and Al-Qaeda members that had managed to bribe their way out of the Coalition Forces prisons to an Afghan facility where they were able to bribe the local prison officials and carry out military operations against the Coalition Forces with impunity!!

- At no time during our incarceration were we ever, I emphasise, ever, given access to an official translator for any dealings with the prison and/or judicial authorities. This included our respective "interrogations", "investigations", "court proceedings" etc. The fact that the legal system "allows" for this does not necessarily mean that it is/was applied. In the case of all "foreigners" I encountered during my incarceration, none were ever given access to an 'official' (reliable) translator.

- Regarding "disciple" and "punishment" by the prison authorities towards us, we were often "targeted" by the various guards for bribes/"gifts" etc, and if we did not acquiesce to their "demands", they would get the local Afghans to instigate trouble against us. An example was when Capt Khalik (Taquif) wanted money from us, something we didn't have, he then got a bulimic prisoner to hurl his vomit at us, not once or twice but on several occasions – all the time watching us and what was going on. As soon as we grabbed the prisoner and tried to take him to the prison guards so as to make him stop his actions, we were shackled and locked up in stress positions from the prison doors, with the 'word' from the prison authorities being that we, as "infidels", had "dared to attack a Muslim". The prisoner who had instigated the matter was allowed to remain 'free', with the reason being that "he was crazy". On another occasion, an Afghan prisoner started a fight with Anthony, who was subsequently shackled to the doors in a stress position by the prison authorities, but the Afghan prisoner was left free, and then proceeded to spit on Anthony numerous times – all the while with the guards looking on and laughing.

- Witnessing torture was an everyday occurrence, with a ANP General (name known) beating prisoners at "Taquif" and then taking them away to the National Directorate of Security (NDS) for further "questioning/interrogation". At Pul-i-Charki, we witnessed:-

  - Prisoners being held in stress positions;

  - Being doused with cold water from a hose and then left outside overnight in winter – also in a stress position;

  - The beating of prisoners with Asp batons, not only to the limbs but directly to the head (contrary to safe Standard Operating Procedures for the use of this piece of equipment);

  - The spraying of teargas into the eyes of prisoners at point-blank range (contrary to safe Standard Operating Procedures for the use of this piece of equipment);

  - The beating of prisoners on the soles of their feet with a think electric cable (an "old technique" employed by the former Khad, trained by the former KGB);

  - Prisoners were left in solitary confinement, water switched off to the cell, and denied food/water, and the lights left on 24/7; and

  - As previously mentioned, we were subject to this behaviour from time-to-time. It is worth noting that when we did raise these issues with the UK Prison Mentors (names known), however, they chose to deny that any such "behaviour" by the guards took place, and stated that if we had issues, to take them up with the relevant Afghan authorities. The only "recourse" we had, was to speak to the US Prison Mentors (CSSP) and inform them of what was going on, it was then that this "behaviour" towards us was halted. In fairness to certain members of the US CSSP programme (names known), they went out of their way to "help/assist" us in making our imprisonment "more bearable".

BEVAN CAMPBELL

I know and understand the contents of this statement.

I have no objections in taking the prescribed oath.

I consider the oath to be binding on my conscience.

Dated at _____ on this the _____ day of December 2014.

I HEREBY CERTIFY that the Deponent has acknowledged that he/she knows and understands the contents of this affidavit, which SWORN TO, and SIGNED before me at _____ on this _____ day of December 2014, the provisions contained in Government Gazette 1649 R1258 dated 21 July 1972 having duly been complied with.

_____

COMMISSIONER OF OATHS

دافغانستان اسلامی جمهوریت
لو ی سفارت ـ لندن

سفارت کبرای جمهوری اسلامی
افغانستان ـ لندن

Embassy of the Islamic Republic of Afghanistan – London
Defence Attaché Office

شماره : 51

تاریخ 1385/8/ 13

به وزارت د فا ع ملی   ج.ا.ا
ریاست کشف!
احترا ما مینگارم.

نظر به تقاضای کمپنی(ایلت) انگلستان اسامی (انتونی صالون) جهت بازدید
وتهیه گزارشات کمپ های تعلیمی و از عملیات اردوی ملی دیدن نماید.
وبه دفتر اتشه نظامی مقیم لندن مراجعه کردند از این طریق به شما معرفی گردید
امیدوا رم طوریکه لازم میدانید همکاری لطف نماید.

باا حترام
دگروال احمد مسلم حیات
ا تشه نظامی افغانستان لندن

(Above from Military) Members of the British Army in Iraq with Uday's (Saddam's sons) Gold AK47 (Below from Author) Terrorist weapons in Western Iraq

(Above, Below From Author) Surface to Air Missiles found along the Iraq/Syrian border. Terrorist IED in Northern Iraq

(Above, Below from Author) Combat patrolling with members of 101st Airborne Division in Northern Iraq

(Above) Remembering the fallen Brothers in Arms from 101st ABD in Iraq. (Below) Baghdad Airport.

FCO/BEK personnel in 'order':

-Lawrence Jenkins – Consul
-Trudy Kennedy – Vice-Consul under Lawrence Jenkins and the Consul following Lawrence Jenkins being 're-assigned'
-Jan Everleigh – Consul, she replaced Trudy Kennedy who was sent home to the UK on "stress leave"
-Simon Thomas – Vice-Consul under Jan Everleigh

ISIS

The Islamic State of Iraq and Syria (ISIS), also known as the Islamic State of Iraq and the Levant (ISIL), or the Islamic State of Iraq and ash-Sham, or Islamic State (IS), or Daesh which ISIL considers derogatory, because it sounds similar to the Arabic words Daes, "*one who crushes something underfoot*", and Dahes, "*one who sows discord*"!!

Came into being in 1999 as the *Jamā'at al-Tawḥīd wa-al-Jihād*, joined Al-Qaeda in 2004 but declared itself a 'state' in Iraq in 2006, and in the 'Levant' in 2013. After the Syrian Civil War began in March 2011, the ISI, under the leadership of al-Baghdadi, sent delegates into Syria in August 2011. These fighters named themselves the al-Nusra Front, and established a presence in Sunni-majority areas of Syria, specifically in Ar-Raqqah (ISIS Headquarters), Idlib, Deir ez-Zor, and Aleppo. In April 2013, al-Baghdadi announced the merger of the ISI with al-Nusra under the name ISIL. However, Abu Mohammad al-Julani and Ayman al-Zawahiri, the leaders of al-Nusra and al-Qaeda respectively, rejected the merger. After an eight-month power struggle, al-Qaeda cut all ties with ISIL on 3 February 2014. On 29 June 2014, the group proclaimed itself to be a worldwide caliphate, with Abu Bakr al-Baghdadi being named its Caliph. As a caliphate, it claims religious, political and military authority over all Muslims worldwide, and that "*the legality of all emirates, groups, states, and organisations, becomes null by the expansion of the khilāfah's [caliphate's] authority and arrival of its troops to their areas*", claiming territory in Libya, Egypt, Algeria, Saudi Arabia, Yemen, Afghanistan, Pakistan as well as parts of India, the North Caucasus and Central Asian militants groups, such as the Islamic Movement of Uzbekistan, support ISIS. ISIS has control over territory occupied by 10 million people in Iraq and Syria, and through loyal local groups, has control over small areas of Libya, Nigeria and Afghanistan. The group also operates or has affiliates in other parts of the world, including North Africa and South Asia.

Its 'ideology' is based on Wahhabism/Salafi Jihadist, being led by, and mainly composed of, Sunni Arabs from Iraq and Syria. For their guiding principles, the leaders of the ISIS are clear about their commitment and adherence to the Wahhabi movement of Sunni Islam. The group circulates images of Wahhabi religious textbooks from Saudi Arabia in the schools it controls. In the ISIS capital of Ar-Raqqah it is reported that "*all 12 of the judges who now run its court system ... are Saudis*". Saudi Wahhabi practices also followed by the group include the establishment of religious police to root out "vice" and enforce attendance at salat prayers, the widespread use of capital punishment, and the destruction or re-purposing of any non-Sunni religious buildings. ISIS leadership are all Sunni, and adherents of Wahhabism. One of the biggest differences between ISIS and other Islamist and Jihadist movements, including al-Qaeda, is the group's emphasis on apocalypticism, a belief in a final Day of Judgment by God, and specifically, a belief that the arrival of one known as Imam Mahdi is near. ISIS believes that it will defeat the army of "Rome" at the town of Dabiq, in fulfilment of prophecy. Following its interpretation of the Hadith of the Twelve Successors, ISIS also believes that after al-Baghdadi there will be only four more legitimate caliphs.

That ISIS is an 'army' cannot be disputed when one looks at the numbers. Its 'strength' varies from between 53-200,000, with CIA estimates between 20,000-30,000. By 2014, ISIS was viewed as a militia rather than a terrorist group, but as major Iraqi cities fell to ISIS in 2014, Jessica Lewis (a former U.S. Army intelligence officer at the Institute for the Study of War), described ISIS as "*not a terrorism problem anymore*", but rather "*an army on the move in Iraq and Syria, and they are taking terrain. They have shadow governments in and around Baghdad, and they have an aspirational goal to govern*". Lewis has called ISISL "*an advanced military leadership... that have incredible command and control with a sophisticated reporting mechanism from the field that can relay tactics and directives up and down the line. They are well-financed, and they have big sources of manpower, not just the foreign fighters, but also prisoner escapees*".

ISIS has captured huge quantities of weapons, primary sources being from Saddam Hussein's Iraqi stockpiles and weapons from government and opposition forces fighting in the Syrian Civil War and during the post-US withdrawal Iraqi insurgency. The captured weapons, including armour, guns, surface-to-air missiles, and even some aircraft, enabled rapid territorial growth and facilitated the capture of additional equipment. Perhaps more 'concerning' is the use of 'unconventional' weapons. We should all be used to the truck and car bombs; suicide bombers and IEDs; but ISIS has used chemical weapons in Iraq and Syria in the past, and had an active 'chemical weapons research team' in its ranks. In September 2015 a US official stated that ISIS was manufacturing, and using mustard agent in Syria and Iraq. There are even hypothetical scenarios where ISIS might be able to get its hands on nuclear weapons and/or nuclear material to make a 'dirty bomb', not too far-fetched when we consider that Hussein Laghmani (Al-Qaeda Logistics Officer), knowing that Bevan was South Africa and that the South African Defence Force had decommissioned its nuclear arsenal, calmly asked Bevan one day if it was "possible for him to get material to make a small bomb". We laughed about it and said it was not something we could do, but the scary thought was that he had even considered it.

In August 2014, ISIS captured the cities of Zumar, Sinjar, and Wana in northern Iraq, forcing thousands of Yazidis to flee the militants. They fled up Mount Sinjar, a place I once 'broke bread' with the then-Col Lennington as we smoked a cigar. The stranded Yazidis' needed food and water, prompting American intervention in dropping supplies to the Yazidis but at the same time conducting an aerial campaign against the militants, who had threatened the Yazidis with genocide.

By January 2015, ISIS was coming into conflict with al-Qaeda in the Arabian Peninsula (AQAP) as ISIS went on a recruitment drive in Yemen. In February 2015, some *Ansar al-Sharia* members had broken from al-Qaeda and pledged allegiance to ISIS. At the same time ISIS established a 'military presence' in Afghanistan, and started a recruitment drive there. In January 2015 alone they were able to recruit over 150, but suffered losses of the militants, either by capture or death, at the hands of the Taliban. This was not 'unusual' for militants to oppose each other, Bevan and I had witnessed this many a time in Pul-i-Charki as allegiances changed and new ones sprung up. A further blow to ISIS in Afghanistan was the death of their 'recruiter-in-chief', Mullah Abdul Rauf, who was killed in an American drone strike in February 2015. ISIS's reach now stretches from Nigeria, in West Africa; across the Sahara to Somalia in East Africa; up the

Arabian Peninsula and into the Middle East itself, with Syria and Iraq at the epicentre; all the way across to Afghanistan and Pakistan.

ISIS creates fiefdoms of conflict in Afghanistan. In the east of Afghanistan, ISIS is gaining momentum, launching coordinated attacks on the Afghan National Security Forces (ANSF) in Nangarhar province. ISIS's growing activities in Nangarhar reveal the inability of the ANSF to maintain the fight against Taliban-ISIS militancy in the long run; and negates the assumption that Taliban-ISIS animosity will weaken the two groups in their fight against the government. In April 2015, ISIS claimed responsibility for a suicide bombing in Jalalabad (Nangarhar) that killed 35 people. Even the United Nations has issued a report claiming that ISIS is recruiting followers in 25 of the country's 34 provinces. ISIS was starting to make contact with Afghans and Pakistanis, and trying to recruit people to come to the fight in Syria and Iraq, but then they were able to gain a foothold in the country. This is despite the fact that the domineering and exclusive agenda of ISIS, which seeks to create a transnational Islamic caliphate, has emerged as a dividing rather than unifying factor in Afghanistan. ISIS has challenged Taliban 'nationalist' Jihad, while the Taliban in response has not only rejected ISIS but even begun to fight it. Bevan and I witnessed this with the al-Qaeda faction in Block-10. The Al-Qaeda element was the 'international' side of the jihadi movement, whilst the Taliban wanted to concentrate on the 'national level' and just get rid of the 'foreigners'. Interestingly enough, we witnessed the 'conversion' of Wais Hudien from 'national' to 'international' mujahedeen. In Nangarhar, even as Taliban and ISIS clashed, they continued fighting the government. The clashes between them, and against the government, have turned Nangarhar into a volatile province, with the Taliban dominating some parts, while others have an ISIS presence. ISIS is a declared a transnational threat and that there are potential ISIS sympathizers among the Taliban therefore also renders the Taliban a threat beyond Afghanistan. No one knows exactly how many ISIS badged fighters are now, but even 'official estimates' put the number at around a thousand fighters. The main areas where ISIS holds sway are in districts in the eastern province of Nangarhar, which borders Pakistan, as well as parts of Zabul in the south and Kunduz in the north. By some 'strange co-incidence' all three of these areas also happen to be major narcotics smuggling routes, something Jihadi groups will use to fund their operations. It is an 'open secret' that the 'war on drugs' in Afghanistan has failed dismally, and being the world's largest producer of illegal heroin, this area also has an economic element to it. By July 2015, ISIS had defeated the Taliban in three districts in Nangarhar situated in the foothills of the White Mountain (Spin Ghar), namely: Achin, Shinwar and Khogyani. The Taliban and ISIS in Afghanistan are not involved in a fight against only the Afghan government; in the long term they challenge the state system in the broader region. With fighters in Afghanistan now flying the flag of ISIS too, the natural concern is whether what happened in Iraq and Syria could happen in Afghanistan.

Why the 'conflict' between the two Islamist elements? The extent of ISIS activities and presence in Afghanistan remain ambiguous, but the Taliban have started to feel the group's impact. The Taliban has warned Abu Bakr al-Baghdadi, the leader of the Islamic State and its self-styled caliph, that *"jihad against the Americans and their allies [in Afghanistan] must be conducted under one flag and one leadership.*" The Taliban in Afghanistan, and Pakistan, largely remain loyal to the 'spirit' of Mullah Omar, the Taliban's deceased leader who held the title of *Amir al-Mu'minin* (Commander of the Faithful).

Pakistan is not alone in facing the ISIS threat. It is set to face another violent and deadly threat as ISIS has gained a foothold near Afghanistan-Pakistan (Af-Pak) border, and is able to spread its influence among people living on the border areas. This threat comes when Pakistan's offensive against terrorism in its tribal borderlands was moving towards a tentative 'conclusion'. ISIS has virtually established its writ in Federally Administered Tribal Areas (FATA) as they found it a safe haven full of resources and manpower. The White Mountains (Spin Ghar) in the area have become natural barrier to the spillover of the ISIS from Afghanistan's Nangarhar province to the adjacent areas of FATA. The Afghan Taliban have been displaced from the area and Afghan government has no control over these areas. People who belong to Shinwari tribe have taken shelter in Jalalabad .

Perhaps something of more concern is the attempt by the Pakistani ISI trying to merge Taliban and ISIS. Most of the ISIS fighters belong to Orakzai Agency. They have restored abandoned infrastructure of the Afghan Mujahideen in Achin district. A report submitted by the Balochistan government in November 2014 has also confirmed a large-scale recruitment for the ISIS in Kurram, Orakzai and adjacent Hangu district. The location where ISIS has established its stronghold is important. Movement in the 16,500ft high White Mountain may be difficult but not impossible. Cross-border movement takes little effort in the area where White Mountain ends which links Paktia province in Afghanistan with Kurram Agency, a sensitive area in Pakistan. Pakistani forces have no or little presence in the area. Kurram is home to 'heretic' population, according to the ISIS dogma, which the group has applied in Iraq and Syria. The ISIS elements are gaining ground in Afghanistan due to financial resources, but Islamabad and Kabul are busy in blame game. Both the countries have yet to evolve a joint strategy to tackle the emerging threat in the shape of the ISIS in the region.

So, how does that affect the European Union? In 2015 ISIS let it be known that it had infiltrated members into the European Union, often disguising themselves as civilian refugees who were emigrating from the war zones of Syria, Iraq and Afghanistan. Fighting between ISIS, the Taliban, and government forces and allied militias has displaced a new wave of Afghan civilians, many of whom have made the treacherous journey across the Mediterranean Sea to seek refuge in Europe. Claims by ISIS of thousands of fighters having been successfully smuggled into Europe, as part of the refugee 'flood', cannot be ignored, especially in light of events in Paris and Brussels, where attacks were carried out killing 130 people and a city paralysed by fear of a Paris style attack. Authorities were able to prove after the attacks that some of the jihadists had entered the EU posing as refugees! In July 2015, a raid by American Special Forces on a compound housing the ISIS's chief financial officer, Abu Sayyaf, produced evidence that Turkish officials had dealt directly with ranking ISIS members. Documents and flash drives seized during the Sayyaf raid revealed "undeniable" links between Turkey and ISIS, something that could not only have a profound effect on American and Turkish relation, but which should be a warning to the European Union that Turkey is not called the "Gateway to Jihad" for nothing. It is commonly regarded as a 'transit country' for such fighters. Turkish border patrol officers have repeatedly been reported as having deliberately overlooked those entering, or exiting Syria, sometimes upon payment of a small bribe. A report by Sky News exposed documents showing that passports of foreign Islamists wanting to join ISIL by crossing into Syria had been stamped by the Turkish government. Again, these 'tactics' were nothing 'new'. I had briefed American Military Intelligence and Greg/Jeff (CIA) that this was all part of the Modus Operandi of the Jihadists, to "swim with the fishes" as The Fox would say, it also happened to be one of his favourite quotes. Not even Russia is immune from ISIS attacks, as we witnessed with the downing of the MetroJet Airbus 321 over the Sinai Peninsula, killing 224 people using a device spirited away in a soda can. This was in reprisal for Russian military involvement in Syria, in support of Bashar al-Assad. I think it's safe to say that ISIS will be a thorn in our flesh for the short to medium term unless there is some political will, a "coalition of the willing" as George W. Bush said, to take the fight to ISIS by unconventional means so as to try and stem the tide. The last thing we want on the streets of Europe is the sound of gunfire, explosions and mayhem, but the question to be asked is: "Is there the political will to fight this by whatever means necessary to put an end to the barbarism that is ISIS".

Printed in Great Britain
by Amazon